xhibition: Selections and Additions • Reginald Marsh's New Y
Life: Hollywood Photographs • Raymond Hood: City of Tow
n Paintings & Musical Instruments 1770–1910 • On 42nd Str
al City: 1930s–1950s • Art for the Masses 1911–1917: A Radi
Sculpture • The Photography of Imogen Cunningham • Urb
Likeness: Twentieth-Century Portrait Drawings • Walter Mu
e Viewer as Voyeur • The Social Graces, 1905–1944: Prints a
nstallations • Precisionist Perspectives: Prints and Drawin
iature Environments • Isamu Noguchi: Portrait Sculpture •
ly Years • The (Un)Making of Nature: Installations by Mich
pressionism: Other Dimensions • Painted Forms: Recent Me
80–91 • Immaterial Objects • Ellen Driscoll: The Loophole
w Boat • Gary Simmons: The Garden of Hate • Y. David Chu
zanne McClelland: Painting • Amalia Mesa-Bains: Venus E
d) • Maren Hassinger: Window Boxes • Expanding the Collect
otographs of New York City • Lorna Simpson: Standing in
onald: Double Foolscap • Works on Paper • Photographs • Ja
art Davis and Reginald Marsh • Carmen Lomas Garza • Alte
: Harnessing Nature • Jane Dickson: Paradise Alley • Ik-Joo
nare Bearden in Black-and-White: Photomontage Projectio
n • Tunnel Visions: Photographs by Accra Shepp • Pictures
ián, by Ming Fay • Who What When Where: An Installation
rbulent • **25 YEARS** • The Long Twilight: An Installation by Ly
e Studio Stripped Bare, Again • Lee Boroson: Underpass • F
nd Ellsworth Kelly • Shahzia Sikander: Acts of Balance • Pasto
: Two or Three Corridors • A Way with Words • Do-Ho Suh: So
: G-Force • Alex Katz: Small Paintings • Jane Hammond: Ba
e Owls, and the Others • Five by Five: Contemporary Artists
m, Ryan Humphrey, Mike Kelley • Paul Henry Ramirez: Spa
endee, Ester Partegàs • Haluk Akakçe: Illusion of the First Ti
ay Goodbye to Substance • Mark Bradford: Very Powerful Lo
Urban Myths Part II (Return of the Hyp   hitect
ght or Flight: Kristin Baker, Amy Gartrel   Wange
Past Presence: Childhood and Memor   • And
on Ebner, Karyn Olivier, Iván Navarro, Michael Queenland, Ka
a Cooper, Tara Donovan, Charles Goldman, Jason Rogenes,

Whitney
Museum of
American
Art at
Altria

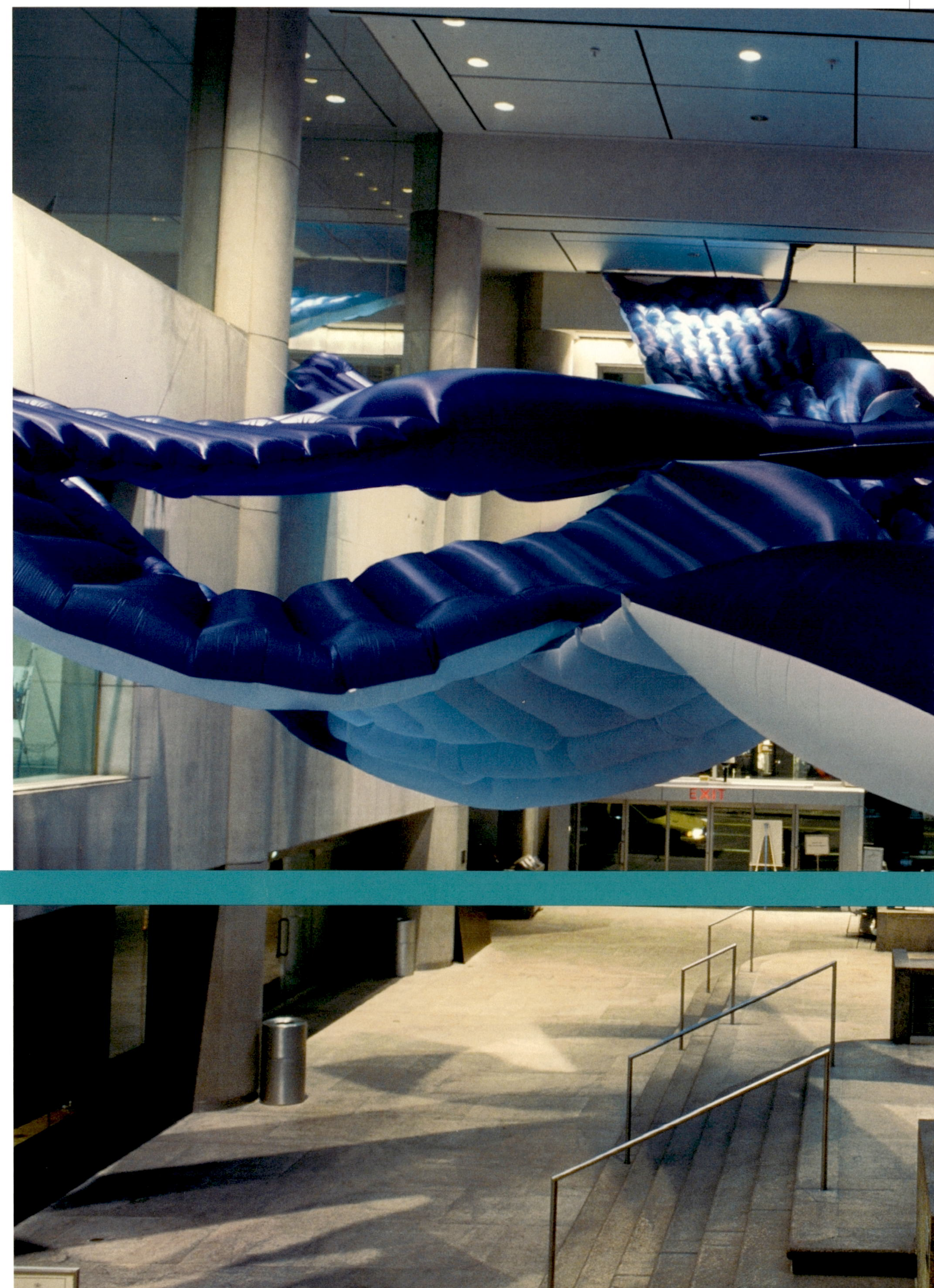

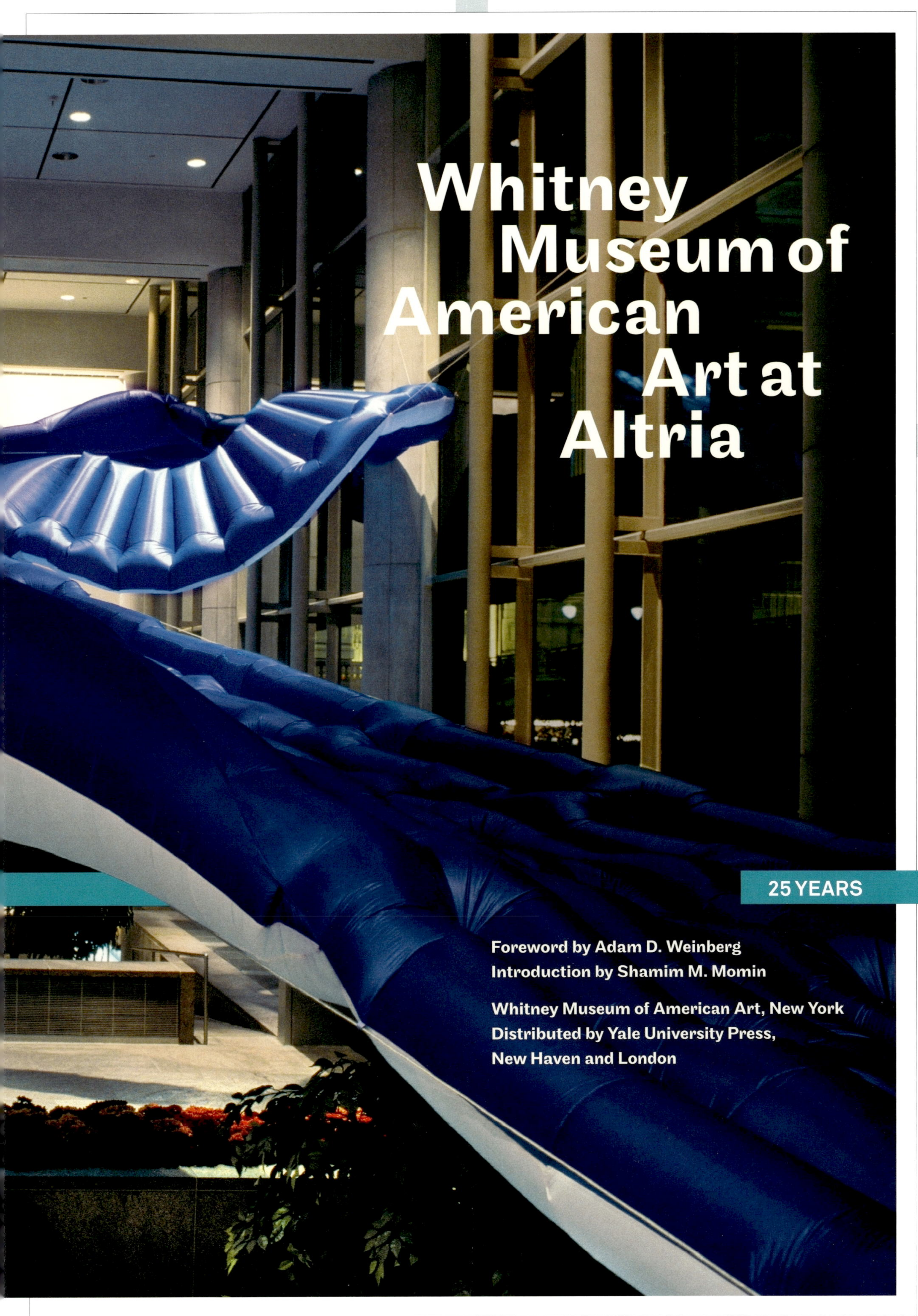

Whitney
Museum of
American
Art at
Altria

25 YEARS

Foreword by Adam D. Weinberg
Introduction by Shamim M. Momin

Whitney Museum of American Art, New York
Distributed by Yale University Press,
New Haven and London

Published in celebration of the twenty-five-year history of the Whitney Museum of American Art at Altria, 1983–2008.

WHITNEY

Whitney Museum of American Art
945 Madison Avenue at 75th Street
New York, New York 10021
whitney.org

Cover: Photograph by Marianna Pegno
Frontispiece: Installation view of *Lee Boroson: Underpass* (see page 90).

Library of Congress Cataloging-in-Publication Data

Whitney Museum of American Art.
Whitney Museum of American Art at Altria: 25 years / foreword by Adam D. Weinberg; introduction by Shamim M. Momin.
p. cm.
"Published in celebration of the twenty-five-year history of the Whitney Museum of American Art's branch at Altria (formerly Philip Morris), 1983-2008"—T.p. verso.
Includes index.
ISBN 978-0-300-13933-4
1. Whitney Museum of American Art at Altria.
2. Art—New York (State)—New York. I. Title.
N618.A88 2008
709.73'0747471—dc22
                    2008017698

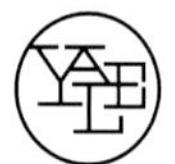

Yale University Press
302 Temple Street
P.O. Box 209040
New Haven, Connecticut 06520
yalebooks.com

Contents

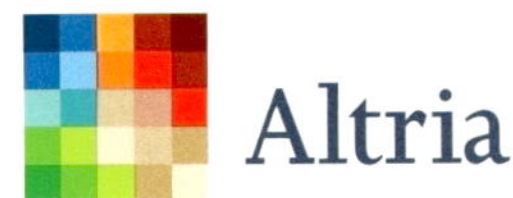

Since the Whitney Museum of American Art first opened its branch at our company's headquarters at 120 Park Avenue in New York City, it has made an indelible mark on the art world, while profoundly enriching our everyday work life and experience. This unique space has touched each and every one of us. It has been a source of inspiration, a catalyst for conversation, and a living testament to the power of the arts. For that, we are most grateful.

Sponsor's Statement

We thank and applaud each of the branch directors, staff members, and artists who over the past twenty-five years have created the most extraordinary exhibitions, installations, performances, and educational programs. The branch location in the heart of Manhattan, just steps away from Grand Central Terminal, has given hundreds of new and emerging artists the opportunity to share their innovative vision with the people of New York City and far beyond.

We are truly proud to support this important anthology documenting the history of the Whitney Museum of American Art at Altria and to celebrate its achievements. There is no doubt that the Whitney at Altria has forever broadened the cultural landscape of our city, and perhaps more importantly, our individual perspectives on the world.

On April 1, 2008, Altria Group, Inc., relocated its corporate headquarters to Richmond, VA.

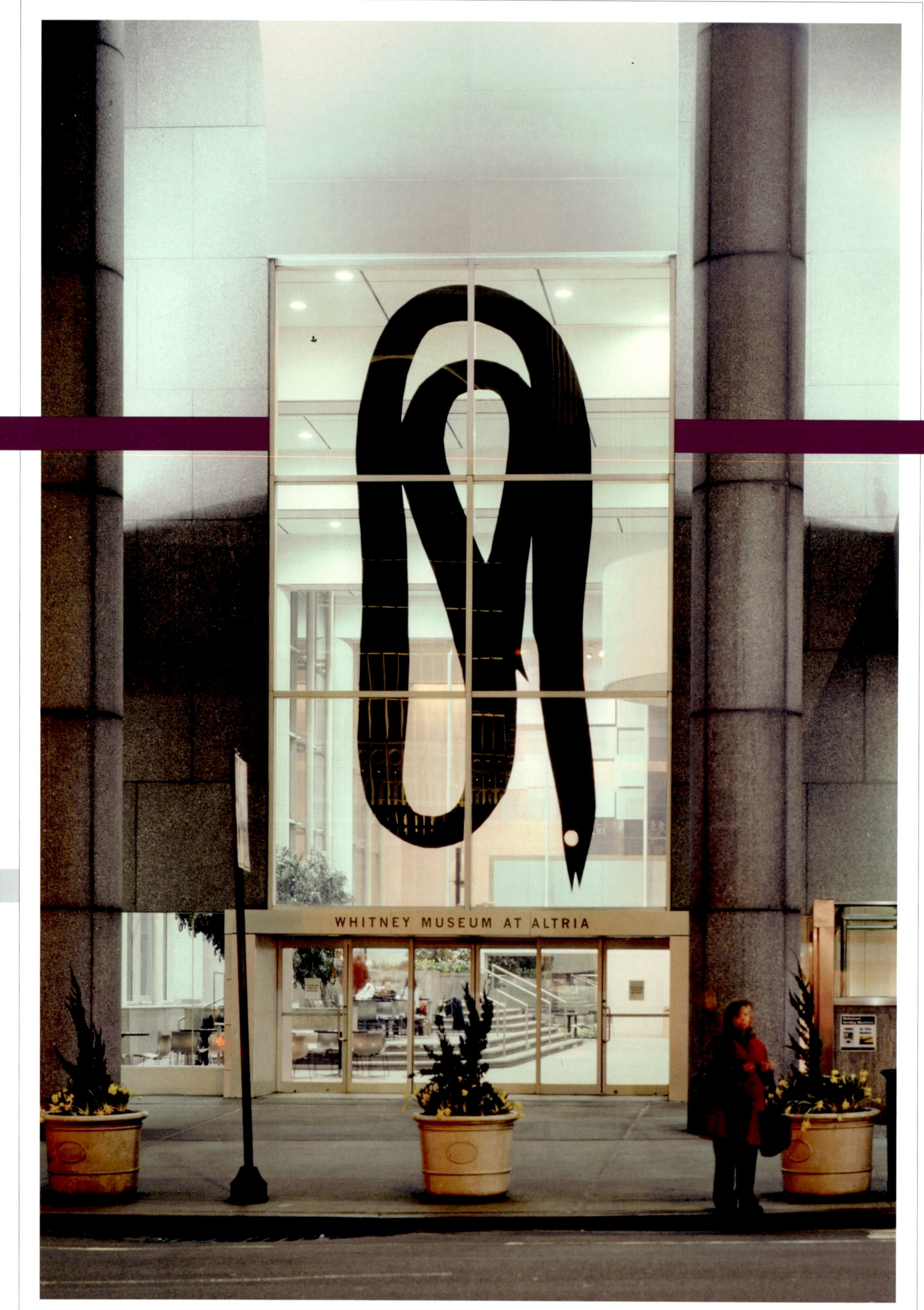
WHITNEY MUSEUM AT ALTRIA

In April of 1983 the Whitney Museum of American Art opened a branch museum at the new Philip Morris headquarters, strategically positioned at the crossroads of New York City, on 42nd Street and Park Avenue across from Grand Central Terminal. As of January 2008, this branch—the last of four Whitney branches—has closed. This closing does not simply mark the end of the great and long-term generosity of Altria Group (known until 2003 as Philip Morris) but the end of an era for the Whitney and American museums in general.

The Whitney Museum opened its first branch in 1973 on 55 Water Street in downtown Manhattan. The fact that it was referred to as a branch, an outgrowth of the Whitney on Madison Avenue and 75th Street, causes one to consider this initiative in light of the great American public library system, which made its intellectual resources accessible to as broad a public as possible through its neighborhood branch system. The establishment of the downtown branch museum, the brainchild of then Whitney director Tom Armstrong, was with the intent "to provide cultural activities in an area of the city which has no comparable program." In the populist spirit of the early 1970s it was also an effort to make the Whitney's growing permanent collection more accessible to a larger and more diverse public as well as provide opportunities for contemporary artists to exhibit new work. It was in effect "outreach"—one of the most popular political terms of the period—to bring the art to the people. In this spirit, admission to the branch museum (as well as the three subsequent branches) was and continued to be free-of-charge as were the performances, education programs, and publications.

The branch museum concept also signified a new relationship between America's flourishing corporate sector and the country's museums during a period of quantitative growth in the 1980s. This ambitious type of corporate sponsorship coincided with the lavish underwriting of large-scale exhibitions that occurred at museums throughout the United States. While the first Whitney branch was operated by contributions from thirty local businesses, the branch museums of the 1980s were not shoestring operations. The Philip Morris branch—as well as the Champion and Equitable branches—was conceived of as a self-contained, semi-autonomous unit with a director/curator, educator, and support staff who had their offices onsite. This situation enabled each branch to have a substantial impact on the neighboring community. And, while it maximized benefit for the company's employees and burnished the corporation's image as a cultural leader, it must be acknowledged that the creation of a museum branch also provided the corporation with certain zoning and tax benefits. (These incentives were established by New York City to encourage corporate give-back for the public good.)

The idea of establishing the branch at Philip Morris was initially encouraged by Ulrich Franzen, the architect who had designed the headquarters of Champion International in Stamford, Connecticut, the site of the second Whitney branch, and George Weissman former chairman and CEO of the Philip Morris Companies, an

View of the Whitney Museum of American
Art at Altria from 42nd Street during the exhibition
Matthew Brannon: Where Were We, 2007.

enlightened and culturally-involved executive. Given the great spirit of social service through cultural involvement at the time it is not surprising that the architect conceived a spacious public court with seating and plantings as well as an enclosed gallery space. The court enabled the Whitney to install large sculptures and eventually Museum-commissioned sculptures and installations in this casual setting that bridged the public sphere of the street with the private zone of the corporation. While the gallery allowed for traditional small-scale exhibitions, the projects and performances conceived for the court were among those that most distinguished the programs of the Whitney at Altria.

From 1983 until 1991 the Whitney at Philip Morris was primarily utilized for thematic exhibitions of works from its permanent collection and small loan exhibitions organized by the Whitney and other museums such as *Calder: Selections from the Collections*; and *The Changing Likeness: 20th Century Portrait Drawings*. However, many exhibitions responded to the specificity of the midtown location, among them: *On 42nd Street: Artist Visions*, *The Viewer as Voyeur*, *Urban Figures*, and *The Surreal City 1930's–1950's*.

From 1991 forward, the Whitney branches served as laboratories. While they had periodically presented commissioned works and installations before this time, the early 1990s marked a new direction for the branches especially as they offered exhibition spaces that could accommodate the increased scale and burgeoning number of contemporary works. In addition, there was increasingly a need for space to introduce the work of emerging artists and to provide opportunities for the presentation of new works by mid-career artists. Many important artists were given their first one-person museum exhibitions at the Whitney's branches.

The Altria branch was not only a testing ground for art and artists but also a platform for aspiring directors and curators. The lineage of these directors and their subsequent accomplishments is indeed impressive. Lisa Phillips, who initiated the branch at Philip Morris, became a celebrated and seasoned curator at the Whitney uptown and today is the Toby Devan Lewis Director of the New Museum of Contemporary Art; Susan Lubowsky Talbott, the second director, subsequently held numerous directorial posts and most recently was appointed director of the Wadsworth Atheneum; Josephine Gear, her successor, is currently an independent curator and writer as well as an adjunct associate professor at New York University's graduate program in museum studies; Thelma Golden, who initiated the project-based program at the branch, is presently director and chief curator of The Studio Museum in Harlem; Eugenie Tsai, curator of branches in the late 1990s, has since held numerous curatorial posts and is now John and Barbara Vogelstein Curator of Contemporary Art at the Brooklyn Museum; Debra Singer continued her curatorial career at the Whitney uptown and is today director of The Kitchen; and last, but far from least, Shamim Momin, who in addition to her role at the branch is an associate curator at the Whitney, has just completed co-curating her second Whitney Biennial. It is to these passionate and inventive curator/directors and their staffs that the Whitney Museum of American Art at Altria owed its great success.

ADAM D. WEINBERG
ALICE PRATT BROWN DIRECTOR, WHITNEY MUSEUM OF AMERICAN ART

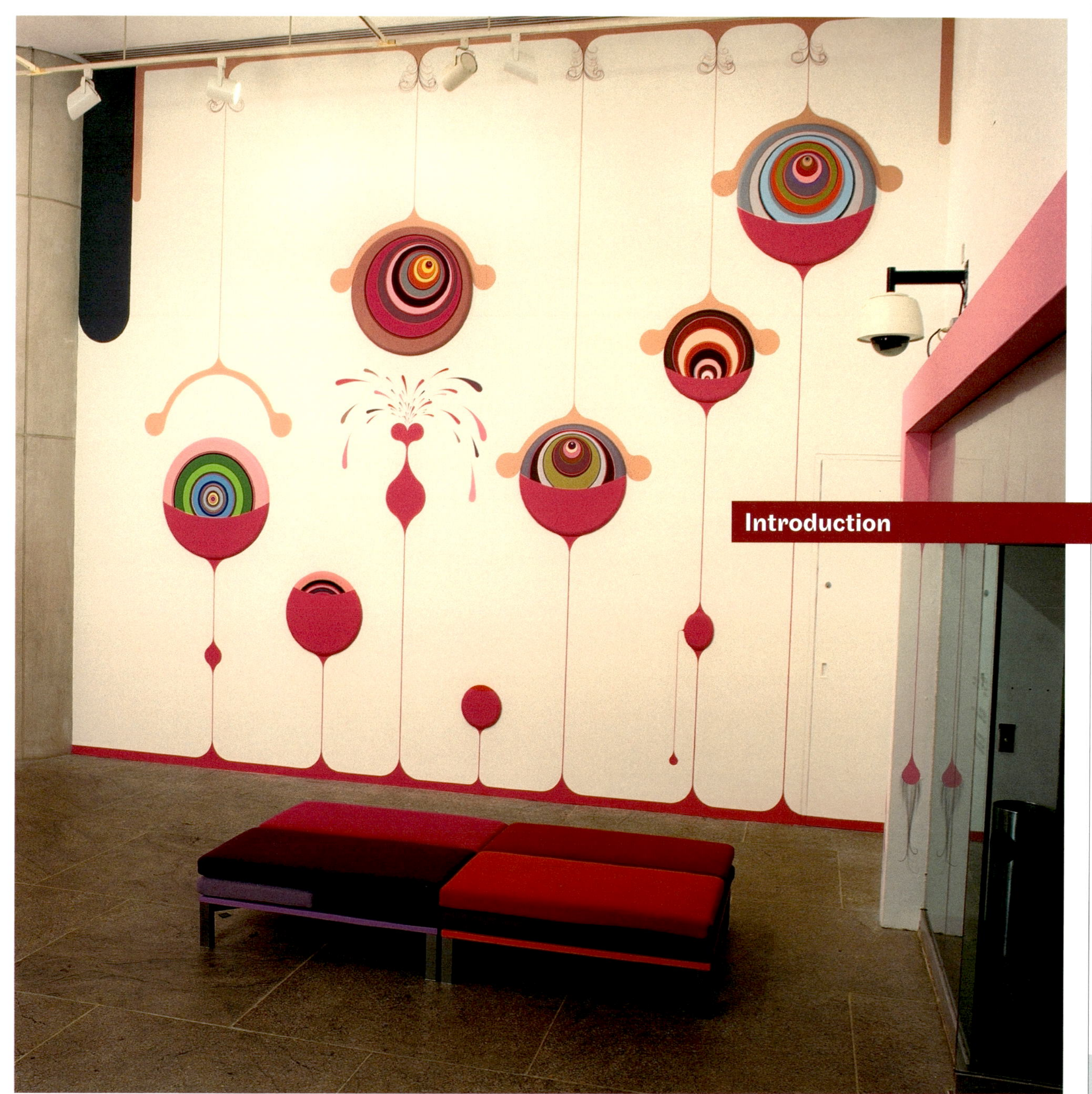

For the past twenty-five years, since its inauguration in April 1983, the Whitney at Altria (known as Philip Morris until 2003) has been a venue supporting the visual and performing arts, and has proven itself as a leader in the field of organizing and producing contemporary art projects by emerging and mid-career artists. Throughout the majority of its history, the central focus of the Whitney at Altria has been site-specific projects highlighting the relationship between artist, site, and institution. Built specifically to house the Whitney branch, the 5200-square-foot street-level plaza/sculpture court and 1100-square-foot gallery of the Altria Group headquarters housed the longest-running of the Whitney's branch museums. The past quarter century has also provided an opportunity for the Whitney to expand its reach, whether through the branch's countless innovative education programs, the hundreds of exhibitions and performances, or by providing an escape from the

Installation view of *Paul Henry Ramirez:*
Space Addiction (see page 122).

chaos and anonymity of midtown Manhattan. Therefore, it is with great fondness that we take this opportunity to look back on the past and look forward to the future.

In creating this anthology highlighting the creative achievements of the Whitney at Altria, the staff and I have been able to rediscover the initial plans for the branch and speak to many of those who influenced its evolution. The primary intention for the space was to enable the public, as stated by the first press release, "to view important works of art, which, because of their scale, can rarely be shown at the main Museum on Madison Avenue." George Wiessman, Philip Morris Companies chairman and chief executive officer at the time, noted that the partnership "adds a unique dimension to our business and daily life. It suggests, I hope, new ways in which American business can work with museums in offering art to the American people." Lisa Phillips, the Whitney's director of branches, was responsible for the set-up, hiring, managerial structuring, and opening programming (a precursor experience to her most recent endeavor, building and opening an entirely new home for the New Museum of Contemporary Art). She recently reflected on the experience: "It was a wonderful opportunity to be able to share some of the great masterpieces from the Whitney's permanent collection with the midtown work force and tourists coming out of Grand Central Terminal in a free public space. It was also not without its challenges—like animating the rather cold corporate, monumental architecture with works of art that could tolerate and change the environment. For the opening of the space, I invited a number of sculptors to create or place pieces in the atrium—including George Segal, John Chamberlain, and Claes Oldenburg. Louise Lawler chose to photograph details of the sculpture in the space for a series of photos of collections and installations. The small exhibition gallery was devoted to drawings by sculptors from the permanent collection of the Whitney." In a way, this idea of working directly with Whitney artists to create or locate their works in the space prefigured the more well-known incarnation of the branch as a commissioned project space. Phillips also worked closely with Stephanie French, who for many years was the guiding force within Philip Morris' philanthropic giving department, and who was invaluable in helping to shape the branch museum as an autonomous curatorial space. Entirely devoted to assisting the Whitney Museum with outreach and accessibility, French was adamant that the space and all of its programming remain free to the public.

Susan Lubowsky Talbott, the branch's first director, was charged with developing a full program that echoed the activities carried on uptown but that would also reach new audiences. She established the multilevel offering that became the core of the branch's activities: a full educational program that in later years functioned as the entire arts programming for a number of underfunded New York City public schools, a performance program that took place on the architectural "stages" of the sculpture court, and an exhibition program that largely highlighted works from the permanent collection, often on the recurring theme of the "city." The gallery also housed exhibitions curated by students of the ISP (Independent Study Program), a seminal and signature education program of the Whitney Museum, founded in 1968 and continuing to this day to foster emerging curators, critics, and artists. Lubowsky Talbott recalls this time: "The populist ideal of art that emerged during the formative years of the Whitney Museum was at the heart of the branch's activity. . . . Our audience was perhaps the most diverse in the city—from office workers and executives at Philip Morris and nearby businesses and corporations, to bicycle messengers who visited the exhibitions, welfare mothers from West Side SRO hotels who brought their children after school, and artists and art lovers who were our core audience. The branch truly reflected the diversity of the city itself."

In 1991, the branch shifted its focus to presenting commissioned exhibitions and projects by contemporary artists, thus forming an entirely unique niche within the New York art world. As a free exhibition space that functioned both under the aegis of the Whitney Museum and maintained its own autonomous identity, the Whitney at Philip Morris enjoyed great programmatic freedom, offering exciting new work while simultaneously maintaining the qualitative rigor of a major museum. The branch, now under Thelma Golden supported progressive, cutting-edge projects by contemporary artists, many of whom have become major art world figures. Building on the populist gesture of the previous years, Golden sought to explore the potential of a quasi-public, multi-use exhibition space (the sculpture court has over the years housed several different stores, cafes, and of course has functioned as a seating and meeting area as well), and to redefine for artists how and where a commissioned project might function and live: "It seemed to me that the space could provide an amazing laboratory to offer artists the chance to test their ideas in a site-specific format, but also, from the other side, to really engage the audience without the usual barriers inherent in a traditional institutional building. The space allowed for a direct conversation with the public about contemporary art, and moreover a public not necessarily coming to the space for that reason. It could provide an introduction to a much more diverse range of art and artists without the dimension of institutional authority attached that can often feel alienating or off-putting—and the audiences were consequently more open in that experience to what they were seeing and engaging with."

At the same time, the Performance on 42nd series had grown in reputation and audience demand to such a degree that the branch staff now included a dedicated performance curator, Jeanette Vuocolo. For many years, in fact, the branch's performance program served as the Whitney's main venue for such activity, as the Breuer building uptown had no space comparable to the sculpture court. The program functioned analogously to the mission of the visual arts exhibitions. Vuocolo recalls, "I saw the program as an open laboratory where artists interested in performance could work in a public space under the embrace of the museum and in the gaze of the corporate world. I loved the planning process when artists came in the space and envisioned what was possible. I enjoyed the unpredictable in performance . . . the commuters glancing in, the mash-up between the corporate folks, the artists, and the museum . . . all for the goal of presenting fresh new ideas and artists in the contemporary performing arts world. I loved how the artists 'took on' the space: using, being fascinated with every inch and always pushing the boundary of what was permissible. It was a rich time, a very creative time, a very public time, a kind of romance between the museum world, the corporate world, the public, and the artists."

In subsequent years, the branch maintained this general profile, though with certain shifts pursuant to the specific visions of the curators in charge. Eugenie Tsai continued to expand the diversity of the artists invited to engage with the branch space during her stewardship there, while Beth Venn (currently curator of modern and contemporary art at the Newark Museum), who was the director of branch museums from 1999 to 2000, instituted a program at the uptown Museum that used the smaller scale of the branch spaces (both the Philip Morris and Champion spaces were still active at that time) to its advantage, presenting focused group or "dialogue" exhibitions intended to carry on as part of the Whitney's Traveling Exhibitions Program, which she also initiated. Deb Singer, who began as the branch's performance curator and then took over as director, felt that this dual programmatic role allowed for "the opportunity to conceive of programming in the most holistic way, where all types of work both object-based and performative was considered as a total organism, each element in balance with, or presenting a challenge to, another."

As for my tenure at the branch, I took over the reins in 2000, and over the past eight years have tried to continue that mission of support for contemporary artists but in an expanded way that reflects shifts and developments in artistic practice, while also being attendant to our now long-standing public. I modified Venn's focused collection projects through a series called "Contemporary Artists on Contemporary Art," in which invited artists were asked to use the permanent collection as the locus for their proposed commission. I revised the programming format somewhat in order to present fewer exhibitions but with more ambitious scale and which could increasingly take on the mammoth space of the sculpture court as well as work with the more traditional gallery space. We also engaged a performance curator again, Boo Froebel, who approached the challenge of presenting progressive contemporary work with a similar vision, "When I think of the atrium, I remember the huge walls of windows looking onto 42nd Street and Park Avenue, where tourists and locals alike would stand and look in, becoming a part of the piece; the granite floor (sorry dancers!!); the five stories of reverberation; the different levels; and the trees with real trunks and fake leaves. I tried to program artists who were inspired by the space, and used it in ways that reflected/exploited its singularity. . . . It was wonderful to put performance in that space, in the heart of New York City—and surprise countless strangers who just happened onto magical happenings as they left Grand Central, or walked down 42nd Street. . . . The Whitney at Altria was an important part of the New York performance ecosystem and it will be missed."

In 2006, the Whitney Museum at Altria presented an exhibition in both its sculpture court and gallery spaces entitled *Small Liberties*, a very ambitious project by Andrea Zittel that involved more than a dozen customized "wagon station" modules. These pod-like forms were intended to present intimate, personal environments tailored to the invited inhabitants' ideas of what would best provide a small space of freedom, one that could function in the desert (at Zittel's compound in Joshua Tree, for example) as well as it could in midtown Manhattan, where its incongruous presence might challenge notions of personal space—small acts of subversion that might create "small liberties" within what is often felt to be a cold, anonymous architectural and urban environment. While this exhibition—as with any other art presentation in a public space—came with its familiar difficulties, what struck me then, and at so many other moments in my years at the Whitney's Altria branch, was the amazing sense of care, of protection, and of personal ownership our audience felt over the space, and the work presented within. On several occasions, for example, our "regulars" were captured by security cameras preventing other visitors from tampering with the wagon stations, all of which had very easily removable elements. In other exhibitions employing delicate or easily damaged material, it was remarkable how careful our visitors were—often, it seemed, more so than in the museum space proper. While there were certainly incidents to the contrary over the years, in general I found that our audience, when given the respect to engage challenging and often provocative contemporary projects, would step up to that opportunity in remarkable ways. Similarly, the artists that we worked with over the course of the branch museum's history have consistently impressed the art world with their sense of innovation and commitment to stretching the bounds of what commissioned public art projects can be and can achieve.

In recent years, working closely with our amazing team at the branch, we developed hybrid programming intended to reflect the shifting state of contemporary practice. In concert with Howie Chen, for example, we initiated "Breakout Sessions," an artist event series reflecting the diverse ways in which artists engage and present visual culture. As a departure from conventional formats, the series invited artists to present work, performances, and ideas that spoke to the constellation of influences informing their overall creative practice. Promoting an "open studio" format, the series provided rare access to artists' visual inspirations ranging from works by fellow artists to interdisciplinary elements of pop culture. This way of working, inspired directly by the extraordinary privilege of working closely with an artist throughout the development of a commissioned project and the discourse about the way he or she works that was central to that process, has been deeply formative in my curatorial practice overall.

Whitney Museum of American Art at Altria: 25 Years would not have been possible without the significant and continued support of a range of organizations and individuals. First and foremost, I would like to thank Altria Group, Inc. and its chairman and chief executive officer, Louis C. Camelleri—not just for their support of the branch throughout its twenty-five-year history, but also for their understanding of the need to chronicle that history in a permanent and accessible fashion. This book, made possible entirely by Altria's generous financial support, allows the important contributions of the many wonderful artists, performers, and curators who worked within the space to become a part of art historical scholarship, as it should be. In particular, I would like to thank Jennifer Goodale, vice president, contributions, and Diana Echevarria, manager, contributions, for their steadfast support of the branch's mission, and for recognizing the importance of creating this publication. My thanks as well to Adam D. Weinberg, Alice Pratt Brown Director, Whitney Museum of American Art, and the directors that preceded him, as well as to the entire Whitney staff for their unwavering support of the branch museum throughout its history.

The book itself would have been impossible to produce in such a concentrated time frame without the extraordinary efforts of the Whitney at Altria staff. In particular, Howie Chen, senior curatorial coordinator at the branch, spearheaded the production of this catalogue with indefatigable dedication and efficiency, spending countless hours sifting through the extensive archives for material, and coordinating the many different voices, elements, and input to create a coherent yet accurate reflection of the branch's history. His efforts were immeasurably enhanced by the commitment of Marianna Pegno, our intern, who dedicated herself entirely to the project for many months. Additional assistance came from Lee Clark, curatorial assistant at Altria when the book was first conceived, Graham Coreil-Allen, gallery assistant, and Elizabeth Lovero, curatorial assistant. In the Whitney's publications department, I am indebted to the tireless commitment of Rachel de W. Wixom in her role as head of publications, as well as to Beth Turk, assistant editor, for her rigorous editing of the publication's texts and Anita Duquette, manager, rights and reproductions, for ensuring that all images were correctly captioned and credited. Nerissa Dominguez Vales coordinated the production with dedication and skill, and Barbara Glauber, assisted by Erika Nishizato, designed an original and elegant volume that captures the essence of Whitney at Altria's mission and impact.

SHAMIM M. MOMIN
BRANCH DIRECTOR AND CURATOR, WHITNEY MUSEUM OF AMERICAN ART

NOTE TO THE READER: *This anthology is intended to function both as a means of capturing the spirit and mission of the branch museum and as a sourcebook for readers interested in the institutional history of contemporary art in New York. To that end, we have provided multiple points of access for the reader: chronological spreads of either excerpts or full reprints of brochure essays accompanied by visuals from the exhibitions and selected images from concurrent performances that provide a sense of tone and experience, followed by comprehensive listings of all of the exhibitions and performances, indexed chronologically and by artist. Texts without attributions were produced by the staff of the Whitney Museum of American Art.*

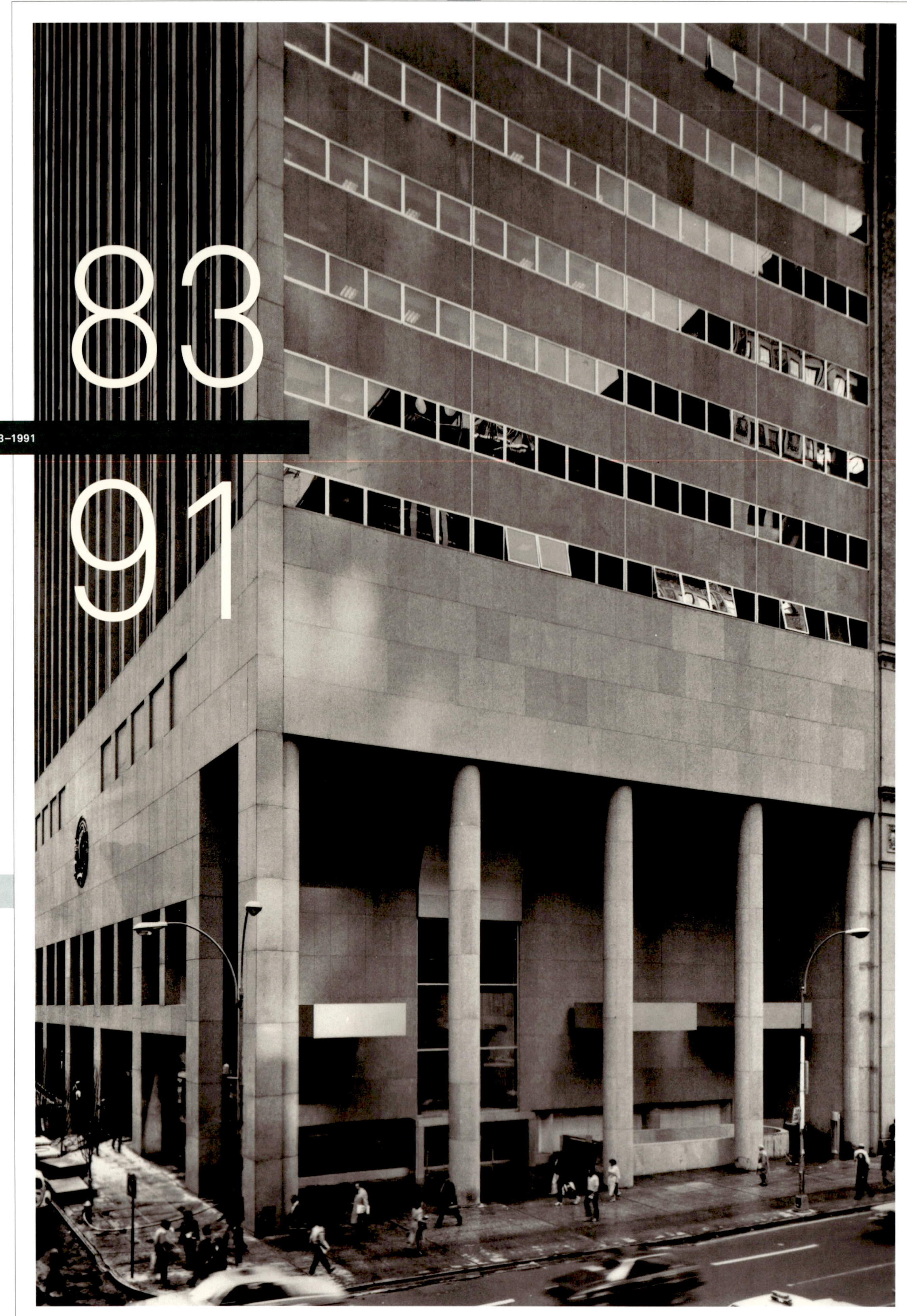
83
91
1983–1991

In 1977, the Whitney Museum was invited by Philip Morris Incorporated to consider operating a branch museum in the new Philip Morris headquarters to be built at Park Avenue and 42nd Street, one of the busiest intersections in the world. For the first time, a corporation was proposing to act as host for a cultural facility....

The arrangement first suggested by Philip Morris, whereby a corporation supports American art—primarily the work of living artists—for the benefit of the public, is especially noteworthy. In essence, the corporation is publicly and proudly identifying itself with the achievements of American artists. —TOM ARMSTRONG, DIRECTOR, WHITNEY MUSEUM OF AMERICAN ART

The opening of the Whitney Museum of American Art at Philip Morris is the culmination of several years of planning and discussion. Without the support of our host, Philip Morris Incorporated, the project would never have been conceived and realized. Those artists who have created works especially for the Sculpture Court—John Chamberlain, Mark di Suvero, and George Segal— deserve the deepest gratitude for their exceptional contributions. —LISA PHILLIPS, ASSOCIATE CURATOR, BRANCH MUSEUMS

Twentieth-Century
Sculpture: Process and Presence

April 8 to May 11, 1983

Modern art has taken as its principal challenge the testing of its own definitions. This is why much work, when it is new, often seems to have departed from everything previously known as art. By necessity, the testing must take place in those borderline areas between art and non-art. —LISA PHILLIPS, ASSOCIATE CURATOR, BRANCH MUSEUMS

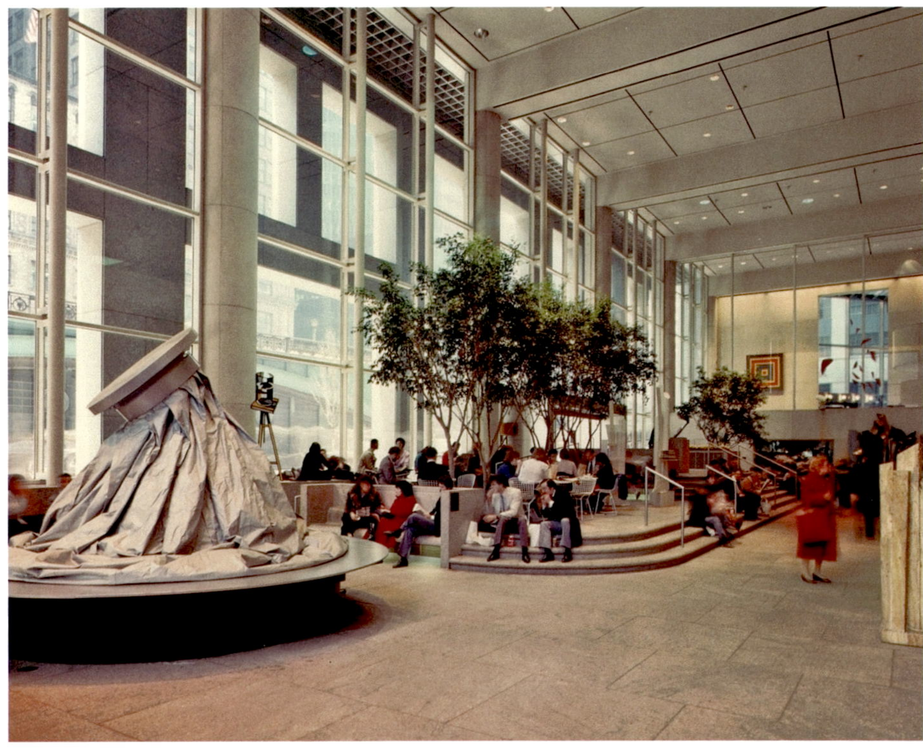

Left to right: Claes Oldenburg, *Ice Bag–Scale C,* 1971; Roy Lichtenstein, *Gold Fish Bowl,* 1977; Frank Stella, *Gran Cairo,* 1962; Alexander Calder, *Big Red,* 1959 (installation view of *Twentieth-Century Sculpture: Process and Presence*).
OPPOSITE: Exterior view of Whitney Museum of American Art at Altria (Philip Morris), c. 1983.

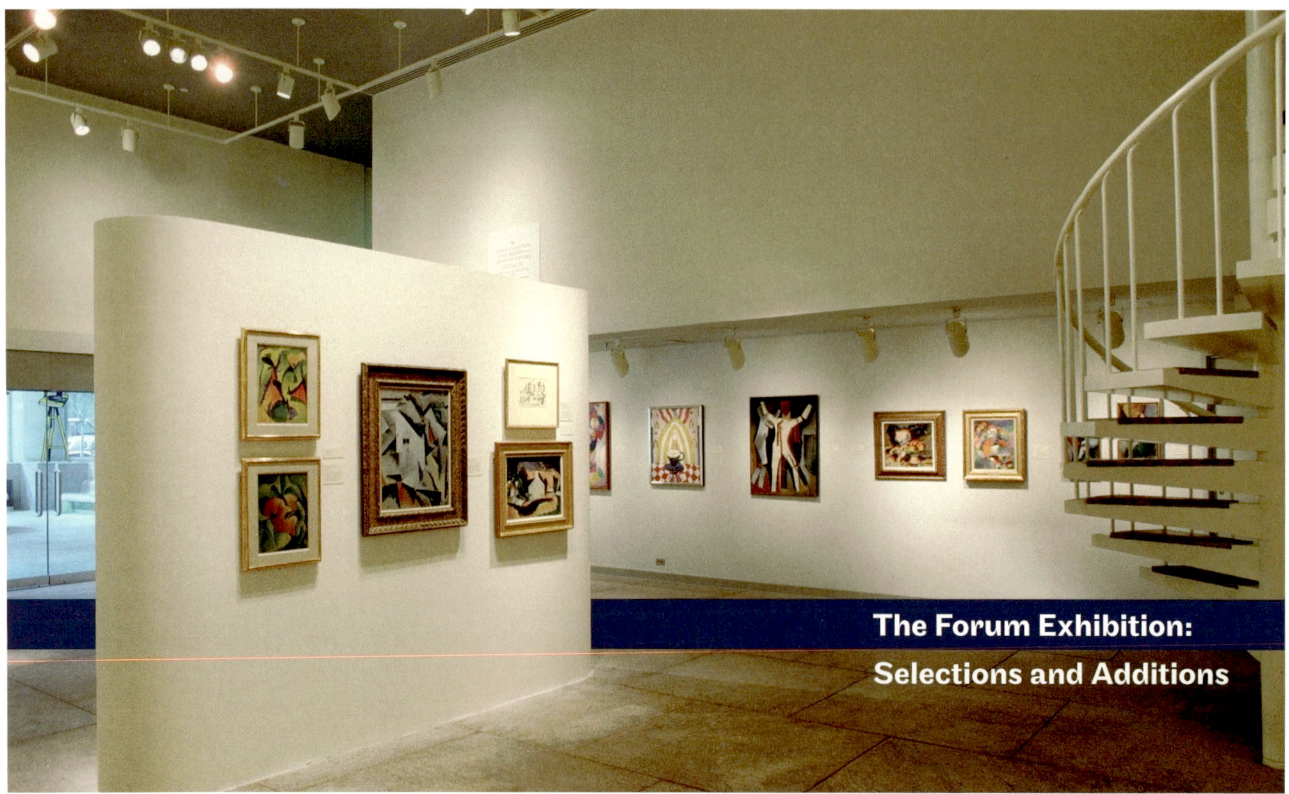

Installation view of *The Forum Exhibtion: Selections and Additions.*

S.E.M Ensemble

New York
Grand Opera Singers

Hanne Tierney

Bill and Mary Buchen

Mel Wong
Dance Company

Sally Gross

Peter Griggs

The New York
Kammermusiker

Margaret Leng Tam

New England Bach
Festival Ensemble

Joan Jonas

Theodora Skipitares
& Company

The Forum Exhibition:
Selections and Additions

May 18 to June 22, 1983

The Forum Exhibition of Modern American Painters, held at the Anderson Galleries in New York in 1916, was the single most important exhibition of its kind during the early years of the twentieth century. The exhibition was organized as America's response to the Armory Show's European section, which received unprecedented attention and interest at the expense of America's native art. It's partial re-creation here offers us not only an excellent opportunity to rediscover and reassess the early work of many of the painters who were later to be considered among America's foremost modern artists, but also to examine their role in the development of modern art in America. For most of these modernists, the paintings they exhibited at the Anderson Galleries remain the most original and experimental of their careers. . . .

. . . Although the present exhibition cannot be considered a definitive reconstruction, it does represent a serious, comprehensive attempt to locate all of the paintings included in the original exhibition. —ANNE HARRELL, HELENE RUBINSTEIN FELLOW, WHITNEY MUSEUM INDEPENDENT STUDY PROGRAM

The Box Transformed

February 15 to April 25, 1985

Box-like configurations have appeared with exceptional frequency in postwar American sculpture. As a container for assemblage, the box functions as a frame—a kind of miniature tableau. For Minimalist artists and their successors, it became an ideal form for their reductive aesthetic. The box has thus undergone extreme transformations— transformations that belie its ostensible simplicity and testify to the imaginative range of the sculptors.

—CORINNE DISERENS, PAM MASLANSKY, AMY MIZRAHI, ELIZABETH SHRIVER, AND ZIBA DE WECK, HELENA RUBINSTEIN FELLOWS, WHITNEY MUSEUM INDEPENDENT STUDY PROGRAM

July 19 to October 3, 1985

The Masses, published in Greenwich Village between 1911 and 1917, brought together a talented group of artists, intellectuals, and activists in an atmosphere of creative impertinence and political concern. The magazine not only examined the social issues of its extraordinary era, but made a lasting contribution to the history of American graphics by publishing some of the best and most characteristic drawings by the urban realists now known as the Ashcan School.

—REBECCA ZURIER, GUEST CURATOR

Art for The Masses 1911–1917:
A Radical Magazine and Its Graphics

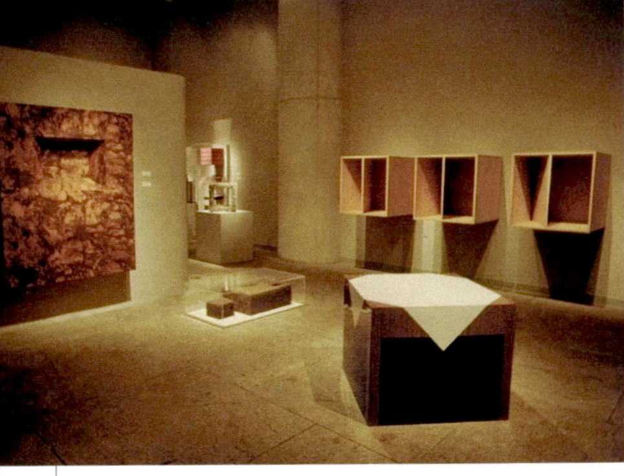

Left to right: Richard Artschwager, *Construction with Indentation*, 1966; *Hair Box*, 1969; *Hair Box 3*, 1969; Lucas Samaras, *Box #56*, 1966; *Untitled*, 1964, Donald Judd, *Untitled*, 1978; Richard Artschwager, *Description of a Table*, 1964 (installation view of *The Box Transformed*).

Jeff Way

Robert Sherman

PERFORMERS 85

The Microscopic Septet

Scott Johnson

Blondell Cummings

Elodie Lauten

Metropolitan All Stars

The Bronzino Duo

Lenny Pickett

Marco Rizo and His Latin-Jazz Quartet

Susan Marshall & Company

Perry Hoberman

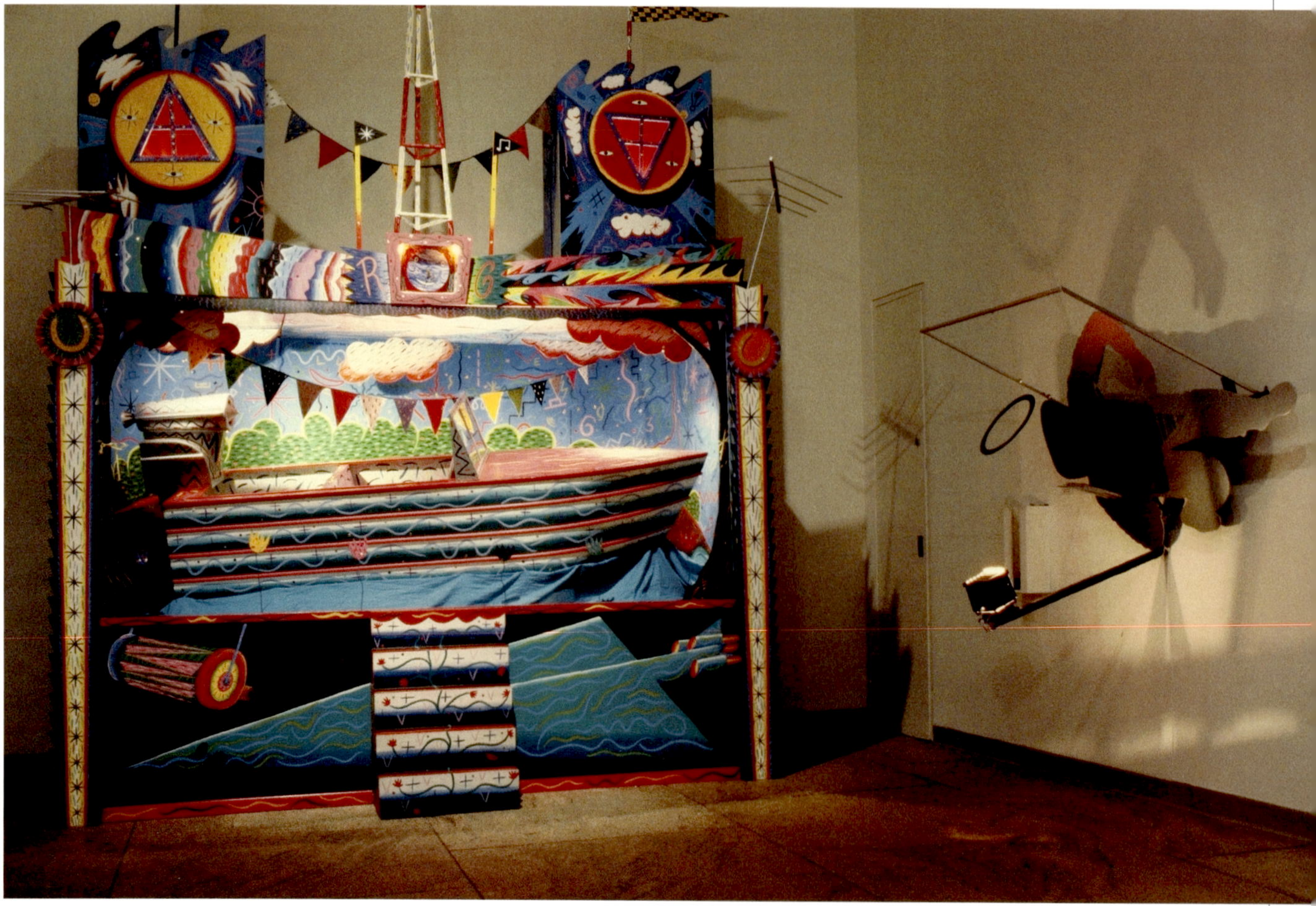

Left to right: Rodney Alan Greenblat, *Boat*, 1981; Perry
Hoberman, *Arms Length*, 1985.

The Ordinaires—
Ton Simons and Dancers

Fred Houn and
The Asian American
Art Ensemble

Bebe Miller and Company

Neil B. Rolnick

S.E.M Ensemble

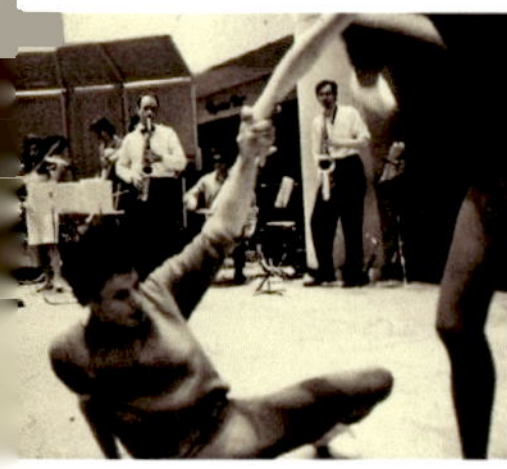

The Ordinaires, 05–01–86

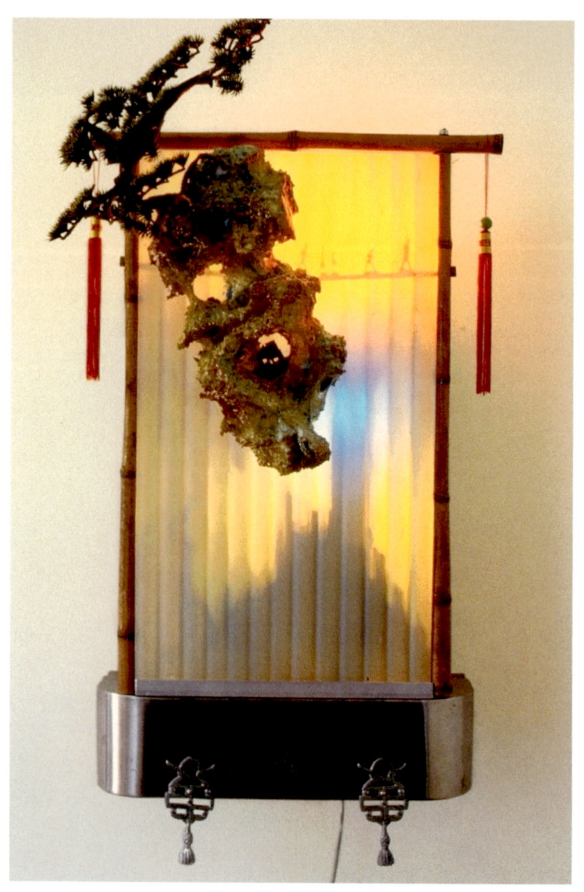

Jon Kessler, *Third Floor Fountain*, 1985 (installation view of *Modern
Machines: Recent Kinetic Sculpture*).

October 11 to December 5, 1985
Through the playful treatment of the
utilitarian, the distortion of physical
properties, and the juxtaposition of moving parts exposed or hidden, the power
of human ingenuity is at certain times
reaffirmed and, at others, viewed with
suspicion. Whatever its form, at present or
in the future, the machine has become
a central feature of twentieth-century art.
—SUSAN LUBOWSKY, BRANCH DIRECTOR

Modern Machines:
Recent Kinetic Sculpture

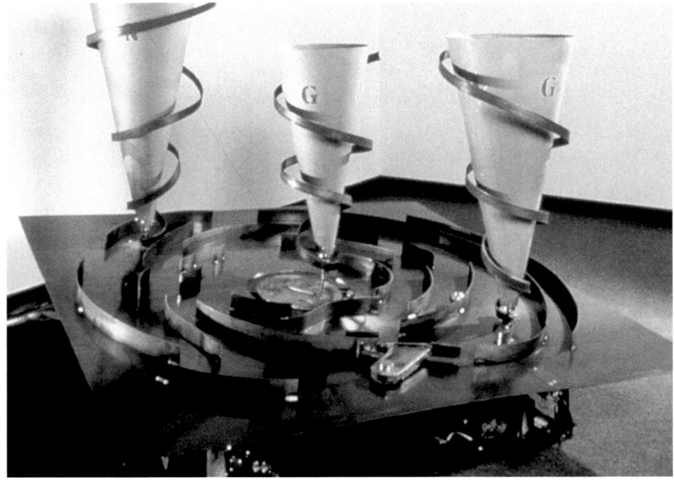

Alice Aycock, *Greased Lightning*, 1984 (installation view of
Modern Machines: Recent Kinetic Sculpture).

David Tudor

Uwe Mengel

Dianne Ruth McIntyre's
Sounds in Motion
Dance Company

Johann Carlo and
Michael Butler

Frankie Mann

John Zorn

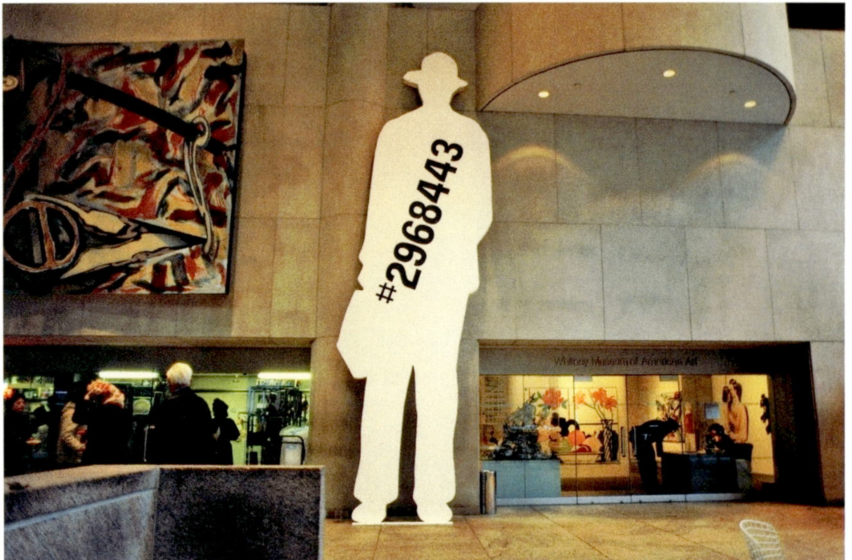

TOP: Left to right: Frank Stella, *Dove of Tanna*, 1977; Jonathan Borofsky, *Man with Briefcase #2,968,443*, 1986 (installation view of *Contemporary Cutouts*). **BOTTOM:** Stuart Davis, *Place Pasdeloup*, 1928.

Contemporary Cutouts

November 26, 1986 to February 17, 1987

During the 1960s, in the wake of Abstract Expressionism, artists began to question the traditional distinction between sculpture and painting. The cutout was one of the new art forms that emerged to challenge these conventions. Figurative artists such as Red Grooms, Alex Katz, Roy Lichtenstein, and Larry Rivers either cut out or reinterpreted images from their paintings, thus removing them from the artificial world of the picture plane to create a form of two-dimensional sculpture....

...No longer reflecting the Pop culture of the 1960s, the cutout asserts its place in contemporary art, not only as an art object, but as an icon of our time. —SUSAN LUBKOWSKY, BRANCH DIRECTOR

Stuart Davis:
An American in Paris

October 2 to December 10, 1987

In Paris, he remained essentially a Cubist painter, unaffected by the avant-garde styles then predominant—Surrealism and various forms of geometric abstraction. For this reason, Davis' Paris sojourn, in the eyes of some critics, interrupted the progress of his art. "Seduced" by his surroundings, as Brian O'Doherty put it, Davis "confected idealized stage sets for a nostalgic musical of an American artist

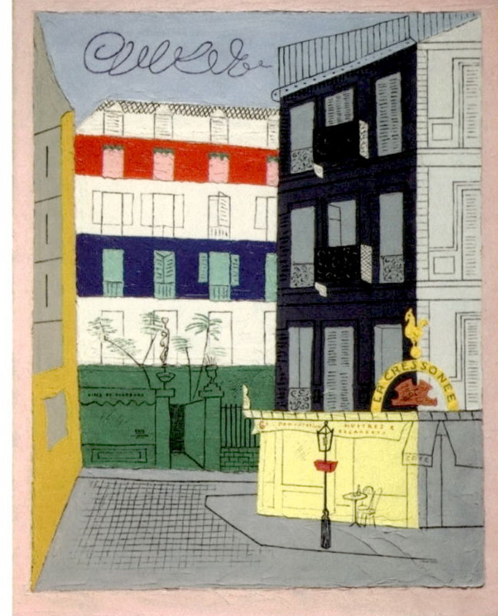

in Paris." Those who view Davis' art as a march toward abstraction have therefore found no place for his more realistic Paris paintings. —LEWIS KACHUR, GUEST CURATOR

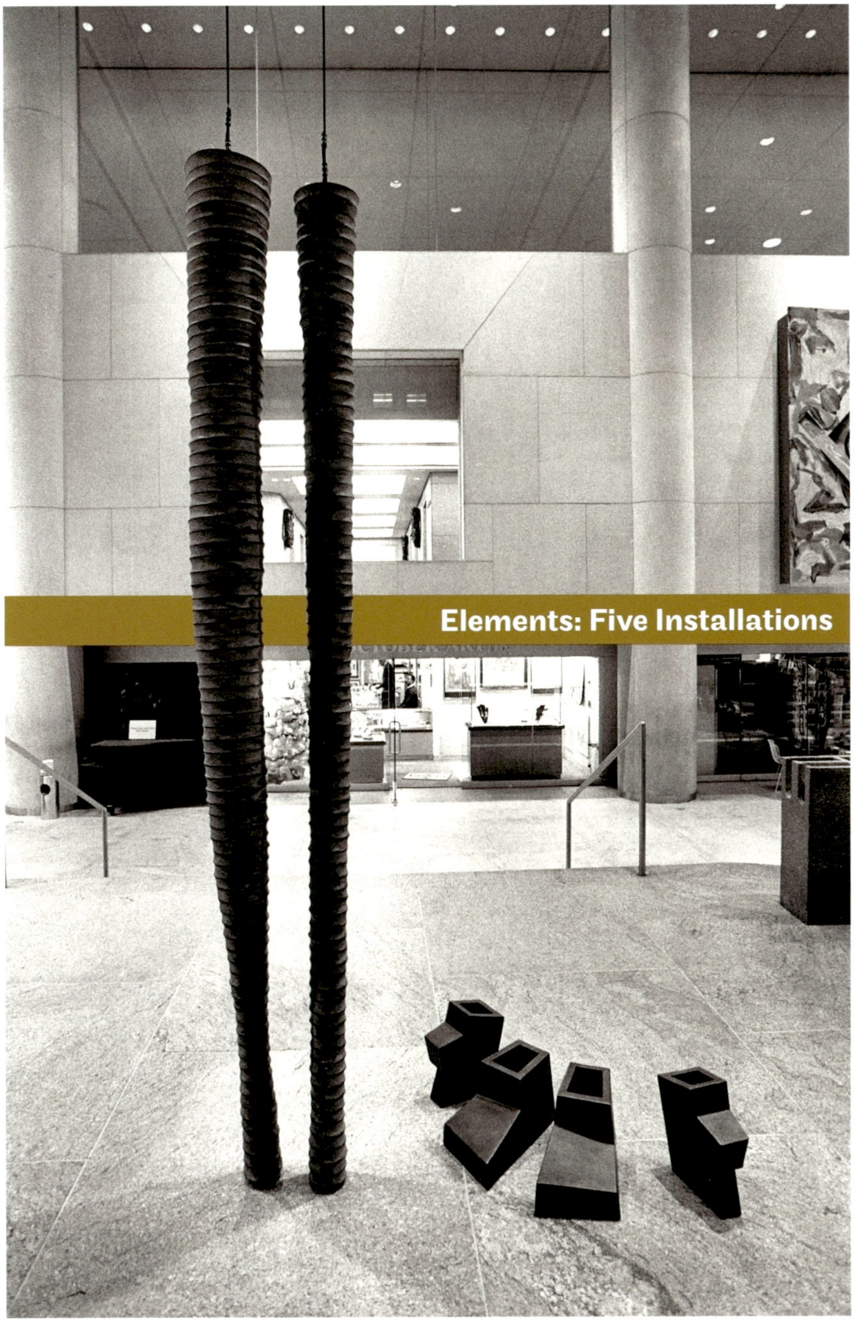

Left to right: Peter Shelton, *Big Legs*, 1983;
Shoes, Gloves, 1983 (installation view of
Elements: Five Installations).

December 18, 1987 to February 18, 1988
The works of the five artists represented
in this exhibition are united by concept
rather than visual similarity. Petah Coyne,
Mineko Grimmer, Ann Hamilton, Eric Orr,
and Peter Shelton are concerned with
the harmony, balance, and process of natural elements and the contradictions
found in nature itself. Although the works
take many different forms, with references sometimes direct but often oblique,
they all project a sense of the familiar
and intimate. The materials used—
water, air, light, stone, metal, wood—form
part of our collective associations,
our personal experiences and memories.
By using phenomenological information
about the universe, each of these artists
has produced an independent language
of feeling; they tell us something about
ourselves, how we respond, and what
happens in our real or imagined rapport
with nature. —KATHLEEN MONAGHAN,
GUEST CURATOR

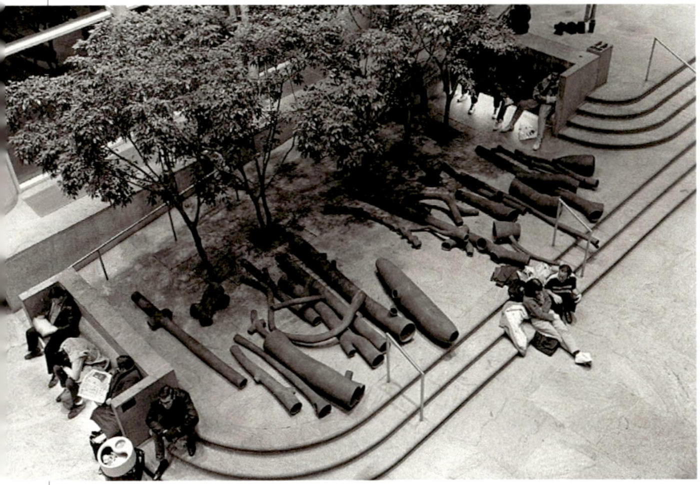

12
–
18
–
87

02
–
18
–
88

Peter Shelton, *TUB, tubes and pipes*, 1987
(installation view of *Elements: Five Installations*).

Akbar Ale and the Black
Swan Quartet

Yoshiko Chuma and
The School of Hard Knocks

Urban Bush Women

David Moss Desne Band

Merián Soto and
Pepón Osorio

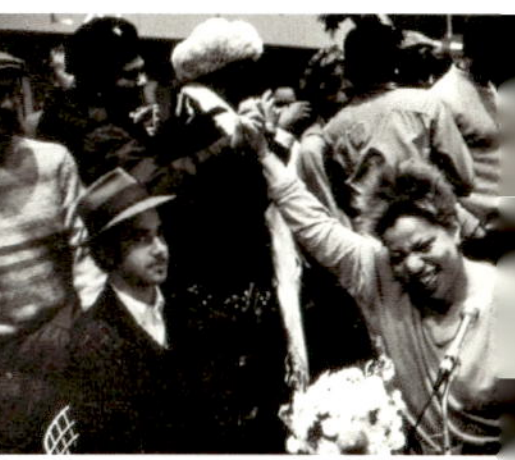

Urban Bush Women,
in Process Re: Heat, 11–11–87

May 6 to September 22, 1988

The most publicized portraiture shocks us out of that stable acceptance of the way part relates to implied whole and performance to being.

As many portraits have lately shown, playacting has gained such dominance, at the expense of the player, that it seems utterly quaint and useless to wonder about who the person portrayed was or is. For the sitter's pictorial guise has absorbed into itself all of the merely idiosyncratic possibilities of a character—has sucked them away into a bright or a sullen grimace. If the viewer is led to anything, it could only be to that which has replaced personality.

—MAX KOZLOFF, GUEST CURATOR

Real Faces

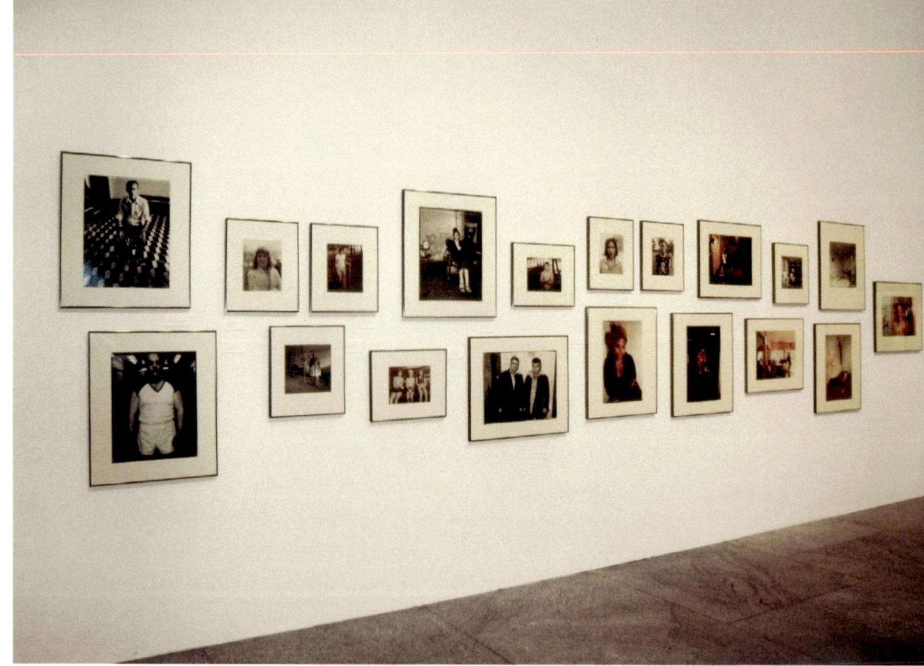

Installation view of *Real Faces*.

The Reggie Workman Ensemble with The Maya Milenovic Dancers

Fast Forward and Ishmael Houston-Jones

Alice Farley and Company

Horvitz, Morris, Previte Trio

Guy Klucevsek

Edwina Lee Tyler & A Piece of the World

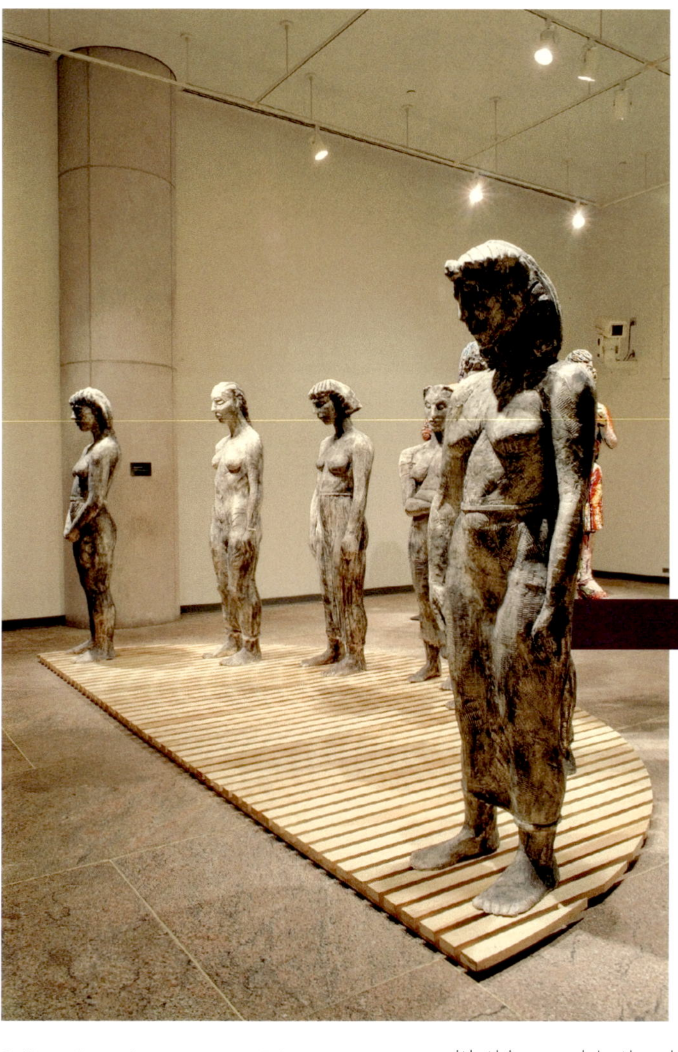

Deborah Masters, *Circle*, 1988
(installation view of *Urban Figures*).

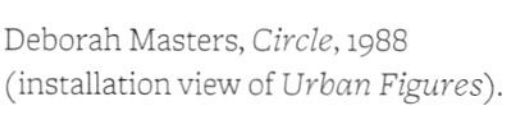

Urban Figures

Gallery: November 17, 1988 to February 15, 1989
Sculpture Court: November 1, 1988
to November 1, 1989

Plato had little time for representations of the material world. He believed that such illusions beguiled people into mistaking the everyday world for the only truth or reality. And representational art, aided by its seductive illusionistic powers, may even prevent the quest for truth which, for Plato and his followers, lies in the metaphysical realm. Platonic thought, revived in later centuries as Neoplatonism, has a long and intertwined history with art. . . .

Urban Figures includes the work of two generations of artists who took issue with this creed. In the older generation, George Segal was impatient with the Abstract Expressionists, while in the next, Jonathan Borofsky reacted with equal force against the Minimalists and Conceptualists. Many of the artists in this exhibition began their careers as abstract painters, but eventually turned from painting to figurative sculpture out of a desire to make art, ideas, and the representation of the human condition accessible again to a larger audience.

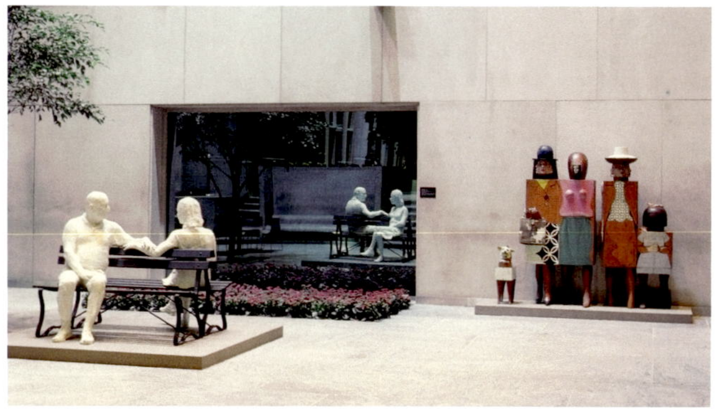

Left to right: George Segal, *Couple on Two Benches*, 1985;
Marisol, *Women and Dog*, 1964 (installation view of *Urban Figures*).

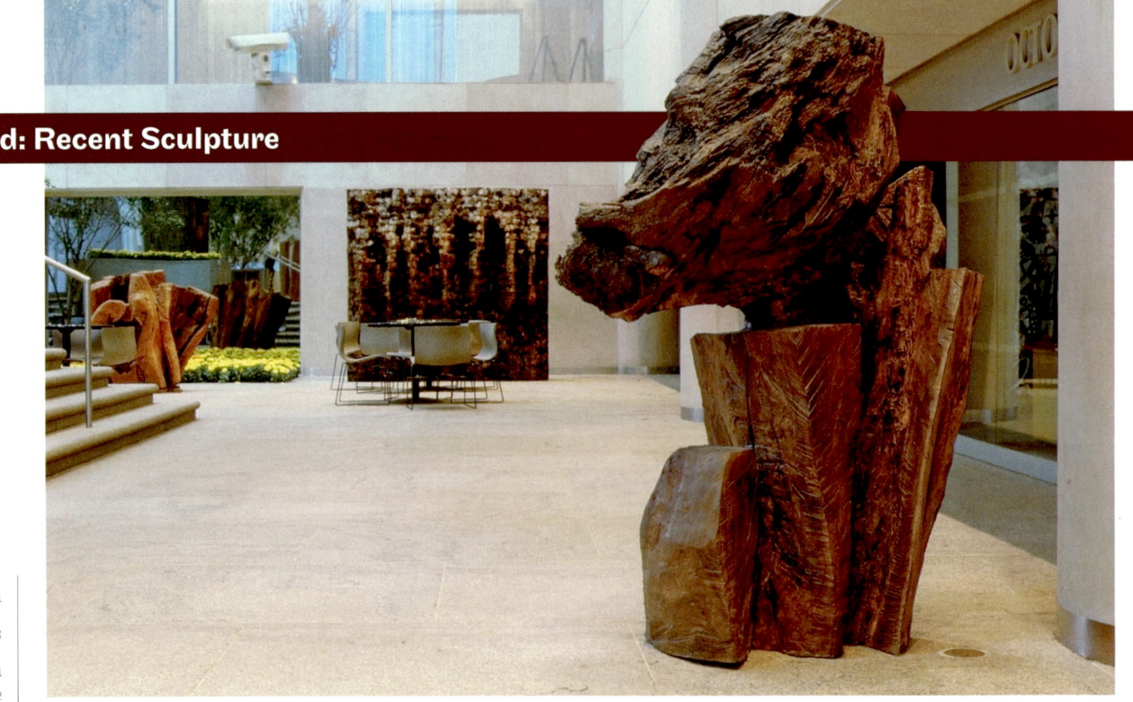

Out of Wood: Recent Sculpture

TOP: Left to right: Raoul Hague, *Feather Farm Cherry*, 1983; Ursula von Rydingsvard, *Lace Mountain*, 1989; Raoul Hague, *Bökens Satire*, 1986 (installation view of *Out of Wood: Recent Sculpture*). **BOTTOM:** Ursula von Rydingsvard, *Ursie A's Dream*, 1988.

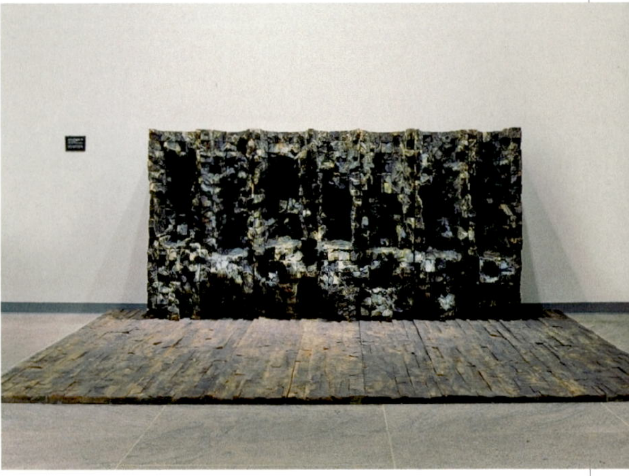

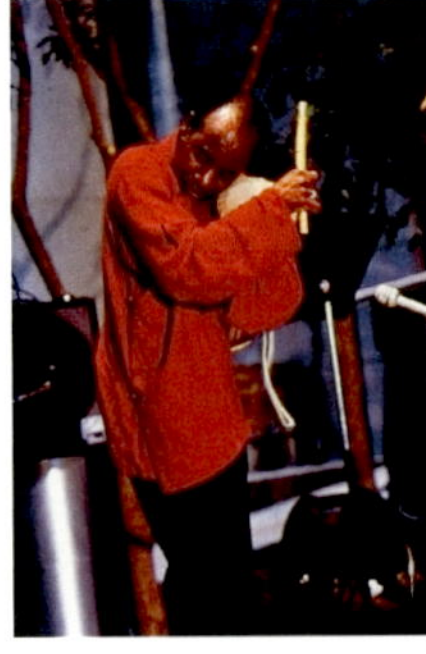

Jalalu-Kalvert Nelson
and Trumpets of Desire,
with TUBATIME, and
The Devastators,
Moving Music, 06–07–89

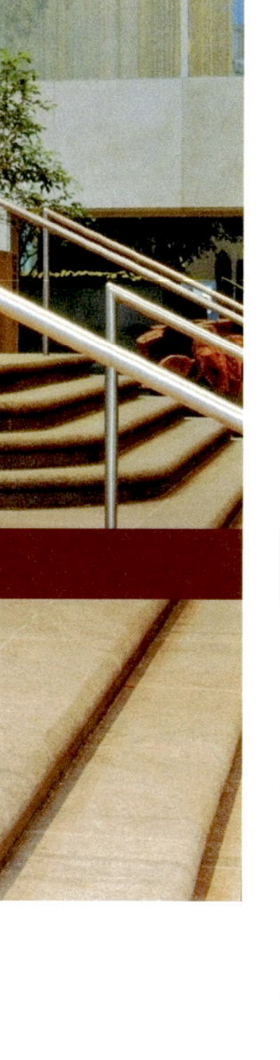

Gallery: December 15, 1989 to February 20, 1990
Sculpture Court: December 1989 to
December 1990

Nature has been a general point of departure for abstraction since the generation of Cézanne and Gauguin. In the twentieth century, biomorphic shapes drawn from organic forms became the mainstay of Surrealism. What came to be known generically as organic abstraction underwent a revival in the early 1970s as artists reacted against the hard-edged rigors of Minimalism. In this context, all the works in the exhibition make reference to natural forms. But they also depend on the special properties of wood. Work of any kind leaves a permanent mark on wood, a mark that cannot be painted over or melted down, which then becomes an integral part of the sculpture. Moreover, all the pieces in the exhibition evolve from the fundamental shape and characteristics of the tree. The artists invent new, raw configurations of sylvan forms and profiles and, through hacking, hewing, sawing, shaping, cutting, and carving, they create a new awareness of the grand physicality as well as the formal and sensual dimensions of wood in its natural state.
—JOSEPHINE GEAR, BRANCH DIRECTOR

Malika Lee Whitney's
The Pickney Players

Fred Hopkins,
Diedre Murray, and
Richard "Shake-A-Leg"
Thomas

Brenda Wong Aoki

Constance De Jong

Peter Gordon

PERFORMERS 90

Peter Cook and Kenny
Lerner

Helen Thorington

New American Radio

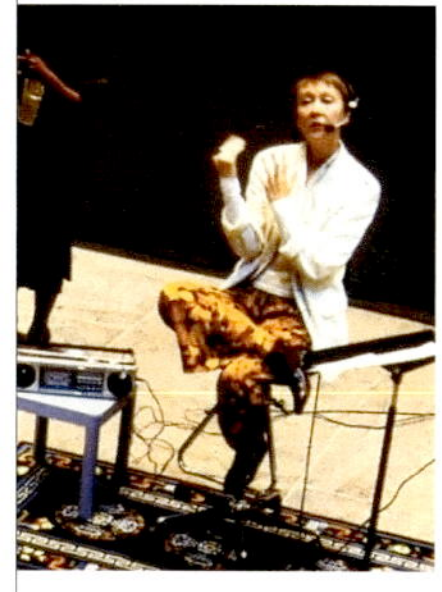

Constance De Jong,
Vanishing Acts, 06–06–90

TOP: Left to right: Raoul Hague, *Willy's Bride*, 1981-82;
Jene Highstein, *Tree Form*, 1988 (installation view of
Out of Wood: Recent Sculpture).

Clockwise from top: Steve Keister, *Anisotropy*, 1990, and *Epigene*, 1990; George Sugarman, *White and Gray Vertical*, 1987–89; Melvin Edwards, *Asafokra*, 1990; John Chamberlain, *Fuccimanooli*, 1990 (installation view of *Painted Forms: Recent Metal Sculpture*). **OPPOSITE:** Installation view of Lucky DeBellevue, *Khlysty, the Owls, and the Others* (see page 120).

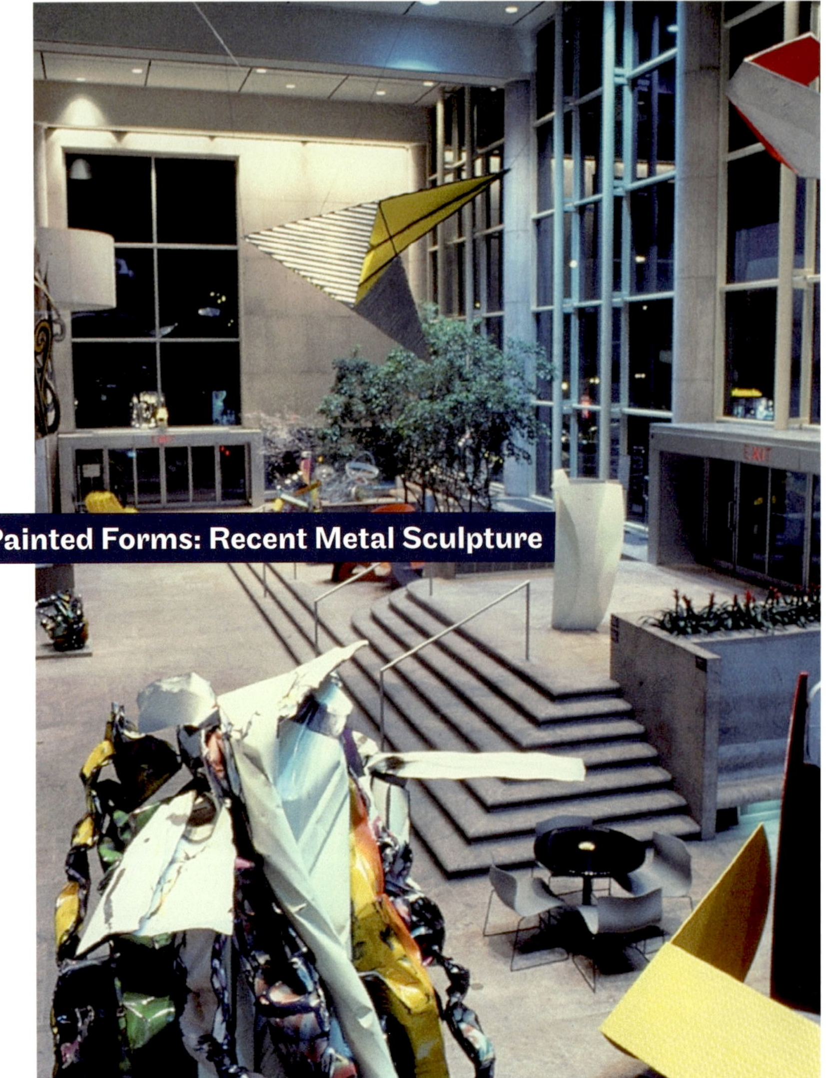

Painted Forms: Recent Metal Sculpture

**Gallery: December 19, 1990 to February 20, 1991
Sculpture Court: December 19, 1990 to
December 1991**

Painted sculpture stands out against the kaleidoscope of our urban environment, yet it fits right in with it, providing a mirror of the city's movement and dynamic interaction of form and space. Like a wild card, color also offers the artist a full range of strategies and the public a challenge; we need some savvy to catch all the subtleties. —JOSEPHINE GEAR, BRANCH DIRECTOR

June 12 to September 5, 1991

For sixty years, the Museum has been committed to the risks and rewards of this ongoing engagement with the

Drawing Acquisitions,

1980–1991: Selections from the Permanent Collection of the Whitney Museum of American Art

contemporary. This exhibition is not a historical survey propelled by a single idea or ideal, but a very small selection of drawing acquisitions made in the last decade; it serves as a highlighted cross section of the Museum's dialogue with the dialogue of art.

The process of selection for the exhibition was also affected by extra-artistic criteria: the size of the gallery space at Philip Morris; the availability of individual works (some are on loan to outside institutions, some will shortly be seen in other Whitney spaces); the strictures of the market; and the inter-action of the drawing curator with the acquisition committee.

—KLAUS KERTESS, ADJUNCT CURATOR, DRAWINGS, WHITNEY MUSEUM OF AMERICAN ART

Mickey Davidson,
Jeanne Lee, and
Ntozake Shange

Lambs Eat Ivy

Carol Emanuel and
Zeena Perkins

Geri Allen and
Don Pullen

Dierdre Murray

Zella Jackson Price

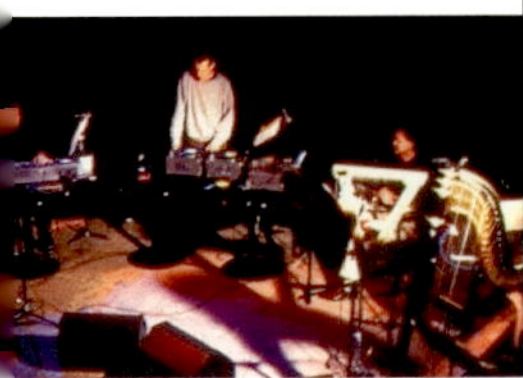

Carol Emanuel and Zeena
Perkins, 03–19–91

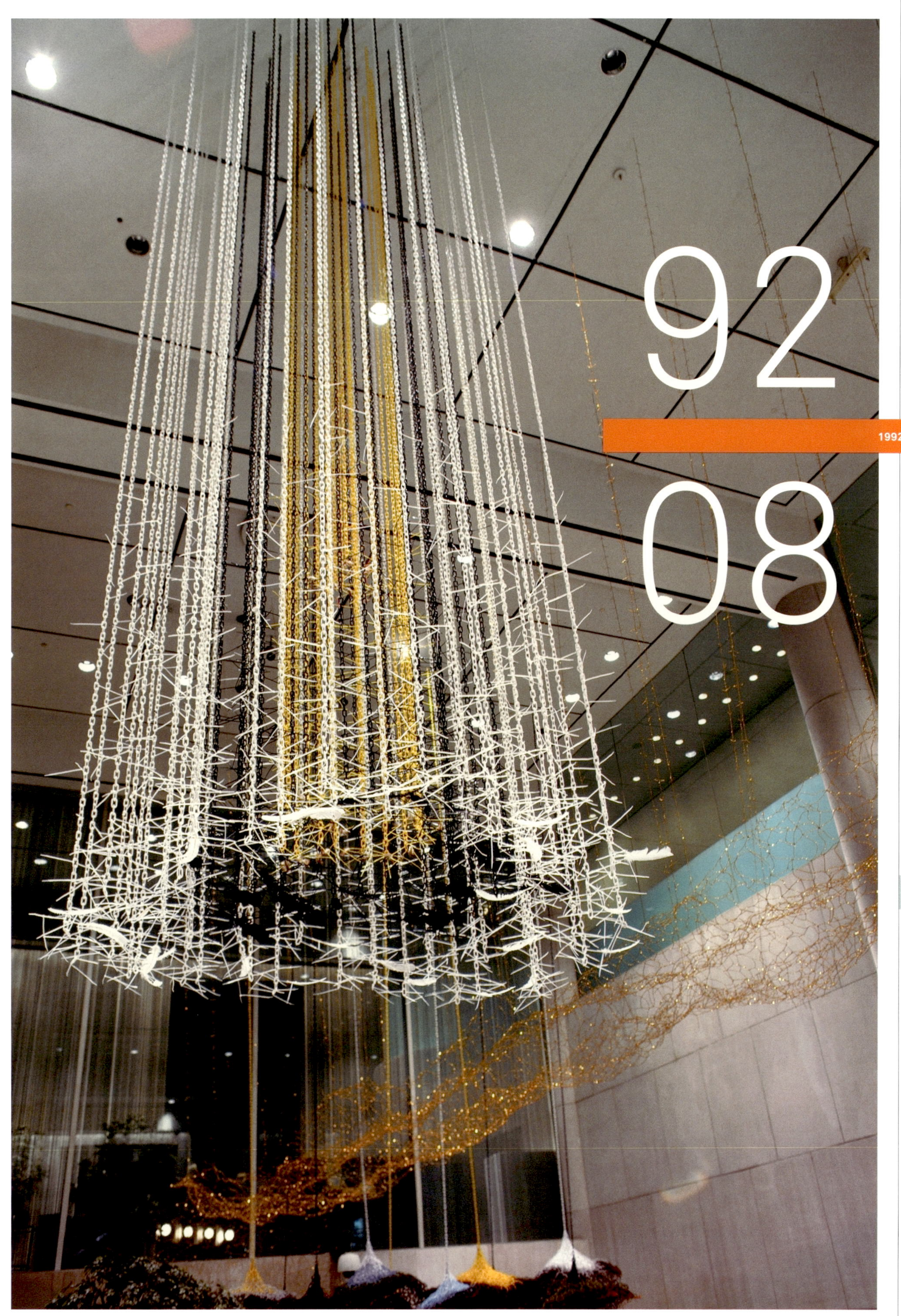
92
08
1992–2008

December 4, 1991 to February 8, 1992

In 1861 Harriet Jacobs published her autobiography, *Incidents in the Life of a Slave Girl, Written by Herself*, under the pseudonym Linda Brent. In the tradition of slave narratives, the autobiography details the circumstances of her life as a slave in North Carolina and her attempt to escape from her physically and psychologically abusive master. This attempt was initially thwarted, and Jacobs had to be concealed in the eaves of a shed in her grandmother's home for seven years, until she could safely escape to the North. In this cramped, dark garret she was able to create a small aperture for herself by boring a drill bit through the wall. It was through this small loophole that Harriet Jacobs maintained contact with the outside world during her years of confinement. This narrative is the reference for Ellen Driscoll's installation *The Loophole of Retreat*. Using a sculptural vocabulary, Driscoll enters Jacobs' text and creates a physical experience loaded with the metaphorical implications of the story. With primitive photographic techniques and a cone that suggests the physical space of the eaves, the installation psychologically intimates the darkness, compression, weightlessness, and loss of self elucidated in the autobiography. —THELMA GOLDEN, BRANCH DIRECTOR

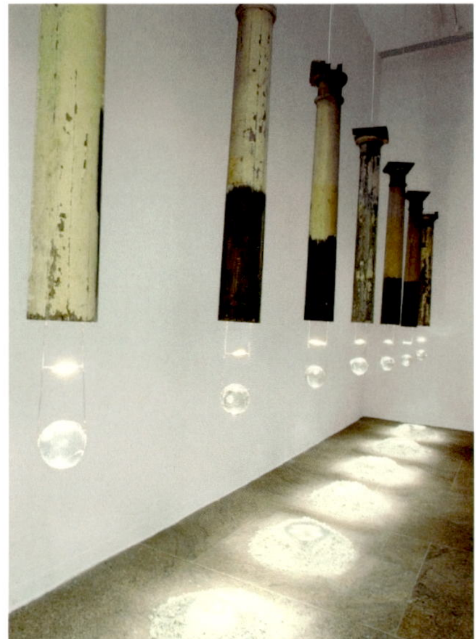

Ellen Driscoll: The Loophole of Retreat

Installation views of *Ellen Driscoll: The Loophole of Retreat*.

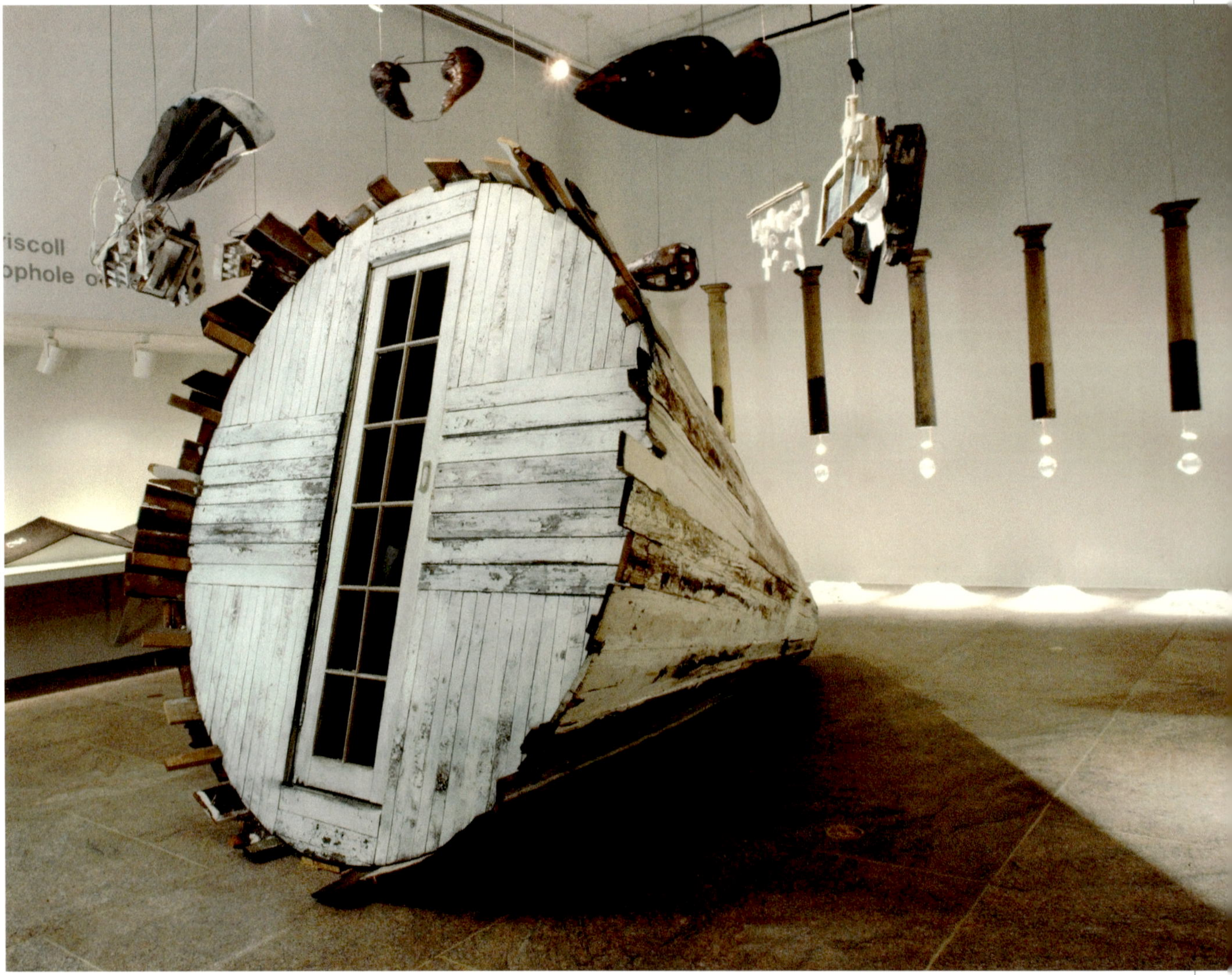

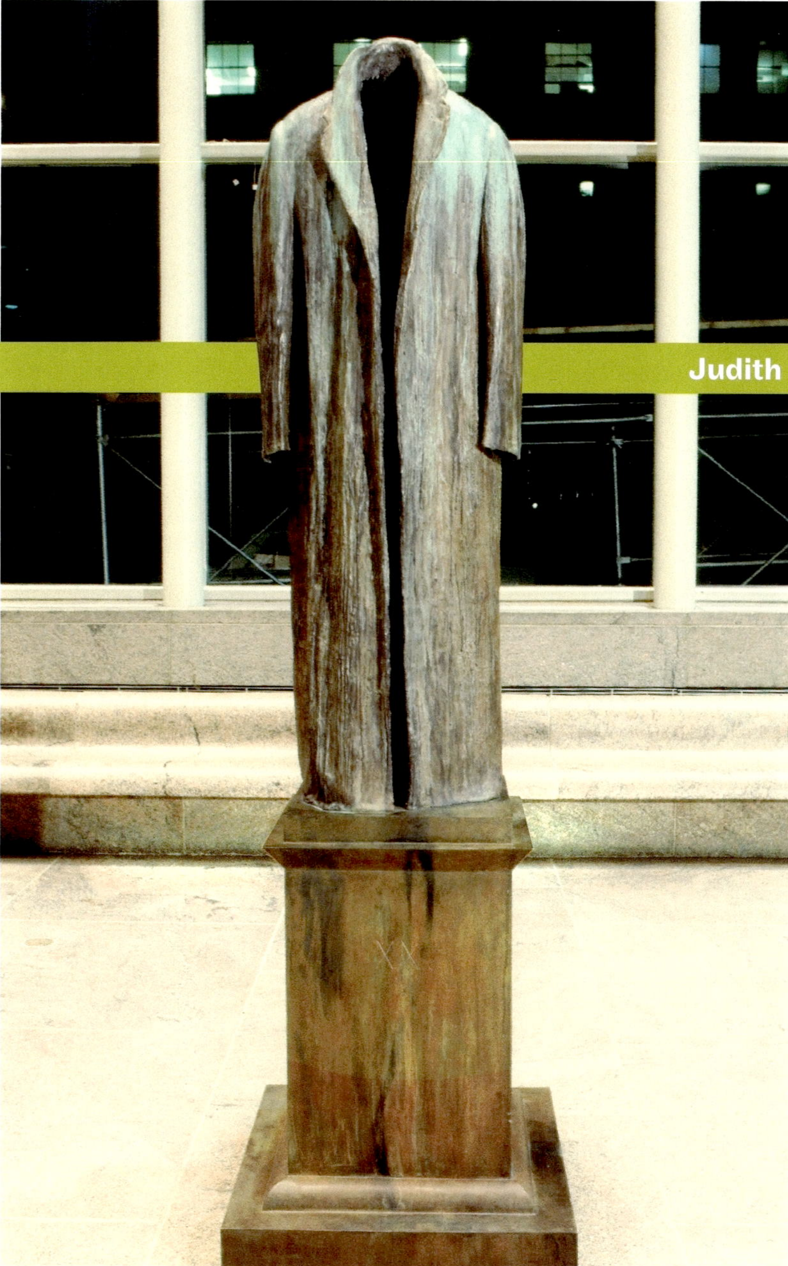

Judith Shea: Monuments and Statues

February 20 to June 20, 1992

At this particularly embattled moment in the history of Western culture, and in the aftermath of the toppling of national statuary in Eastern Europe, Judith Shea has set out to dissect the language of classical monuments. Her installation comprises a progression of three recent bronze sculptures and a new wood sculpture. Both valorizing and deconstructive, they exemplify the feminist impulse to revise history, intervening with the meaning of the monument while reinventing the life of a statue. These works also continue Shea's career-long contemplation of the relationship between the body and its covering. In the mid-1970s, she was among a group of artists who were reinvestigating the role of the figure in

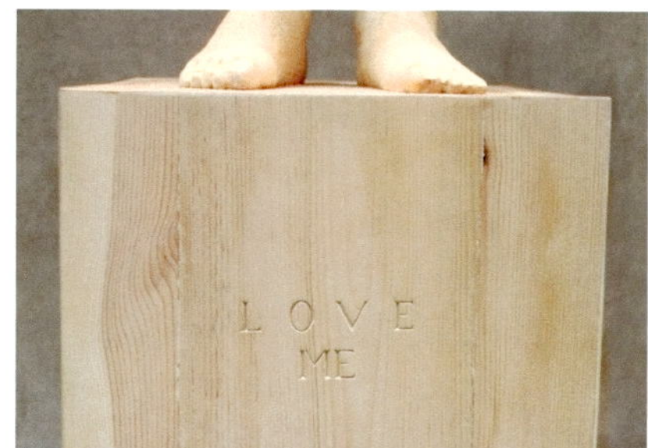

Judith Shea, *Post Balzac*, 1990 (installation view of *Judith Shea: Monuments and Statues*).
RIGHT: Judith Shea, *The Object*, 1992 (installation view of *Judith Shea: Monuments and Statues*).

contemporary sculpture. For Shea, the enterprise continues, and her current pieces confront both the classical past and the imminent future of figurative sculpture. —THELMA GOLDEN, BRANCH DIRECTOR

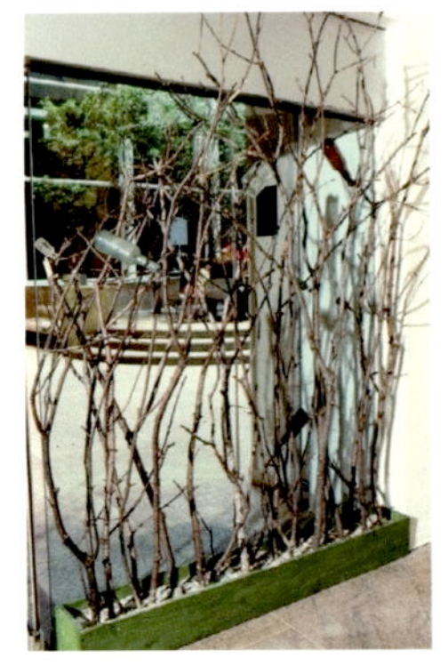

Alison Saar: Slow Boat

Toni Dove

Helen Thorington

Matt Heckert

Hans Moravec

The Wooster Group

Perry Hoberman

92   PERFORMERS

Rachel Rosenthal

Sussan Deyhim

Richard Horowitz

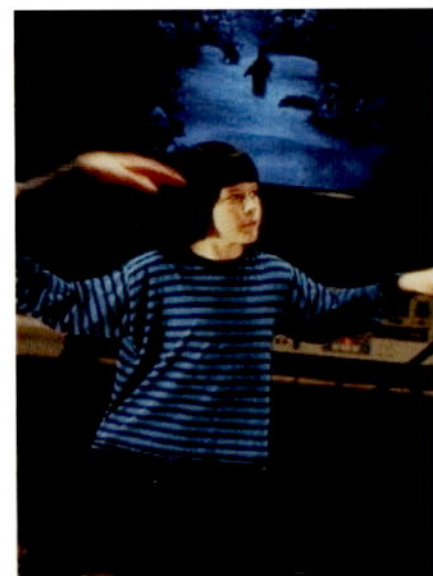

The Wooster Group,
*Rae Whitfield and the
Johnsons Present Dances
from the Wuji Islands,*
04–01–92

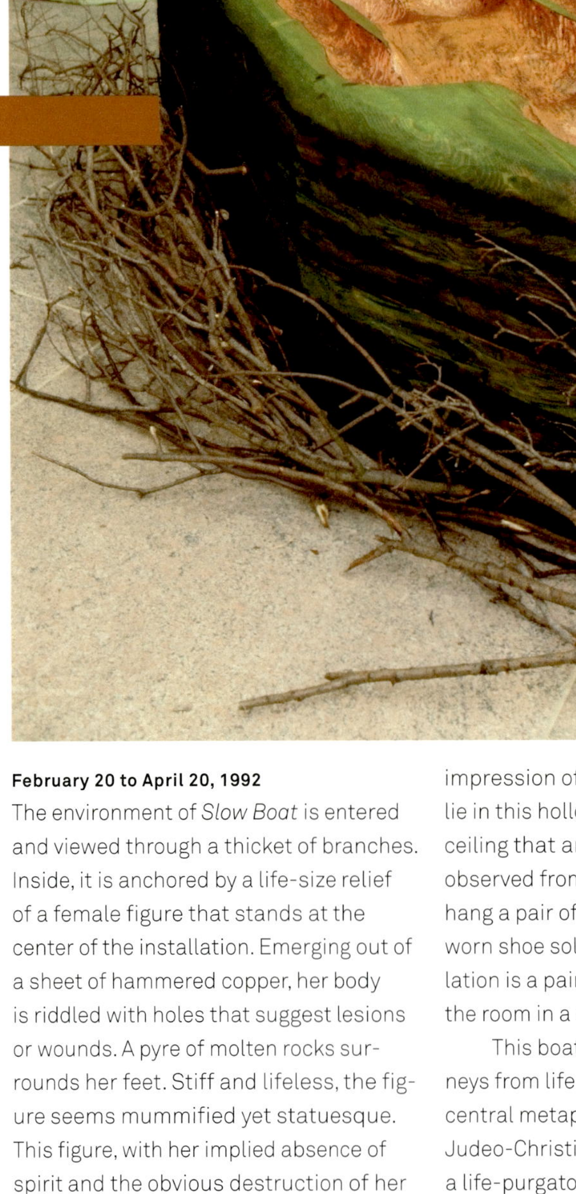

February 20 to April 20, 1992

The environment of *Slow Boat* is entered and viewed through a thicket of branches. Inside, it is anchored by a life-size relief of a female figure that stands at the center of the installation. Emerging out of a sheet of hammered copper, her body is riddled with holes that suggest lesions or wounds. A pyre of molten rocks surrounds her feet. Stiff and lifeless, the figure seems mummified yet statuesque. This figure, with her implied absence of spirit and the obvious destruction of her flesh, exists halfway between a corpse and a live body. Not dead, but dying, succumbing to her decline. In front of the figure is a large, solid rowboat dragging a long strip of satin in its wake. Hollowing out the wood of the boat has left the impression of a 6-foot body. When viewers lie in this hollow, they see aspects of the ceiling that are unintelligible when observed from a standing position. Above hang a pair of wings fashioned from well-worn shoe soles. Surrounding the installation is a painted backdrop that encloses the room in a shadowy, blue-tinged haze.

This boat, this slow boat, which journeys from life to death, conveys Saar's central metaphor. Saar comments on the Judeo-Christian tradition, which sets up a life-purgatory-heaven- or hell sequence of events, each separate in its meaning. *Slow Boat* posits that this passage between life and death has no definitive markers; the living and the dead, the spirit and flesh are intertwined in the voyage of dying.

—THELMA GOLDEN, BRANCH DIRECTOR

Installation view of *Gary Simmons: The Garden of Hate.*

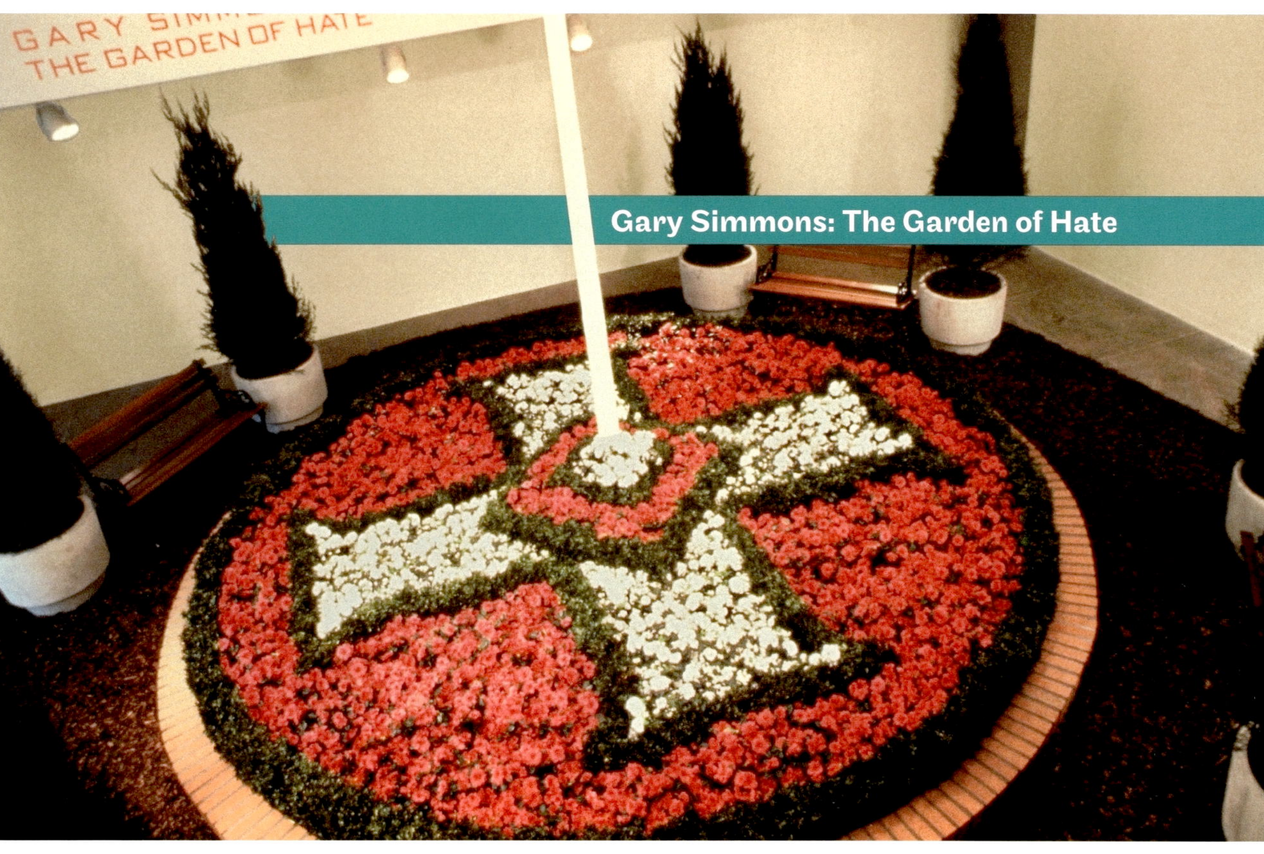

Gary Simmons: The Garden of Hate

May 5 to July 2, 1992

The Garden of Hate is an installation by Gary Simmons. The garden consists of a round flower bed filled with red and white azaleas in the shape of the Ku Klux Klan's cross. Rising from the center is a flagless flagpole. Through the semiotics of garden design, the installation comments on one group's domination over another.

Gary Simmons and Thelma Golden on *The Garden of Hate*:

TG: What was the impetus for this work?

GS: I was thinking about how racism and hate are cloaked and sometimes covered up. I wanted to show how a garden is a symbol of wealth, and that as such it also stands in for institutional racism.

TG: This installation is a real contradiction: you are going to walk in, smell and see the flowers, and then when you really look at them discover a very potent symbol of the Klan.

GS: Right. This work is also about the fallacy of the American dream and the way in which people are supposed to aspire to this dream.

TG: So you are using the KKK as both a literal symbol and as a metaphor for the covert supremacy which exists in this society?

GS: This country was born with hate. . . .

July 17 to September 25, 1992

Chung creates a narrative out of personal experience and the larger epic of immigration that defines America's history. While there are two sides to every story there often are not two willing storytellers. Y. David Chung's art, which investigates this collision of cultures, offers a visual narrative that begins to recount never-told stories. It was very easy for the media to mistakenly identify the Korean immigrant merchants in Los Angeles as part of the problem rather than as necessary participants in the search for a solution. This media coverage presented a monolithic, often one-sided vision of the Korean immigrant experience, stressing their successes in the vacuum of the present with no concrete reference to their past. In this installation, Chung examines the present as well as the past in a Korean immigrant's life. The viewer is offered the immigrant's reflections, milieu, dreams, and a perspective on the complex multi-ethnic matrix in which he exists. With its interrelated stream of visual vignettes, *Turtle Boat Head* fills in the missing chapters of this new history of America as it is being written by those who continue, at all cost, to pursue the American dream. —THELMA GOLDEN, BRANCH DIRECTOR

Y. David Chung: Turtle Boat Head

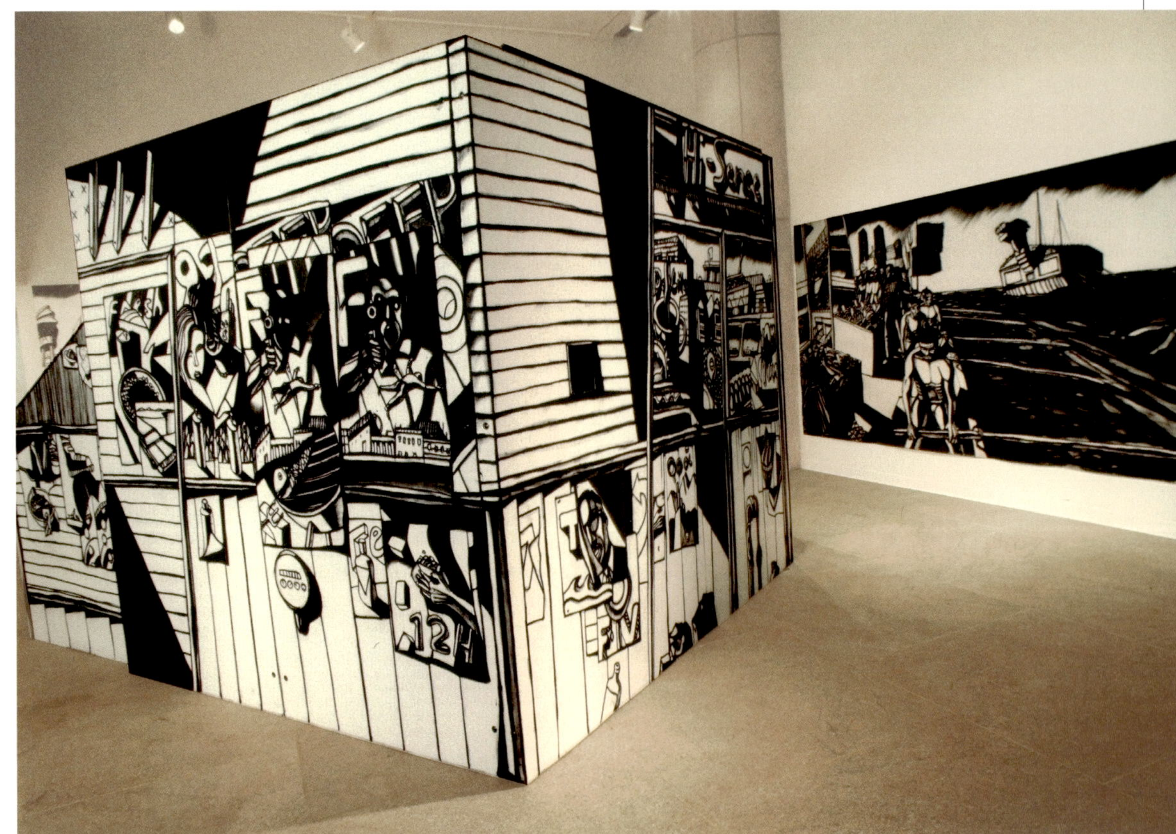

Installation views of *Y. David Chung: Turtle Boat Head*.

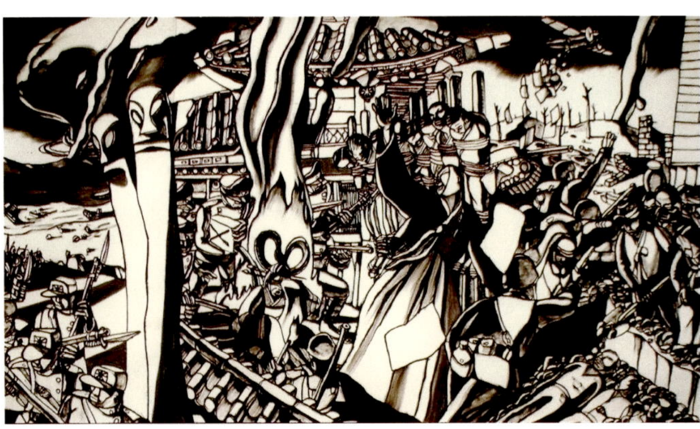

Glenn Ligon: Good Mirrors Are Not Cheap

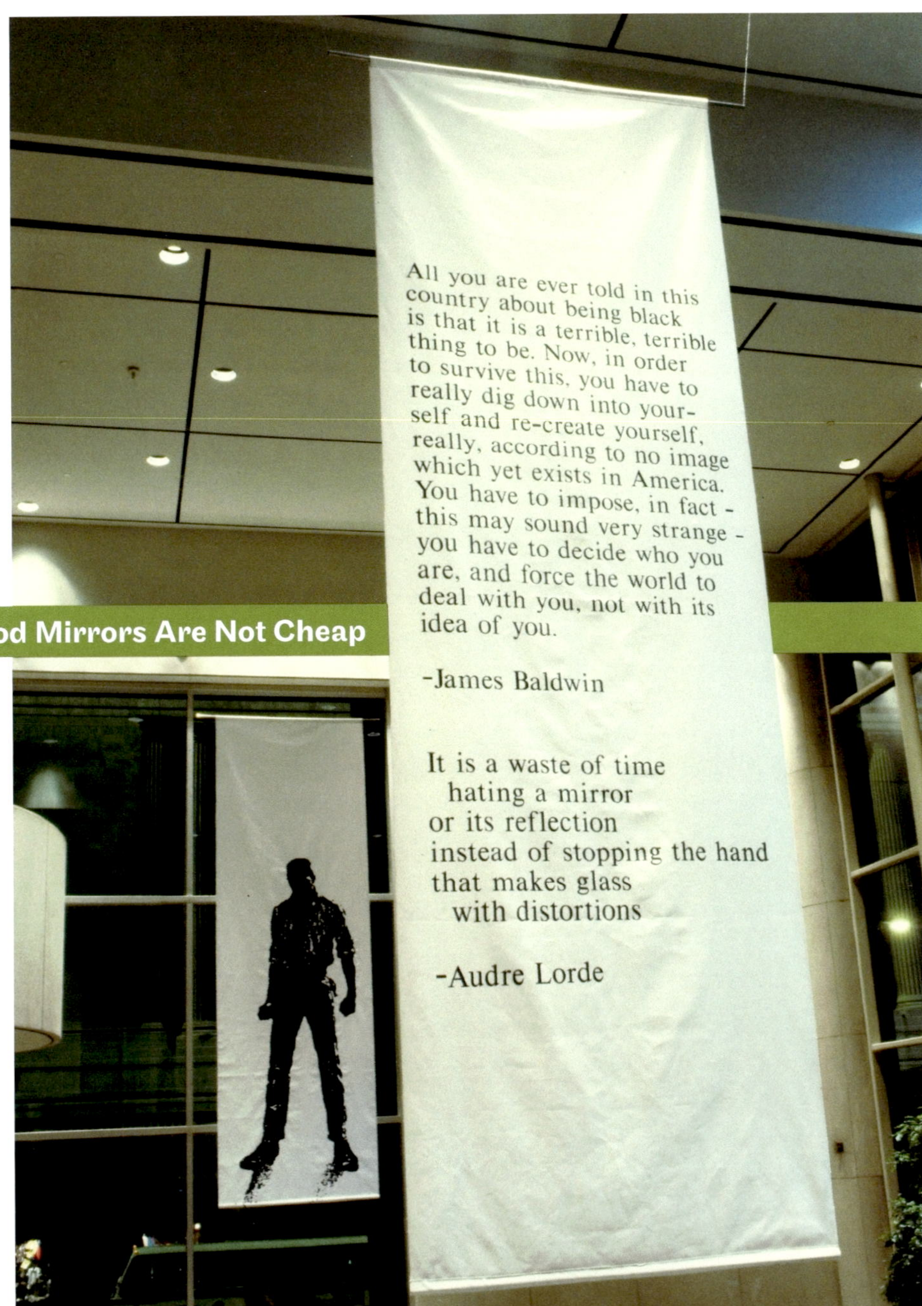

July 17, 1992 to January 1, 1993

An image is commonly understood as a picture, a visual sign system easily recognizable and read. But in the discussion of the construction of images of blackness,
this definition is inadequate—too constricted, too quickly read in the shorthand
language of stereotypes—to convey the depth and complexity of the African-
American identity. Pictures are thus no longer the most reliable tool in an examination of the manifold states that can be called black culture. It is the written word
that has become the oppositional voice which replaces visual representation.

Glenn Ligon is a painter. His canvases operate on dual levels involving the
written text and the images that text conveys. Using words, phrases, and bodies

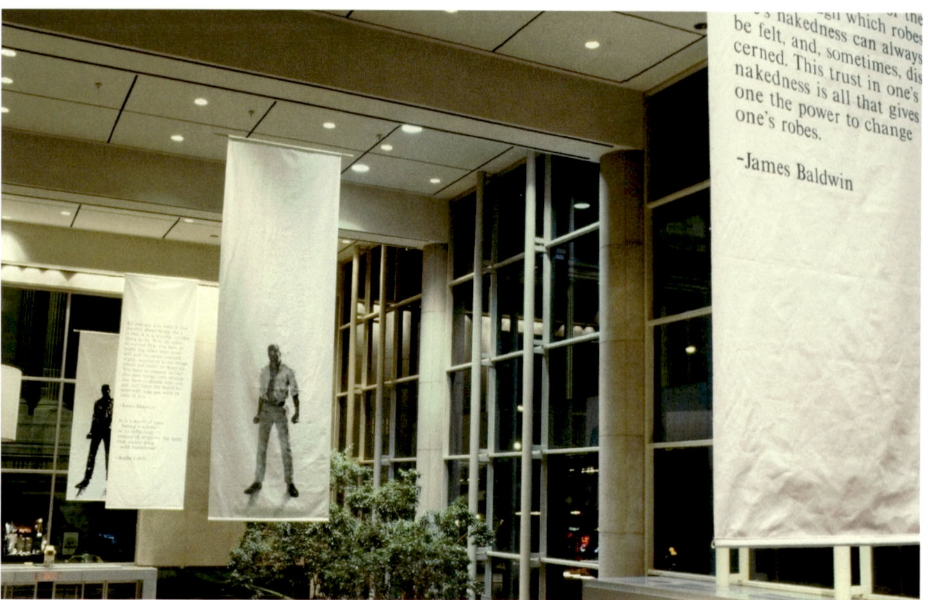

of text as a formal device, he fills his surfaces with type reminiscent of an ancient typewriter. Words chosen both for their evocative quality and as an alternative system of representation are reduced to the most economic form on canvas. The painter's hand becomes evident in the slightly off-register quality of the letters, with the text or repeated phrases disintegrating into patches of pigment. The effect of Ligon's configuration of texts, whether read or seen, is to interrogate notions of whiteness and blackness and the construction of identity as it evolves in the language of literature and the media.

In *Good Mirrors Are Not Cheap,* Ligon works with banners instead of canvases, seeking a more temporal form of communication. Four double-faced banners soar above the viewer, each with an image on one side and text on the other. Whereas the paintings replicate the silent experience of an individual viewer with the printed page, the scale of the banners creates a mode of public address. The image on all four banners is of a black man, standing firm with fists clenched. Ligon appropriated it from the cover of the first paperback edition of *Black Rage* (1968), a landmark study by African-American psychiatrists William H. Grier and Price M. Cobbs. The image carries contemporary connotations, from Bigger Thomas, the protagonist of Richard Wright's 1940 novel *Native Son,* the archetypal literary construction of black rage, to Walter Lee Younger, the black Everyman striving for his rightful place in American society in Lorraine Hansberry's 1959 play *A Raisin in the Sun*. The image relates directly to Grier and Cobbs' treatise, which explains the development of a growing anger among African-Americans whose hopes, dreams, and desires are thwarted by racism—a *de facto* racism that persists despite civil rights legislation. As a counterpoint to the chosen texts, the image looms and recedes and varies in size.

The texts range chronologically and thematically from Zora Neale Hurston to Essex Hemphill. They weave a narrative that argues the construction of the African-American identity from many vantage points. Ligon seeks to abolish the monolithic reading of what blackness is and, more important, is not. The text of the first banner begins with Zora Neale Hurston's "I remember the very day that I became col-

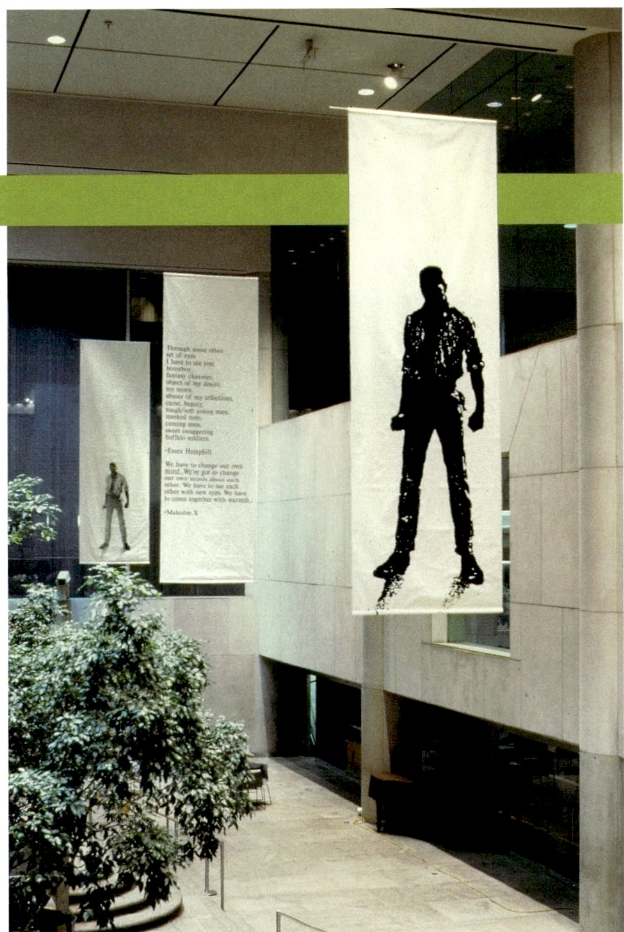

ored" from her autobiographical essay "How It Feels to Be Colored Me." Hurston's (and Ligon's) intention is to examine the point of recognition of difference, of coloredness and, most specifically, of blackness. The next two quotations from James Baldwin, on the first and second banners, speak in his stentorian tones about the internalization of negative images and the recognition that the dominant culture needs to construct and maintain these images. The fragment taken from Audre Lorde's poem "Good Mirrors Are

It is a waste of time
hating a mirror or
its reflection instead
of stopping the hand
that makes glass with
distortions . . .
—AUDRE LORDE

Through some other
set of eyes I have to see
you, homeboy, fantasy
charmer, object of
my desire, my scorn,
abuser of my affections,
curse, beauty, tough/
soft young men, masked
men, cussing
men, sweet staggering
buffalo soldiers.
—ESSEX HEMPHILL

Not Cheap," from which Ligon's project takes its title, appears on the third banner. It reads: "It is a waste of time hating a mirror / or its reflection / instead of stopping the hand / that makes glass with distortions. . . ." Lorde, like Baldwin, questions the source of this distortion in the African-American's self-perception.

Other texts on the third banner speak about learning to change one's perception. Taken from contemporary poet Essex Hemphill as well as Malcolm X, they use eyes as a metaphor and portend a self-investigative need for personal and public love. The fourth banner ends with text from James Baldwin, who metaphorically blasts the notion of the monolithic definitions of identity. He advocates the power of individuality (nakedness) and the ability to adopt and shed complex selves—informed by experience, not skin color—with the ease that one changes clothes.

With his selection of these texts, Ligon underscores the calcifying impact of language on the discourse of self-definition. By subverting the objective readings, he engages in the empowering process of self-representation. Like a dialogue which spans generations and crosses lines of gender and sexual preference, the texts relate, reflect, and at times resist one another in Ligon's interrogation of an everchanging identity. —THELMA GOLDEN, BRANCH DIRECTOR

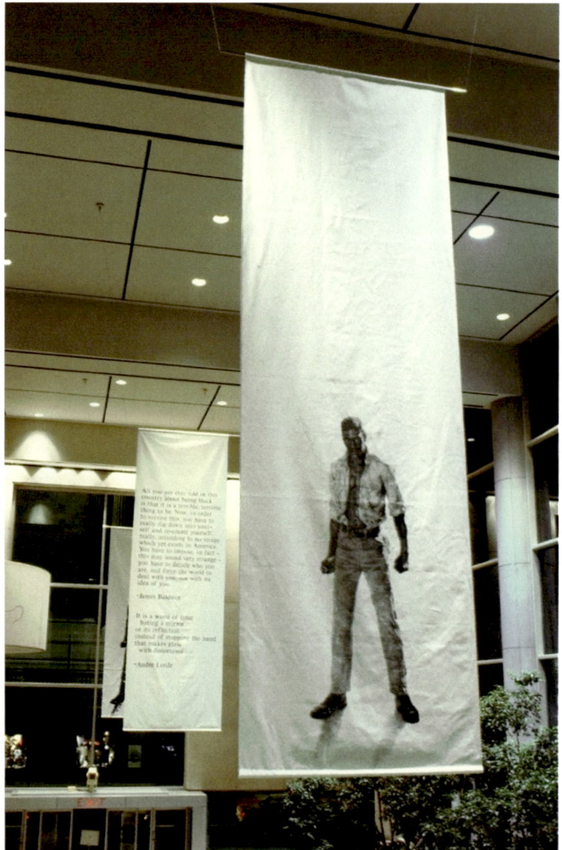

October 29 to December 31, 1992
This project evolved from a desire to explore the process of painting—the process by which an idea becomes a work of art and manifests the artist's struggle along the route. The discussion of the "new" abstraction is foremost in my mind in relation to process. An ongoing installation seems to be the most effective way to explore process. Installation, however, is often seen as the domain of three-dimensional and conceptually based artists, whose practices are sometimes called "new" forms. In this system, painting and particularly

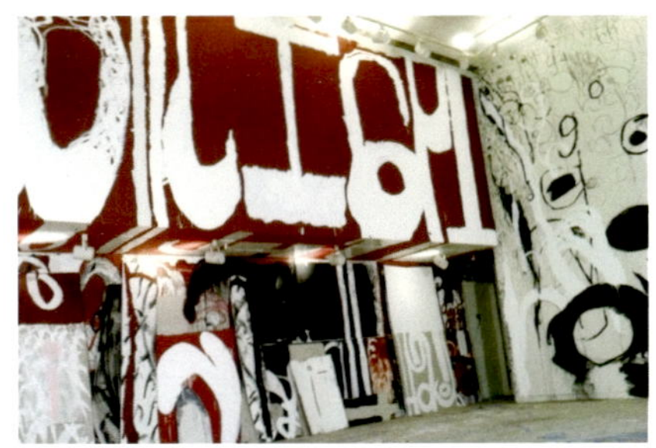

abstract painting are relegated to the traditional exhibition format. To banish some of the assumptions hidden in the discussion of media and site (the insidious assumptions about who makes what, what it is about, and how it should be shown), this project would explore painting as installation, with the mu-

Suzanne McClelland: Painting

seum as its site. New York-based painter Suzanne McClelland had been confronting these arguments in her work and our concerns as artist and curator collided in what seemed like a perfect collaboration.
—THELMA GOLDEN, BRANCH DIRECTOR

Installation views of *Suzanne McClelland: Painting.*

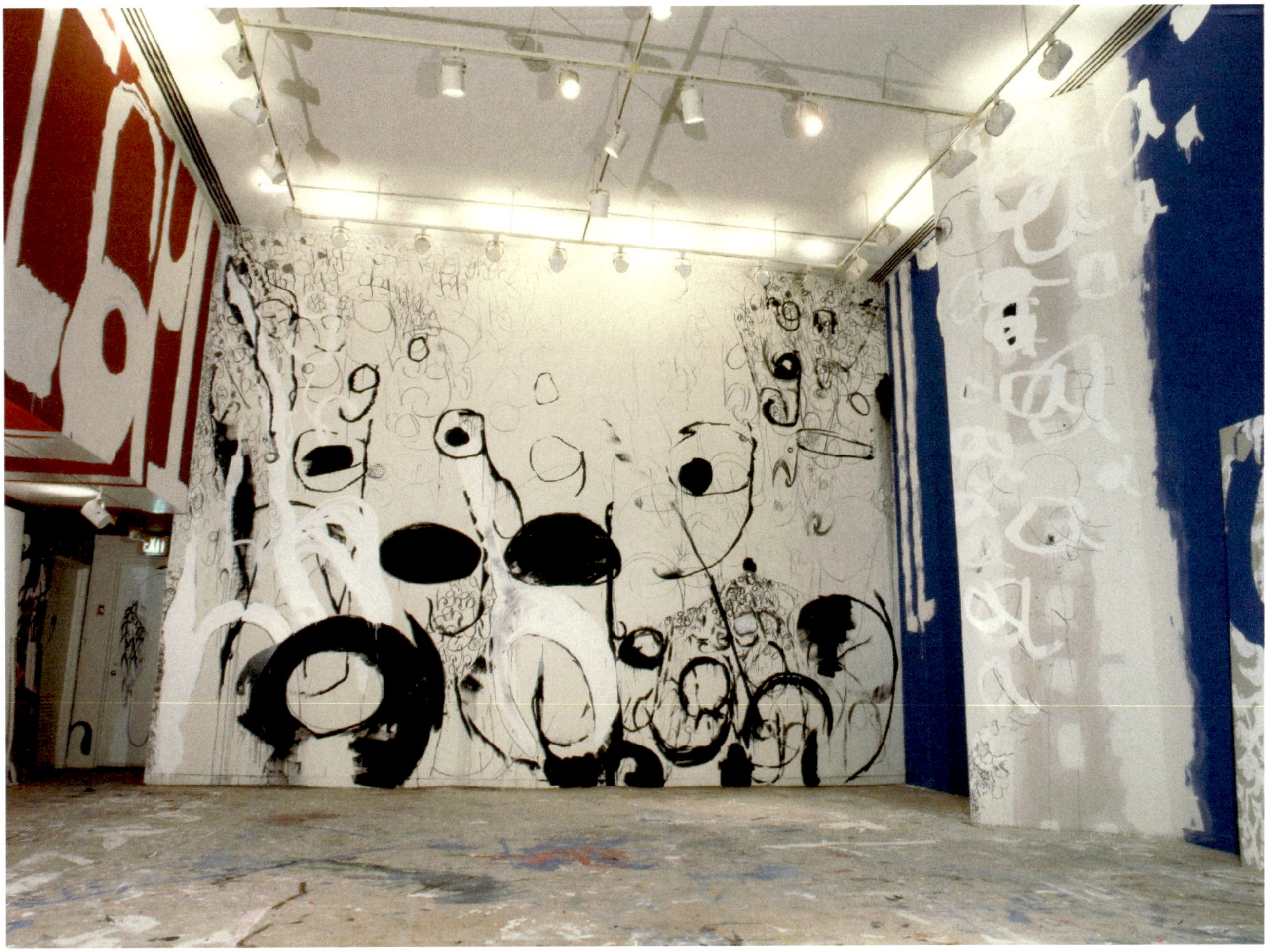

January 19 to April 5, 1993

Venus Envy Chapter One (or the First Holy Communion Moments Before the End) is the first part of a planned trilogy that will serve as a kind of retrospective. Although Mesa-Bains' altar installations are normally dismantled after exhibition, *Venus Envy* will remain intact; in conjunction with the two parts to be completed, it will create a sense of permanence in an otherwise ephemeral body of work. The installation revolves around three characters, the virgin, the nun, and the bride, each of which informs the three sections of the work. . . .

. . . *Venus Envy* resonates with Mesa-Bains' voice and those of the women close to her. As the subtitle indicates, the artist is focused on finalities: the end of innocence, symbolized by the first holy communion, or the larger metaphor of death, which reverberates throughout the work. The installation combines the experience of a variety of different spaces. Sanctuary and salon are intermingled with a museological presentation. Using a narrative system within a sensually charged space, Mesa-Bains joins the sacred and the secular, envisioning a reconciliation of body and soul.

—THELMA GOLDEN, BRANCH DIRECTOR

Amalia Mesa-Bains: Venus Envy Chapter One
(or the First Holy Communion Moments Before the End)

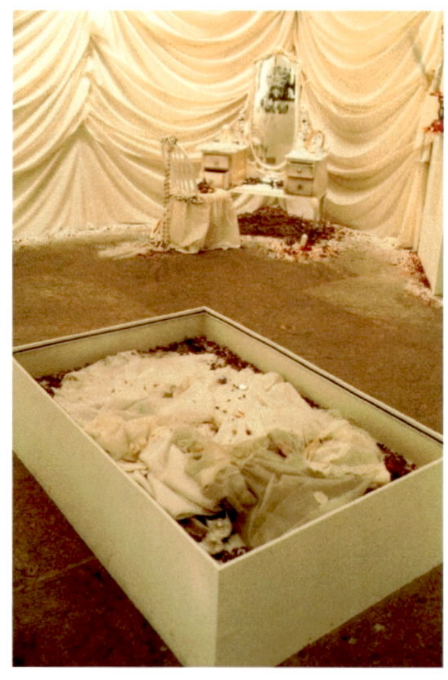

Installation views of *Amalia Mesa-Bains: Venus Envy Chapter One (or the First Holy Communion Moments Before the End)*.

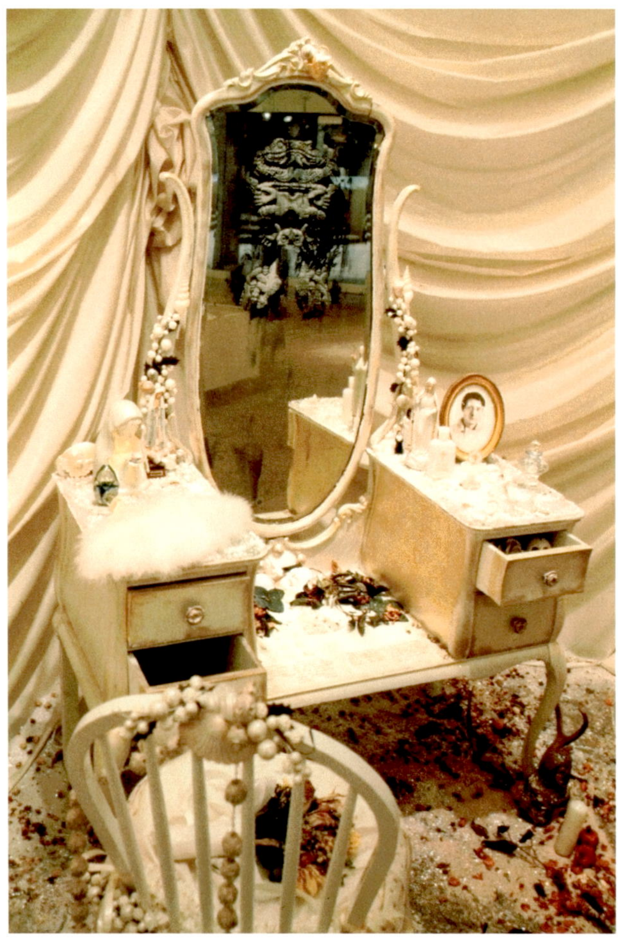

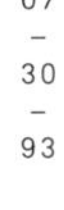

Maren Hassinger: Window Boxes

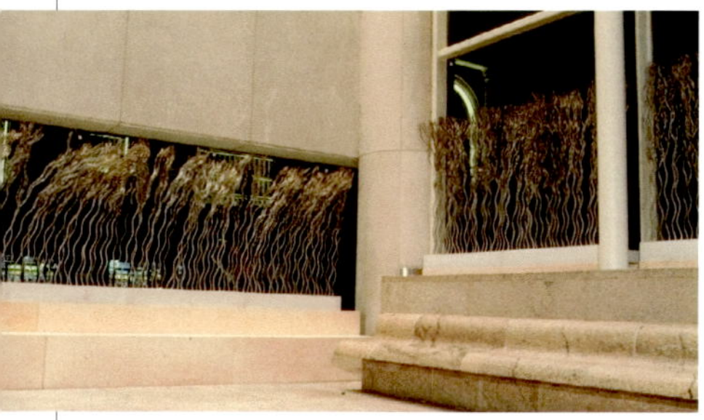

February 20 to June 20, 1992

Maren Hassinger has always worked with public spaces. In her early performance pieces, sculptural forms provided an environment for movement and sound. As her aesthetic vocabulary developed, the conjunction of the public and private, the natural and the industrial began to command her aesthetic vocabulary. Made predominantly with industrial materials such as galvanized wire rope, Hassinger's structures nevertheless resemble natural forms—a weed or a branch—that are then configured into haystacks, grass, bushes, and trees.

Window Boxes, which uses the window ledges of the Sculpture Court, again confronts the dualistic character of spaces. Fashioned of twenty-two individual concrete boxes with 5-foot lengths of galvanized steel rope, it acutely demarcates the once fluid definitions between inside and out. Hassinger's irregular growths reiterate the steel veins that outline the Sculpture Court windows, so as to mock the window's formal geometry. Moreover, while the industrial materials echo the man-made quality of the corporate space, their configuration takes on the feel of "nature." At the same time, however, the absence of nature is critiqued: the windblown forms, for example, evoke an element lacking inside the space. *Window Boxes* also suggests a hedge interrupting the previously seamless view from inside to out. Accepting the challenge of using a public interior space, Hassinger has created a work which, in its contrast to the environment, transforms the viewer's experience of that space. —THELMA GOLDEN, BRANCH DIRECTOR

Marga Gomez

James Luna

PERFORMERS   93

Kip Fulbeck

Robbie McCauley

Mac Wellman

John Kelly

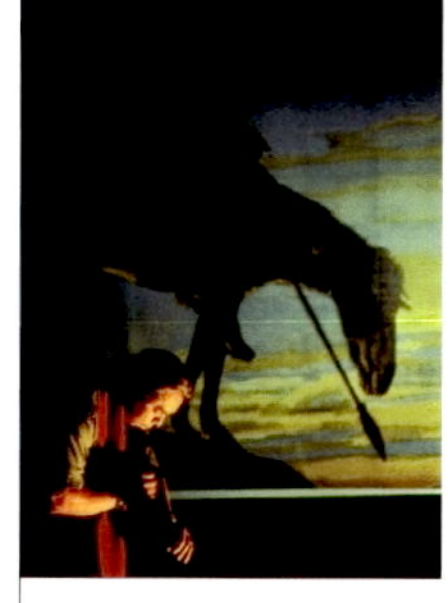

James Luna, *UNPLUGGED: The Shame-Man*, 04–21–93

Expanding the Collection: Biennial Acquisitions

Sylvia Plachy: The Call of the Street: Photographs of New York City

Installation view of *Sylvia Plachy: The Call of the Street: Photographs of New York City*.

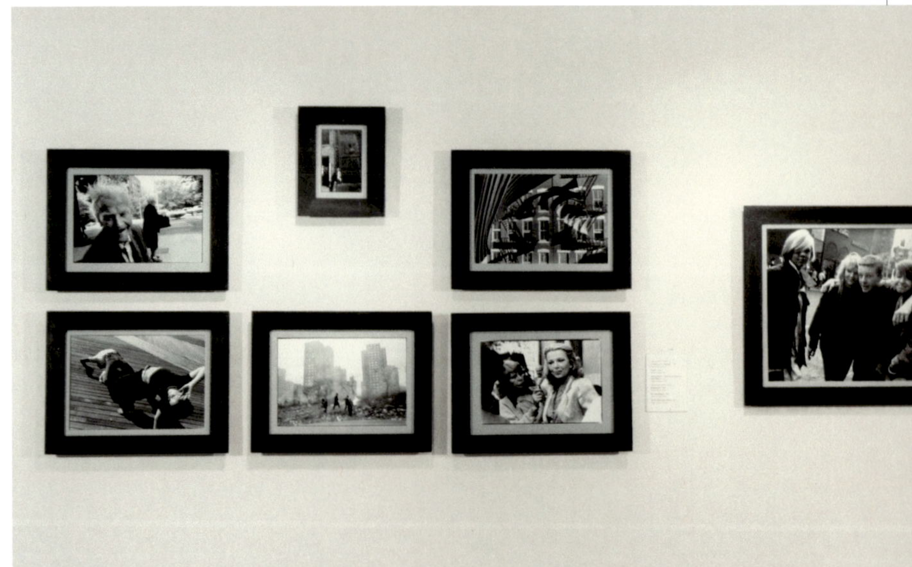

September 28 to December 31, 1993
Conversation: Thelma Golden and Sylvia Plachy

TG: *Many of your photographs, including many of the images in this exhibition, capture the spontaneous nature of New York City streets as you experience it—all the very strange things that can happen, all the very strange people you can meet.*

SP: I like the kind of chance experience that for just a moment choreographs itself into an image. You have only a second to dive into it like into an ocean and to catch it; aware all at once of the dangers as well as the wonderful things that are around you. . . .

SP: There are many things that have influenced my work: art, music, literature, and life itself. When I started college, I knew a little about art but not much about photography beyond looking at snapshots. It was something I learned slowly as I looked at books and magazines. While still at Pratt, I visited photographers André Kertész and W. Eugene Smith, whose work I liked very much. André Kertész and I became friends. We had a common bond not only because we were both from Hungary but also because emotion and intuition were important to both of us. I don't know of any direct links between my work and other photographers. There may be. What do you see?

An Interview with Lorna Simpson by Thema Golden

Early on Lorna Simpson acknowledged that words weren't enough. Or sometimes too much. And most often inadequate to describe the complexity of fact and emotion. Her art practice, which began with documentary photography, matured in a style that joined photographs with text to explore a range of formal and ideological concerns. She harnessed a highly peripatetic voice to an acute sense of image to create an astonishing body of work.

This new installation, *Standing in the water,* signals an inspired departure. Consisting of three separate but interrelated components, the work is centered around a video and combines objects and images in unexpected forms. One enters the space around a diaphanous off-white fabric scrim. The scrim cuts the space off from the outer sculpture court space, creating a conscious divide between inside and out. On the floor, leading progressively to the video monitors imbedded in the far wall, are three 5 x 12-foot lengths of felt. The felt pieces are printed with a photograph of the ocean. Each of the three wave images becomes subtly clearer as the viewer moves from the entrance of the gallery to the video monitors. The felt pieces are punctuated with 12 x 12-inch glass squares, each etched with a photograph of a pair of shoes. The images, although the same on each square, range from light to dark, which visually insinuates varying levels of depth. The video is shown on two 2 x 4-inch monitors, one directly on top of the other, placed at eye level. The image on the top monitor is of a water pitcher, that on the bottom of moving waves. Both have text that continuously scrolls down the screen and describes water in a variety of manifestations. The video is accompanied by a soundtrack comprising a multitude of water-involved sound effects.

What follows is a small part of an extended dialogue Lorna Simpson and I have been having for a long time. We talk about everything, her work, my work, her life,

Lorna Simpson: Standing in the water

THIS PAGE AND FOLLOWING:
Installation views of *Lorna Simpson: Standing in the water.*

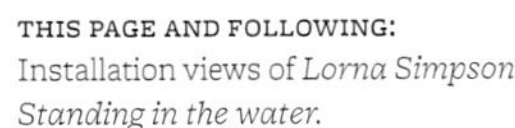

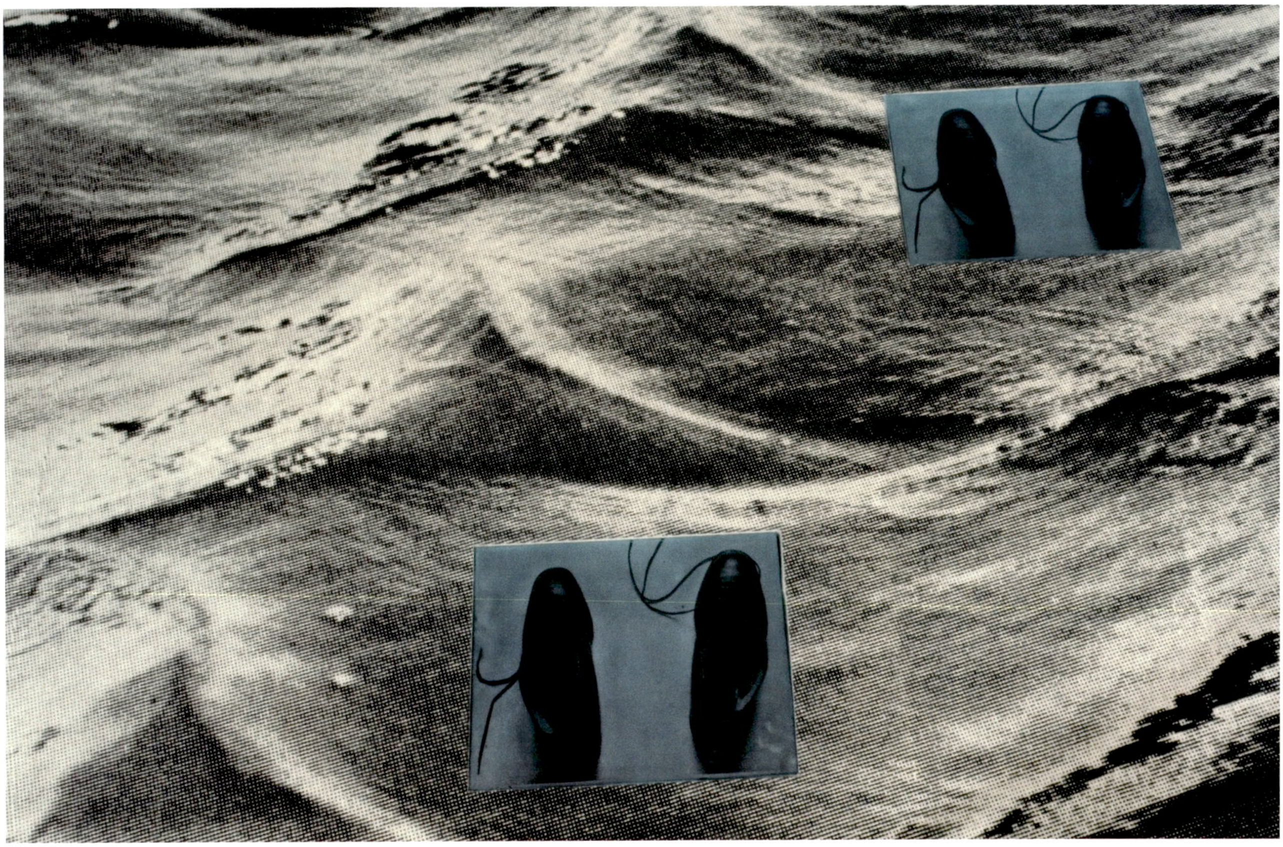

my life, everything. This ongoing dialogue led to the realization of this new installation. After indicating my desire to continually challenge the gallery space and notions of site specific work in general, Lorna expressed her desire to work three dimensionally and expand her relationship to photography, text, and media. In this conversation, held a few weeks after the installation opened, we discuss the results.

TG: *Could you talk about the ideas that led up to this piece and specifically about the title?*

LS: "Standing in the water." . . . I think that in working with water there's initially the problem of it falling into a religious connotation. I didn't want the piece to be read as a work about baptism or about walking on the water or wading in the water.

TG: *Water has profoundly religious connotations; purification, redemption by water.*

LS: I wanted the viewer to experience the power of being mesmerized by the water, stopped dead, standing in the water. So I don't want the title to refer to a religious experience, but really to the body and this experience of confronting water in all of its meanings.

TG: *Water also has cultural meanings, but it seems as if you are working toward less rooted meanings. You've used references to water in other work. What surprised me most about this work was the image of the silver water pitcher in the video, which I immediately recognized from one of your seminal early works,* Waterbearer, *of 1986. Water was also an integral component of* 5 Rooms, *the installation you created in 1991 for* "Places with a Past" *in Charleston, South Carolina, in collaboration with Alva Rogers.*

LS: In this particular piece, for the first time, my use of water is more about its sensuality, its seductive surface. This is what drew me back to using water in my work. In earlier work the reference was more specific—*Waterbearer* is about memory and disappearance, the Charleston piece was about the Middle Passage. Both these references appear in a way in this work, but what made me want to use water again was the stylistic change going on in my work and the desire to create a different set of references or parameters. So in my decision to avoid the figure and other elements that I consistently used in the past, I am allowing myself to approach my ideas from a variety of new perspectives.

TG: *How did these interests come into the piece?*

LS: The picture I used to create the water image in this piece is actually from a photograph in a book which shows the effect of varying sound waves on water and the particular wave patterns the different sound waves create in an artificial environment. Something about the way those waves look is mesmerizing.

TG: *What also struck me about this work is something you have already referred to: the absence of the figure.*

LS: You mean the figure in its totality.

TG: *Yes, because the image of the shoes in this work is a cipher for the human figure—the part as symbol for the whole, a device also used before. But the figure, your colored, gendered figure, seems to have moved out of the work. Our colleague Kellie Jones, our homegirl, art historian, and curator, and I have only half jokingly referred to this shift by titling the new piece "Bye, Bye Black Girl."*

LS: Oh, no!!! (She laughs)

TG: *But I think I understand this shift. When I first came to know your work, I connected with it on a very personal level, and as I continued to spend time with it I held my "specific" reading to be a general one. I saw "myself" but I knew the work was about a variety of experiences. I am sure the loaded connotations of the engendered, colored body, the black woman's body, made it seem hard for the work to be read as very localized, very specific. It was always interesting to me, for example, that the simple white shift you used in many works to clothe your models was often read as a slave girl dress or sometimes a hospital shift. Never as, say, a designer dress or a non-western costume.*

LS: A lot of the same over-determined connotations are continually applied to the work.

TG: *Is the absenting of the figure a way to bring forward the issues that have consumed you in past work but have been somewhat obscured in this less figurative approach? By denying viewers a figure are you disallowing them a place to "site" the issues so specifically, as you have similarly denied access to a face in the past?*

LS: Not really, I wanted to get away from a figurative representation of the body. It was actually a purely selfish maneuver I developed in order to make *Standing in the water*. The formula for working with the figure was such a contained set of elements that it got to a point where for me to expand as an artist I had to abandon the formula and create a new one in order to move further. In some ways, I don't feel I have abandoned everything because in *Standing in the water* there are texts which deal with issues I have explored before. There are references to the Middle Passage and the idea of the occupation or "ownership" of land that refer to both African and Native American histories. So there are references in the text to the body and to the black body within the American context and what that experience has meant over time. So I haven't abandoned the body, I am just trying to work through these issues without an image of a figure. My interest in the body remains. The text in this piece refers to both political and personal concerns.

TG: *So the meaning attached to the figure is still there.* Standing in the water *also continues your interest in working three dimensionally—beginning with your early screen pieces, which were meant to be viewed in the round, to the Charleston installation, to your installation in the 1993 Whitney Biennial,* Hypothetical, *to your 1994 piece* Group Dynamic, *which directly precedes* Standing in the water. *Is this concern ongoing?*

LS: Intensely! I have more of an interest in working in installation or architecturally.

TG: *But those two-dimensional works relate to the installations because quite often you included objects within the figured images; now you are making objects and placing them in the foreground.*

LS: When I was in art school in California in the early 1980s Conceptual art practice was prevalent. It wasn't about making precious objects or making an elaborate installation to represent an idea, but rather a more conceptual approach to how one might get the idea across with some expediency, with efficiency. I think I still work in this manner.

TG: *You are moving around both sculptural and architectural practices. With this work, you not only made objects but altered the gallery space to contain the objects.*

LS: I think this is derived from work by other artists that I have had in the back of my mind.

TG: *Like?*

LS: Although I don't think of my work as similar, I feel an affinity to the work of David Hammons and Vito Acconci. Seeing both of them work in many, many different environments and seeing how they "work" these environments—this has been very influential for me. And some of the works of Louise Bourgeois.

TG: *That's interesting because I think an important component of her work is beauty, even when the subject is ugly. Even when the subject (or text) of your own work belies this, beauty is also a leitmotif. Curator Lowery Sims spoke about your transgressive, yet subtle emphasis on the beauty of your models. These new objects, which comprise part of the installation, also are beautiful. My sense is that in your object beauty is paramount in your formal vocabulary. Are their any other artists, specifically photographers, who influence and inform your work?*

LS: Certainly Adrian Piper, Carrie Mae Weems . . . there are lots of links. I'm very interested in process and try to see and understand process—sometimes I'm much more interested in the process than in the completed work.

TG: *This piece seems to indicate a beginning and an end in the progression of your work. It feels like a transition. I won't say change because.*

LS: Why?

TG: *Because change seems very final and this work, along with the successive bodies of work before it, has gradually encompassed new elements without fully abandoning everything that came before.*

LS: I am working on a new show right now, and while I have something of an idea of what it might be, for the first time I really don't know because I have created this new way of working, with a new visual vocabulary. I feel a great sense of possibility when I work without the constraints of "knowing" my work.

TG: *Everything is wide open.*

LS: Completely open. I had been working in a consistent way for almost ten years. I knew how to do it. Now I think I am challenging myself more. I surprise myself. It has made me more relaxed, more open to experiment.

TG: *Central to your work has been your use of text in conjunction with images. In your earlier work, the text and the images remained somewhat separate, as two discrete objects. Text captioning photograph. In this work you join the text and image in the form of the video. Let's talk about this difference.*

LS: I have been moving more and more into video. The floor pieces, the felt with the glass plates, are very static and I wanted the work to have a kind of fluidity that would complement the soundtrack. So that's why I used the looped image of moving water on one of the monitors to contrast the still images of the waves printed on the felt. The other monitor has an image of a water pitcher. There I was working both with a play on words, pitcher vs. picture, referring to the thing and the image as well as the conjunction of the image of the ocean and that of the pitcher, which is a vessel or container of water.

TG: *What is the relationship between the top and bottom images?*

LS: The top monitor, with the image of the pitcher, carries the descriptions of things that occur in water, and the bottom monitor's texts, over the ocean image, are a literal description of the soundtrack.

TG: *How did you create the soundtrack?*

LS: I culled sounds from a library of sound effects and edited them together.

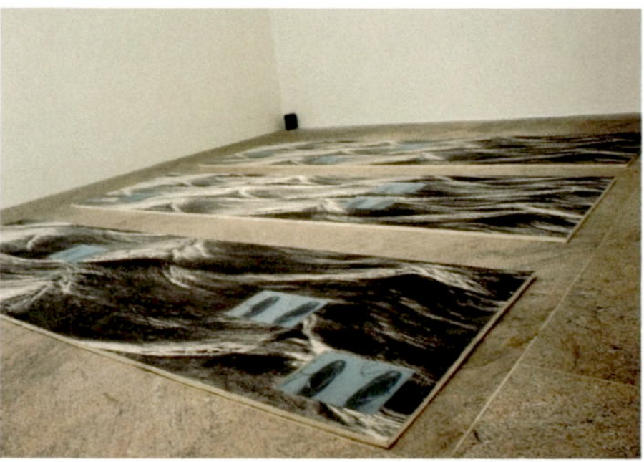

TG: *The sounds range from highly evocative to very mysterious to weirdly symphonic. They include a bathtub filling with water, a fire hose. . . .*

LS: A garden hose spraying, water dripping in a bucket, footsteps through water.

TG: *Spliced together to create something oddly musical.*

LS: Yes. I picked effects that were clear and discrete, which had their own beauty and sound, somewhat Cageian.

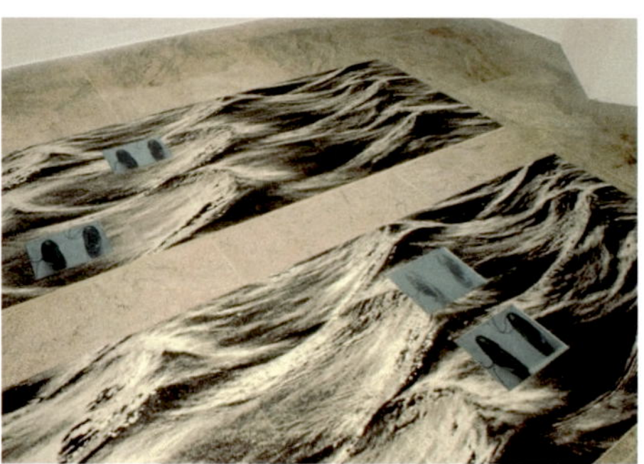

TG: *The text in your work has always ranged from the journalistic to the poetic, from the vernacular to the technical, and the descriptions in this piece are now different. I am going to read some of them and I would like you to talk about the sources and/or the*

meanings. *"They were both shot while collecting water from the public water spouts in Bosnia."*

LS: The news and the newspapers of the past months. I was thinking about the association between political crisis and water.

TG: *"Flooding the rice fields on purpose."*

LS: Reference to the acts of insurrection by enslaved Africans.

TG: *"Her vagina and buttocks are suspended in liquid in a jar in Le Musée de l'Homme."*

LS: A fact about the Venus Hottentot, Sarah Baartman, a South African woman who was displayed as an oddity in Paris early in the century.

TG: *"The promise of showers."*

LS: World War II concentration camps.

TG: *"One day during a smooth sea and moderate wind, the two who had been chained together somehow made it to the deck, through the netting, and jumped into the sea."*

LS: A description from a narrative of the Middle Passage of two Africans jumping ship.

TG: *"First time pissing in a pool, first time pissing in the ocean."*

LS: Everybody's done it!

TG: *"Disappeared by the river"*—is that a reference to your work Waterbearer?

TG: Yes.

TG: *Where is this going?*

LS: I cannot say where the work is going right now. I can say it addresses several issues that I have developed in earlier work but I don't think I have ever known exactly the evolution of the next body of work ahead of time.

Sam Gilliam: Golden Element Inside Gold

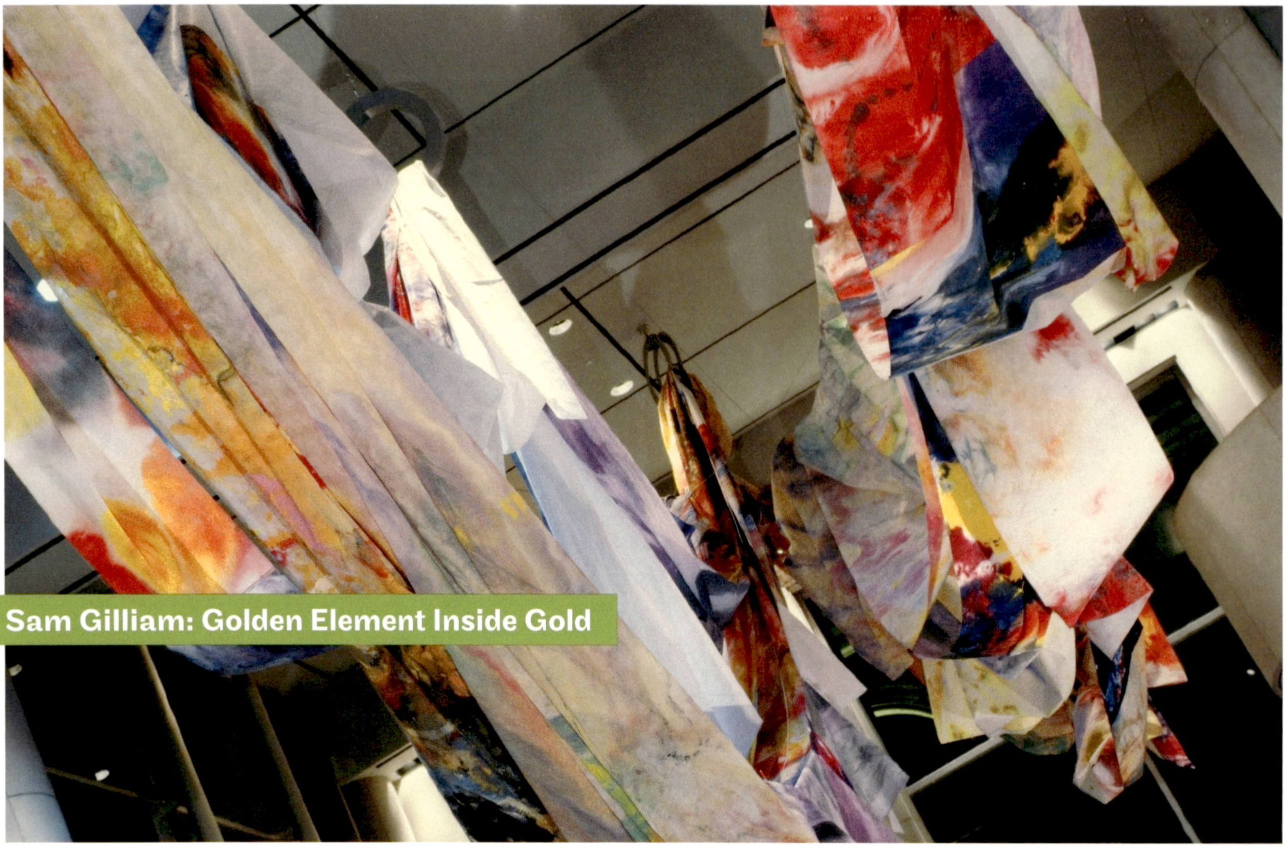

Installation view of *Sam Gilliam: Golden Element Inside Gold.*

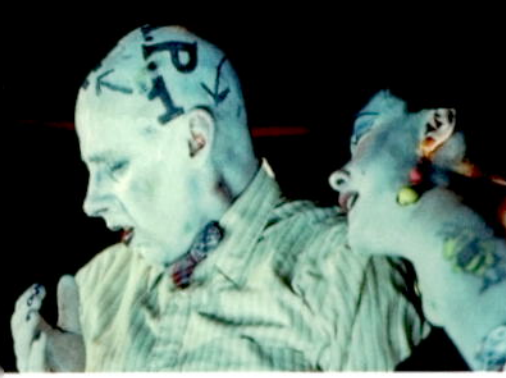

Sledgehammer Theatre,
*No Time Like the
Present (A Rosary to Mary
Frankenstein on the
Occasion of the Rapture),*
04–13–94

January 20 to July 1, 1994

Golden Element Inside Gold, a new site-specific installation of Drape paintings by Sam Gilliam, will be presented in the Sculpture Court at the Whitney Museum of American Art at Philip Morris. Gilliam (b. 1933) forged an early reputation with this body of work in 1968, and quickly gained international recognition. His Drape paintings were among the works representing the United States at the Venice Biennale in 1972. . . .

Gilliam's Drape paintings, characterized by expressive spontaneity and saturated color, are large unstretched canvases gathered and hung like curtains from walls and ceilings, then shaped to fit the particular spaces in which they are presented. These opulent works reflect his association with the Washington Color Painters, a group that included Morris Louis, Kenneth Noland, and Howard Mehring, who explored

a technique developed by Helen Frankenthaler of staining colors into raw canvas. Unlike many Color Field painters, Gilliam's technique frequently entailed splashing and mopping the paint onto rolled, folded, and crumpled canvas to enhance the color effects.

In the mid-1970s, Gilliam abandoned the improvisational process of staining and use of unstretched canvas in favor of a more controlled exploration of sculptural form. He has recently returned to a new phase of Drape paintings after a nearly twenty-year hiatus and his new works incorporate many of these formal concerns. The new works explore more sculptural and tactile possibilities than their predecessors, evoking complex architectural spaces and rich metaphorical possibilities with their elaborate folds and textured application of paint.

In *Double Foolscap*, hundreds of sheets of textured paper wrap around the walls of the gallery to form a monumental grid or contrasting monochromes. Beyond its reference to Minimalism and Color Field painting of the 1960s, the installation holds within it another, and more hidden, history: that or its own making. Over the course of a year, the artists produced these pages from their personal clothing. They literally shredded, boiled, soaked, pulped, and pressed their wardrobe into more than one thousand sheets or paper.

Defying the conventions of papermaking, Leone & Macdonald used not only cottons, linens, and silks as their source material, but synthetic and highly processed garments such as lycra bathing suits, velour shirts, polyester pants, mixed-blend sweaters, and suede winter coats. The extraordinary papers which resulted, deeply saturated in color and densely layered in texture, function both as painterly abstractions and empty pages awaiting inscription. . . .

In *Double Foolscap*, the artists macerate their combined wardrobe into a blank field of paper, an open grid awaiting new inscriptions. Yet, as they themselves note, such blankness remains something or a "fantasy," a fool's dream of infinite possibility. Clothing marks both our public persona and our private sense or self, cloaking and contouring our bodies in ways which carry legible signs of gender, class, and sexual preference. While *Double Foolscap* stages a spectacular escape from the artists' own wardrobe, it also reminds us how powerfully our clothing—and our closets—continue to define our lives. —RICHARD MEYER

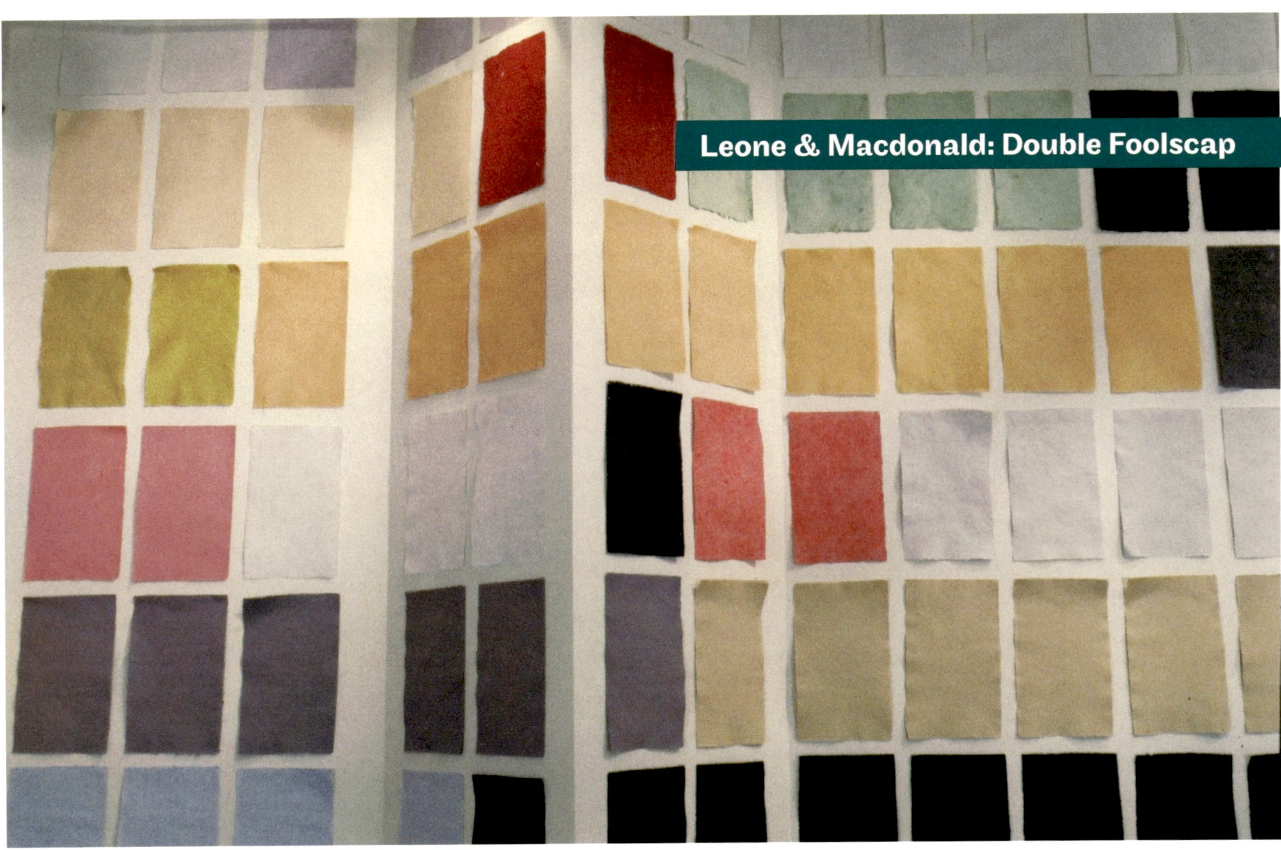

Hillary Leone and Jennifer Macdonald, installation view of
Leone & Macdonald: Double Foolscap.

Works on Paper: Selections from the Permanent Collection of the Whitney Museum of American Art

Jean-Michel Basquiat, Ross Bleckner, Bruce Conner, Carroll Dunham, Robert Gober, April Gornik, Sol LeWitt, Glenn Ligon, Brice Marden, Bridge Study, Suzanne McClelland, Donald Moffett, Stephen Mueller, Tom Otterness, Martin Puryear, Michael Rees, Jim Shaw, Kiki Smith, Philip Taaffe, Sue Williams

04–08–94

07–01–94

07–13–94

10–14–94

Photographs:

Selections from the Permanent Collection of the Whitney Museum of American Art

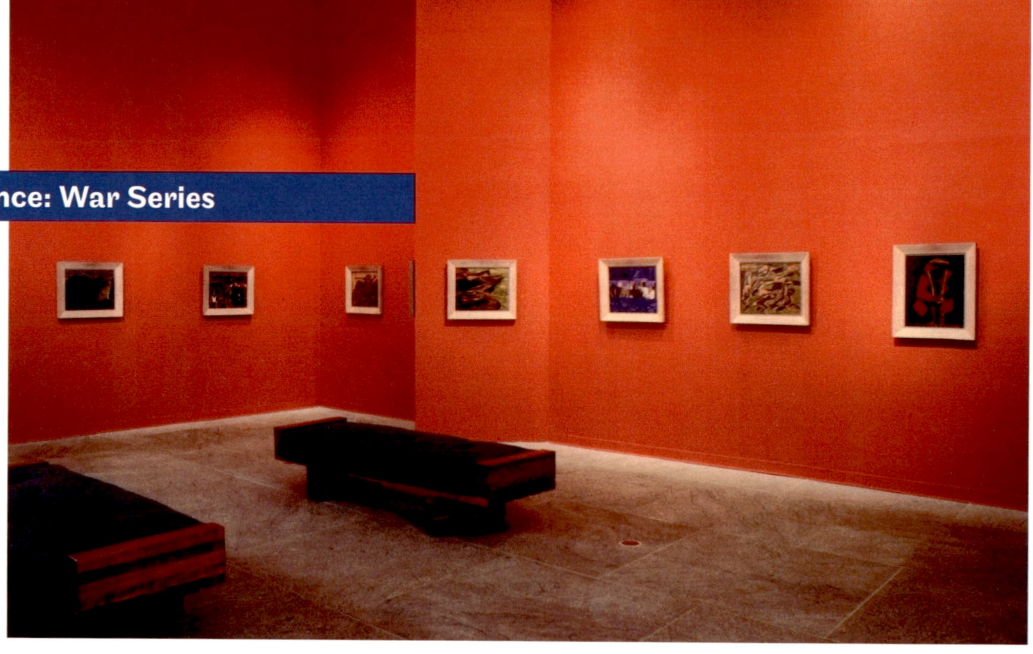

Jacob Lawrence: War Series

January 11 to March 31, 1995

Born in 1917, Jacob Lawrence is one of the most prominent African-American artists of this century. His War Series painted in 1946 and 1947, and purchased by the Whitney Museum in 1951, chronicles his experience in the United States Coast Guard from 1943 to 1945. . . .

A narrative painter whose work has spanned more than five decades, Lawrence has devoted his career to exploring diverse aspects of the African-American experience. . . .

. . . Through abstract organization Lawrence depicts an emotional reaction an event of daily life in war. The series does not document specific battles nor does it glamorize war and heroism, rather, the artist has synthesized the experience of war into remembered images and particular experiences.

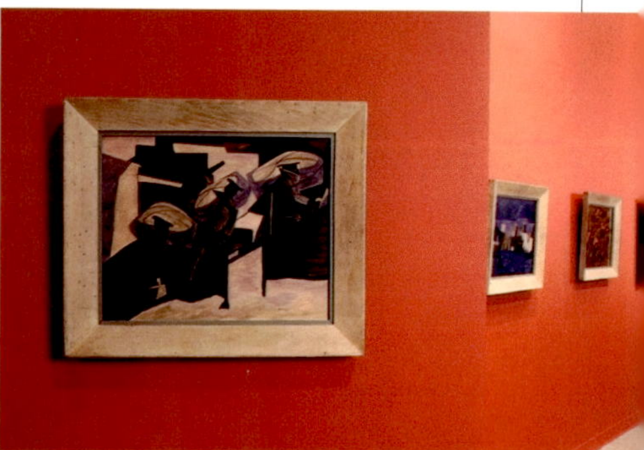

Installation views of *Jacob Lawrence: War Series*.
BOTTOM: Jacob Lawrence, *Another Patrol*, 1946.

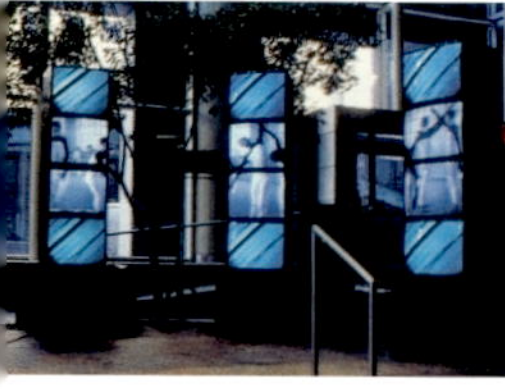

Cunningham Dance Foundation, *Beach Birds for Camera: A Music Video Event*, 03–01 to 03–03–95

Double Take: Views of Modern Life by
Stuart Davis and Reginald Marsh

April 10 to July 7, 1995

Double Take: Views of Modern Life by Stuart Davis and Reginald Marsh juxtaposes two artists who take modernity—"the immediate life of the day"—as the subject of their work. Overlapping angular shapes, bold vibrant color, and radically flattened space characterize Stuart Davis' mature paintings. The riffs and syncopated rhythms created by the interplay of shapes, colors, and space are analogous to those found in jazz, a form of music the artist loved. In contrast, keenly observed urban types, from burlesque queens to Bowery bums, populate Reginald Marsh's canvases. These animated figures in contemporary settings suggest narratives similar to the lively, topical plots found in movies of the late twenties and thirties, which Marsh frequented. In different ways, the works of Davis and Marsh capture the exhilarating pace of life during the first three decades of the century. . . .

Although the traditions of realism and commercial illustration inform the work of Davis and Marsh, each transforms the given tradition in strikingly different ways. Grounded in the everyday world, Davis' paintings and prints single out telling fragments—words or objects—that represent modernity and render these icons in an abstract visual language. Marsh, on the other hand, focuses on the costumes and behavior of men and women in their urban surroundings, simultaneously updating the Renaissance figurative tradition and transcribing the look of commercial illustration into paint and print. Ultimately, the commitment shared by Davis and Marsh to represent the essence of modernity far outweighs their stylistic differences. —EUGENIE TSAI, BRANCH DIRECTOR, WHITNEY MUSEUM OF AMERICAN ART AT CHAMPION

July 19 to September 22, 1995
Carmen Lomas Garza is an artist whose work powerfully expresses the Chicana/o experience. Through the deployment of memory, she creates a visual language that narrates Chicana/o rural life. Cel-

Carmen Lomas Garza

ebrations, myths, healing ceremonies, family stories, and everyday life are visually rendered in the framework of tradition and innovation. Working in the tradition of the chronicler, Lomas Garza recollects and recasts reminiscences in a visual narrative. The chronicle of things past is grounded in the polyphony of ballads, tales, myths, and *chisme* (gossip) that make up the oral tradition. Lomas Garza reworks shared images, signs, and metaphors through anecdote, a device that invites the viewer to enter the marvels of her pictorial language. In *Abuelitos Piscando Nopalitos (Grandparents Cutting Cactus)* (1980), Lomas Garza's *monitos* (doll-like figures) harvest a poor yet delectable delicacy cherished since Pre-Columbian times.

Three generations of rural Tejanos (Chicano Texans), participate in a seasonal and family ritual. *Nopalitos* (cacti), apart from their place in the Chicano culinary tradition, are also symbols of the greatness and adversity of life; if not cut and handled with care, they prick. Also pictured is a barbed wire fence dividing the arid landscape, which has been opened to allow the family to cross and cut the cacti. This division mirrors the geo-historical as well as spiritual experience; it is a sign that triggers diverse layers of signification, from imposed borders that divide families and demarcate the usurpation of land to contemporary reclamations of place. —VICTOR ZAMUDIO-TAYLOR

Altered and Irrational: Selections from the Permanent Collection of the Whitney

Museum of American Art

Jared Bark, Michael Byron, Jim Love, Rona Pondick, Lucas Samaras, Cindy Sherman, Kiki Smith, Mike Todd, May Wilson, Joel-Peter Witkin

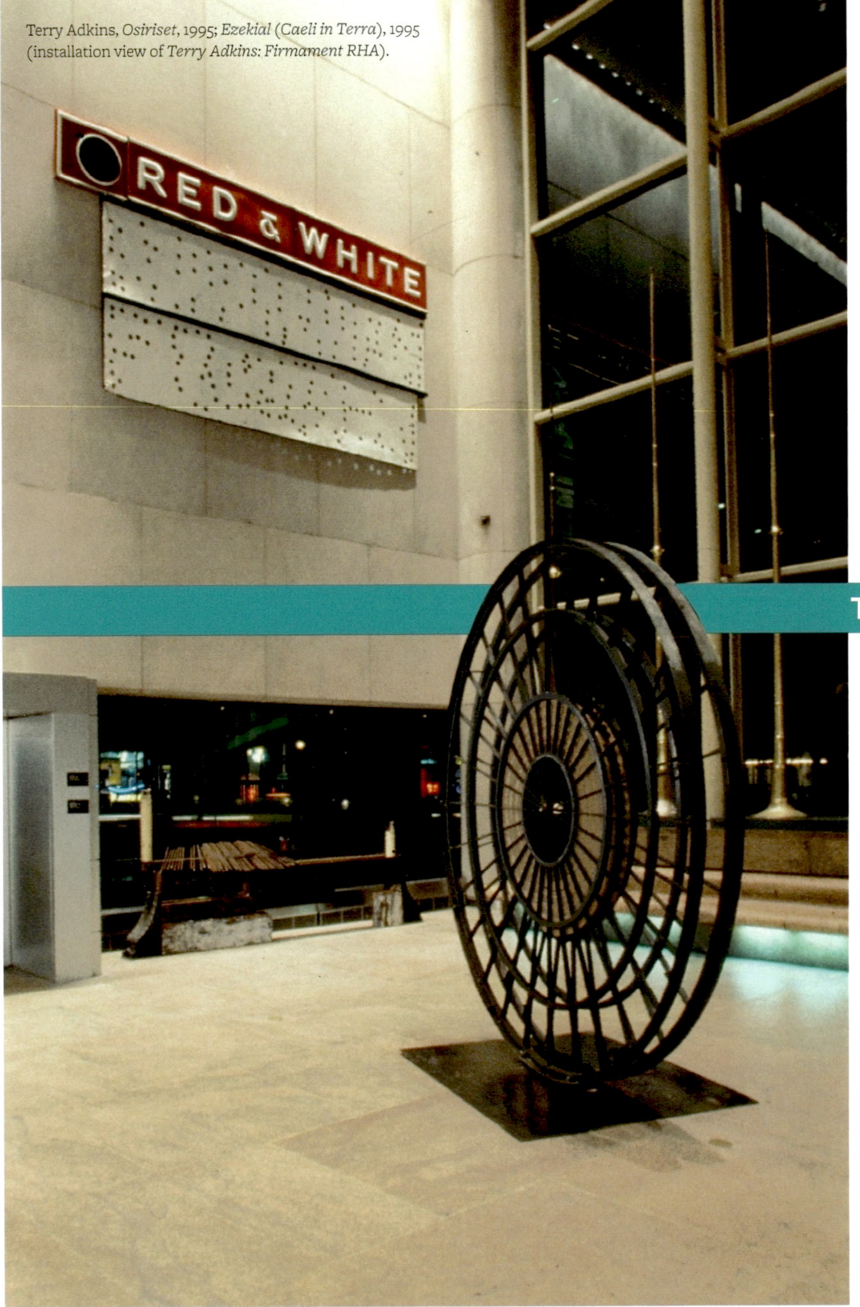

Terry Adkins, *Osiriset*, 1995; *Ezekial (Caeli in Terra)*, 1995 (installation view of *Terry Adkins: Firmament RHA*).

Terry Adkins: Firmament RHA

October 18, 1995 to March 29, 1996

The works, all constructed in 1995 specifically for the Philip Morris sculpture court, will be both freestanding and mounted on the walls to make full use of the large open space. "The work will extend vertically upward to the heavens ('firmament' means 'the vault of heaven') and the infinite. Its horizontal extension will be temporal and backward, thereby making reference to . . . memory and ancestry," Adkins says. "The thematic focus of *Firmament RHA* concerns the soul and its transcendence from the corporeal to non-manifested states of being," he says, adding that he incorporates such symbols as ladders and boats to allude to culturally based ways the soul makes that journey.

01
–
17
–
96

03
–
29
–
96

Installation views of *Matthew McCaslin: Harnessing Nature.*

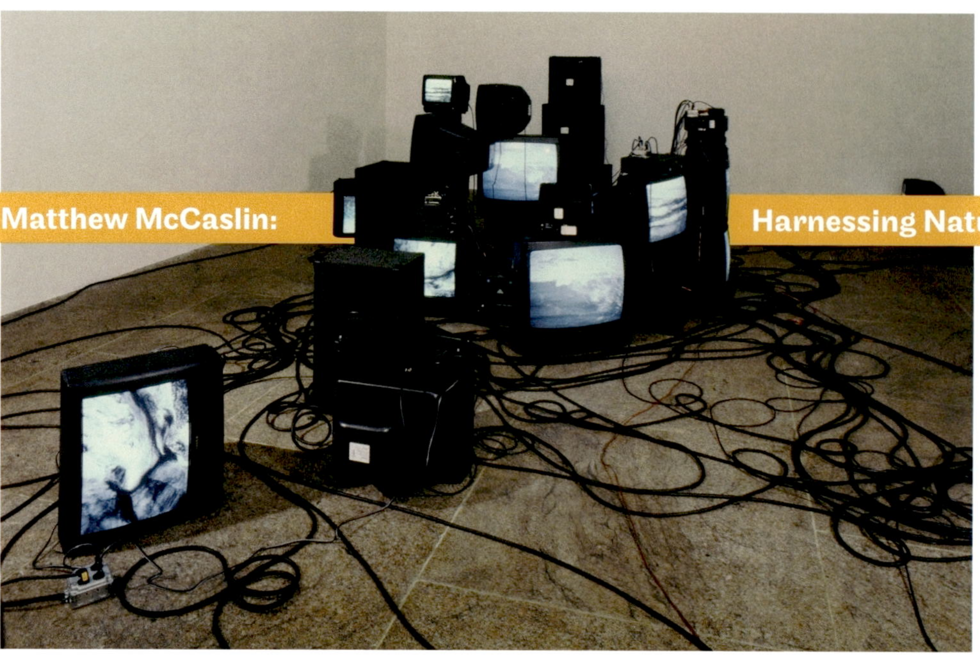

Matthew McCaslin: Harnessing Nature

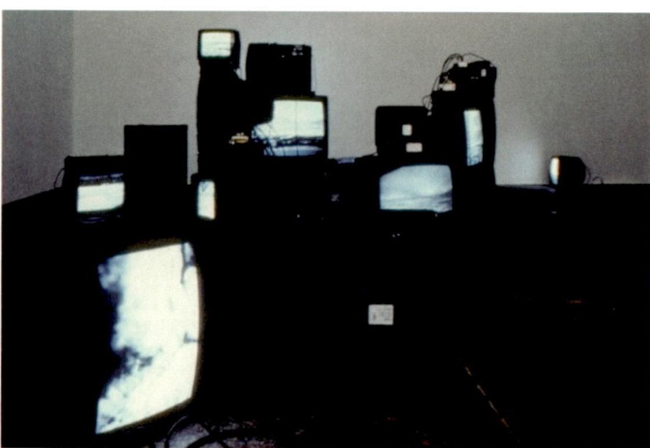

January 17 to March 29, 1996

Using industrial materials of construction, with their polished finishes and carefully engineered constructions, McCaslin's sculptures and installations transpose the interior structures of building and engineering to visible space. The exhibition room, not unlike a room in a modern home—four walls, ceiling, floor, electrical outlets, etc.— becomes a shell in which those interior structures and trapped energies extend through the walls. We are looking at both the room, constructed from these structures and conduits, and the unprotected, skeletal forms themselves as elements of an art installation: an interior/exterior view....

...In his newest work at the Whitney Museum of American Art at Philip Morris, ocean waves crest and break in an unending crescendo. Similar to the destabilization of a television's vertical hold, which produces the effect of "vertical roll," this constant, visual repetition makes us aware of the television's objectness—that the image we see on the monitor is not a magical experience but a mechanical or electronic one. The television monitor becomes an object or container of the event. But unlike a narrative work, in which a linear story is told through multiple images, here one or several similar movements repeat, capturing a single mood or emotion. —MATTHEW YOKOBOSKY, ASSISTANT CURATOR, FILM AND VIDEO, WHITNEY MUSEUM OF AMERICAN ART

April 11 to June 28, 1996

During the day, the city is the locus for a continuous series of changing impressions or "shocks": sights, smells, sounds, the exchange of glances with a steady stream of anonymous passersby. At night, the pace slows down and electric lighting makes dazzling facades for even the dumpiest of quarters. Even so, a mute brutality dominates the relative emptiness. Typically, one would expect luminosity from Dickson's windows, but she begins by painting her canvases black. Sometimes she prepares the ground with Roll-A-Tex, a readymade texturing compound. Over this, she often sketches the scene in oilstick with highly saturated colors. Dickson's technique is keyed not so much to the conventional depiction of reflected light as it is to that of direct light sources. These oilstick strokes have a slightly cruddy feeling, beads of the substance congealing against the grain of the canvas or Rolotex. The brute yet deadened physicality of the stroke as such becomes an analogy for the everyday shock of urban experience. —JOHN MILLER

Jane Dickson, *Paradise Alley*, 1983 (detail).

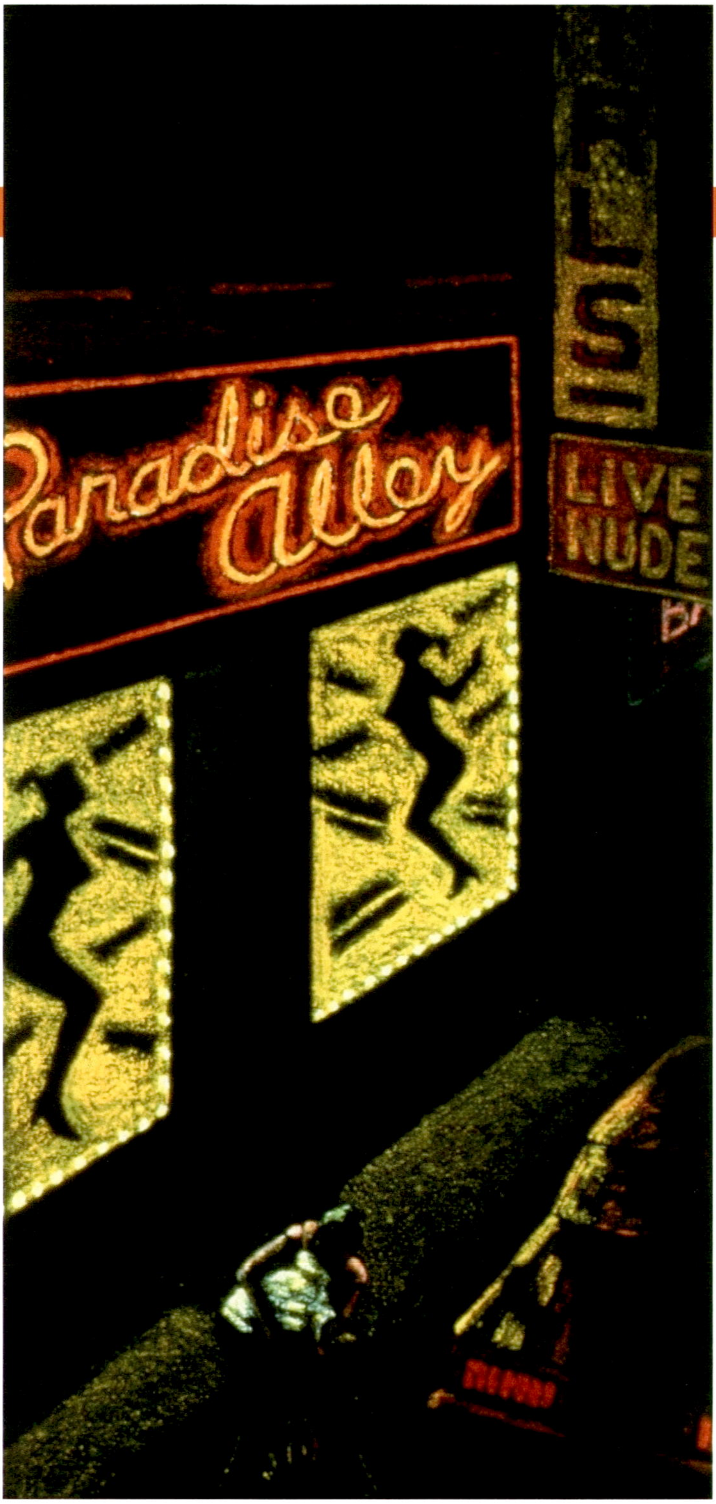

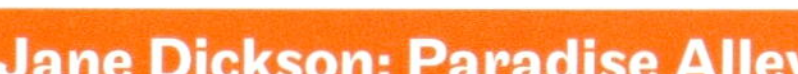

PERFORMERS	96

Terry Adkins

Lé Thi Diem Thúy, Le Tuan Hung and Dang Kim Hiem, and The Far East Side Band

The Mark Hennen/ Toby Kasavan Piano Duo

The Cooper-Moore/ John Blum Duo

Double Edge (Edmund Niemann and Nurit Tilles)

Anthony de Marc and Kathleen Supové

Liz Prince and Zé Luis Oliveira

Shelley Hirsch

Ik-Joong Kang: 8490 Days of Memory

July 12 to September 27, 1996

Ik-Joong Kang's *8490 Days of Memory* is an installation composed of 8490 squares of chocolate hung on foil-covered walls, and the same number of polished clear plastic cubes amassed on the floor below. Each 3-inch square bears an insignia from the US Army cast in relief; each 3-inch cube contains a memento from the artist's childhood. Stacked cubes form a pedestal which supports a 9-foot-statue of Korean war hero General Douglas MacArthur entirely coated in chocolate. For Kang, the sweet scent and taste of creamy chocolate play the role of the tea-soaked madeleine in Proust's novel *Remembrance of Things Past*, bearing in their essence "the vast structure of recollection." In *8490 Days of Memory*, the combination of materials and imagery coalesces into an elegiac evocation of Kang's twenty-four years in Korea—exactly 8490 days—prior to immigrating to the US in 1984. This evocation of Kang's past includes the complex interplay between Korean and American cultures, which continues into the present. —EUGENIE TSAI, BRANCH DIRECTOR, WHITNEY MUSEUM OF AMERICAN ART AT CHAMPION

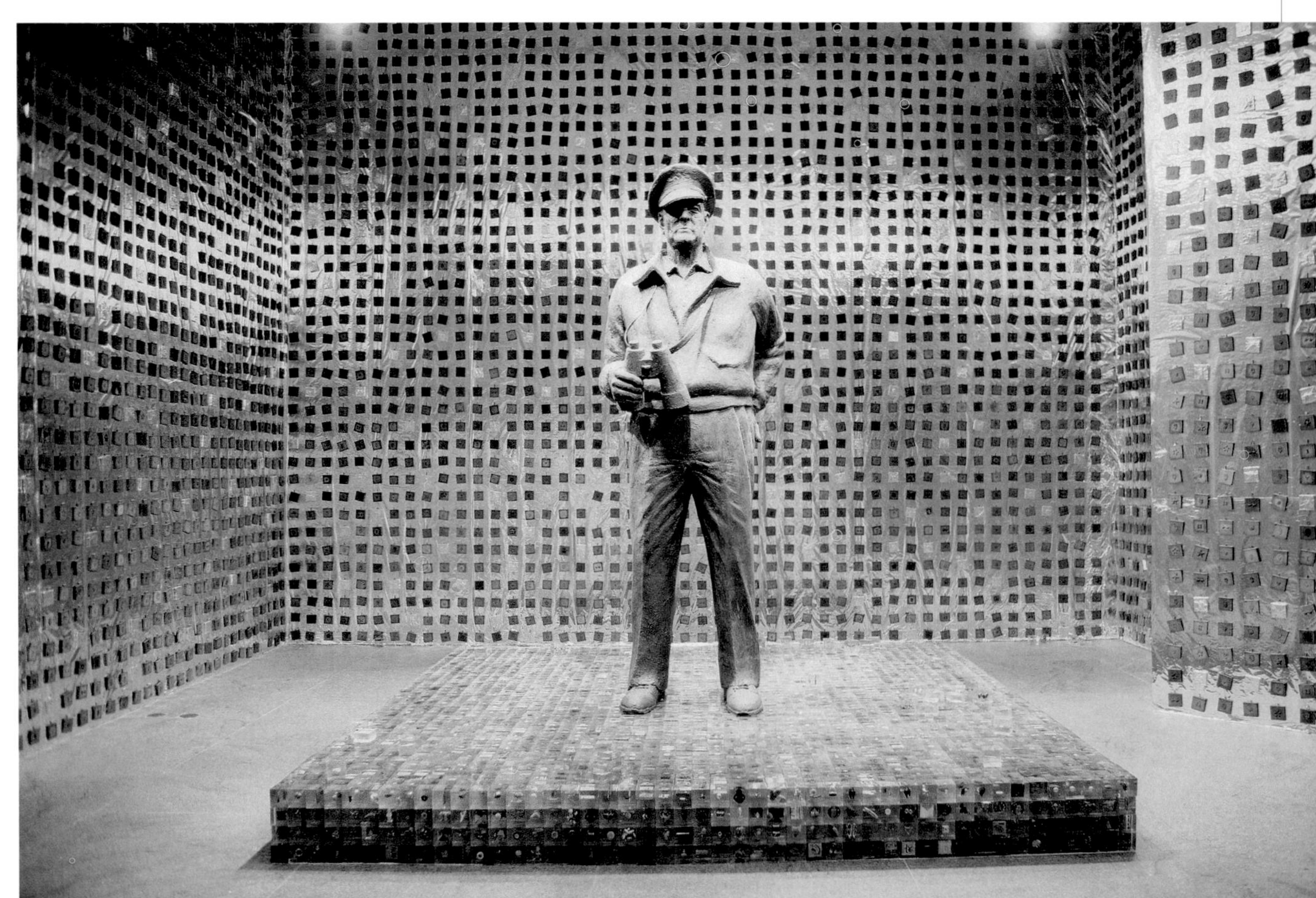

Installation view of *Ik-Joong Kang: 8490 Days of Memory*.

This exhibition of the work of contemporary sculptor Beverly Semmes features a motorized yellow dress with elongated sleeves, entitled "She Moves." Created for the Philip Morris gallery space, the piece developed from Semmes' investigations of fabric and women's garments. Influenced both by Surrealism's change of scale and Minimalism's creation

10
–
17
–
96

Beverly Semmes: She Moves

01
–
04
–
97

of spatial surround, Semmes distorts known forms and objects. The soft sewn or woven pieces, often women's dresses, emphasize handmade gesture and physical presence to investigate issues of body, gender, and identity.

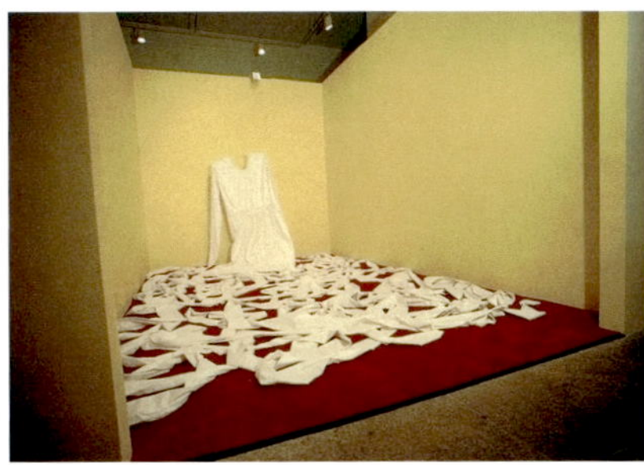

Installation views of *Beverly Semmes: She Moves.*

Romare Bearden's Photomontages developed out of his involvement with the politically oriented artists' group, Spiral, formed in 1963. After the group abandoned the idea for a collaborative collage that addressed the position of African-Americans in society, Bearden completed the collage himself and developed the "projection." The term refers to Bearden's process of making a collage in color (usually about the size of a sheet of writing paper) and then enlarging it through a black-and-white photostat to create a photomontage work.

The Photomontages of 1964 mark a radical departure from Bearden's abstract work of the 1950s in their photographic and documentary quality. Using images culled from the media and other pictorial sources, they provided a means through which Bearden could respond to the issues raised by the social and political upheaval around the civil rights movement. His work, however, is neither militant nor didactic, but rather a powerful evocation of community life and spirituality. "History is made explicit in these works through visual narratives Bearden created about the African-American experience. His own life provided the details of what could be encapsulated as a retelling of the primary experience of many African-Americans," writes Whitney curator Thelma Golden, in her catalogue essay for the exhibition.
—SHAMIM M. MOMIN, GALLERY ASSISTANT, EXHIBITION PROGRAMS

01
–
17
–
97

Romare Bearden in Black-and-White:
Photomontage Projections 1964

03
–
20
–
97

97 PERFORMERS

Savion Glover and
Eli Fountain with
Incognergroes

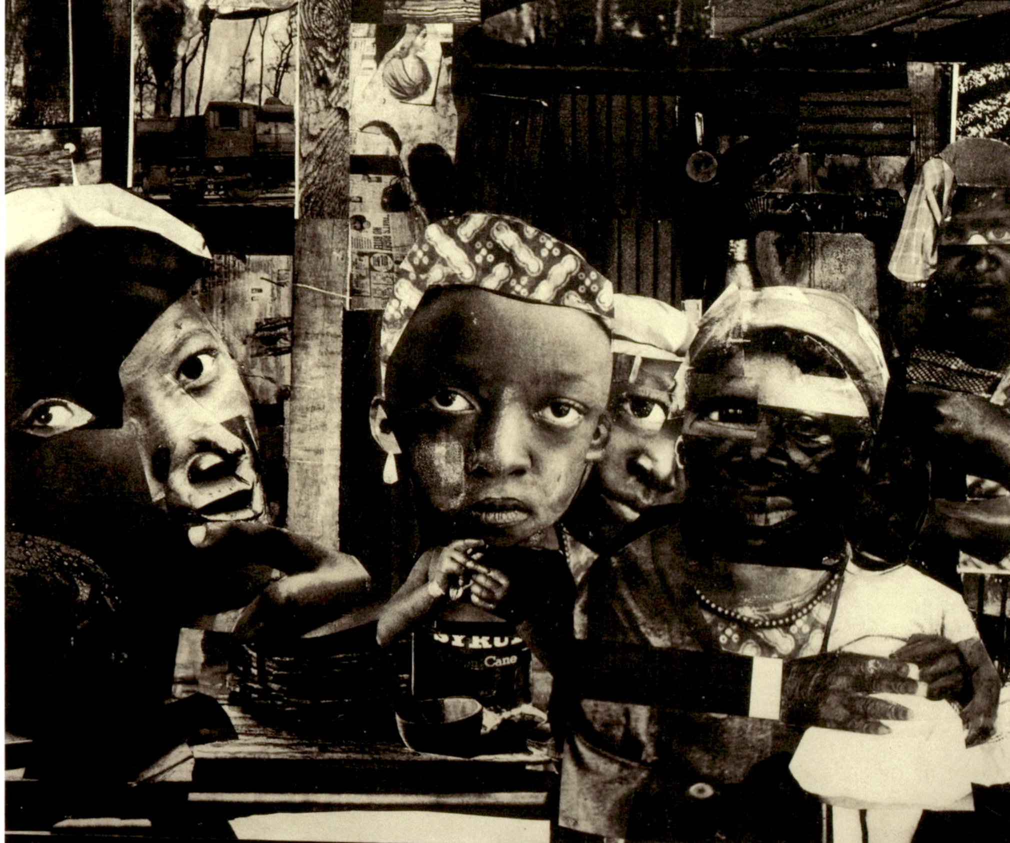

Romare Bearden, *Mysteries*, 1964.

March 31 to June 27, 1997
Harold Edgerton (1903–1990) may not be a household name, but many of the dramatic microseconds he captured on film—a drop of milk splashing into a cup,

Quicker Than A Wink: The Photographs of Harold Edgerton

a bullet splitting a playing card in two, a hummingbird hovering in midflight, a tennis ball flattened by the strings of a racquet—are already icons in our repertory of cultural images. *Quicker Than a Wink: The Photographs of Harold Edgerton* presents a selection of eighty works from a recent gift by the estate of the artist to the Whitney Museum of American Art. This new addition to the Whitney's Permanent Collection spans Edgerton's entire career, from the 1930s through the 1980s. It includes a concentration of images from the thirties, an exciting and productive decade during which Edgerton invented the process of stroboscopic photography. This technological innovation revolutionized photography, allowing microseconds to be captured on film with great clarity, and resulted in arresting photographic images that have forever altered our view of ordinary events. —EUGENIE TSAI, ASSOCIATE CURATOR AND CURATOR OF BRANCHES

Installation view of *Tunnel Visions: Photographs by Accra Shepp.*

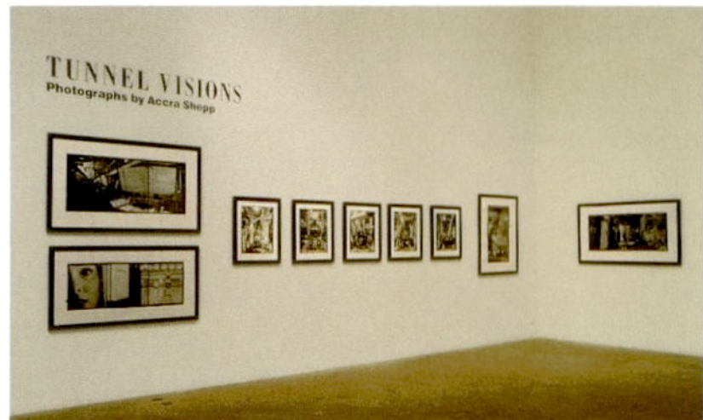

Tunnel Visions: Photographs by Accra Shepp

July 1 to October 10, 1997

The underground station represented in Shepp's photographs is as private as the station above is public, as dark as its counterpart is light, and as devoid of people as the upstairs is full. This is a world filled with utilitarian structures—pipes, ducts, machinery, generators, and gauges. This is the heart of Grand Central Terminal, the infrastructure that provides power for the trains and heat and light for the huge station above. This is the command post, where dispatchers route incoming and departing trains.

Shepp photographed the nether regions of Grand Central Terminal from April through August 1993, after receiving an invitation to participate in a project about 42nd Street. Deliberately avoiding the Times Square area, and looking for an underexposed aspect of this all-too-familiar midtown district, he settled on Grand Central Terminal as the subject of his investigation. His view of the station differed markedly from that of guidebooks, which inevitably highlight the terminal's distinctive architectural character. To Shepp, the terminal above ground is only part of a much larger and more integrated vision: "Grand Central Station is a Beaux-Arts edifice, a marble colossus. This of course is only part of the Terminal, in fact, only a small part. The building is actually like a tiny ornate cap atop a giant underground behemoth of tunnels and chambers and machines."
—EUGENIE TSAI, ASSOCIATE CURATOR AND CURATOR OF BRANCHES

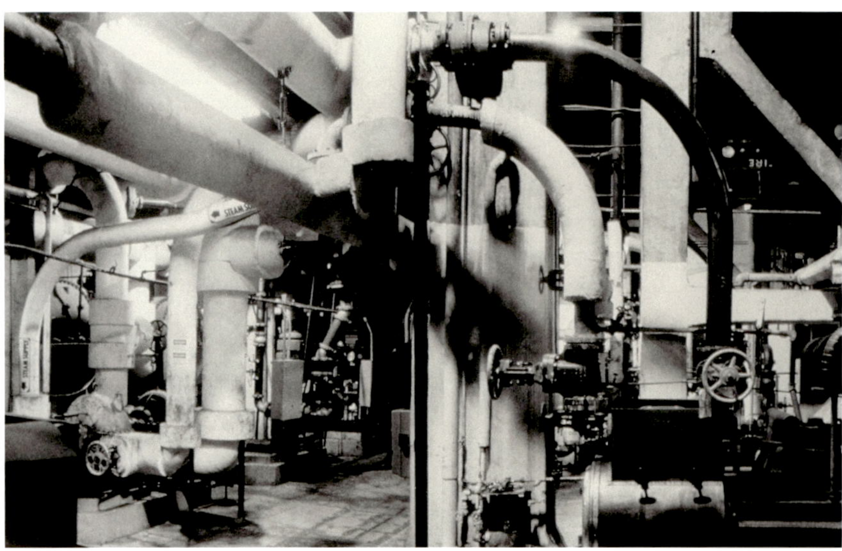

Accra Shepp, *Untitled* (from the series *Steam Plant*), 1993.

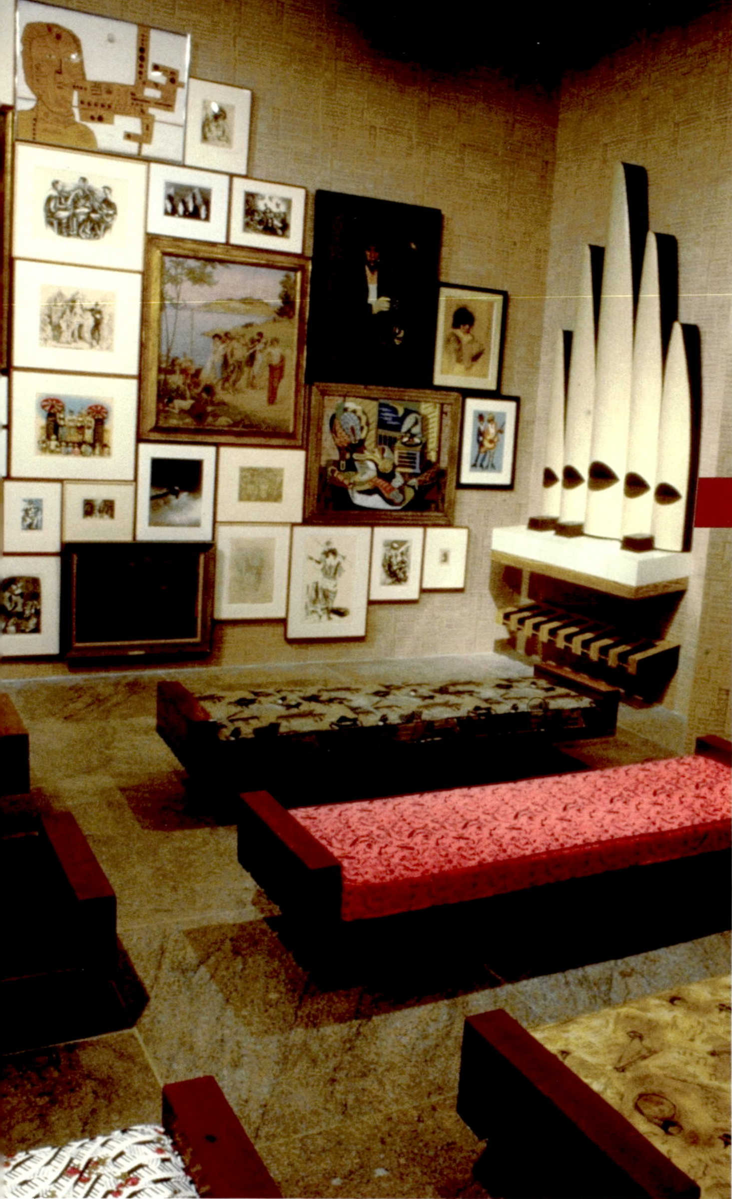

Pictures at an Exhibition:
An Installation by Christian Marclay

October 24, 1997 to January 25, 1998
Curatorial Counterpoint

Assuming the diverse roles of curator, interior decorator, and exhibition designer, Christian Marclay produced *Pictures at an Exhibition,* a lively and eclectic mix of works of art, furniture, and wallpaper. For this installation, Marclay worked with the collection of the Whitney Museum and selected objects that treated the theme of making music or producing sound. Sifting through some twelve thousand pieces, he found about fifty, in a variety of media. Drawings, prints, photographs, and paintings cover the rear wall of the gallery, densely hung from floor to ceiling. Six benches, designed in the 1960s for the main building of the Whitney Museum on Madison Avenue, sit directly in front of the wall. Configured in two rows of three, they suggest a musical or theatrical performance. A plethora of patterns on the wallpaper and reupholstered benches, incorporating pages of sheet music, piano keyboards, and Elvis Presley's head, underscore the musical theme of the installation. Although music has provided the impetus for Marclay's production since his student performances of the late 1970s, *Pictures at an Exhibition* is one of several recent collaborations with museum collections that suggest a new and fruitful area of exploration.

Marclay took the title, *Pictures at an Exhibition,* from an eponymous piano composition, written in 1874 by the Russian composer Modest Mussorgsky. The composition consists of ten short pieces, each inspired by a drawing by the artist Victor Hartmann, to whom the music was dedicated. Through his choice of title, therefore, Marclay introduces the theme of the installation—the intimate relationship between image and sound.

The works on view from the Whitney's collection include examples by familiar figures—Richard Artschwager, Thomas Hart Benton, Elizabeth Catlett, Stuart

Davis, Yasuo Kuniyoshi, William H. Johnson, Reginald Marsh, John Sloan, and Joseph Stella—as well as lesser-known artists, whose works have rarely been shown. Many of the selections are prints; most date from the first half of this century. Although the link between music and abstraction in art is a significant topic in discussions of twentieth-century American art, Marclay deliberately avoids abstraction in favor of figurative images. He feels these more effectively evoke the experience of hearing music through the act of looking. Indeed, gazing upon Benton's *I Got a Gal on Sourwood Mountain,* we can hear the rhythmic toe-tapping tune of the fiddle, whereas sitting before Artschwager's *Organ of Cause and Effect III,* we might hear strains of the "Wedding March." Unexpected jux-

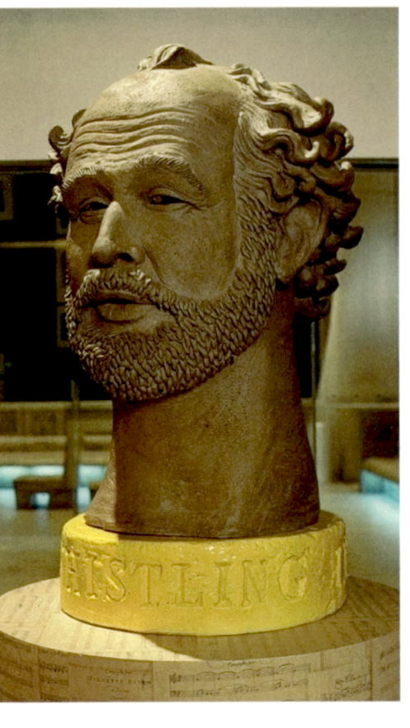

Robert Arneson, *Whistling in the Dark*, 1976 (installation view of *Pictures at an Exhibition: An Installation by Christian Marclay*).

tapositions occurred in the process of Marclay's improvisational arrangement of the works on the wall. The salon-style arrangement creates an "orchestra of images" or a "wall of sound," an interweaving of visible image and remembered sound that pro-vides a different experience for each of us.

Although *Pictures at an Exhibition* is Marclay's first collaboration with a museum collection in the United States, for the past few years he has been cre-ating similar site-specific installations in Europe. The first was *Accompagnement musical* at the Musée d'Art et d'Histoire, Geneva, in 1995. Artifacts from all of the departments of the museum, including fine arts, drawings, prints, photographs, furniture, archaeology, musical instruments, coins, and ancient arms and armor were at Marclay's disposal. In addition, he was given access to the holdings of other

Christian Marclay

Toshio Kajiwara

DJ Olive,
The Audio Janitor

museums affiliated with the Musée d'Art et d'Histoire—ceramics from the Musée Ariana, watches from the Musée de l'Horlogerie, musical instruments from the Musée d'Ethnographie, and books from the University Library. Using more than four hundred objects, Marclay filled different period rooms in the museum with a variety of installations. The only thing consistent throughout was a chosen object's relationship to sound. Sometimes an installation looked like misplaced storage, with paintings leaning randomly one against another, or against furniture strewn casually about an elegant Neoclassical salon. In another installation, empty storage cases belonging to a variety of stringed instruments were propped open and neatly laid out on an oriental rug for the viewer's inspection. Marclay's decision to display these objects, not characteristically shown in museums and therefore rarely seen by visitors, suggests a desire to defy aspects of conventional curatorial practice.

The following year, Marclay took part in "Helvetia Sounds," at the Villa Merkel in Esslingen, Germany. He decided to redecorate an entire floor of the villa, six rooms surrounding an atrium, by adding wallpaper and floor-to-ceiling curtains. The rooms were empty, except for one which had cushions lying on the floor. By playing off the bold and delicate patterns and colors of the wallpaper, curtains, and cushions, he created environments with disparate moods, rhythms, and syncopations. In the atrium, paintings with a musical theme, drawn from the municipal art collection, were hung somewhat lower than usual—at a height perfect for viewers seated in the chairs lined up in front of the works. The fabrics used to make the curtains and cushions in the rooms covered the seats of the chairs.

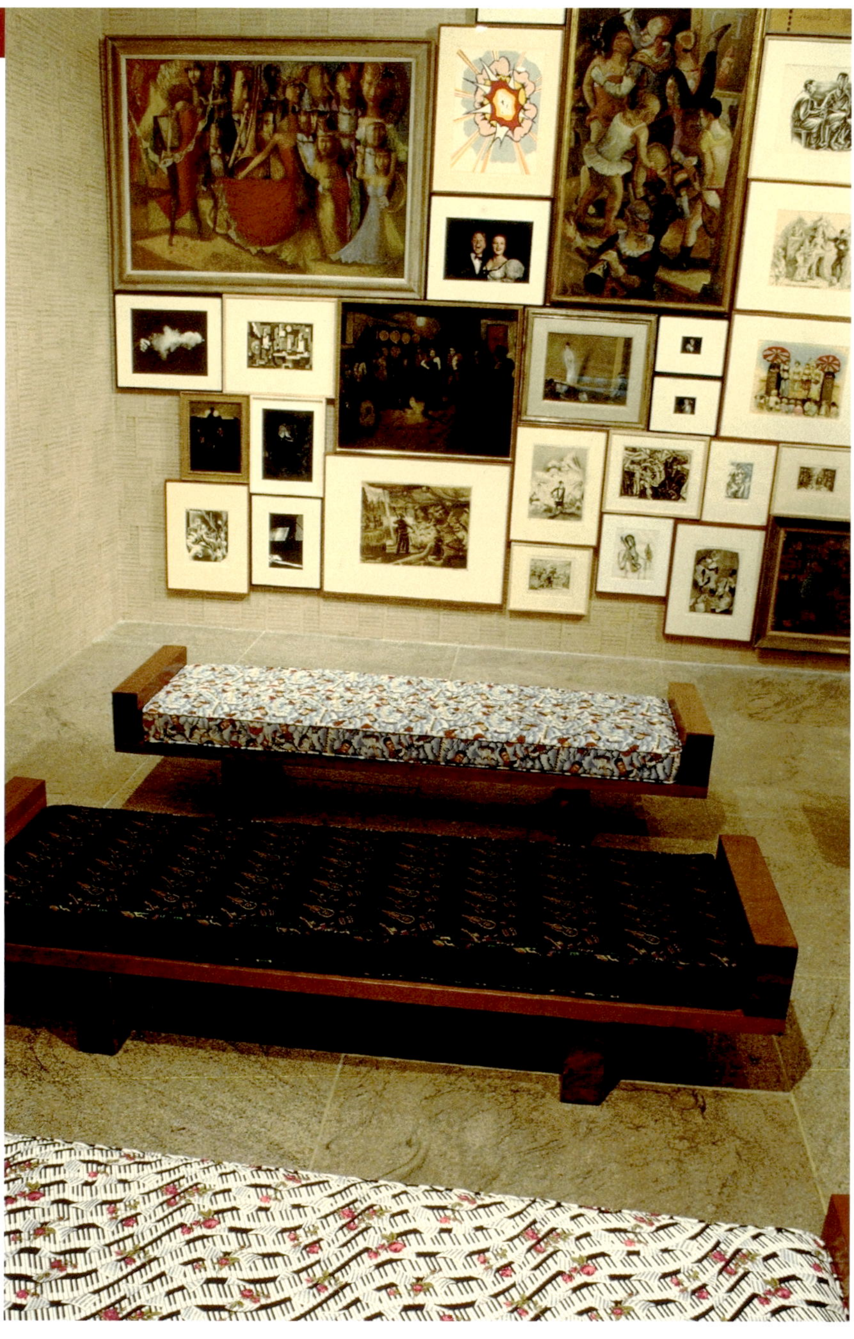

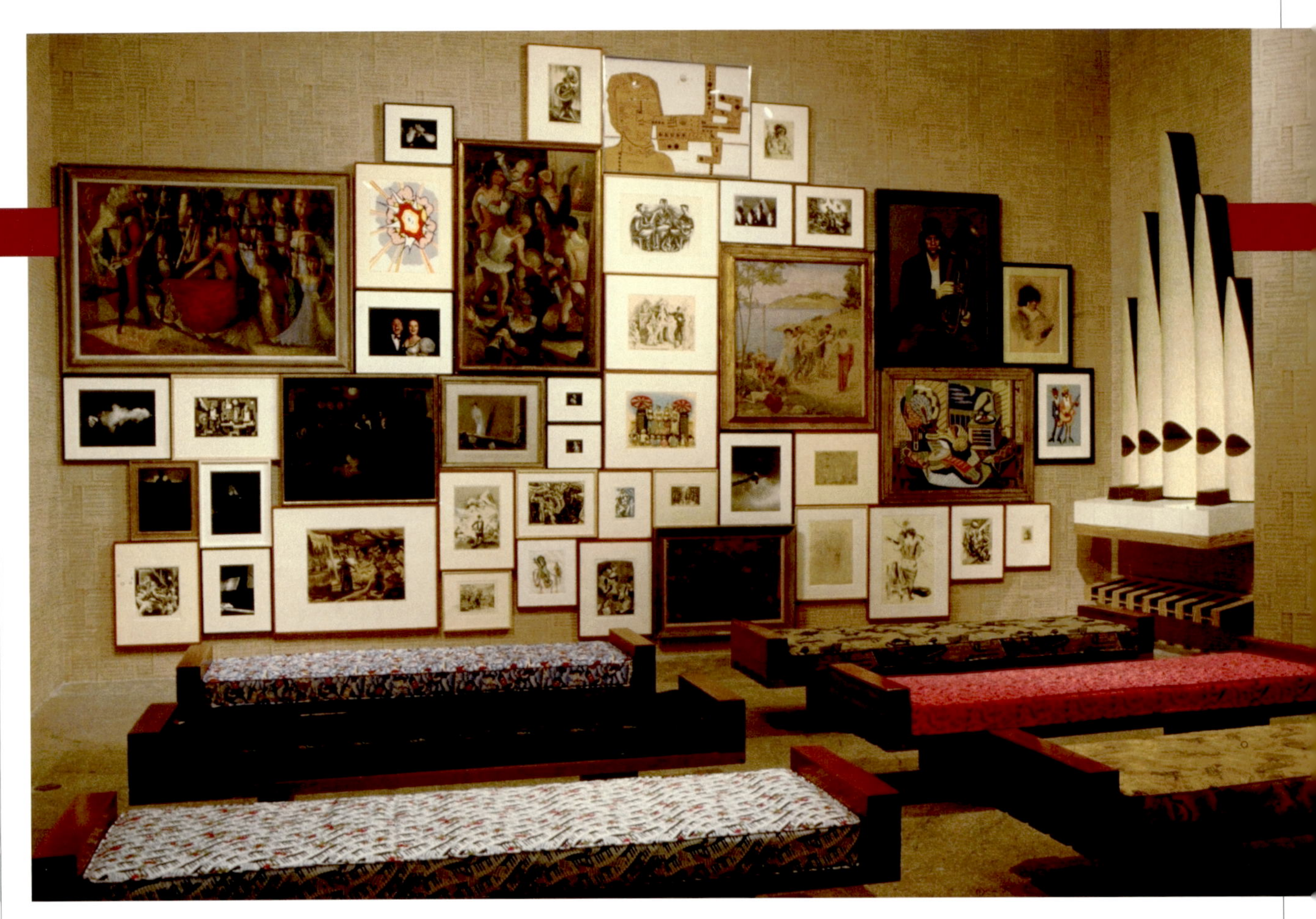

Most recently, Marclay created *Arranged and Conducted* at the Kunsthaus Zurich. More than a hundred paintings, prints, drawings, and photographs from the collection, all on the theme of people playing music, hung frame-to-frame on a large wall. Sixty chairs, each upholstered with a different fabric with a musical motif, stand before the wall. Marclay even designed uniforms for the guards, combining various fabrics to create harmonious and discordant juxtapositions. The Zurich installation also included a new component, Marclay's private collection of images and objects entitled *Scrapbook*. Vitrines hold neatly arranged pictures of people talking on the telephone—snapshots, record album covers, photographs from magazines and newspapers—a grouping of telephone receivers, images of people dancing, and plates decorated with figures making music. Comparing the two components of the Zurich installation, we find two different approaches to the accumulation of material, one highly structured and institutional, the other intuitive and intensely personal.

Marclay developed a taste for music and performance as an art student in Geneva during the mid-1970s, when he attended performances organized by Ecart, a contemporary Fluxus group. He left Switzerland in 1977 to study sculpture at the Massachusetts College of Art. In the United States, Marclay discovered punk rock, as well as the performance work of Dan Graham, Vito Acconci, and Laurie Anderson. He formed his first performance group, The Bachelors, Even—the name a nod to Duchamp—a duo with a guitarist. In 1980, after he moved to New York City, he formed a second group, Mon Ton Son. Some of his performances incorporated a sculptural component in the form of "recycled records," created by slicing, fragmenting, and reconstructing the vinyl discs. When played on a turntable, they emitted sounds described by the artist as "loud and gritty." During the early 1980s, Marclay focused on performance, appearing at the Kitchen and other downtown venues.

In 1987, Marclay had his first exhibition in New York, an installation of about 850 vinyl records, laid like tiles on the floor of the Clocktower Gallery. Footprints on the shiny surface recorded the presence of visitors. At the same time, he made sculpture from found objects that made reference to sound and, in the spirit of Dada, often incorporated a visual pun. In 1989, Marclay created *Tape Fall,* one of his best-known sculptures,

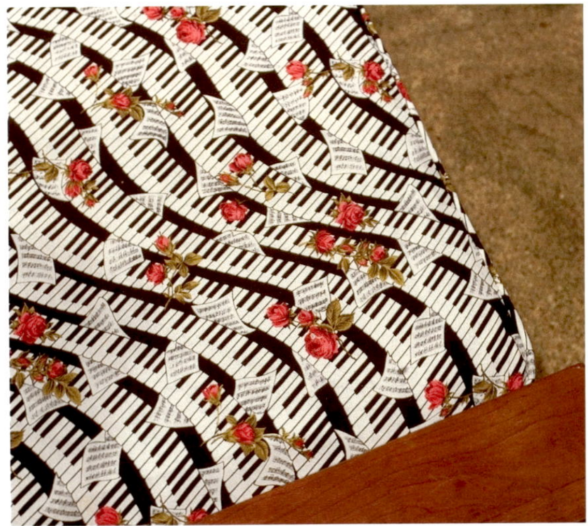

Detail of bench from *Pictures at an Exhibition:*
An Installation by Christian Marclay.

a tapeplayer without a takeup reel, which played the sound of trickling water as the tape cascaded and pooled onto the floor. A related piece of the same year, *The Beatles,* consisted of a pillow crocheted out of magnetic tape that contained recordings of all the music by the Beatles. The following year, Marclay began to stitch collages together from found album covers. The images on the covers lined up to form composite bodies, like the Surrealist game known as the "Exquisite Corpse." Male-female hybrids often resulted, which commented on the role of sexuality in the marketing of music.

The approach Marclay employs in *Pictures at an Exhibition* presents a striking contrast with more conventional curatorial practices in terms of selection and installation. *Pictures at an Exhibition* does not attempt to present a historical survey on the theme of music-making, nor is it is a connoisseur's choice of masterpieces. Once the artist decided to choose only representational works depicting music-making, thus setting parameters for selecting works from the Whitney's collection without prior knowledge of its contents, the element of chance took over. The process of selection is key to his art-making. In addition to selecting the works of art, Marclay selected the title of the exhibition, the fabrics for the slipcovers on the gallery benches, and the wallpaper. In many ways, Marcel Duchamp provides the model for Marclay as artist-curator. Duchamp, creator of Fountain, the urinal-qua-work-of-art, believed it was the selection and designation of found or readymade objects and the context of their display that made them art. In this case, the museum setting helps to establish the identity of *Pictures at an Exhibition* as an art installation, rather than an offbeat display in, say, a home furnishings store. Like Duchamp, Marclay avoids judgments about "quality." As long as a work of art falls within his set parameters it will be part of the exhibition, hung democratically on the wall as part of an ensemble.

Marclay is one of a number of artists who have curated museum exhibitions over the past twenty years. (They include Joseph Beuys, Marcel Broodthaers, Christian Boltanski, Joseph Kosuth, Bertrand Lavier, Claes Oldenburg, Daniel Spoerri, and Andy Warhol.) A recent example in New York is the series of artist-organized exhibitions initiated in 1989 by The Museum of Modern Art. Various artists were each invited to create an exhibition from the museum's collection according to a personally chosen theme or principle. For example, the series opened with Scott Burton making a selection of sculpture by Brancusi. In the most recent exhibition of the series (1995), Elizabeth Murray chose works by women artists. Clearly, in addition to featuring the collection of the host institution, each of these exhibitions revealed elements of the artist-organizer's taste, artistic interests, and formative influences. They did not question the authority of the museum as an institution.

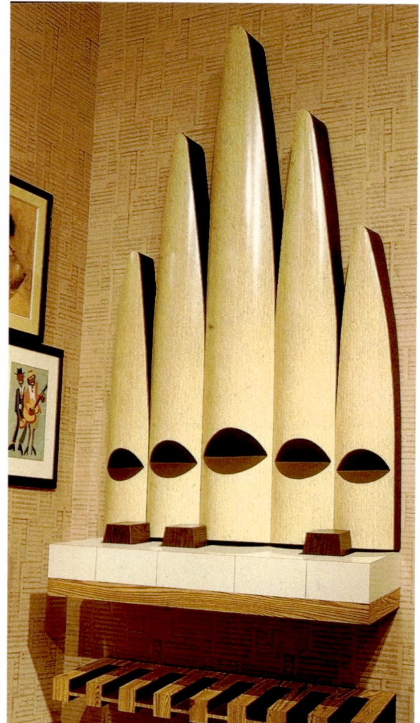

Richard Artschwager, *Organ of Cause and Effect III,* 1996 (installation view of *Pictures at an Exhibition: An Installation by Christian Marclay*).

Recently, artists like Fred Wilson have been working with museum collections to examine institutional power, a purpose that differs significantly from that of the artist-organized exhibition. In his yearlong project "Mining the Museum" at the Maryland Historical Society, his reinstallation of the permanent collection critically examined the relationship of the collection to the local community. Conceived with input from the staff of the Historical Society, from the maintenance staff to the director, Wilson's reinstallation examined the assumptions underlying the institution itself—the formation of its collection, its view of history, how it was told, by whom and for whom, and the imbalance of power between administration and audience. Wilson regards his interventions of this sort as works of art in and of themselves.

Pictures at an Exhibition shares common ground with the artist-organized exhibition and the institutional critique. Marclay's installation reveals the significance of music and performance in his overall production. His choice of the works of art, the fabrics, and the wallpaper speaks volumes about his unique sensibility and his improvisatory ability to skillfully combine seemingly disparate elements into a dynamic whole. At the same time, by selecting and remixing this particular slice of the Whitney's collection, *Pictures at an Exhibition* invites us to consider the process of collecting, the formation of collections, as well as the ever-changing notions of quality and taste. Perhaps most important of all, *Pictures at an Exhibition* invites us to pause during our frenetic day, to sit, to look, to wonder, to enjoy, to hear the music that lies within us all. —EUGENIE TSAI, ASSOCIATE CURATOR AND CURATOR OF BRANCHES

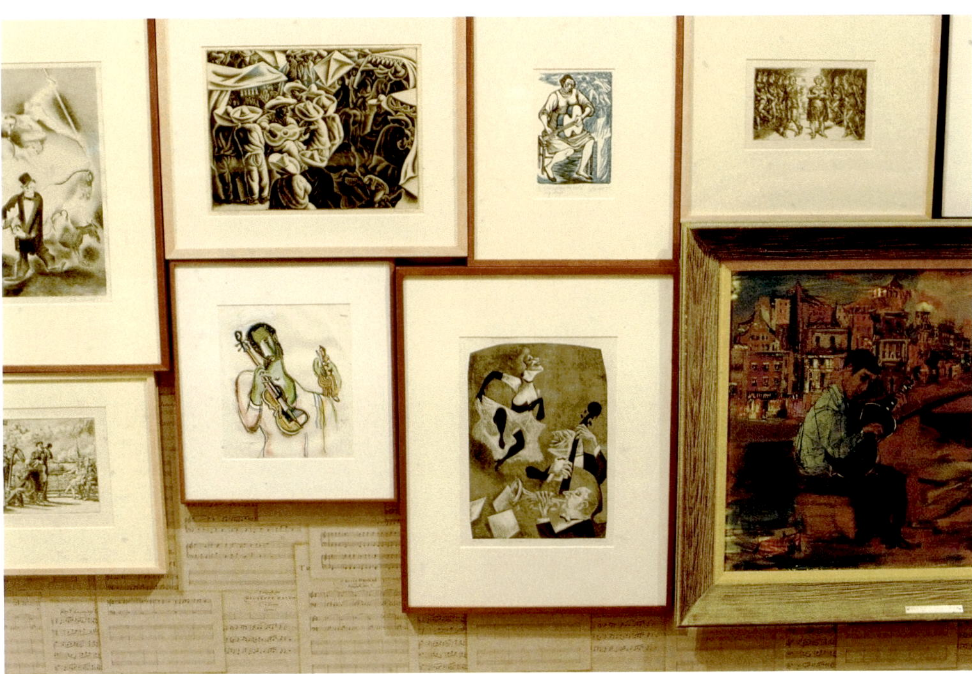

Garden of Qián, by Ming Fay

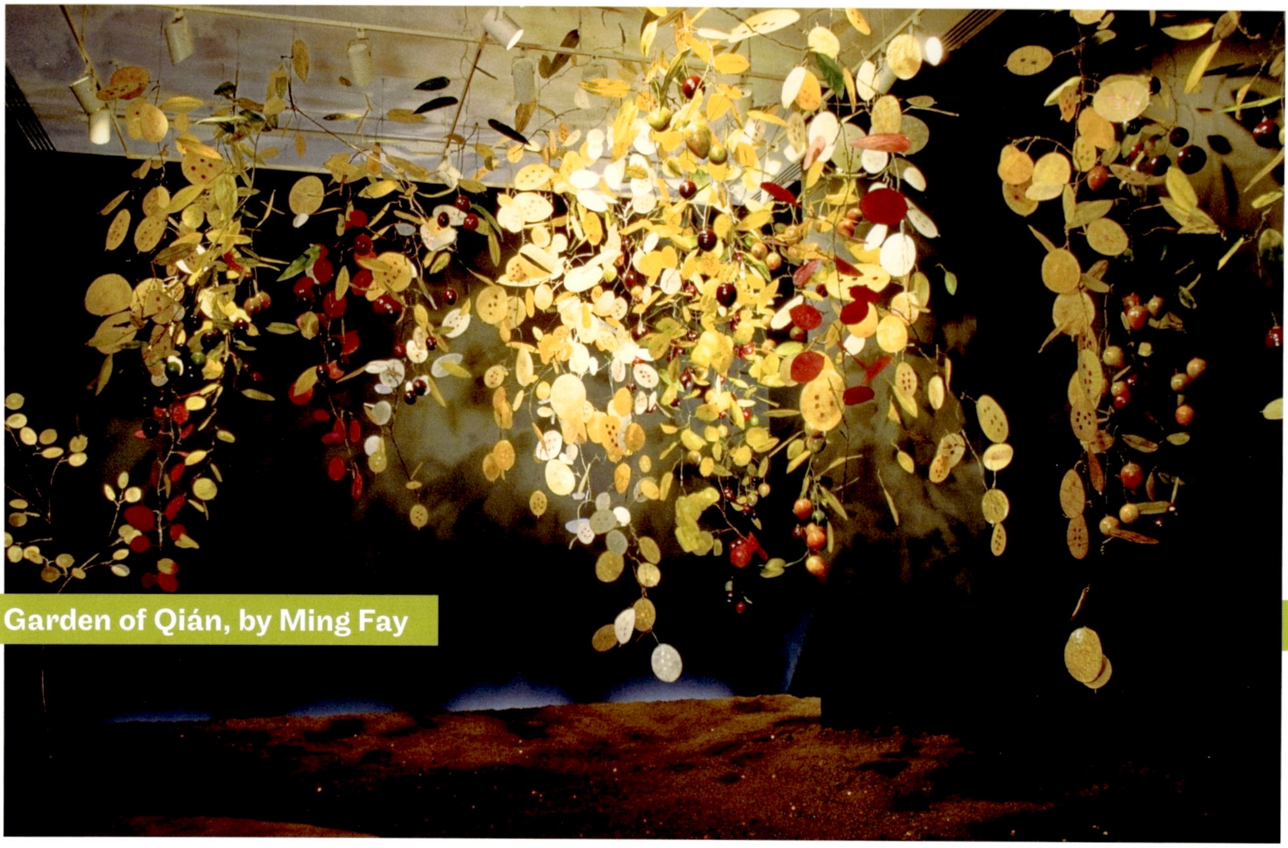

Installation views of *Garden of Qián, by Ming Fay.*

February 6 to April 17, 1998

Seated on a craggy rock contemplating Ming Fay's *Garden of Qián* prompts flights of fantasy in the viewer, flights to realms far removed from the urban jungle. The installation begins with fruit-laden branches suspended high in the Sculpture Court and expands into a lush garden inside the gallery. Intertwining fruit and foliage hang above a bed of soil embedded with gleaming pennies. While the vegetation looks familiar to us, close examination reveals that nothing can be identified with certainty—this is no ordinary garden. Rather, it is a garden containing Fay's sculptural transformations of acutely observed natural phenomena....

Garden of Qián grows out of Fay's fascination with the concept of the garden, with its implications of cyclical decay and renewal. —EUGENIE TSAI, ASSOCIATE CURATOR AND CURATOR OF BRANCHES

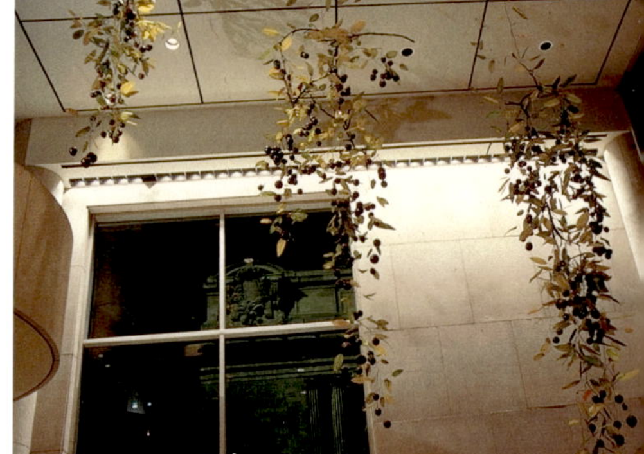

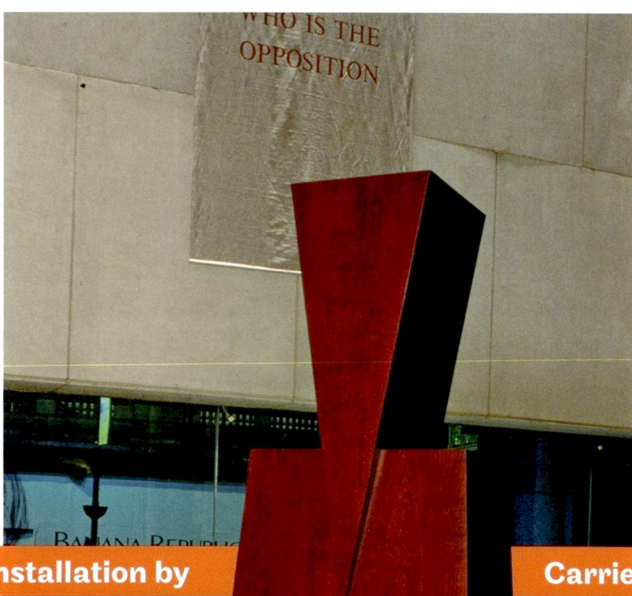

Carrie Mae Weems, *Sometimes a Great Notion*, 1998 (installation view of *Who What When Where: An Installation by Carrie Mae Weems*).

Who What When Where: An Installation by Carrie Mae Weems

May 1 to July 16, 1998

Through the use of evocative images, objects, and words, Weems' installation critiques capitalism's seemingly un-questioned authority, and considers the artist's and the viewer's responsibility to talk seriously about how power is wielded, dealt with, and challenged in our society. The installation will feature a small-scale, steel model of Vladimir Tatlin's never-realized tower, the *Monument to the Third International* (1920), as well as three banners depicting images, created by Weems, that draw upon the work of artists Kazimir Malevich and El Lissitzky. By referencing works by these three early 20th-century Russian Con-structivist artists, all of whom believed in affecting societal change through their work, Carrie Mae Weems explores the role of artist as social activist. On other banners, the questions "Who is the oppo-sition?" "What is the opposition?" "When is the opposition?" and "Where is the opposition?" are printed, inviting viewers to think about their own roles in oppos-ing authority and challenging the status quo....

... For over a decade, Weems has presented her beautiful and provocative photographic installations with an eye toward confronting and challenging viewers' understandings of class, race, gender and—more broadly—human relationships.

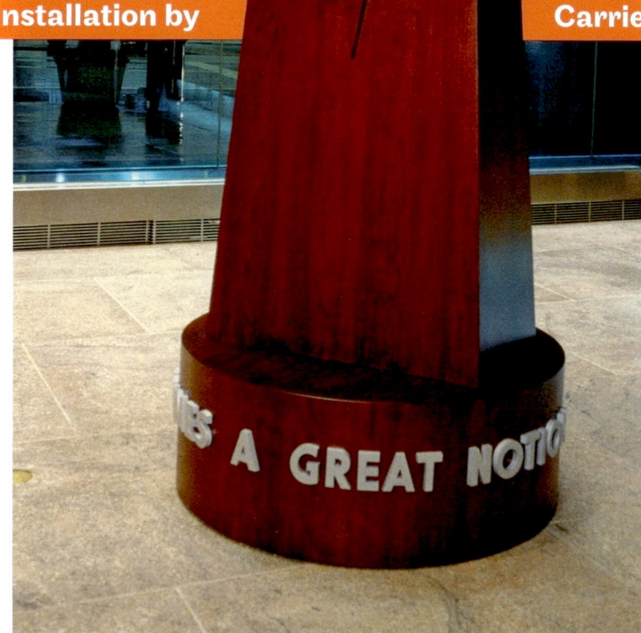

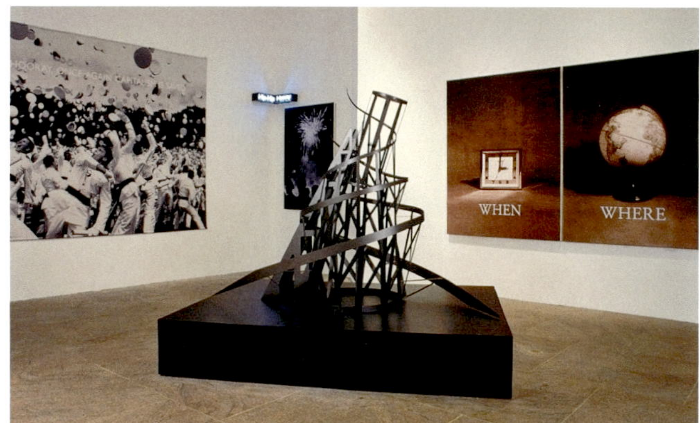

Installation view of *Who What When Where: An Installation by Carrie Mae Weems*.

PERFORMERS	98

David Antin

Eleanor Antin

Dael Orlandersmith

Lawrence Goldhuber and Heidi Latsky with Lesley Dill

Theo Bleckmann and Kenneth Goldsmith with Skuli Sverrisson and John Hollenbeck

July 24 to October 9, 1998

In *Water Life*, the combination of photographs and shells evokes Mecox Bay, a site of harmonious reconciliation between people and nature, and a place of personal healing for the artist. Despite the apparent contradiction between the world of nature represented in Sandrow's art and the overtly urban environment of the Whitney Museum at Philip Morris, the artist draws connections between the two realms. Reading about the history of midtown Manhattan, she discovered that the area was once a marshy meadowland, with rocky bluffs and streams. A river ran northwest from Kips Bay past where the Whitney Museum at Philip Morris currently stands. There was, moreover, an abundance of shellfish in the area. A third element of the installation, the sound of running water, audible in some parts of the gallery, evokes this river that might still run through the depths beneath the Museum. With this recording, Sandrow invites us to imagine what Manhattan was like in the past, when its flora and fauna resembled that of present-day Mecox Bay. . . .

. . . The photographs and the shells in *Water Life* evoke not merely a place of extraordinary beauty in the natural world, but a place of personal significance, where Sandrow can be born anew, whole and unbroken. —EUGENIE TSAI, ASSOCIATE CURATOR AND CURATOR OF BRANCHES

Hope Sandrow: Water Life

Installation views of *Hope Sandrow: Water Life*.

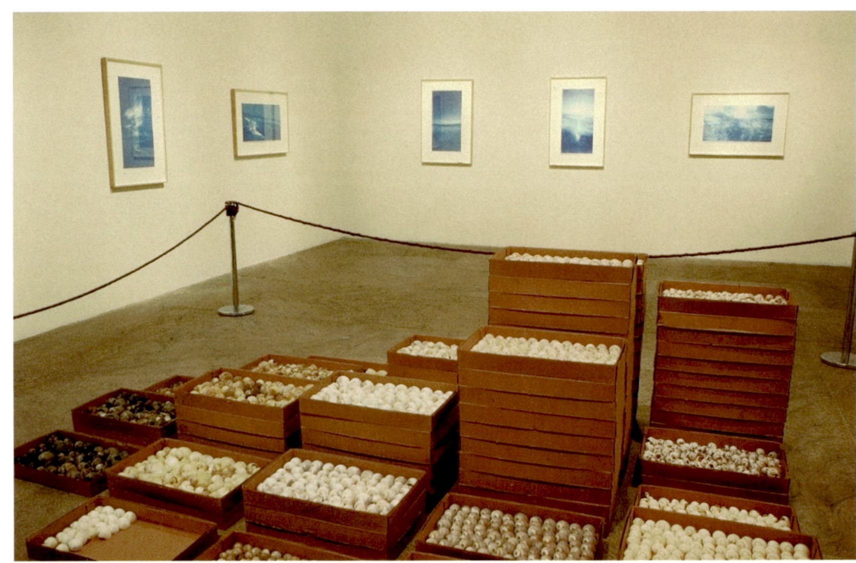

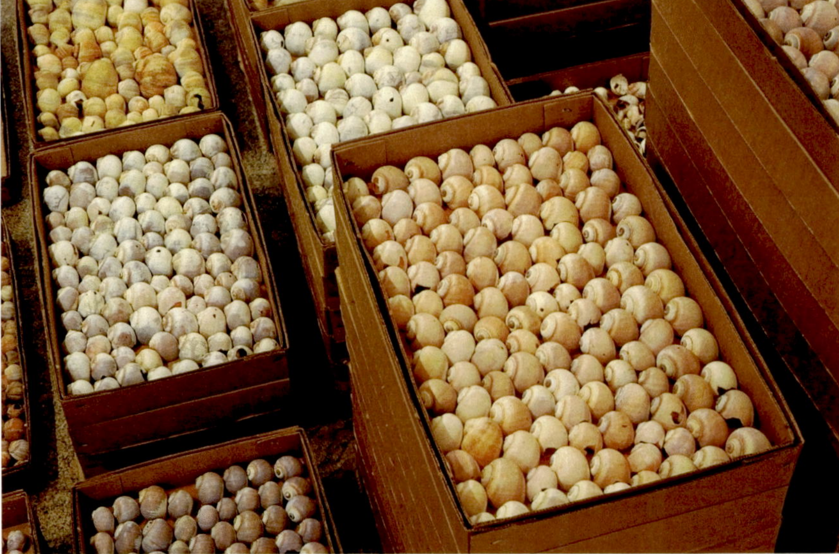

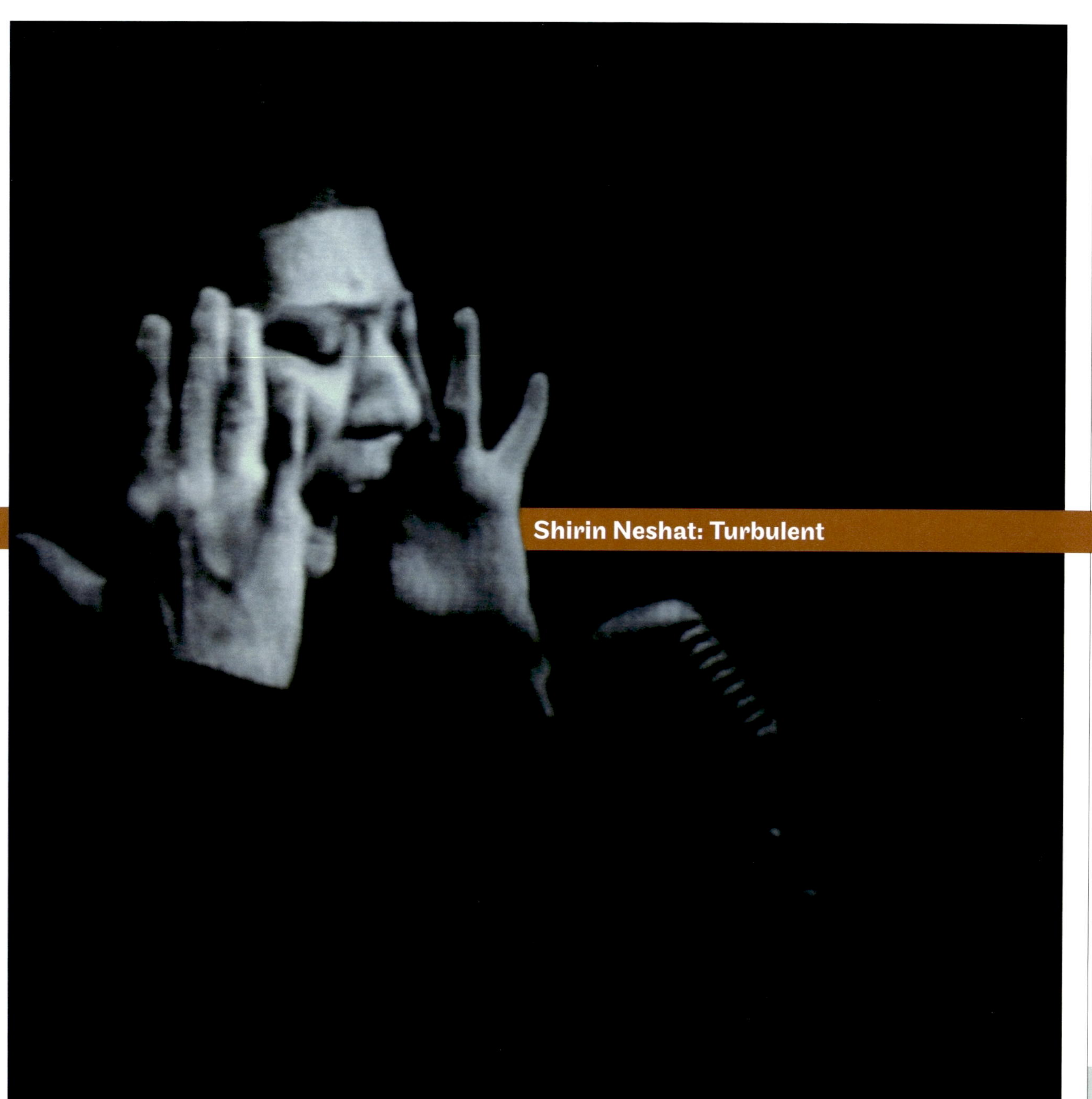

THIS PAGE AND FOLLOWING: Stills from
Shirin Neshat: Turbulent, 1998.

October 23, 1998 to January 15, 1999

A Not-Yet-Named Third Space

According to the great Babylonian epic poem "Enuma Elish" (c. 2000 BC), Tiamat and
Apsu, the god and goddess of chaos, once ruled the world. But in the next generation,
the god Marduk appeared. Because he represented a patriarchal concept of nations
and the paradigm of order, there was conflict over how the world ought to be run.
This conflict led to a social transformation. Tiamat and Apsu were demoted and
Marduk became the chief god of Babylon. To celebrate his victory over the death
of chaos and his establishment of a new world order, Marduk devised a New Year's
festival that lasted eleven days and was celebrated everywhere. Virtually identical
festivals were held for two thousand years in Egypt, Crete, and Canaan.

One contemporary interpretation of this myth argues that those annual
celebrations acted as a reminder that chaos was evil and, therefore, had to be de-
stroyed and replaced by order. To some modern thinkers, however, the world has

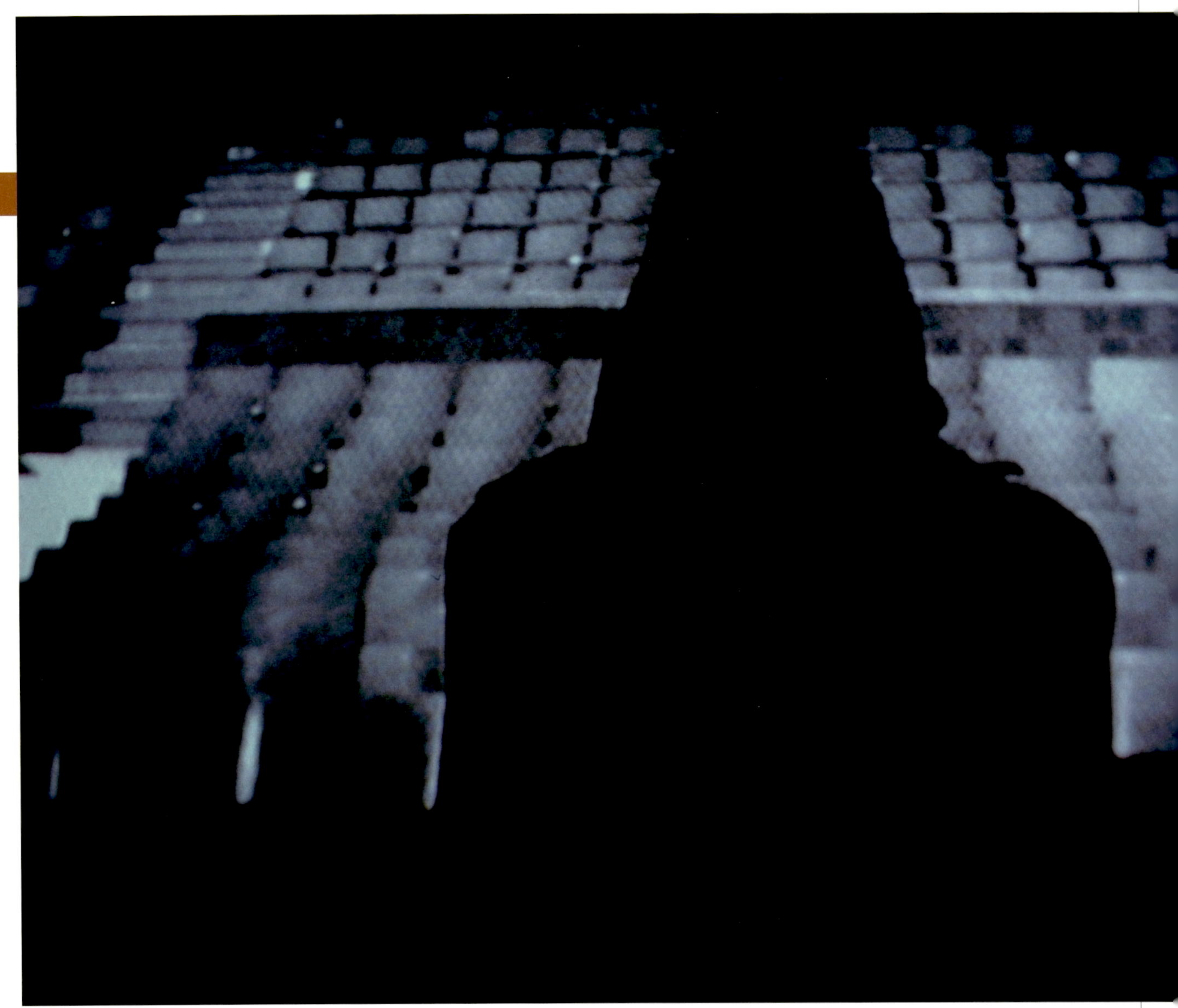

suffered for four thousand years due to the repression of chaos, which is identified as the embodiment of the feminine, the intuitive, and the creative. The resulting obstruction of imagination—among other things—has led to today's ecological problems, while denying us the ability to fully exercise our poetic capacity to seek solutions or mediate conflict.[1]

Shirin Neshat's emblematic photographs and compelling video installations can be seen as a poetic attempt to re-create the creative chaos that governed the world in the reign of Tiamat and Apsu. Neshat symbolically disrupts the exclusionary positioning of women within fundamentalist Islamic societies, the ideological parallels to which, as this essay argues, can also be found within Orientalist perceptions of Western cultures. In this latter context, Neshat chooses to work with the photographic medium, where the camera and its gaze stand as a hidden metaphor for Western invention, and by extension colonial intervention. Neshat's simplistic, almost reductive, iconography is a ploy that evokes the essentialist nature of fundamentalism, whether religious or national.

The effectiveness of Neshat's work depends on the idea that a photograph represents the truth, as does an advertisement. Thus her seemingly banal, sensationalized, and digestible mode of delivery recalls, as well as mocks, strategies employed in advertising. For instance, the frontally shot, life-size black-and-white self-portraits which depict the artist's partially veiled body—sometimes highlighted with colored props such as guns, swords, and flowers, or ornamented with Islamic texts that accent her face, hands, and feet—feed our curiosity about the stereotypical image of the exotic "Oriental" woman while also re-routing such myths. As Ella Habiba Shohat reminds us, "The Orient as a metaphor for sexuality is encapsulated by the recurrent figure of the veiled woman. The inaccessibility of the veiled woman, mirroring the mystery of the Orient itself, requires a process of Western unveiling for comprehension. Veiled women in Orientalist paintings, photographs, and films expose flesh, ironically, more than they conceal it. It is this process of exposing the female Other, of literally denuding her, which comes to allegorize the Western masculinist power of possession, that she, as a metaphor for her land, becomes available for Western penetration and knowledge."[2]

Somewhat related in strategy are the mimetic and abstract qualities of the Islamic calligraphy that Neshat appropriates to ornament images of her body, in the process transforming this centuries-old activity into an intermediary site. On one

level, such juxtapositions have a sensory appeal to the viewer; on the other, they turn the object into a re-presentation of another kind of social reality. It is for this reason that ornamentation has been favored and exploited by the historically marginalized world of women, and other deprived patrons, makers, and users of art.[3]

By forging such contested sites, Neshat also questions the gendered space within the current patriarchal culture of her native Iran. In *Anchorage*, a single-monitor, life-size video projection, the viewer encounters light-skin colored images of (the artist's) body parts (hands, feet, and face) floating in an otherwise blackened space; the sound is that of Neshat chanting a poem at an accelerated pace corresponding to the fast beats of a heart, which keeps the comprehensibility of her words at bay. Halfway through this four-minute piece, her figure appears in full, pulls out a gun, aims it at the viewer, and fires. The story ends with the same figure whirling, slowly, as in the beginning of a Sufi meditative dance, to suggest a form of renewal or hope, no matter how Utopian or temporary.

Neshat's 1997 video installation *The Shadow Under the Web,* shot in Istanbul, lacks the optimism of *Anchorage*. All four monitors, placed above eye level on separate walls of the gallery, repeat the same narrative at slightly different intervals. Each depicts the artist, dressed in traditional Islamic attire, running continuously in and out of different public spaces within the labyrinthine city (once known as Constantinople) that has come to designate the crossroads of East and West. While running aimlessly through mazelike souks, quiet old neighborhoods, and ancient city gates, the artist also maps for us the various cultures (Greek, Christian, and Ottoman) that have left their marks on this modern metropolis, where fundamentalism has been on the rise in the past few years. The lack of a clear destination, combined with the monotonous pace of running and the constant sound of uncomfortable breathing, project a feeling of endlessness which makes Neshat's search (and ours) for a place to belong or rest, even if momentarily, a disorienting and, ultimately, an impossible experience.

What is not explicit in Neshat's re-imaging or re-imagining of the predicament of displacement is that the symbolic disembodiment or marginalization of the Muslim woman (and, by extension, of underprivileged men and other minorities throughout the Middle East) has its parallels in the broader experience of deterritorialization and reterritorialization of what used to be called Persia—which in turn shares a long and deeply rooted colonial history as part of a region once known as the Ancient Near East or the "Orient."

Like "Orientalism," the "Orient" is a term that we no longer use but, as Mahmut Mutman elaborates, its implications are dispersed and continuous: "Orientalism is hegemonic not simply because it is a dominant idea to which people consent, but because it is a *signifying force* that is multiplied and reproduced in different texts and contexts to such a degree that it is not even recognizable as a separate entity. . . . The Orient occurs on multiple levels (academic, political, epistemological, literary, cultural, moral) . . ."[4]—and sexual, I might add.

The "unveiling" of the fragmentation experienced by modern Islamic societies in general and Iranian culture in particular as a consequence of Orientalism is best invoked in Neshat's present video installation, *Turbulent*. As its dramatic title suggests, *Turbulent* is about the existential tension of two singers, a man and a woman, who have a common passion for music. But their different yet related creative potentials are confined to the hierarchized and separated gender roles in contemporary Iran. The installation, which consists of two monitors projected simultaneously on opposite walls, also positions the viewer in a place of in-betweenness, in order to re-create the diasporic space of the artist and her equally displaced Iranian collaborators: actor Shoja Azari; vocalist/composer Sussan Deyhim; and director of photography Ghasem Ibrahimian.

Beginning with its credit lines, *Turbulent* confronts us with a duality—a splitting of the self, or a sense of being from two worlds at once, much like the artist herself, who is both from the "East" and of the "West."

This becomes apparent when the monitor on the right introduces the title and the author of the piece in Latin and English, while the monitor on the left, with Arabic and Persian script, concentrates on an image of a veiled woman standing with her back to us, patiently waiting on a stage, facing an empty auditorium.

The motionless camera of the second monitor portrays a man who appears on the stage of the same auditorium. After bowing to an all-male audience, dressed (like him) in black pants and white shirt, he turns to us, facing a (phallic-looking) microphone, and begins to sing, in the most compassionate voice imaginable, a traditional Persian song. The song is a thirteenth-century Sufi poem by Jalal ed-Din Rumi about divine love, dubbed in the voice of the popular Kurdish-Iranian classical singer Shahram Nazeri. An unfamiliar ear could easily mistake it, however, for a passionate worldly love song. This element of unfamiliarity also invites a more fluid relation between sacred and profane love just as we become conscious of the vulnerability of the text to mistranslation.

As the man's performance ends to a welcoming applause and he resumes a static position on stage, our attention shifts, as does his, to the captivating voice of the woman performer reaching out through the other, thus far muted, monitor. Although her song has no lyrics, or because of it, there is not much room for mistranslation here. On the contrary, what we experience is the communicative power or the universal dimension of music—music as a language capable of traveling across time and place. Also, since literary activities, particularly those related to religious texts, have traditionally been relegated to men in most Middle Eastern cultures,

Deyhim's transcendence of the written word gives her transgressive performance a double meaning.

Through the symbolic gesture of her wordless song, Deyhim first reclaims a space without resorting to the violent strategies that have rendered her invisible to begin with. Second, the wailing and throbbing utterances Deyhim unleashes hit us on a primal level that evokes the transformative powers of a shamanic ritual—an equally marginalized practice. This effect, in turn, makes us hypersensitive to the tone of the entire performance, its mournful lament for an unrecoverable loss.

Is Deyhim mourning the loss of ancient Persia or modern Iran? The answer is neither, yet both. Her trancelike voice, aided by baroque facial expressions and body language, locates the origins of her performance here (West/Occident), there (East/Orient), and elsewhere. In doing so, she creates a not-yet-named third space, where a new understanding of relations between constructs such as homeland/guestland and foreigner/native become possible.

The sound movements within Deyhim's pre- and postmodern composition are at times abrupt and at other moments elongated—accentuated by the erratic and erotic camera movements of Ibrahimian, which follow her in-and-out breathing patterns. The aural and visual effect is to bring us up close and distance us, an alternation that alludes to the schism between the local and the global. Eurocentrism has long perceived the "local" *as* traditional/provincial, hence backward, and in need of help or intervention. The "global," by contrast, connotes contemporary/cosmopolitan, thus progressive and more desirable. By being both local and global at the same time, *Turbulent* dispels such simplistic oppositional categories.

The kind of misconceptions inherent to the perception of "local" and "global," which complicates the act of cultural translation, prevails in other realms as well. For instance, the West perceives "silence" as death, while the East sees it as a sign of strength; minimalism in the West is relegated to formal considerations and a rational activity, while in the East it is associated with the practice of spirituality or mysticism. Somewhat related is the West's undifferentiated space between sensuality and sexuality. In the East, it is more nuanced, to the point where repression, deferral, and even suffering are considered necessary steps, in the attainment of such higher states of consciousness as divine knowledge or ecstasy. In this context, *Turbulent* also blurs the boundary between private and public space, challenging the division between subjective and collective experience.

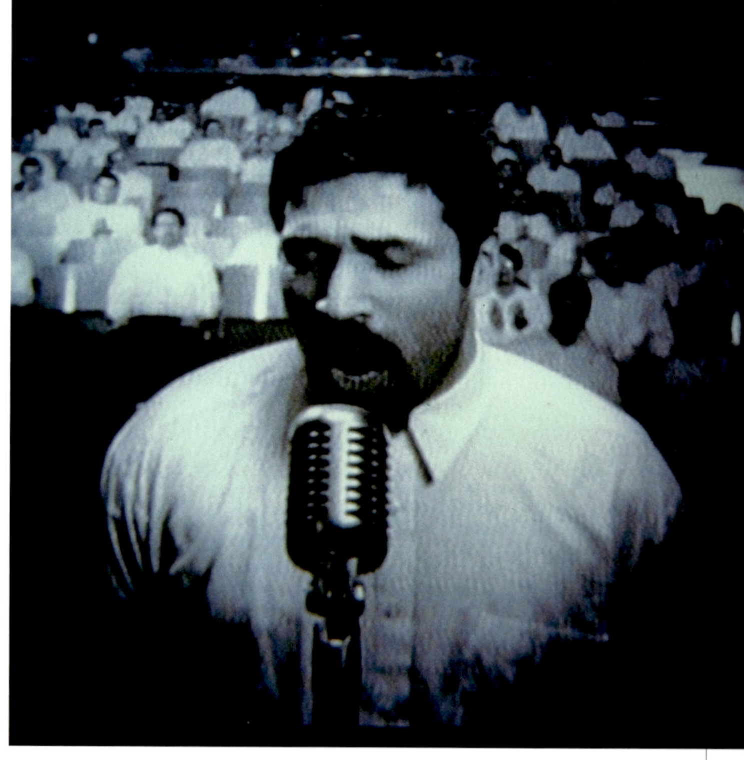

In other words, it is as if the turbulent social space which Neshat essential-
izes so powerfully on a subjective level also reveals the equally displaced religio-po-
litical space of her native country. For in Iran, the marriage between a nation-state
and its religious order begs to be viewed as a response to the country's discontinuous history and its colonial past, or Western imperialism. Neshat, like many other
diasporan artists and intellectuals from the Middle East who live in the West (including this writer), is cognizant of the reality, to paraphrase film scholar and cultural critic Hamid Naficy, that a return to an originary house/home/homeland is structurally impossible.[5] Through *Turbulent*, the artist makes us confront the dilemma
of preserving the glories of a past by repetition—the male singer who desperately
rehearses a medieval poem—or by re-inventing that past—the female performer
who mesmerizes us with her wordless song.

Conceptually, *Turbulent* also recalls Homi Bhabha's observations on locat-
ing culture: "The borderline work of culture demands an encounter with 'newness'
that is not part of the continuum of past and present. It creates a sense of the new
as an insurgent act of cultural translation. Such art does not merely recall the past
as social cause or aesthetic precedent; it renews the past, refiguring it as a contingent 'in-between' space, that innovates and interrupts the performance of the present. The 'past-present' becomes part of the necessity, not the nostalgia, of living."[6]

Turbulent also speaks of tensions related to internal displacement particular to a specific place; it represents the ambivalent taste of a cosmopolitan travel
culture and its corresponding "global aesthetics." *Turbulent* was inspired by the artist's recent visit to Istanbul, where she encountered a young blind girl, one of many
migrant workers from the provinces, trying to earn a living by singing on a street
corner to the music of an off-tune electrical keyboard played by an older man. Although the lyrics were untranslatable, the girl's penetrating voice as she performed
with closed eyes, without a formal stage or audience, reminded Neshat of the predicament and isolation of female singers in contemporary Iran. According to Shi'ite
Muslim laws, women are not allowed to sing in public places, even though they participate in other spheres, such as the military, politics, education, and filmmaking.
Prior to the enforcement of these laws under the Khomeini regime, women singers
in Iran represented a rich tradition, going back about 150 years to the decline of the
Ottoman Empire. This tradition, ironically, ran parallel with the European colonial
presence in the region. Like much of the "Orient," Iran has been subjected to the
mixed blessings—the tensions and contradictory relations—that arose from the
West's seductive project of modernizing the region.

After World War II, with America's new role as superpower, combined with
the climate of cold war politics, pro-West policies intervened with the destiny of
countries like Iran, Iraq, and Lebanon. This in turn alienated, and hence fueled, the

nationalist and fundamentalist tendencies within the region which, once again, was renamed the "Middle East." Here political unrest, civil wars, social instability, imbalance of power, and economic deprivation prevail to this day.

But, as Robert Kaplan points out in a probing article, "There Is No 'Middle East,'" "If we knew a little more about Jalal ed-Din Rumi, the 13th-century Turkic founder of the tariqat that was associated with the whirling dervishes, Islam might not seem incompatible with democracy, and Islamic fundamentalism might not seem so monolithic and threatening. Rumi dismissed 'immature fanatics' who scorn music and poetry. He cautioned that a beard or a mustache on a cleric is no sign of wisdom. Rumi favored the individual over the crowd and consistently spoke against tyranny. Rumi's legacy is more applicable to democratizing tendencies in the Muslim world than are figures of the Arab and Iranian religious pantheons with whom the West is more familiar."[7]

Neshat, similarly, problematizes the artificially constructed boundaries between the two seemingly opposing cultures of "Occident" and "Orient," perhaps to remind us that globalization is not confined to conventional, territorial geographies and that the present mapping of the world is far, far more complex than ever before.

It wasn't too long ago that avant-garde thinkers were debating how "internationalism" as an ideology failed because it assumed that progress reaches everywhere at the same time. "Globalization," a bit more refined and better disguised in its construct, represents the other side of the same coin, only this time in a multicentered world of emerging markets that are competing with one another, as if repeating and multiplying the model provided by the Soviet Union and the United States during the cold war era.

While no one can predict where, when, and how this renewed economic reshuffling of the world is going to settle, Shirin Neshat, like other emerging transnational artists, intellectuals, and cultural producers, helps us "see" the imbalances created within the cracks of contemporary society by unequal power relations and uneven development. In doing so, the artist also facilitates the imagining of new paradigms with which we might better understand the mixed blessings of globalization.

—NEERY MELKONIAN

Ned Rothenberg,
Jerome Harris, and
Samir Chatterjee

Sussan Deyhim

1. Ralph Abraham, Terence McKenna, Rupert Sheldrake, *Trialogues at the Edge of the West: Chaos, Creativity, and the Resacralization of the World* (Santa Fe, New Mexico: Bear and Company, 1992), pp. 44–47.

2. Ella Habiba Shohat, "Gender and the Culture of Empire: Toward a Feminist Ethnography of the Cinema," in Hamid Naficy and Teshome H. Gabriel, eds., *Otherness and the Media: The Ethnography of the Imagined and the Imaged* (Chur, Switzerland, and Langhorne, Pennsylvania: Harwood Academic Publishers, 1993), pp. 57–59.

3. Oleg Grabar, *The Mediation of Ornament* (Princeton: Princeton University Press, 1992), pp. 234–35.

4. Mahmut Mutman, "Pictures from Afar: Shooting the Middle East," in Mahmut Mutman and Meyda Yegenoglu, eds., *Inscriptions 6: Orientalism and Cultural Differences* (Santa Cruz: Center for Cultural Studies, University of California, 1992), pp. 3–4.

5. Hamid Naficy, "The Poetics and Practice of Iranian Nostalgia in Exile," *Diaspora*, 1 (Winter 1991), p. 285.

6. Homi K. Bhabha, *The Location of Culture* (London and New York: Routledge, 1994), p. 7.

7. Robert D. Kaplan, "There Is No 'Middle East,'" *The New York Times Magazine*, February 20, 1994, p. 43.

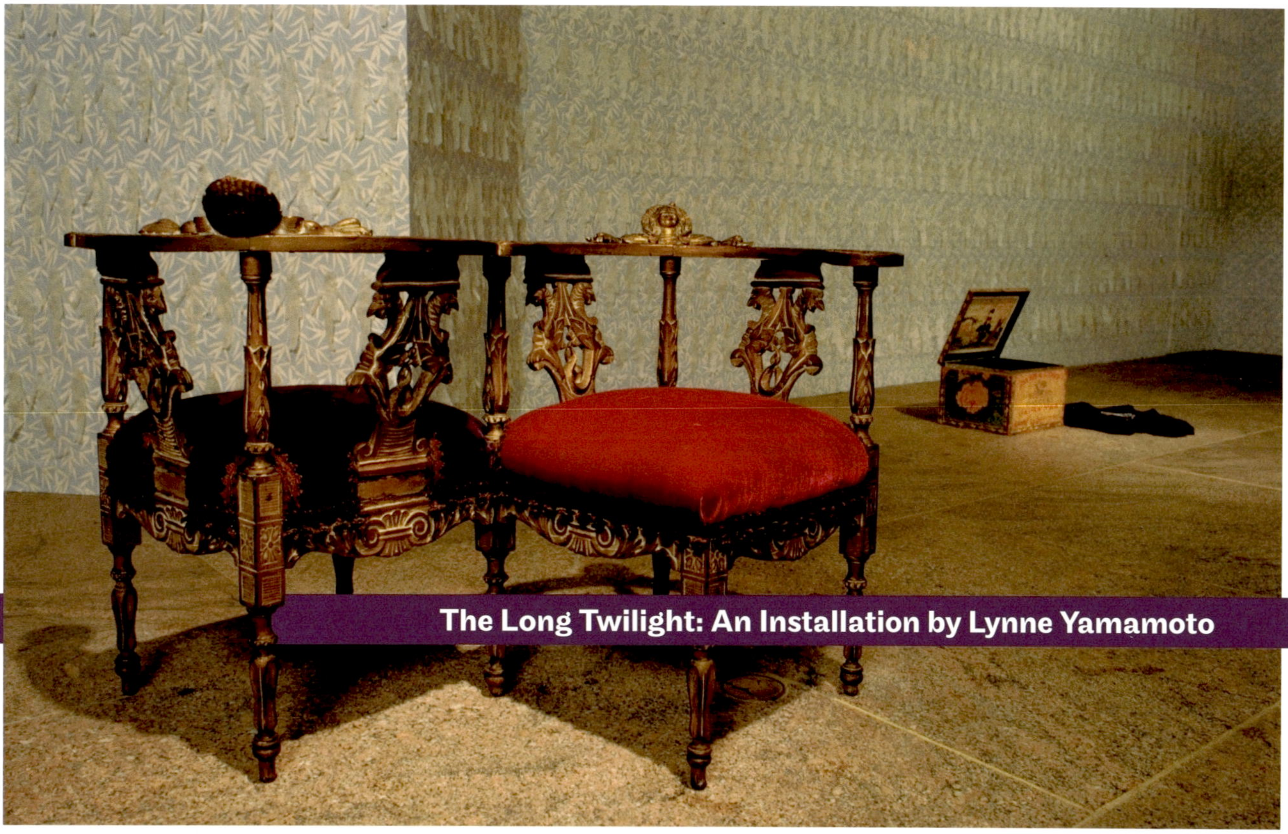

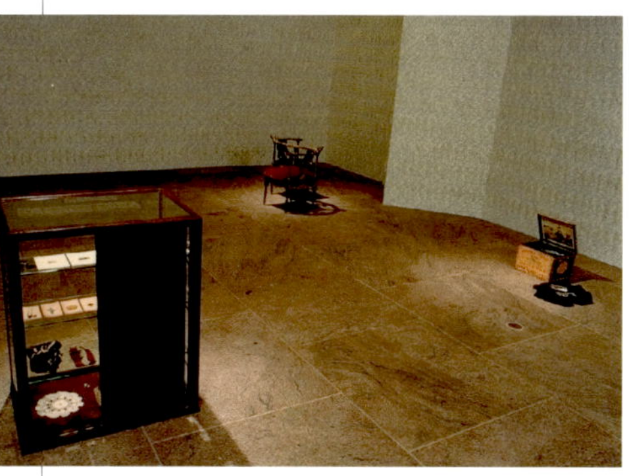

The Long Twilight: An Installation by Lynne Yamamoto

Installation views of *The Long Twilight: An Installation by Lynne Yamamoto.*

January 29 to April 23, 1999

The installation has many things in it, however, that are indisputably facts— that might also be understood as clues to a mystery. I give here an inventory of those facts, laced with interrogatives about what they signify.

The room is papered with a pale blue, willow-patterned wallpaper that evokes a late Victorian *japonisme*. It is hung round with thousands of translucent silk-tissue paper dolls, chains of vaguely twinned little girl shapes (traced and cut from one figure in an old school photograph), delicately moth-eaten with tiny burn holes that further complicate the veiling, shadow-casting overlay of repeated silhouettes on an already busy patterned ground. The silk is evocative material, and its screening effect is resonant too. But of what? The meeting of Anglo and Japanese cultures? The layering of several pasts and presents? The intricacy of relationships that are at once formal and effective, material and immaterial? And the burn holes? They are evocative, too, but it is difficult to say of what, other than indexicality— in other words, the effect of a cause, the trace of an event, the physical marks left by the inscrutable passage of time (between the 1930s of the text, when Ayame's "story ends mysteriously," and the now of this room in New York, fashioned by Lynne?).

—CAROL ARMSTRONG

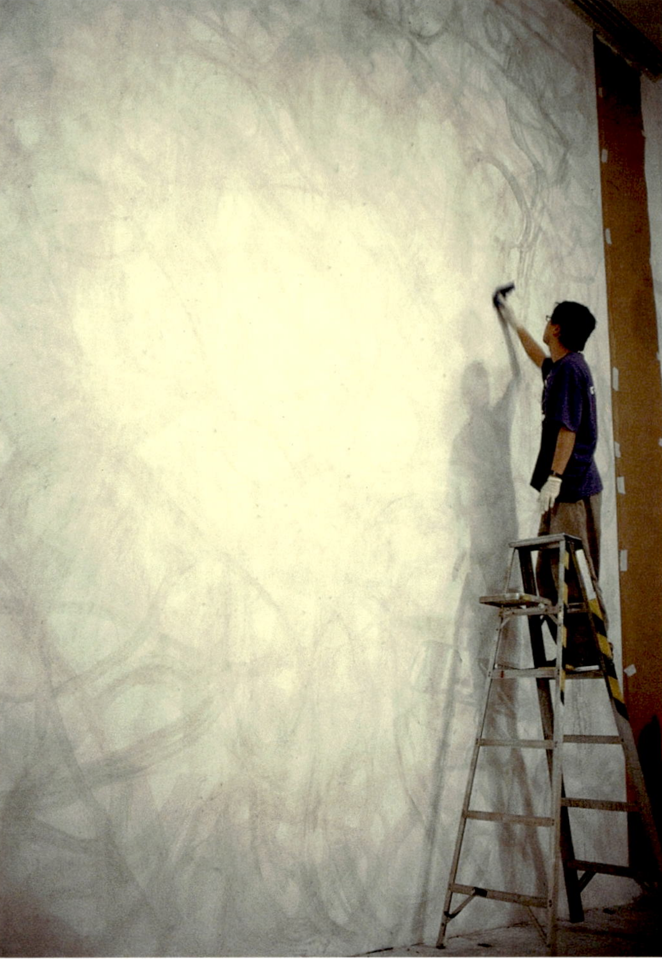

May 7 to July 16, 1999

A Conversation in the Periphery

Two months before the opening of "Whitney Philip Morris," three friends of Byron Kim met to talk about his work. At the time this conversation took place, Kim was deciding what he wanted to do with his exhibition. To varying degrees, each of the three participants—an artist, a poet, and an arts administrator—was familiar with the process Kim was going through to arrive at a

Wall Drawings by Byron Kim

solution, but they knew only that he was thinking of dirtying the gallery's walls with dirt and grime of New York City. Kim provided the group with several quotations (mostly from other artists' writings) and some of his own journal entries, which were central to his decisions regarding the show. Kim was not present, but the resulting conversation became an integral part of the process he used to create this exhibition.

1: Do you think we're here because Byron doesn't want to take responsibility for what is said about what he's doing?

2: I think he wants to be contrarian, and the risk is exciting for him.

3: I DON'T SEE IT THAT WAY AT ALL. HE SEEMS TO BE EXTREMELY NERVOUS ABOUT IT.

1: Don't you think that this is part of his personality? I've listened to him explain this project twice, and both times he kept dancing around what he was going to do. The second time I wanted to kill him. The person he was talking to was trying to get at what he was trying to say, and Byron just would not give it to him. Creatively, things are always happening in the periphery, and artists do this funny dance to get at what they're trying to do, but we never go straight for it. There's something about the way Byron presents himself that fits in with that. That's the way this conversation is set up—we don't really know what he's going to do, but we're trying to talk about it. It's a little bit about him and also about our relationship to him.

2: So in a way he really is in control, because he's getting us to do this.

He came to California for a week and the weather was bad. A friend drove him to the airport and apologized for the gray and gloomy weather. "That's all right," he said. "Gray is my favorite color." Johns always describes himself with a peculiar flat accuracy. He insists he is a poor colorist, with little ability to discriminate between colors he sees. He says he is worse at this than the average person. One is tempted to take him at his word. Then he reports this anecdote: "I was working on a colored numbers painting. When I worked on it for longer than a minute, the entire painting would turn gray to me. I couldn't see any of the colors, and I would have to stop."

—MICHAEL CRICHTON, FROM JASPER JOHNS, 1977

1: Byron's work does that to you, too. He gives you a lot of space, which is really generous, but also really intimidating. And that's how I imagine this installation might be. There will be a very gentle gesture that you can expound on, but the rest is sort of left up to you.

2: A lot of people get annoyed with Byron's work. Sometimes explanation is needed or would be helpful, and this show will be the opposite. Byron is questioning all the time, and he's making the viewer question him—and he doubts himself, and he questions himself, and so the people looking at his work start to see a gigantic ball of questions.

1: The question is whether he's duping them or being generous. When he spoke to my friend and me about the work, he would get us really excited, and then he wouldn't say anything. He would work us all up, and then not deliver the punch line. I guess that's the charm—he's creating a space in which the viewer can exist. Maybe he leaves too much space. It's like the power of the work is being restrained. The mystery of Byron's work, the beauty, is very subtle—it takes time. The viewer who doesn't take the time is going to miss it. It's just going to seem lame.

3: WHY WOULD IT SEEM LAME?

1: Because I think Byron's work is quiet, I think it's slow. I think it's sensitive. I also think it's incredibly subtle. All of that takes a certain sensitivity in the viewer.

2: Byron did the Roche's Point *drawings from Ireland (1998), and they were understated as can be and absolutely beautiful. I resisted, but others said over and over again that they were so refreshing—that they felt renewed by looking at them. The* Roche's Point *drawings looked like Kenneth Noland stripes in the mat, but when you lifted the mats, they were incredibly organic. You could feel the horizon line. Spiritual things are not explainable, you can't articulate them. Of course, it's a dream of some artists to speak the unspeakable, to be able to touch that part in all of us that is a spiritual part. That's the great power of art, that none of us can actually say how you do that or how you touch someone that way. But it is a drive, and you do try to make the spirit world. Those corny movies that try to make a picture of God—they can't do it. When they get to the parts about heaven, you know they're wondering, "How are we going to paint heaven?" They really can't. Maybe Michelangelo did it in the Sistine Chapel's "touch," but you can't do that again. So it is a great opportunity in contemporary art to create that kind of space or to evoke a feeling that transcends, and I think Byron's work goes that way. His daffodil mural (*I Wandered Lonely as a Cloud, *1997) is broad, it's big, and at the same time it's small, like poetry. He wants to do both things, be humble, but big, and to do both is very hard. It's a good thing to spend your lifetime trying to achieve that fine line. It's about me, but then there's the us. How do you bridge that?*

1: It's part of that whole ego thing that Byron is trying to battle with. He gave us that quotation where Andy Warhol talks about the gray in Joseph Beuys' work, and Warhol says that gray is spiritual. That's such a flaky painter's comment. Gray is gray. It's what you do with gray that makes it one thing or another. I was trying to think about what gray is. In Byron's journal entries where he talks about this project, he talks about emptiness. I gave him this quotation from a Buddhist thinker: "See emptiness, have compassion." I have no idea what it means, but I think it means something very important. If you could bring yourself to that, something might really unfold for you. Ultimately, emptiness is about interconnection and impermanence. That's the lack of tangibility in Byron's work. But when you acknowledge this impermanence, you also realize that it connects us all.

2: There is a level of anonymity in people's lives in this city. Especially with 42nd Street. Even though people are always striving for excellence here, they're still so anonymous. Maybe they're not anonymous for a minute, but then they are again. That brings me to the dirt. We don't really know what is going to happen when Byron makes this piece, but he talks about dirt and about New York.

1: What totally grossed me out when I came to New York was that there is this layer, this surface, over everything. When you clean your apartment, it has a kind of oily texture to it. I started thinking about surface; I was thinking about painting. And then Byron was telling me about all of these ideas, of splashing and dripping. We'll see what he does—at first I thought that he might cover the surface of the gallery black, but since then I've pictured it as a monochrome gray.

2: Really? I pictured it with a lot of texture. I thought, oh, the surface is going to modulate. Byron has this great ability to go back and talk to modernist painting, talk to a Rothko. Somehow, his work always makes me think of someone who is trying to stand behind himself. My favorite piece of his is the Clyfford Still piece he did at the Neuberger Museum (Even Stone Is Not Permanent, 1995). It was gigantic, two 30-foot-long walls, but it still stood behind itself. Wow! It was so passive, but also aggressive, and it was absolutely beautiful. Byron thinks too much, and those wall pieces don't let him do that. Inevitably, he gets into the painterly, the push and pull of the paint.

1: Which is really different than the dirty mark on the wall that is there by chance, or the way dirt collects in cracks.

2: Yes, but you could use those to make something else.

1: Byron keeps saying "I tried this, but it was too beautiful. And then I tried this." This whole notion about the Whitney project working and not working, this whole "no-idea" thing. For a while, Byron was interested in the fact that he couldn't get an idea, and that he wouldn't force himself to come up with one until the last second. Or, how he might not have his name on the piece, let it be hardly anything.

3: YOU'RE TALKING ABOUT BYRON'S WORK AS IF HE KNOWS JUST WHAT HE'S DOING. YOU TALK ABOUT THE "NO-IDEA" IDEA AS IF IT'S JUST ANOTHER ONE OF HIS CONCEPTS. BUT LISTENING TO BYRON TALK ABOUT THIS PROJECT AND ABOUT DOING THIS CONVERSATION, I THINK THAT ON A FUNDAMENTAL LEVEL HE DOESN'T KNOW WHAT HE'S DOING.

2: What do you mean he doesn't know what he's doing?

3: WELL, HE MENTIONED IN ONE OF HIS JOURNAL ENTRIES THAT HE CONSIDERED QUITTING THE PROJECT.

1: The creative process is all about doubt and not knowing what you're doing. The minute you stop doubting, you become a really bad artist. We use the phrase Conceptual artist and assume that there is a fully formed idea that gets translated into an object—but that makes the worst art. Because then why make the object at all? Our language is visual, so the meaning has to come out of the making.

In that talk with Lisa [Sigal], Byron was bringing back all of these rejected ideas: somewhere in the unconscious you have the idea, it's already there, you just haven't put it into form yet. In his journal, it's as though the minute an idea becomes viable, he throws it out and starts again from scratch. That's probably a way for him to push himself; it's not about just trying to make a good piece. But the struggle shouldn't make you think that he doesn't know what he's doing.

2: He also gave us that Gerhard Richter quotation that says gray "is suited like no other color to illustrate 'nothing.'" Wanting to illustrate nothing is very contrarian. It's perfect for Byron.

3: THE IDEA OF ILLUSTRATING NOTHING IS ONE THING, BUT TO SAY THAT GRAY IS SUITED LIKE NO OTHER COLOR TO ILLUSTRATE NOTHING—THAT'S A TOTALLY MEANINGLESS STATEMENT.

2: Oh no. Doesn't gray make you feel nothing? I think gray can mean nothing.

3: SURE IT CAN, BUT WHY MORE THAN ANY OTHER COLOR?

2: It can say nothingness. It's very hard to paint nothing with red. Red is something.

3: SO WE DON'T ACTUALLY NEED ART—WE COULD JUST HAVE A SYSTEM WHERE GRAY REPRESENTS NOTHING, RED REPRESENTS ANGER, GREEN REPRESENTS ENVY, WHITE REPRESENTS HOPEFULNESS, AND BLACK REPRESENTS DESPAIR.

1: Eugenie Tsai from the Whitney called Byron and asked him, "Is gray a color or a shade?" I don't know much about painting, but gray is the absence of color in a way that brown is all of the colors mixed, right? The problem you're having is that we're giving these metaphors to color. I'm with you in a certain way. I was having more problems with gray being spiritual than gray being nothing. But then I came all the way around to see it as being emptiness, which seems spiritual, in a sense. I think about language and the way we use "gray." It has a sad connotation, more than being neutral, like a gray day.

2: Right, but nothing's not neutral.

1: Byron's work is not abstraction, it's not monochrome gray. It may look like that when you go into the room, but he's thinking about the context of the walls and the street and the dirt. It may seem like just a gray surface, but in the end that's not what he's interested in at all. And this conversation will exist in the periphery of the work. It won't be necessarily about the work. An essay that says "this is what the piece means" or "Byron says this, so . . ."—that could really squash the work. Ideally, the viewer will have to make a creative leap between what we're saying right now and what they are seeing, and—we hope—the space between those two positions would be a very interesting place to be.

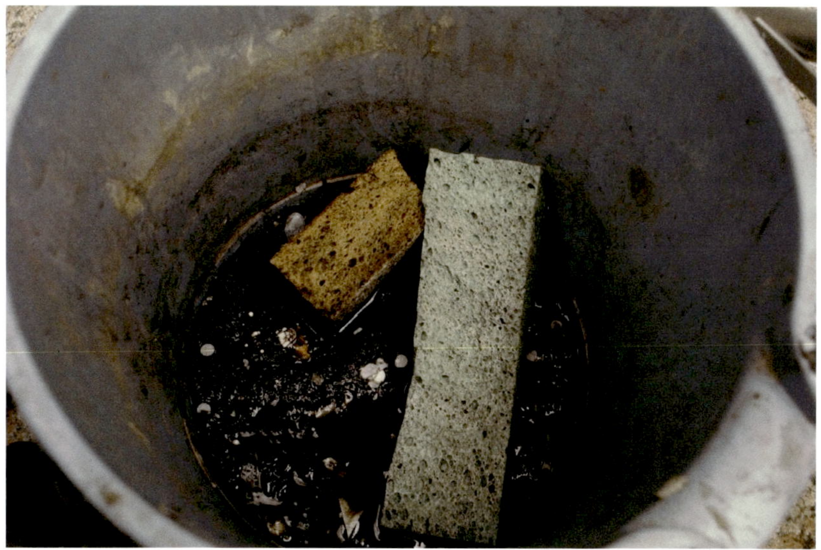

Byron Kim, artist's tools used in the installation.

Entries from Byron Kim's Journal, 1999

JANUARY 22—Eugenie Tsai [senior curator for the Permanent Collection, Whitney Museum of American Art] leaves a phone message to this effect: "Byron, we're trying to answer the question: Is gray a color or a shade? And we figure you're the expert." Since I'm really busy with the kids, I don't get a chance to reply for two days during which I brood about the gray question. It's a ridiculous question, but my response is that gray as a *word* connotes neutrality and is therefore, due to its necessary vagueness, less a color, but this very vagueness makes colors that are gray often difficult to name, which makes gray as *color* richer due to subtlety. I thought that this question might have some curatorial importance, but eventually found out that someone's seven-year-old got the question wrong at school and thought that the Whitney would be an authoritative source.

JANUARY 23—Ran into Lee Mingwei, who was surprised that I could agree to do a show without having an idea. This made me more determined to push it to the limit, giving me the notion to wait until Lynne [Yamamoto]'s show conies down to figure out what to do, a very scary thought. The attractiveness of it is that it can be done virtually only by a painter, yet no one does it.

    In the evening I went to an AC Project Room opening. A bunch of us go to a Chinese restaurant afterwards. Laura Hoptman [assistant curator, Drawings, The Museum of Modern Art] wonders why artists need so many little essays about their work. On the way back from this dinner, I'm thinking about the gray question and wonder what a show that is all gray would be about or would be like.

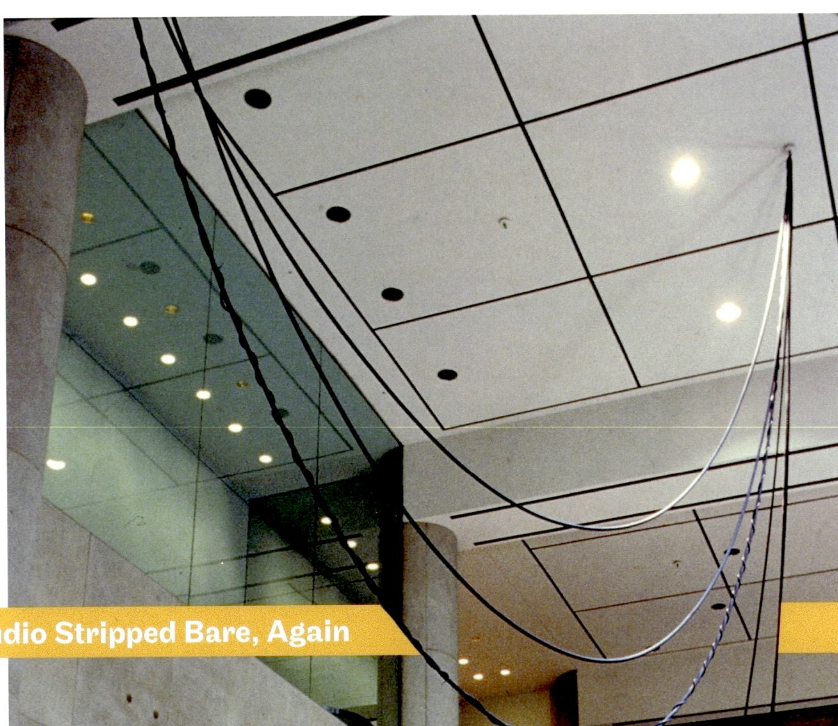

Installation views of *Jeanne Silverthorne: The Studio Stripped Bare, Again.*

Jeanne Silverthorne: The Studio Stripped Bare, Again

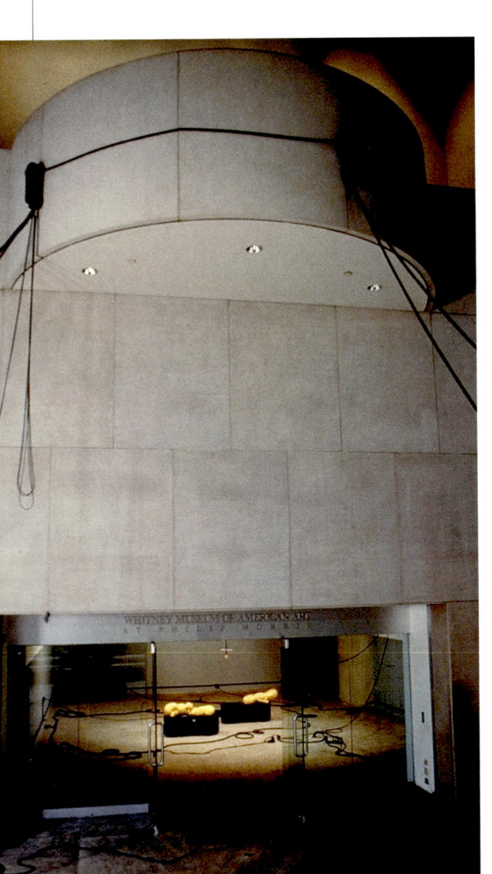

July 30 to October 15, 1999

For this exhibition, Silverthorne produced a large-scale installation that occupies both the Philip Morris Sculpture Court and the gallery. The installation begins with elaborate clusters of rubber wires and circuitry suspended from the Sculpture Court ceiling. These looping, gathered bunches create three-dimensional drawings in space and labyrinthine tangles that dead-end at every wrong turn into dangling, empty light sockets. In the "correct" route of this maze, wires pass through a complex assemblage of rubber electrical conduits and utility boxes, eventually converging into one central wire that leads into the gallery. Once inside, the main wire plugs into a tiny rubber "lamp" equipped with a magnifying glass, which rests on a narrow shelf along with three small, unassuming pieces of Styrofoam. This anti-climactic denouement sets up a ludicrous juxtaposition of scale: the enormous electrical apparatus not only culminates in a product that is outlandishly small, but also terminates in a hanging light bulb that does not function: like the exposed sockets, this fixture fails to illuminate.

—DEBRA SINGER, BRANCH CURATOR

Lee Boroson: Underpass

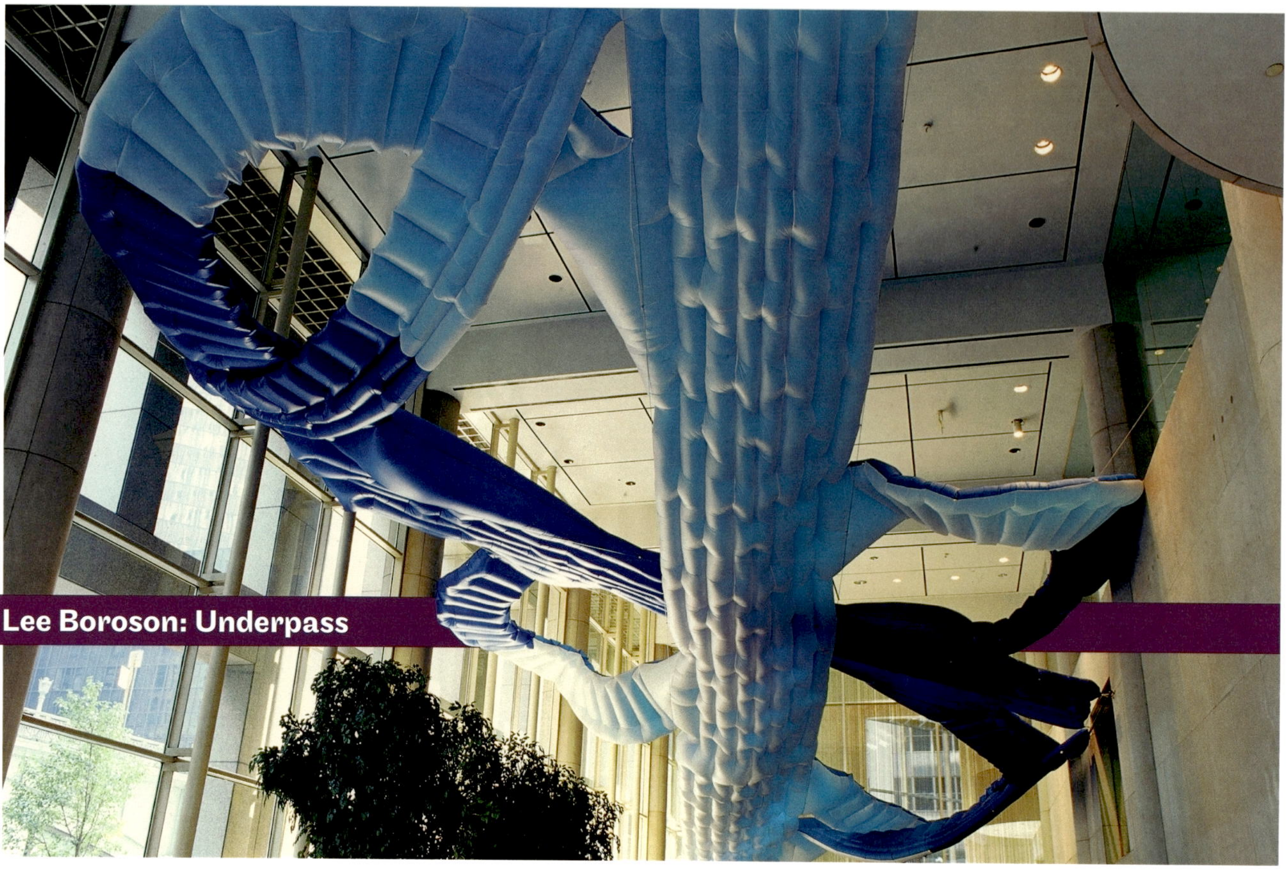

Installation view of *Lee Boroson: Underpass*.

October 29, 1999 to March 17, 2000

The piece, despite its immense size, appears surprisingly airy and light, as its overlapping horizontal planes of blue and white counter the towering vertically of the 42-foot-high surrounding walls. Created from a translucent, silky material generally used to make parachutes, the sculpture takes advantage of the large glass windows on all sides and diffuses light in dramatic ways. How, and to what extent, the piece refracts the artificial and natural light depends on the time of day and on shifts in the weather. By temporarily changing the configurations of the architecture and reflecting color and light, *Underpass* transforms the atmosphere of this unusual atrium-like setting and alters our physical perceptions of being in, and moving through, the Sculpture Court.

Gazing upward at *Underpass*, you might imagine that the outdoors has moved in and that you stand beneath a sky or a running river. The work's organic feel is enhanced by air currents, originating from a fan embedded in the building's crawlspace, which pulse through the piece, causing it to billow and sway, as if it were a living, breathing creature. As the title suggests, however, the sculpture's form relates to more than natural phenomena. The structure is also associated with highway design, specifically a cloverleaf traffic exchange pattern. In this type of road system (and in the sculpture itself), four individual circles loop around a central straight thrust, creating a linear scheme that resembles a four-leaf clover.

—DEBRA SINGER, BRANCH CURATOR

Elliott Sharp and
Orchestra Carbon

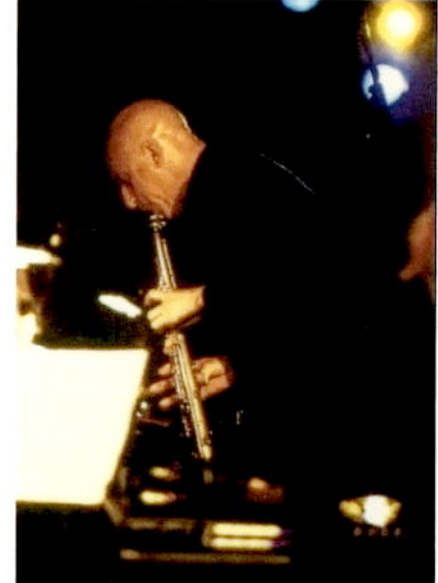

Elliott Sharp
and Orchestra Carbon,
Radiolaria, 12–09–99

Beauty, Desire, Seduction: The Art of Fred Tomaselli

Gravity's Rainbow (Large) (1999) offers intense visual pleasure. Brilliantly colored arcs of varying lengths swoop and crisscross gracefully against a black ground, creating arabesques that loop rhythmically across the five panels of the piece. The visual density and complexity of Fred Tomaselli's piece parallels the structure of Thomas Pynchon's 1973 novel *Gravity's Rainbow,* whose title Tomaselli adopted. The arcs in *Gravity's Rainbow (Large)* resemble festive garlands, or extraordinarily large strands of a beaded necklace. Closer inspection reveals that the arcs are composed of hundreds, sometimes thousands, of individual elements, painstakingly pieced together from unusual sources: pills; leaves from hemp and jimson weed plants; foxglove petals; photographic images of butterflies, flowers, birds, and insects; magazine cutouts of body parts such as lips, hands, eyes, and feet; and painted trompe-l'oeil objects. Each of these units is affixed to the panels and encased in layers of hard, glossy resin.

Gravity's Rainbow (Large) is essentially an elaborate collage, seamlessly blending real, photographically re-produced, and painted objects drawn from the disparate realms of nature and commerce. Its dazzling array of shapes and colors suggests the term "eye can-dy." The abundance of pharmaceutical capsules and tablets used to construct the arcs, however, gives the work an aura of toxicity. Though all the pills are encased in tamper-proof resin, we are reminded that Tomaselli's concept of beauty has a po-tentially dark, poisonous underside.

While *Gravity's Rainbow (Large)* employs materials and techniques Tomaselli has been using for nearly a decade, it is his largest and most ambitious work to date.

Fred Tomaselli: Gravity's Rainbow

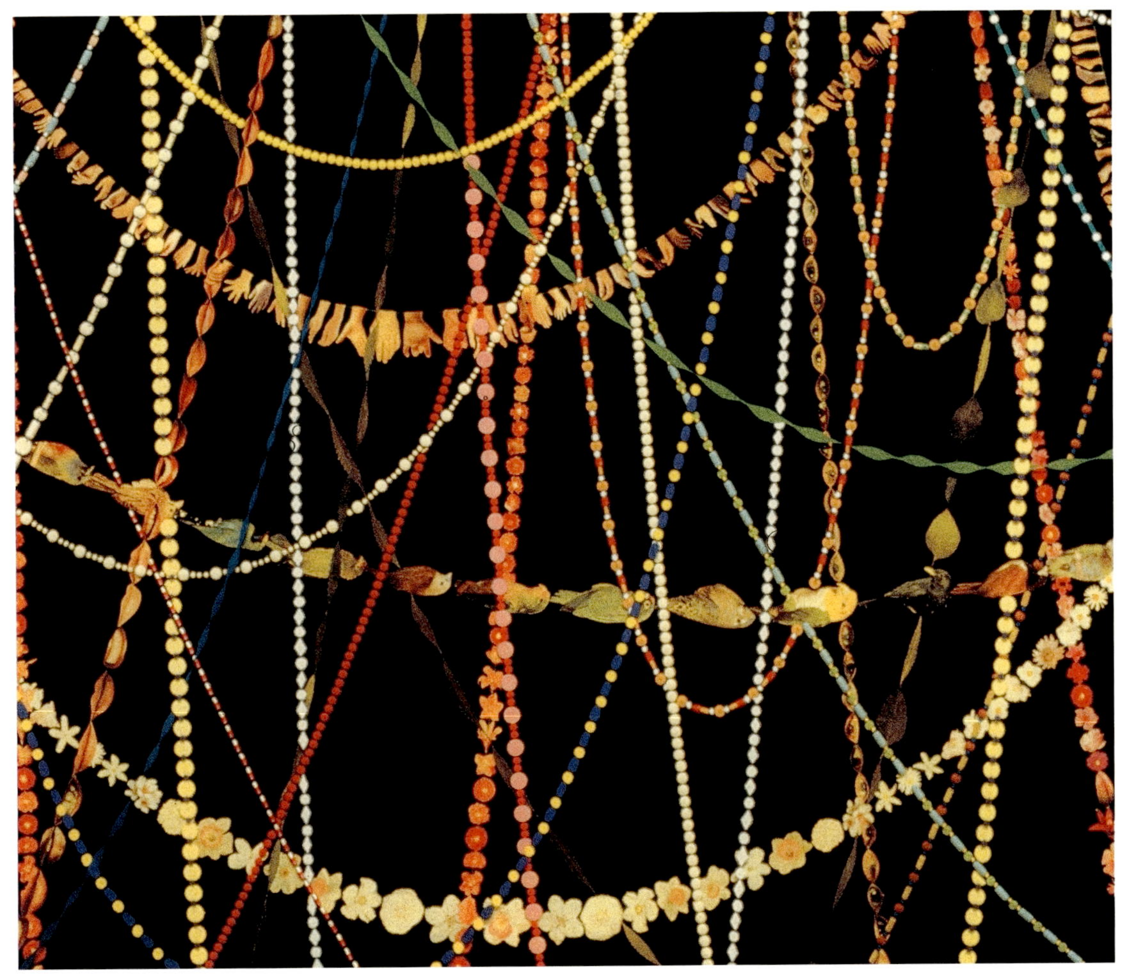

Fred Tomaselli, detail of *Gravity's Rainbow (Large)*, 1999. **THIS PAGE AND FOLLOWING:** Installation views of *Fred Tomaselli: Gravity's Rainbow,* 1999.

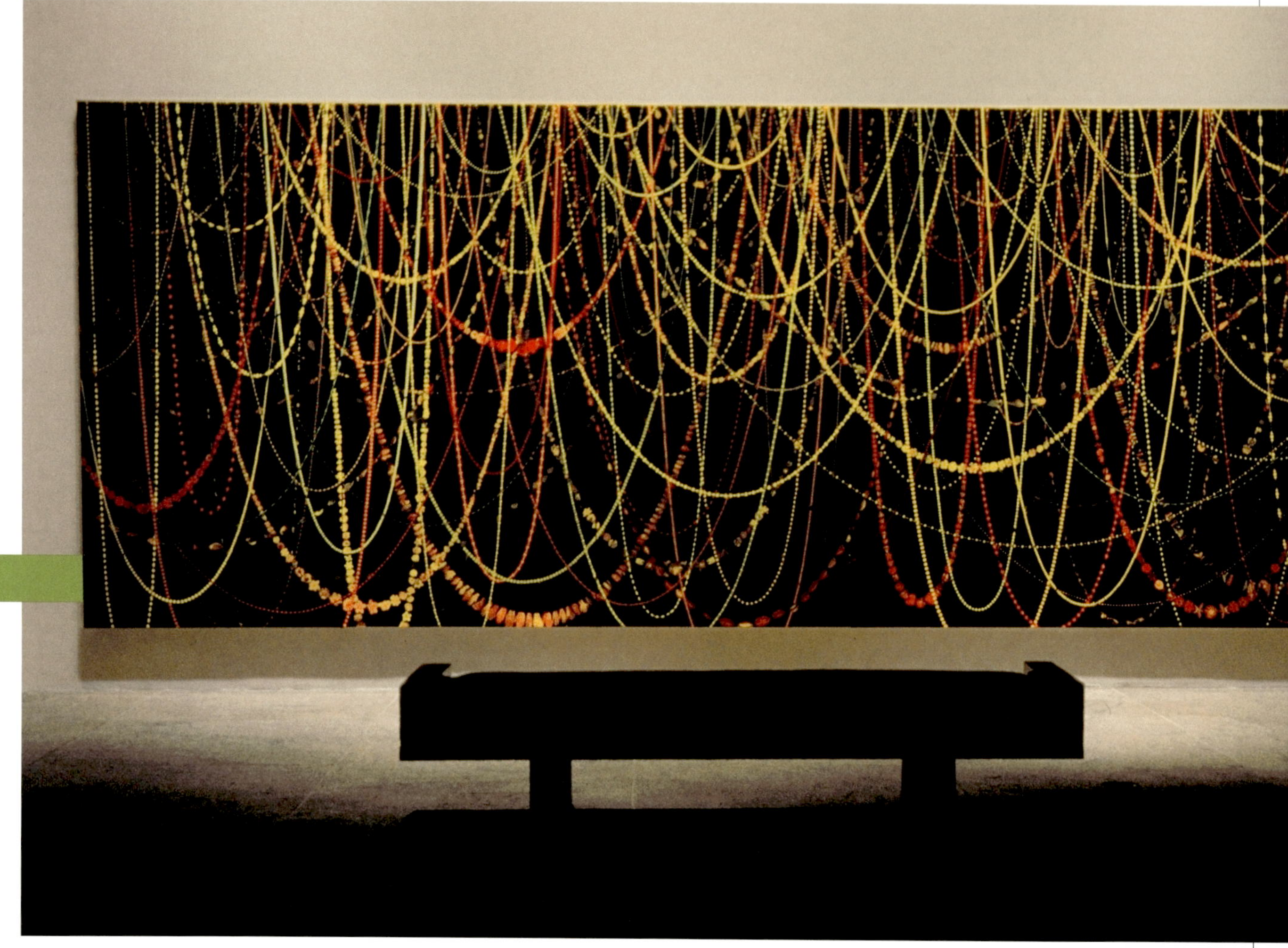

Six months in the making, its size is comparable to the largest of Abstract Expressionist canvases. Like a classic 1950s drip painting by Jackson Pollock, the scale of *Gravity's Rainbow (Large)* awes and overwhelms us. It is large enough to enter. If laid flat, as it was during construction, it becomes an arena in which action (of an obsessive sort) takes place.

In preparation for the piece, Tomaselli and his assistant spent over half a year assembling material for the collage elements: scouring field guides for flowers, insects, and birds; harvesting leaves from plants; and combing fashion magazines for the perfect eyes, feet, hands, and lips. These materials were then laid out on cardboard flats in drawers, meticulously organized by shape, color, and size, genus and species. On a worktable, the pills were sorted into piles, again by shape—round, oblong, and lozenge. Tomaselli regards the pills, archive of cutout images, and organic materials as his palette.

Installation view of *Fred Tomaselli: Gravity's Rainbow (Large)*, 1999.

Tomaselli began by hanging five 8 x 4-foot black-painted panels side-by-side on a wall, abutting one another to create a single expanse. He then pinned each end of an 18-foot pull chain to two different places along the top edge, producing catenaries, arcs that Tomaselli then traced with a white wax pencil. With the same chain, he repeated the process over and over, using different portions of the chain to generate a composition of densely overlapping arcs with a wide range of lengths and curvatures. The process of embellishing the traced arcs began when he laid the individual panels on the floor. The width of each panel was deliberately chosen to enable Tomaselli to reach the center. First he attached the leaves and cutouts, one at a time, over the outlines of the arcs, using gloss medium as an adhesive. Then, using the same technique, he attached the pills. The process of affixing each element is a laborious and repetitive task the artist claims to have enjoyed.

Next, he coated the pills, cutouts, and leaves with more gloss medium to seal them and protect them from discoloration. Over this medium, two coats of ultra-violet protection varnish were applied, and another layer of black paint was brushed around each component to cover the visible residue of the medium. Tomaselli then poured epoxy resin onto the surface of the panel and spread it with a squeegee. He used the heat from a blowtorch to pop visible air bubbles and to smooth the resin surface. After rehanging the panels, he added more arcs with the pull chain and covered them with strands of painted pills, rather than real ones, applied more resin and, using extremely fine steel wool, buffed the surface to a lustrous finish.

The size of *Gravity's Rainbow (Large)* suggests a space parallel to our own, one that we could enter if we pushed aside what seems to be a beaded curtain. The idea of a fictive space had emerged in Tomaselli's earlier installations. A painter by training, one who had experimented with everything from Photo-Realism to Neo-Expressionism, he abandoned two-dimensional art shortly after graduating from California State University at Fullerton in 1982. He wanted to make art that incorporated actual space, to create environments that could affect the viewer's perception. In *Shoreline* (1984), one of his first installations, rows of Styrofoam cups were lined up on the floor and subjected to a gentle breeze created by fans. The following year, Tomaselli moved to New York, where he continued to explore the possibilities of installation art. His first New York exhibition was in 1987 at P.S.1, where he made site-specific work that explored notions of artifice, energy, and nature.

Three years later, in a one-artist show at Artists Space, Tomaselli presented *Remedy* (1989), his first work using drugs as a medium. The piece was a stack of

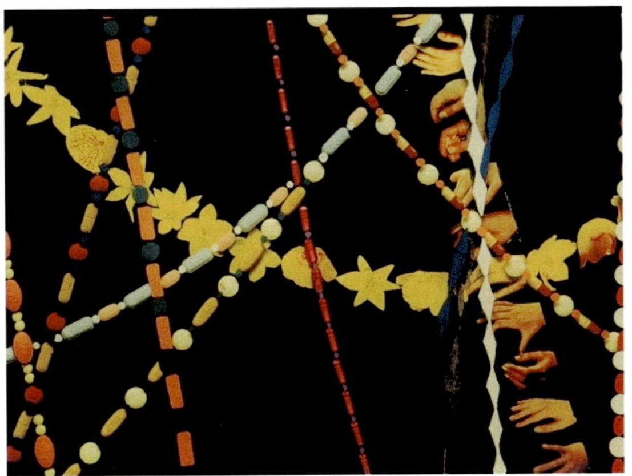

Fred Tomaselli, detail of
Gravity's Rainbow (Large), 1999.

730 aspirin tablets under plexiglass, the number representing the proverbial "two-a-day" for a year. Here we see a shift in Tomaselli's concerns from the body and the environment to a more physiological perspective of pain and its relief. Like *Shoreline*, *Remedy* marks the austere aesthetic of the earlier stages of Tomaselli's career. That same year, he made *Big as Me* (1990), inspired by the work of Bruce Nauman. Circular aspirin tablets alternated with cylindrical Tylenol capsules to create an upright shape resembling a spinal cord. Since then, Tomaselli's choice of drugs has expanded dramatically. Along with over-the-counter drugs such as antacids, caffeine, and acetaminophen, he has added a host of antidepressants, as well as antipsychotic and other psychoactive drugs.

This introduction of psychoactive drugs coincided with Tomaselli's return to two-dimensional work, as he became what he calls an "accidental painter." Abandoning installation art, he began producing pieces that were increasingly ornate. The three works in the Whitney Museum's Permanent Collection demonstrate the range of his output in the 1990s.

Ocotillo Nocturne (1993) could be seen as Tomaselli's answer to Van Gogh's *Starry Night* (1889). Intricately patterned constellations of colorful pills and hemp leaves emblazon an evening sky over a desert landscape. Painted in a smooth airbrushed style, the distinctive vegetation (after which the work is named) is based on snapshots Tomaselli took of one of his favorite places in California's Joshua Tree National Park. Although more abstract and somber in palette, *Split Stalk* (1996) is no less visionary. It is made from a hemp plant split carefully in half and splayed onto a black ground; ephedra stems, attached to look like branches, bear eyeballs, which the artist painted red, white, and blue, lending the piece a surreal aura. Like *Ocotillo Nocturne, Self-Portrait* (1995) plays on a star-filled evening sky, but uses only black and white. Each constellation in this photogram represents a drug the artist remembers taking. In his words, "It is a chemical-celestial portrait—a portrait of inner space and outer space."

As suggested by *Self-Portrait*, the use of drugs in Tomaselli's art has biographical associations. The artist acknowledges the importance of stoner culture when he was growing up in the 1970s in Southern California. He also maintains that a childhood spent in close proximity to Disneyland fostered a theme-park view of reality, one in which the boundaries between the authentic and the artificial were blurred. This cultural landscape also introduced Tomaselli to an awareness of surface treatments through the so-called "finish fetish" associated with cars and surfboards.

The culture of Southern California is only one force that has shaped Tomaselli's art and artistic sensibility. Art historical sources from disparate eras and cultures have also played a role. Among the varied sources of inspiration for *Gravity's Rainbow (Large),* Tomaselli cites Sol LeWitt, Ed Ruscha, Henry Darger, and Indian miniatures, as well as tangkas, ancient Tibetan paintings on cloth. He compares the way he composed the catenaries to LeWitt's use of system to create structure, and the expansive space to the Southern California aesthetic of Ruscha's wide horizontal skies. Also related is the psychological tension in Darger's unsettling depictions of little girls, and the visionary quality of Tibetan tangka paintings—Tomaselli notes the way love and death intermingle in the central grouping of figures, and he is fascinated by the necklace of skulls and severed heads. As an aside, he mentions that his introduction to Asian art came in the debased form of bad psychedelia on record album covers.

Tomaselli's incorporation of drugs has lent his work a certain notoriety, perhaps giving him a reputation for transgressive behavior. Yet to his mind, the attitudes fostered by the 1970s drug culture dovetail completely with a traditional view of painting as a vehicle through which to experience the sublime. Tomaselli sees the role of drugs and art as remarkably similar: both can transform and heal and are capable of altering our perception. Like drugs, art offers an escape from the pains of daily life as well as a means to heighten its beauties and joys. While Matisse regarded art as an appeasing force or mental soother, "a good armchair in which to rest from physical fatigue," Tomaselli's work transports the viewer to new heights of self-awareness, reaffirming the power of vision to change our lives. —EUGENIE TSAI, SENIOR CURATOR, PERMANENT COLLECTION, WHITNEY MUSEUM OF AMERICAN ART

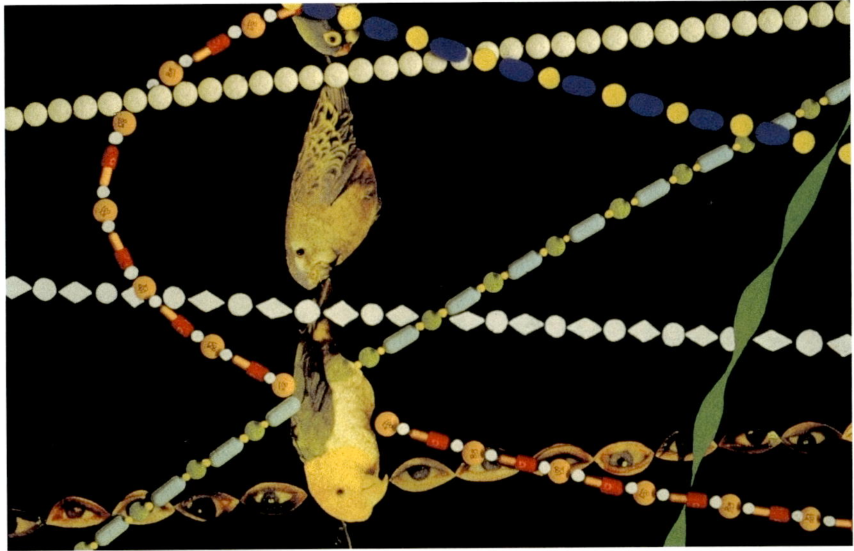

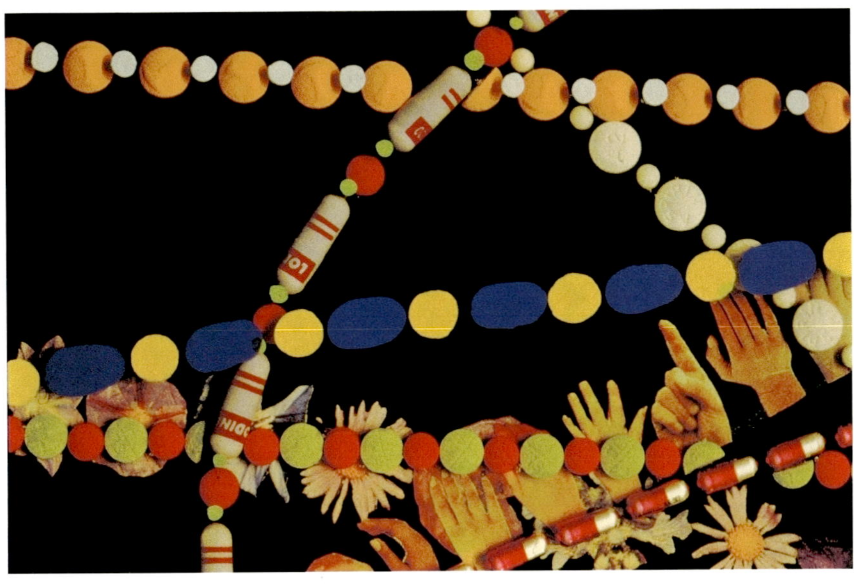

Fred Tomaselli, details of
Gravity's Rainbow (Large), 1999.

January 21 to April 7, 2000

It is a rare opportunity to consider the work of two artists not obviously connected by style, period, or affiliation. Yet the sculpture and works on paper of Isamu Noguchi (1904–1988) and Ellsworth Kelly (b. 1923) pair together effortlessly, each artist's work informing the other in a refreshing play of subtle curves and commanding volumes. Though Noguchi and Kelly, a generation apart, matured under very different circumstances, both forged an abstraction grounded in nature and in keen observation, both sought out the elemental core of simple objects and organic forms, and both believed in truth to materials. Each artist worked alternately in two and three dimensions,

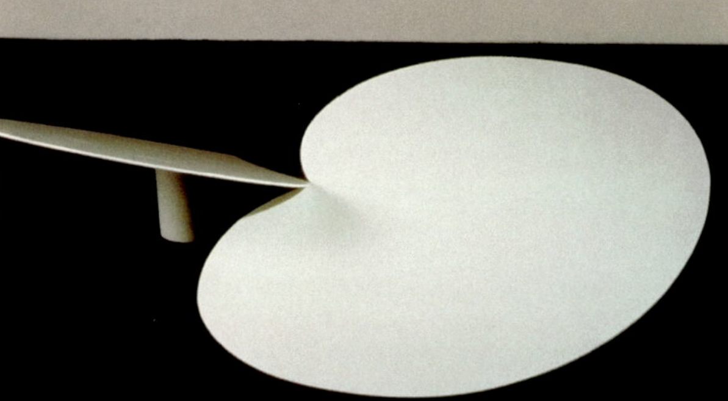

Correspondences:
Isamu Noguchi and Ellsworth Kelly

preferring detail over complete image and shunning figuration in favor of abstraction. . . .

The work of both Isamu Noguchi and Ellsworth Kelly cannot be defined within reigning styles of their times. Each found inspiration in ancient structures: Noguchi identified strongly with primitive forms, noting, "The more archaic and primitive, the better I like it"; Kelly looked toward Pre-Columbian art, finding the "anonymous stonework" and the "object quality of artifacts" more compelling than much of the art of his own time. It is not surprising, then, that the power of both these artists' work lies in its simplicity and clarity of form. Each in his own way evolved an abstraction that fuses modern and historical impulses and hovers in the narrow gap between the geometric and the organic. —BETH VENN, CURATOR, TOURING EXHIBITIONS, AND DIRECTOR, BRANCH MUSEUMS

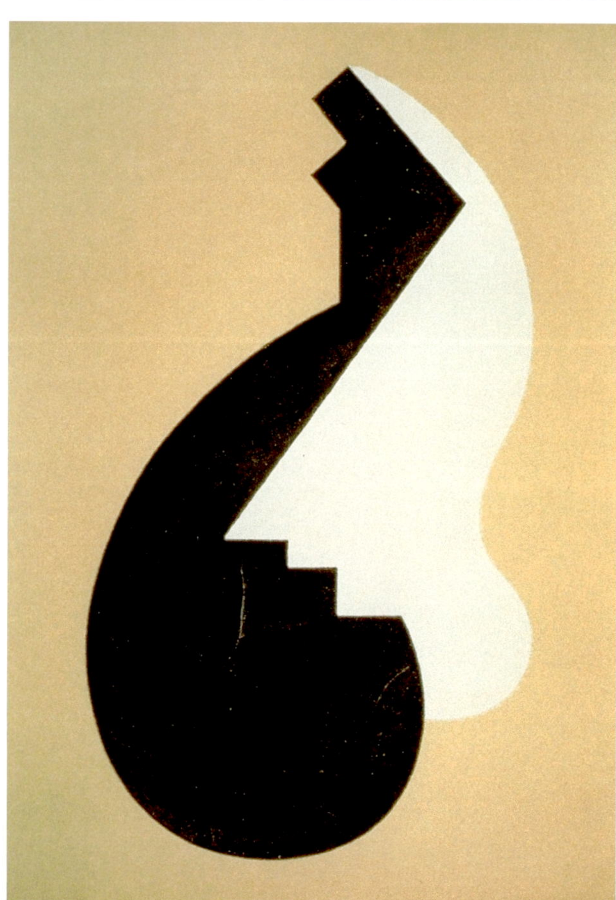

TOP: Installation view of Isamu Noguchi, *Paris Abstraction*, 1927–28.
BOTTOM: Ellsworth Kelly, *Whites*, 1963.

January 21 to April 7, 2000

The Nearness of Difference

As we step off the elevator into Shahzia Sikander's studio, an overwhelming crowd of images instantly rushes into view. Finger-smudged snapshots, crumpled photocopies, torn magazine pages, open books, and scribbled drawings are strewn across the floor, tabletops, and chairs. Tiptoeing around, careful not to place a hand or foot in an occupied space, certain areas gradually come into focus and hints of order emerge. After all, this is not casual clutter, but a creative thought process laid out in clear view, as exposed and vulnerable as it is restless and defiant.

Looking at Sikander's paintings is like walking into her studio. Filled with vibrant layers of images—from figures, animals, and vegetation to architectural structures, geometric patterns, and abstract forms—her paintings immediately draw you in with a hypnotic pull. It then takes time to sort out their complexity. Her compositions integrate not only aspects of Hindu, Islamic, and Western art, but also elements of popular culture from around the world. These widely divergent sources are suggestively and deliberately combined to create pictorial narratives about reinterpreting past traditions, dealing with cultural transitions, and negotiating issues of identity.

Born in 1969 in Pakistan, Sikander first studied painting at the National College of Arts in Lahore, a city often regarded as the country's artistic capital. Unlike most of her peers, who studied Western styles of twentieth-century art, she concentrated on the extremely labor-intensive and technically demanding ancient tradition of Indian miniature painting. This anachronistic art form originally served to illustrate exquisite royal manuscripts and reached its height of sophistication during the Mughal empire (1526–1857), when Islamic rulers from Persia reigned over a predominantly Hindu India. Still taught in many art schools in Pakistan, the highly specific methods and rigorous set of rules for producing miniatures have been

Shahzia Sikander: Acts of Balance

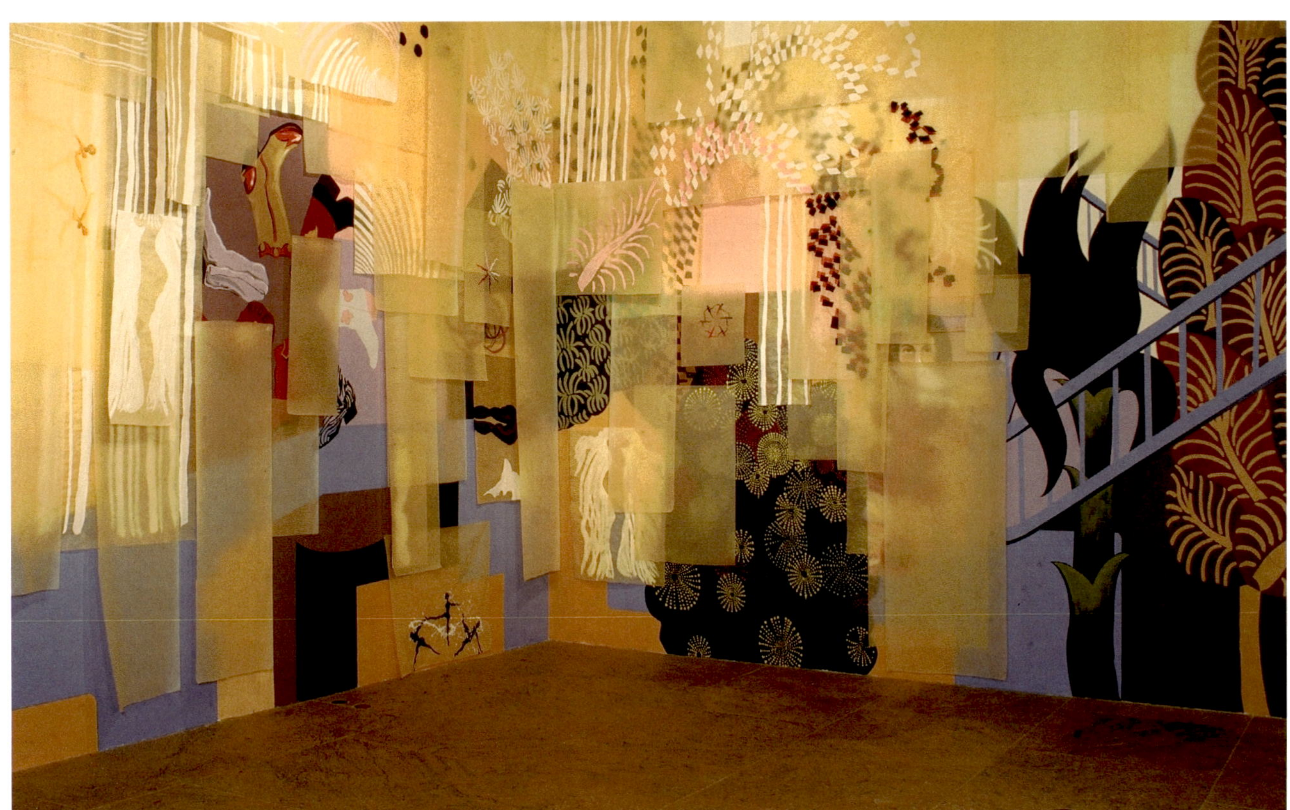

THIS PAGE AND FOLLOWING: Installation view of *Shahzia Sikander: Acts of Balance.*

passed down for centuries. It is only in the last few years that a growing number of younger Pakistani artists like Sikander have started to revive the craft, leading to a noticeable resurgence of miniature paintings.

After several years spent mastering the Indian miniature technique, Sikander moved to the United States in 1992 to attend graduate school at the Rhode Island School of Design. Creating art in a country far from Southeast Asia, one where most viewers were unfamiliar with the style, composition, and iconography common to Indian miniatures, Sikander felt free to manipulate traditional conventions and began to introduce other Eastern and Western artistic styles and symbols into her work. Living in America, she explained, also provided her with access to books and information not available in Pakistan about other schools of Southeast Asian painting, particularly Hindu traditions from India.[1] In addition, the physical distance from her own country gave her the chance to reflect on the difficult, psychologically charged relationship between Muslim Pakistan and a predominantly Hindu India. As a result, she started to produce images that addressed differences between Islamic and Hindu aesthetics, while also incorporating influences from her new life in the West.

Sikander's interest in working through aesthetic differences within Southeast Asian art by juxtaposing Islamic and Hindu elements is a particularly significant endeavor given the complicated history between Pakistan and India. Pakistan was created as an independent Muslim state, separate from India, in 1947, when British colonialists relinquished control over the region. Since that time, territorial disputes have intensified the hostility between the two countries. Sikander's embrace of both artistic traditions in her work, however, not only has contemporary resonance, but also a historical precedent. It echoes the Mughal emperors' peacemaking efforts in the sixteenth and seventeenth centuries, when they encouraged synthesis of Hindu and Islamic art forms to promote understanding between the two cultures.

The specific ways in which Sikander reworks Indian miniature traditions can be seen in an example from the Whitney Museum's collection, *Ready to Leave,* a small painting on paper measuring only about 10 x 8 inches. The title suggests how the artist has left her homeland behind. Immediately apparent are the vibrant reds, yellows, and greens common to Hindu traditions, along with the basic composition of an internally framed image surrounded by a wide border that is typical of Persian Islamic miniatures from the Safavid period (1502–1736). The central portrait depicts a young woman at her toilette. The pose is characteristic of a primarily Hindu style of painting called Kangra. This style, which has strongly influenced all of Sikander's work, developed out of the Mughal school and emerged in the Kangra Valley in northern India in the eighteenth century. Kangra painting was, in part, known for depictions of everyday life imbued with a sense of psychological intensity.[2]

Although the realism of the meticulously executed portrait is in keeping with Mughal traditions, Sikander contrasts this precision with more expressionistic designs evocative of Hindu traditions as well as gestural marks that relate to abstract painting traditions of Western modern art. She then continues to disrupt convention by obstructing our view of the woman's face with a large bluish-gray circle. According to Sikander, the circle denies the viewer access to the woman's identity and blocks the most revered element of a miniature painting, the facial expression. By literally painting over the face, Sikander attempts to repudiate the preciousness of the miniature enterprise.

Sikander also breaks from the past with her handling of the picture's wide borders. In place of the intricate drawings of flowers or animals that would normally fill this area, she presents loosely rendered shapes, patterns, and lines. Moreover, she disregards the normally emphatic separation between border and central image by allowing the forms to move freely around the perimeter of the composition. Among the motifs in this "border" are brightly colored concentric circles. In both Hindu and Islamic cultures, the "circle" is often regarded as a complete, perfect form with spiritual significance. Here they are reminiscent of Hindu *aripanas*, which are part of a folk art custom Sikander first encountered in many villages on a trip through India.

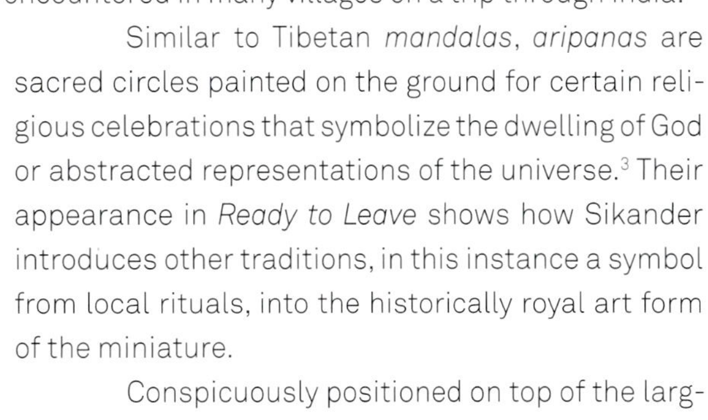

Similar to Tibetan *mandalas*, *aripanas* are sacred circles painted on the ground for certain religious celebrations that symbolize the dwelling of God or abstracted representations of the universe.[3] Their appearance in *Ready to Leave* shows how Sikander introduces other traditions, in this instance a symbol from local rituals, into the historically royal art form of the miniature.

Conspicuously positioned on top of the largest *aripana* is a drawing of a black griffin, a mythological beast—half lion, half eagle—whose head is

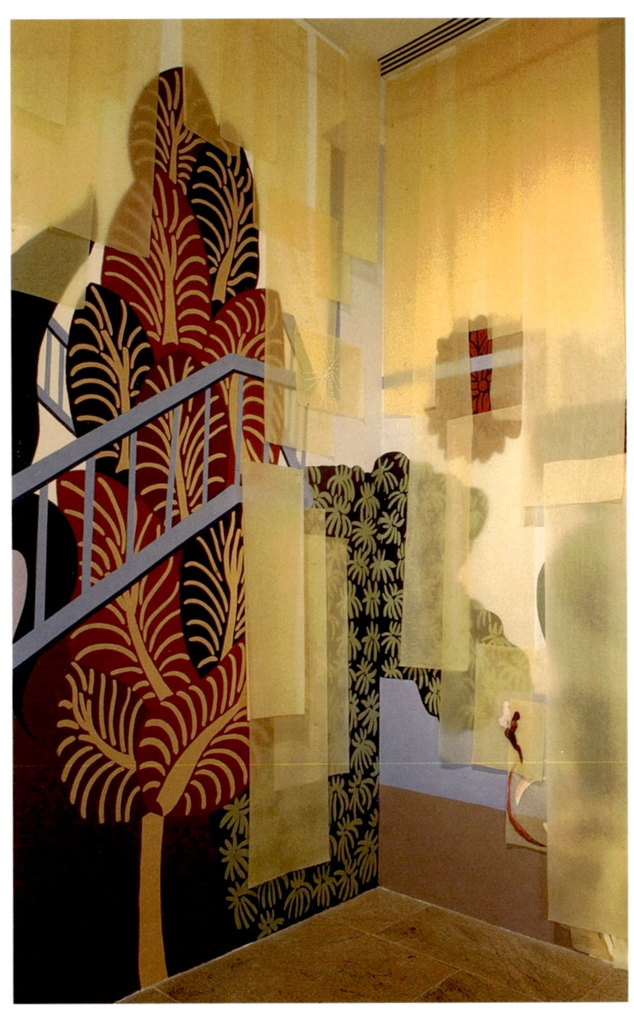

covered by a white, shredded veil. The symbolic griffin first emerged in Greek mythology and then was adapted into local contexts in many parts of India, Western Asia, the Middle East, and Europe where it took on various connotations. Sikander's personal appropriation of the griffin relates both to its reputation as a fleeting creature notoriously hard to track down as well as to its hybrid nature. In the Punjab region of northern Pakistan, Sikander notes, the griffin is called a *chillava,* a term also used to describe a certain kind of personality. In this context, according to Sikander, a *chillava* is

> *somebody who is coming and going so fast you can't pin down who they are. . . . The Chillava has multiple identities, and it reflects the sort of rhetoric or categories that I am confronted with. Are you Muslim, Pakistani, artist, painter, Asian, Asian-American, or what? But it is not my agenda to say that I belong to any of these categories. . . . I am interested in hybridity.*[4]

To the artist, the griffin serves as an icon for the mixed and fluid nature of identity and relates to her experiences in the United States, where she has frequently been questioned about her background. Dressed with an unraveling veil, the griffin is also a humorous reference to the persistent stereotype of the veiled Muslim woman in Western culture and represents Sikander's effort to overturn this reductive signifier of Islamic identity.

How Sikander reshapes her relationships to the past is evident in other ways in the recent miniature *Riding the Ridden.* Like *Ready to Leave,* this small painting depicts an internally framed, partially hidden central image sur-

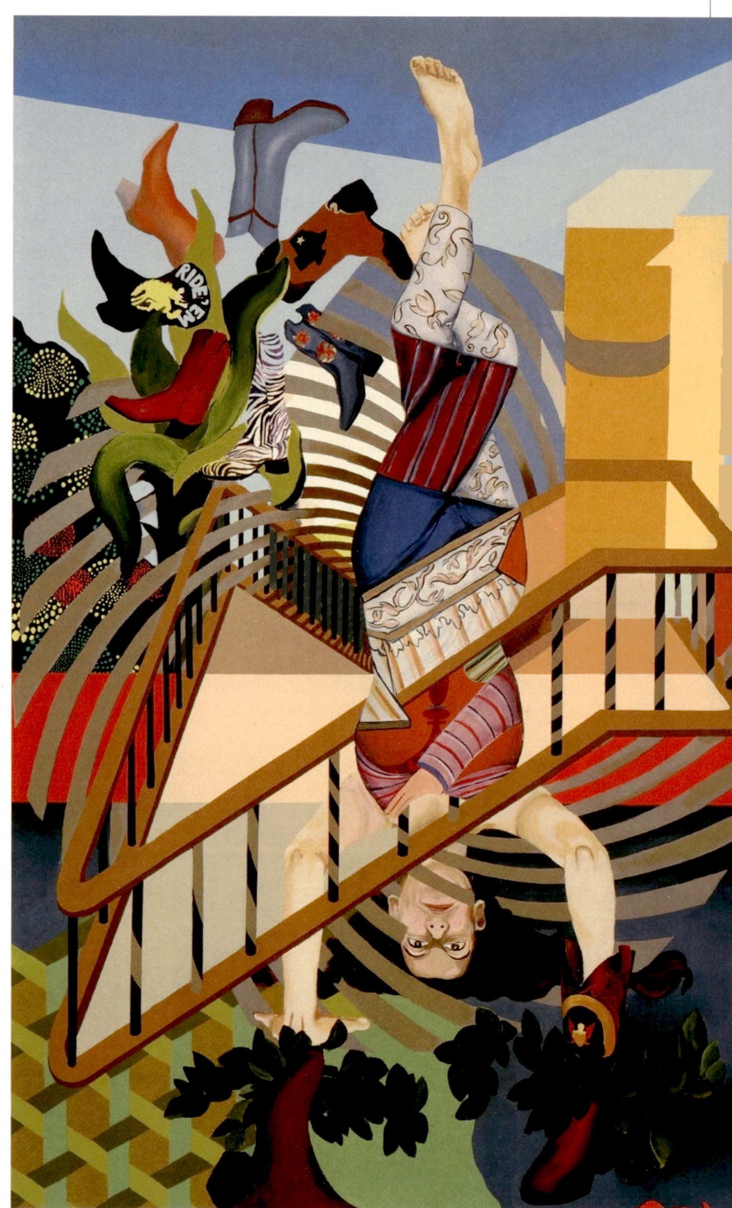

Shahzia Sikander, *Elusive Realities #1,* 2000.

rounded by an elaborate border. A large series of black concentric circles—a form traditionally representing the nine heavens of Islamic cosmology—blocks our view of a silhouetted man and woman in a suggestively romantic encounter. The couple appear as shadowed silhouettes seated on a floral-patterned rug beneath a garden landscape. Both the romantic theme and the stylized rendering of leaves, hills, and lotus flowers are characteristic of Kangra-style painting. Closer inspection of the image reveals that while there are two bodies shown from the waist down, there are actually four upper bodies in the scene. The doubling of the figures' upper bodies is a twist on a miniature convention that signifies movement by repeating the same character in different locations in a single painting.

In *Riding the Ridden,* Sikander again manipulates the border in unusual ways. Flowers from the inner frame spill off the edges and proliferate into red, black, blue, and white dots that migrate across the field. Arranged like sections of a matrix, the dot pattern functions as an important formal device to enhance the effect of parallel, but separate, picture planes existing simultaneously in the painting. The dots also evoke both Eastern Asian and Western references: they are reminiscent of *bindi* dots worn on the foreheads of married women in India, but they also recall Western art's modernist grid and, even more specifically, the signature Benday dots of Roy Lichtenstein's work.

The other prominent motif circulating in the border is cowboy boots, which reflect Sikander's experiences in Texas, where she lived after graduate school.

> *When I first arrived in Houston, I was fascinated with the elaborate*
> *styles of cowboy boots and thought they were incredibly exotic.*
> *They also seemed to be a central part of a specifically "Texan"*
> *identity, one distinct from being "American."*[5]

In the painting, the boots also serve as additional framing devices, containing within them glimpses of other landscapes. Shoes, in general, appear in much of Sikander's work, representing mobility and groundedness. Their multiple meanings refer to Sikander's own transient life, living and working in different cities and countries, which has required her to adapt to many environments.

The elaborate layering of styles and types of images in both *Ready to Leave* and *Riding the Ridden* commingles fragments of discrete worlds, discontinuous time frames, and jumbled memories. How we interpret these fragments is contingent on which elements in the paintings we recognize as familiar and which we regard as foreign or unusual. For example, depending on our experience or background, either cowboy boots or veils might seem out of the ordinary. Through carefully considered juxtapositions, Sikander's paintings propose that popular concepts of identity partly grow out of these processes of recognition. At the same time, she also questions the assumptions underlying those social formations.

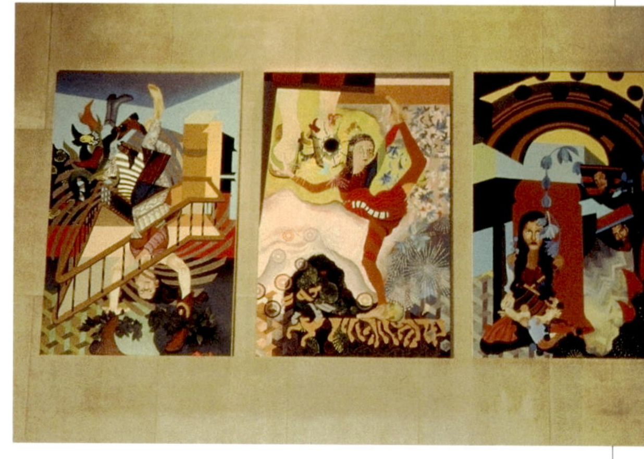

Shahzia Sikander, *Elusive Realities*, 2000 (installation view of *Shahzia Sikander: Acts of Balance*).

While Sikander is best known for her small, jewel-like paintings, this new exhibition features recent experimentations with scale. The large triptych titled *Elusive Realities* translates both the symbols and compositional devices of her miniatures into a grand format. Each of the three canvases is dominated by a central female figure, around which other designs circulate. Apparent in all of the canvases are elements from Sikander's personal artistic inventory—dots, spirals, and other circular forms, cowboy boots, Islamic geometric tile work, and Kangra foliage—as well as compositional conventions that present architectural spaces alongside garden settings. The three paintings in the triptych depict the same woman in three different yoga-based poses: standing on her head, standing on one leg, and sitting cross-legged with her arms twisted behind her back. According to Sikander, this active, flexible, and strong woman is an icon of self-control and independence. Presented in difficult bodily contortions, the figure also metaphorically alludes to the balancing acts women in particular face as they juggle the often competing pressures of familial responsibility, career goals, societal expectations, and the desire for personal freedom.

Sikander has also experimented with another highly developed and revered Indian art, that of mural painting. In the installation titled *Chaman,* the Farsi word for garden, Sikander created a contemplative environment by painting the gallery walls from floor to ceiling with bright areas of green, yellow, lavender, and blue intermixed with earthy tones of beige and ocher. These broad expanses of color serve as the backdrop for oversized plants, boots, figures, and architectural structures whose outsized dimensions dwarf the viewer. Layered on top of these paintings are vertical bands of translucent paper that hang loosely down the walls. It is as if the implied overlay of images in Sikander's smaller paintings has been physically realized in material, three-dimensional form. The bands suggest both Islamic painted scrolls and Muslim veils. Indeed, they function like veils—hiding certain areas , exposing others—to create a playful rhythm of emerging and receding images. These cascading ribbons are painted with simplified, unlabored drawings of swirling geometric patterns and abstract shapes. Their intuitive sensibility contrasts dramatically with the tighter style of painted imagery executed directly on the walls. They possess buoyancy and lightness, as if they were thoughts simply floating in space. Talking about how the tissue drawings contrast with the style of the miniatures, Sikander explained,

> *I try to keep them spontaneous, gestural. There is a rigor behind them, but they are much more open, democratic. They are not fussy or fetishistic. . . . The tissue drawings are not about the exclusivity associated with skill. They are the opposite. . . . It is a mark-making process, a journal or diary.*[6]

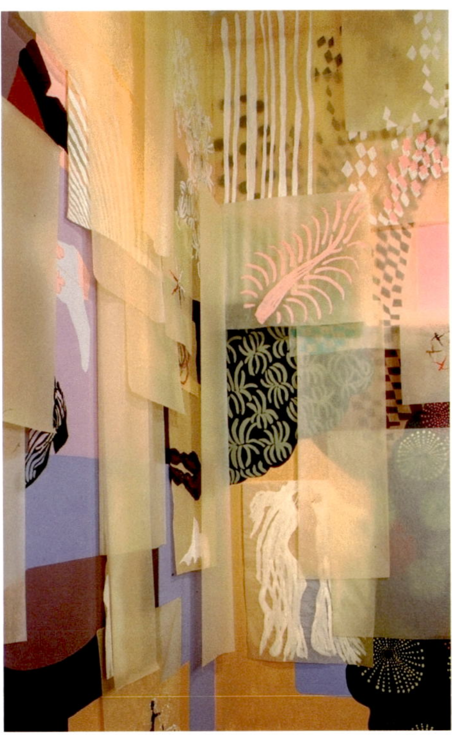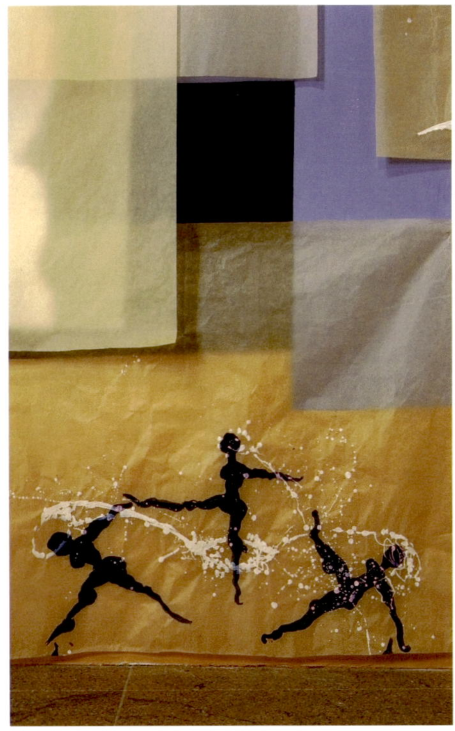

In all her paintings, whether they are small works on paper, large canvases, or expansive wall murals, Sikander puts forth an intricate symbol system that is at once personal, political, and social. Her complex artistic vocabulary tantalizes us with hints of open-ended stories—about travel and displacement, women's independence, contesting identities, and reshaping the past. Rather than encouraging us to draw conclusions, however, her paintings induce us to ask more questions: How much historical knowledge do we need to understand them? What are the consequences of uprooting culturally specific imagery from local contexts? How do traditions of aesthetics relate to constructions of identity? These are some of the issues Sikander's paintings raise as she examines broad distinctions between Eastern and Western art as well as the heterogeneity within the East itself. Her exploration of this latter phenomenon is one that the theorist Homi Bhabha describes as, "the nearness of difference," a phrase used to acknowledge the diversity inherent in any culture or region.[7] Sikander's paintings express this concept as she works through distinctions between the closely intertwined cultures of Pakistan and India, and plays with the notion of a Texan identity separate from an American one. As she moves beyond evident international distinctions to more nuanced intracultural ones, Sikander integrates elements from Hindu, Islamic, and Western traditions to create what she calls an "in-between" space where they can coexist.[8] Her extraordinary array of references are delicately balanced—they neither collapse discrete traditions into one another nor favor certain ones over others. Recalling the unruly site of her studio, this complicated "in-between" space of Sikander's art is paradoxically both fragile and tenacious, reminding us that out of pandemonium the possibility for a new order may emerge. —DEBRA SINGER, BRANCH CURATOR

1. Conversation with the artist, March 2000.
2. Rajaram Narayan Saletore, *Encyclopaedia of Indian Culture* (New Delhi: Sterling Publishers, 1981), pp. 674–75.
3. Yves Véquaud, *Women Painters of Mithila* (London: Thames and Hudson, 1977), p. 28.
4. "Chillava Klatch: Shahzia Sikander Interviewed by Homi Bhabha," in *Shahzia Sikander*, exh. cat. (Chicago: The Renaissance Society at The University of Chicago, 1998), p. 79.
5. Conversation with the artist, March 2000.
6. "Chillava Klatch," p. 20.
7. Elaine Kim and Margo Machida, eds., *Fresh Talk/Daring Gazes: Contemporary Asian American Art* (Berkeley: University of California Press, forthcoming).
8. Conversation with the artist, April 2000.

Muna Tseng Dance Projects with Margaret Leng Tan and Marie Baker-Lee

Zero Boy

Dean Moss with Kacie Change, Marcelo Coutinho, and Stephen Vitiello

Elevator Repair Service

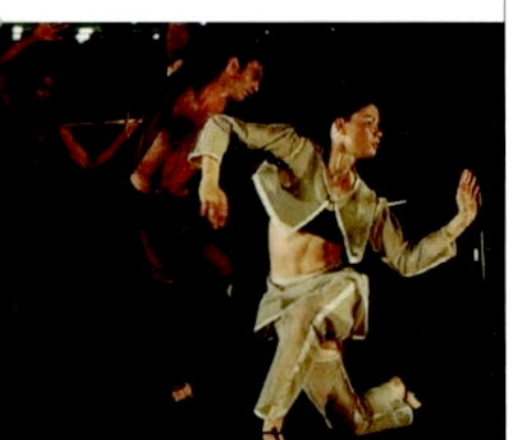

Dean Moss, *Spooky Action at a Distance*, 05–24–00

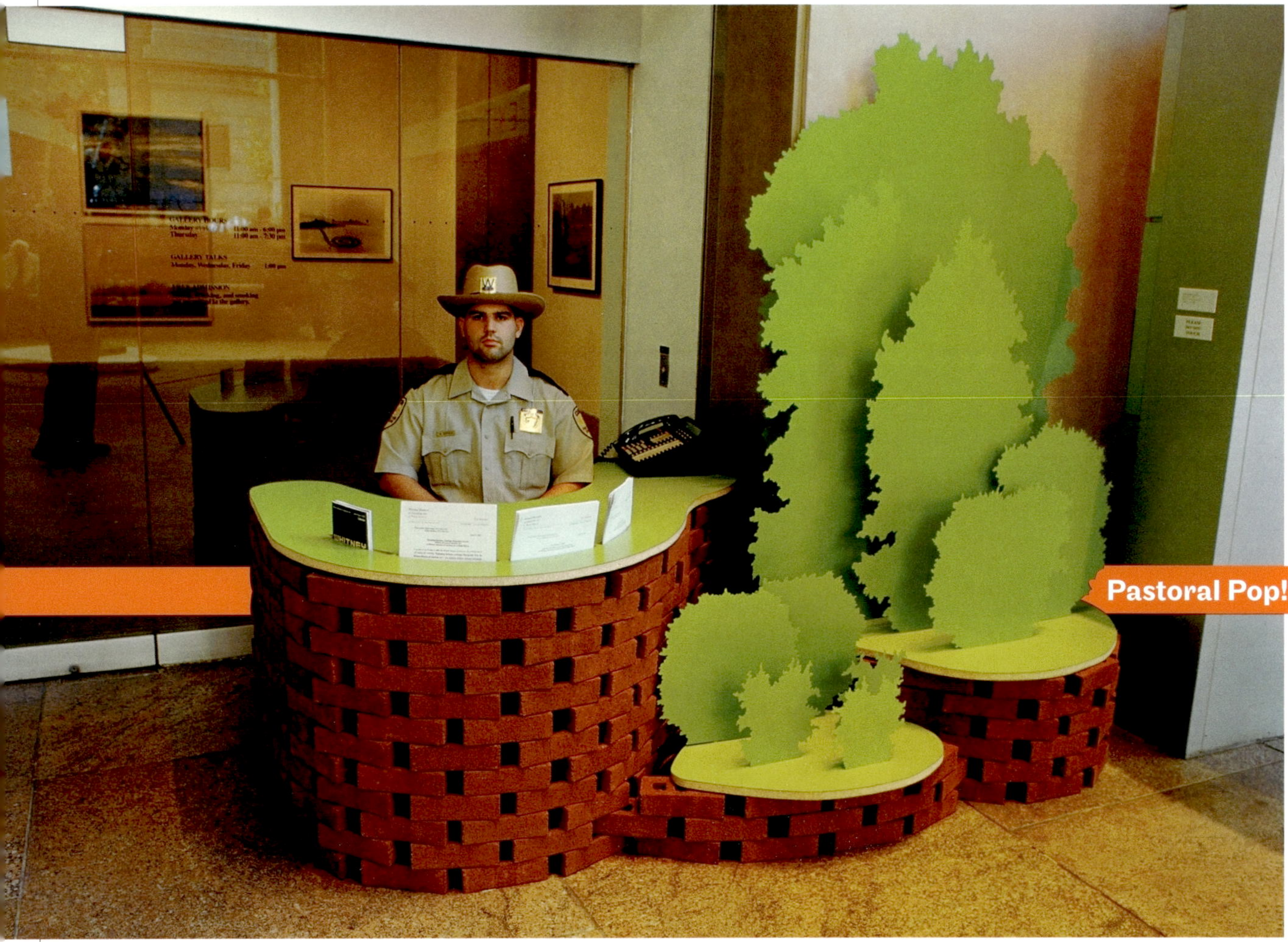

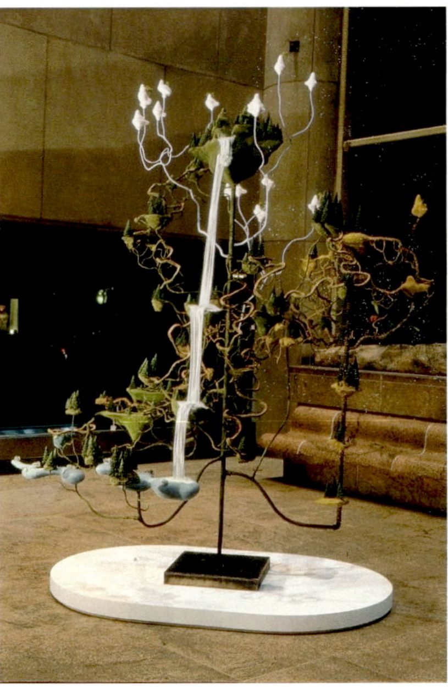

Pastoral Pop!

July 21 to December 15, 2000

Pastoral Pop! features new, commissioned works by Katrin Asbury, Rob de Mar, Rachel Feinstein, Peter Gould, Jason Middlebrook, Lisa Ruyter, and Alyson Shotz. Using the Sculpture Court as their playground, these seven emerging artists employ artificial materials and imagery from popular culture to create sculptures and paintings of fantastical gardens and surreal landscapes. Appropriating elements from an eclectic array of sources—such as advertising, art history, cartoons, technology, office parks, zoos, and fast food joints—these artists mine the legacy of 1960s Pop art to explore how nature in the contemporary moment is no longer separable from mass-media culture. If Pop art proposed decades ago that art is simply another product of consumer society, these artists suggest through their cool, deadpan works that the natural world has now been absorbed into the mix. In addition, by cleverly placing their works in the Sculpture Court's flower boxes, windows, and other idiosyncratic spaces, the group expands on Pop's interest in display, presentation, and spectacle while also playing off of the slippage between sited works of art and landscape architecture.

July 21 to October 6, 2000

The phrase "landscape photography" often evokes mental images of snow-capped mountains, sand-swept dunes, or vernal forests. Such celebrations of pristine, natural beauty can be traced back to photography's beginnings in the second half of the nineteenth century when Carleton E. Watkins, Timothy O'Sullivan, and other pioneer photographers documented unsullied vistas of the American West. Like contemporaneous Romantic painting traditions, their photographs paid tribute to nature's sublime and spiritual qualities and became symbols for a prosperous future as America expanded westward. Ironically, they photographed nature's grandeur just as industrialization and urbanization began to change the face of the land. . . .

Since the late 1980s, however, many landscape photographers have presented nature and culture not as separate visual conditions but as mutually dependent states. They have also once again accepted an aesthetic of beauty defined by older, Romantic ideals. This revival, though, has been qualified by a critical awareness that we can no longer separate nature's splendor from distressing environmental conditions caused by human activity.

—DEBRA SINGER, BRANCH CURATOR

Expanding Horizons: Landscape Photographs from the Whitney Museum of American Art

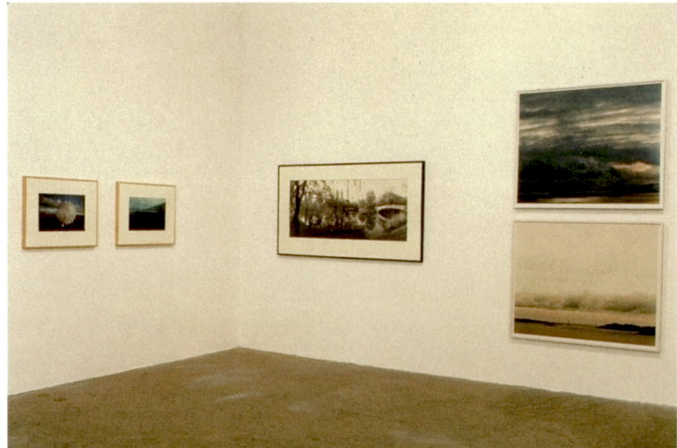

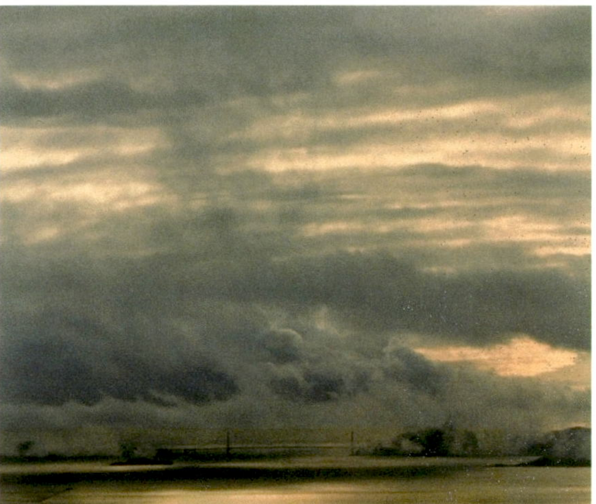

TOP: Left to right: Gabriel Orozco, *Parachute in Iceland, (South)*, 1996; *House and Rain*, 1998; Bruce Davidson, *Bow Bridge, Central Park*, 1991–95; Richard Misrach, *2.21.98 4:46 PM*, 1998–99; *3.19.99 11:14 AM*, 1999 (installation view of *Expanding Horizons: Landscape Photographs from the Whitney Museum of American Art*). **BOTTOM:** Richard Misrach, *2.21.98 4:46 PM*, 1998–99.

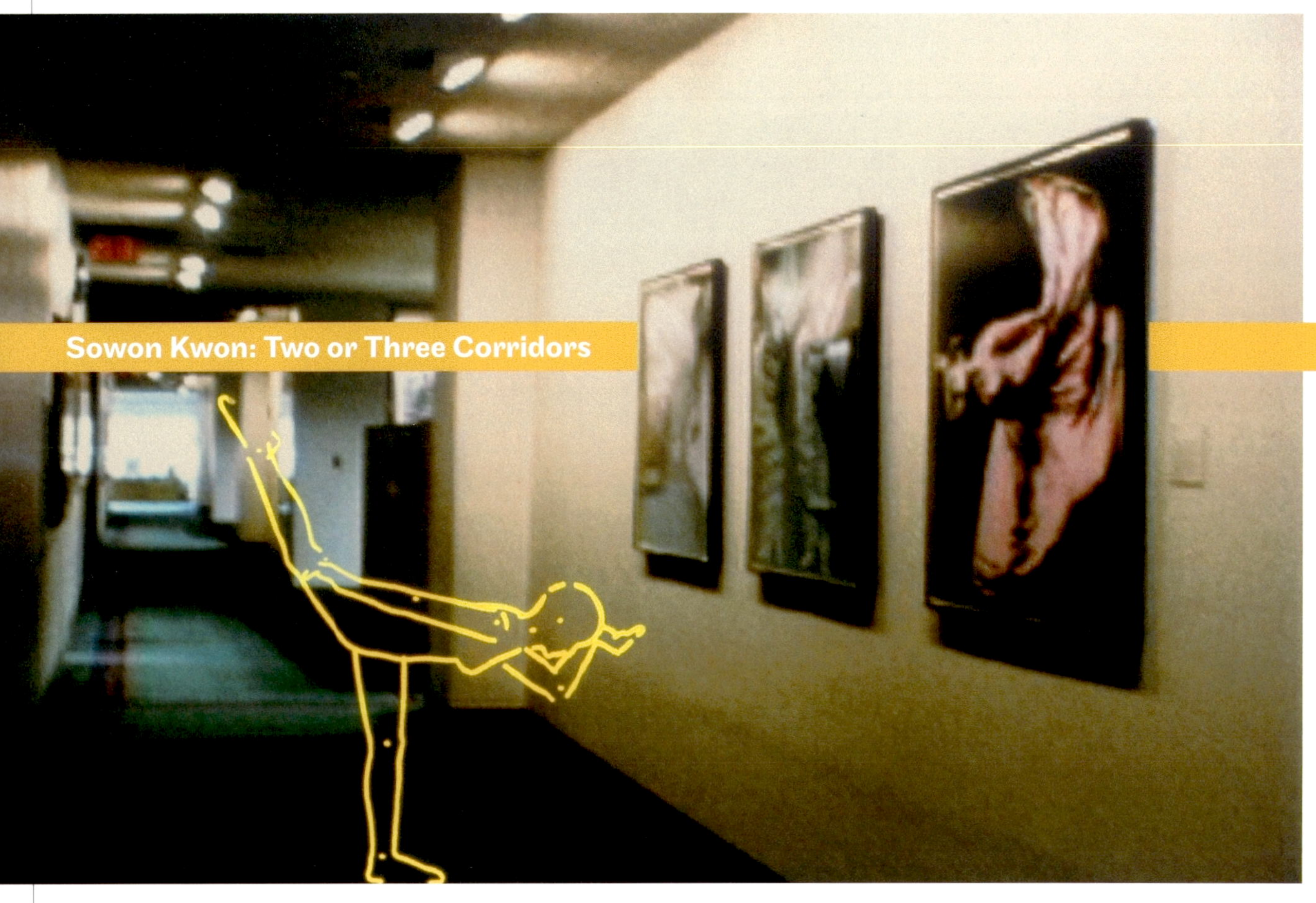

Sowon Kwon: Two or Three Corridors

October 20, 2000 to January 5, 2001

Finding a coffee table, sofa, or desk that you like and can afford is often a frustrating, exhausting, and even painful process. As difficult as such searches may be, the real challenge doesn't begin until you return home with a purchased item in tow. At best, the new object upsets the old equilibrium of the room, setting off a chain reaction of adjustments to accommodate the foreign entity. At worst, the piece that seemed ideal in the store is a glaring disaster at home. Such dramatic shifts in how we view the same piece of furniture in two different settings can also occur with our interpretations of an art work. Seeing it in a museum, for example, and then seeing it in a private home may produce two entirely different opinions. In both instances, our respons-es are strongly influenced by the work's relationship to other items and the surroundings in which it is viewed. . . .

Kwon's gesture of appropriating objects from the Philip Morris collection and repositioning them in the gallery dismantles devices of presentation in order to conduct several discrete investigations of physical context and viewer perception. In so doing, *Two or Three Corridors* leads us to an understanding of "interiors" as both actual places and psychic spaces, conjuring up patterns of responses that connect how we move to how we remember, view, and interpret the visual information around us.

—DEBRA SINGER, BRANCH CURATOR

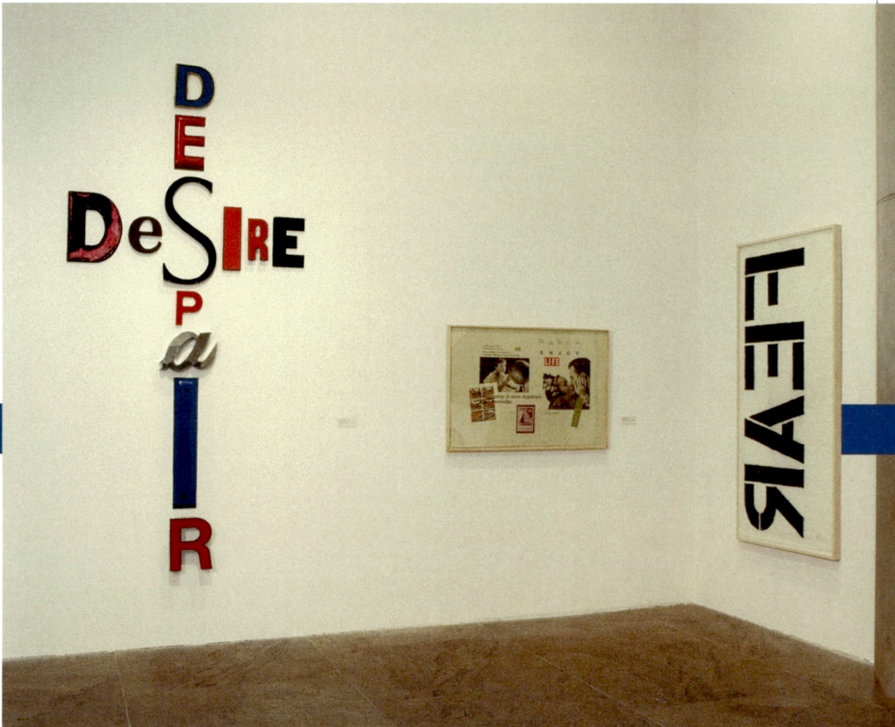

Left to right: Jack Pierson, *Desire, Despair*, 1996; Alexis Smith, *Boy's Life*, 1986; Christopher Wool, *Untitled*, 1990 (installation view of *A Way with Words: Selections from the Whitney Museum of American Art*).

A Way with Words:
Selections from the Whitney Museum of American Art

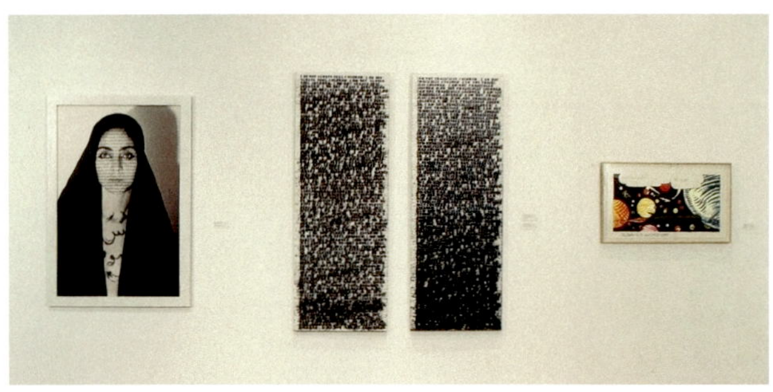

Left to right: Shirin Neshat, *Unveiling*, 1993; Glenn Ligon, *Untitled (I Feel Most Colored When I Am Thrown Against a Sharp White Background)*, 1992; *Untitled (I Do Not Always Feel Colored)*, 1992; Raymond Pettibon, *Untitled*, 1998 (installation view of *A Way with Words: Selections from the Whitney Museum of American Art*).

January 19 to March 30, 2001

The use of text in the visual arts stretches back thousands of years, from identifying inscriptions on ancient wall paintings and sculptures, to the inclusion of biblical passages or saints' names in medieval and Renaissance art, to the Cubist incorporation of language fragments drawn from newspapers and product labels. It was only in the latter half of the twentieth century, however, that language became a primary expressive vehicle in the visual arts. . . .

. . . *A Way with Words*, selected from the Permanent Collection of the Whitney Museum of American Art, includes fourteen works by twelve contemporary artists who employ text as a visual element. The works—by Suzanne McClelland, Shirin Neshat, Raymond Pettibon, Jack Pierson, Lari Pittman, Richard Prince, Lorna Simpson, Alexis Smith, Chris Verene, Carrie Mae Weems, and Christopher Wool—explore the compelling possibilities of word and image from a diversity of perspectives. Taking advantage of the stylistic plurality characteristic of the latter decades of the twentieth century, these artists examine contemporary experience by drawing freely from the complex history of language in the visual arts as well as from literary and popular culture. . . .

Unlike earlier twentieth-century artists, contemporary artists who use text in their work adhere to no generalized conceptual rules or formal manifestos. Instead, they embrace a wealth of sources—from politics to literature, pop culture to American mythology, religion to Hollywood—to create innovative, visually dynamic images that are, above all, fully engaged with the world.

—SHAMIM M. MOMIN, BRANCH CURATOR

The relationship of the individual to the collective is a complex and often uneasy one. Group participation may provide a feeling of safety, the comfort of belonging, relief at diminished personal accountability, and even a sense of virtuousness in unselfishly sacrificing one's own needs for those of the group. But joining with others in the name of con-formity can stifle self-expression—the freedom to act and make personal choices.

These conflicting sensibilities are central to *Some/One* . . . Suh's work investigates notions of personal space and its relationship to individuality, collectivity, and anonymity. In this installation, his first one-artist museum exhibition, Suh uses thousands of newly fabricated dog tags, representing individual identity in its most pared-down, essential form. The tags are linked together into a structure that covers the gallery floor and then swells into a larger-than-life standing form suggesting a royal garment or ancient armor. . . .

Born and raised in Korea but now residing in New York, Suh served a mandatory three-year term in the South Korean military, a seminal experience that continues to inform his thinking. He sees the military, like other institutional, rule-driven groups such as schools, as a microcosmic enactment of social standards and as a training ground where individuals learn how to place themselves within a larger group. The advantages and disadvantages of this social process are embodied in the installation: seen together, the dog tags create a beautiful and strong figure that acts as its own supportive structure; seen as small components of a larger whole, however, the dog tags represent the subjugation of personal identity, the familiar anonymity of the individual in a crowd. —SHAMIM M. MOMIN, BRANCH CURATOR

Do-Ho Suh: Some/One

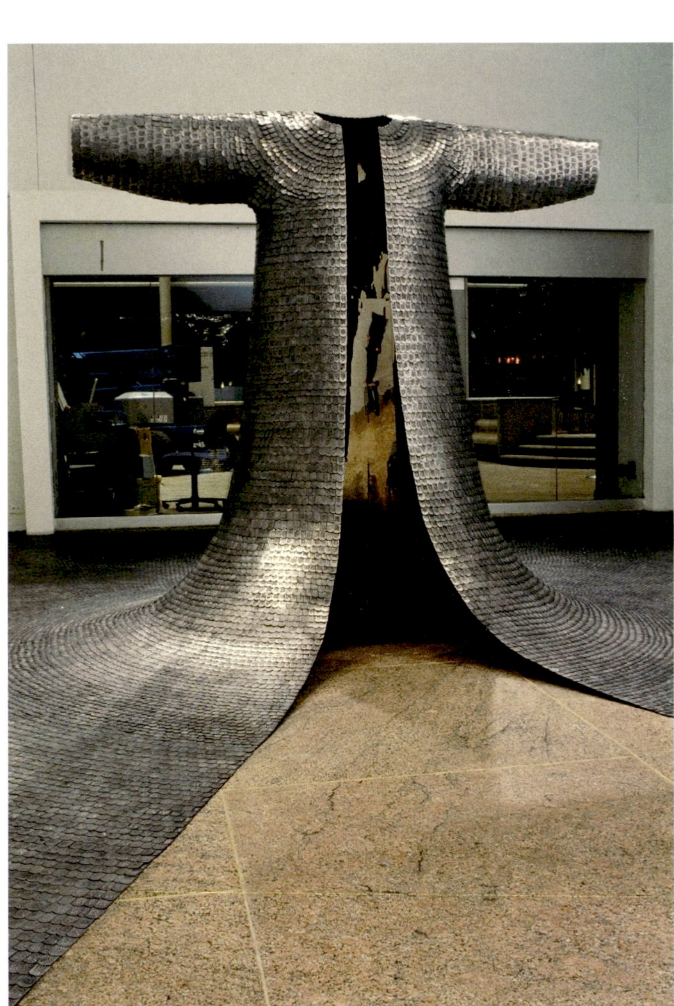

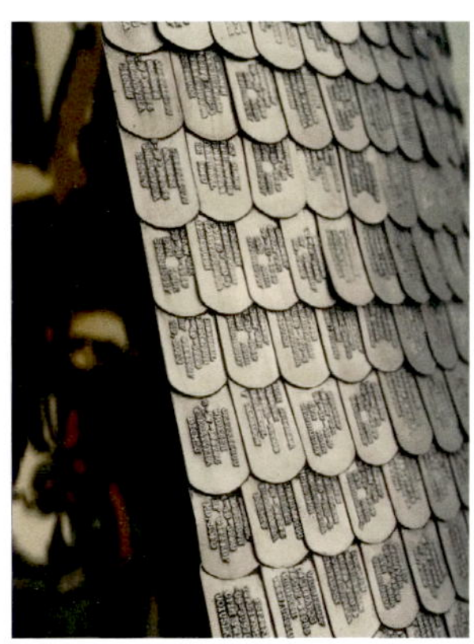

Installation views of Do-Ho Suh, *Some/One*, 2001.

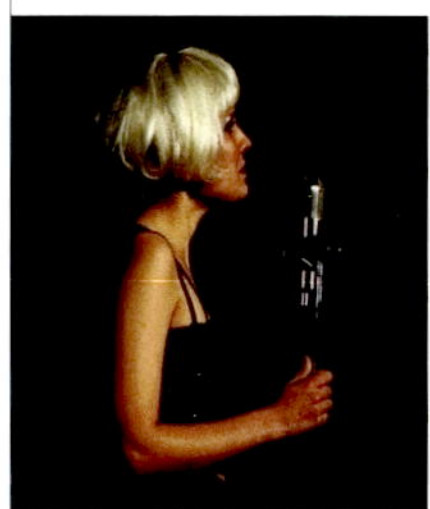

The Builders Association, *Xtravaganza*, 03–26–01

July 13 to September 21, 2001

Miranda Lichtenstein's work explores the ambiguous arenas of sanctuary and fear through subjects ranging from male exhibitionists to suburban houses and byways in Connecticut. Though photography is her primary medium, her new installation at the Whitney Museum at Philip Morris, entitled *Sanctuary for a Wild Child*, consists of a series of drawings and related DVD projections. Inspired by cross-cultural legends of children brought up in the wild, the works are displayed as an installation set within an architectural configuration designed to create a dynamic process of exploration for the viewer.

Miranda Lichtenstein: Sanctuary for a Wild Child

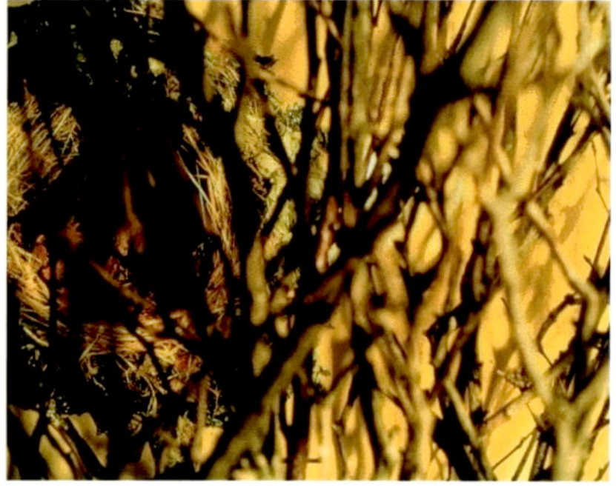

The term "Wild Child" refers to a child who grew up without any contact with civilization. . . .

Lichtenstein proposes no absolute conclusions in the Sanctuary series; rather, she encourages the viewer to look beyond the rigid divisions and assumptions so common to human existence. . . . The Wild Child can be seen to occupy a realm between nature and culture, mythology and science, instinct and language. Lichtenstein affirms the position of the Wild Child in this liminal space as a personification of the gray area that complicates clear, simple dichotomies.

—SHAMIM M. MOMIN, BRANCH CURATOR

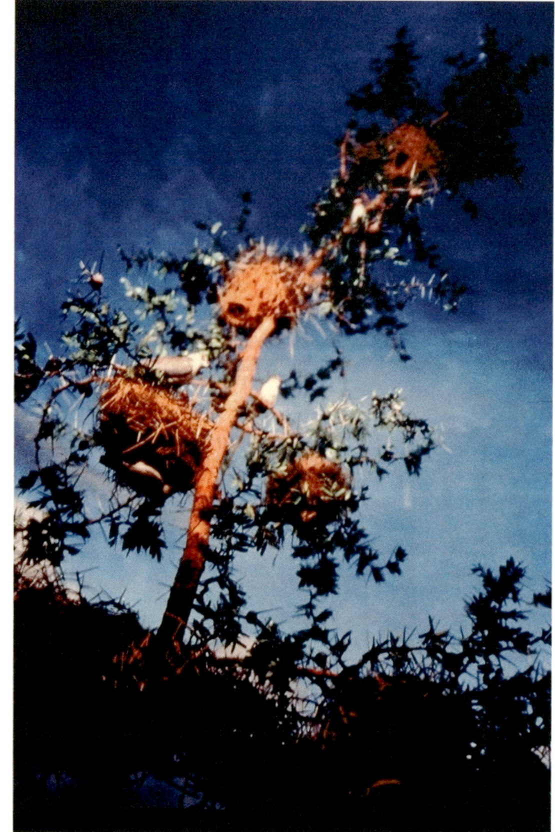

Miranda Lichtenstein, *Lost beyond telling*, 2000–01 (detail of *Sanctuary for a Wild Child*). **LEFT:** Miranda Lichtenstein, *Elsewhere*, 2000–01 (detail of *Sanctuary for a Wild Child*).

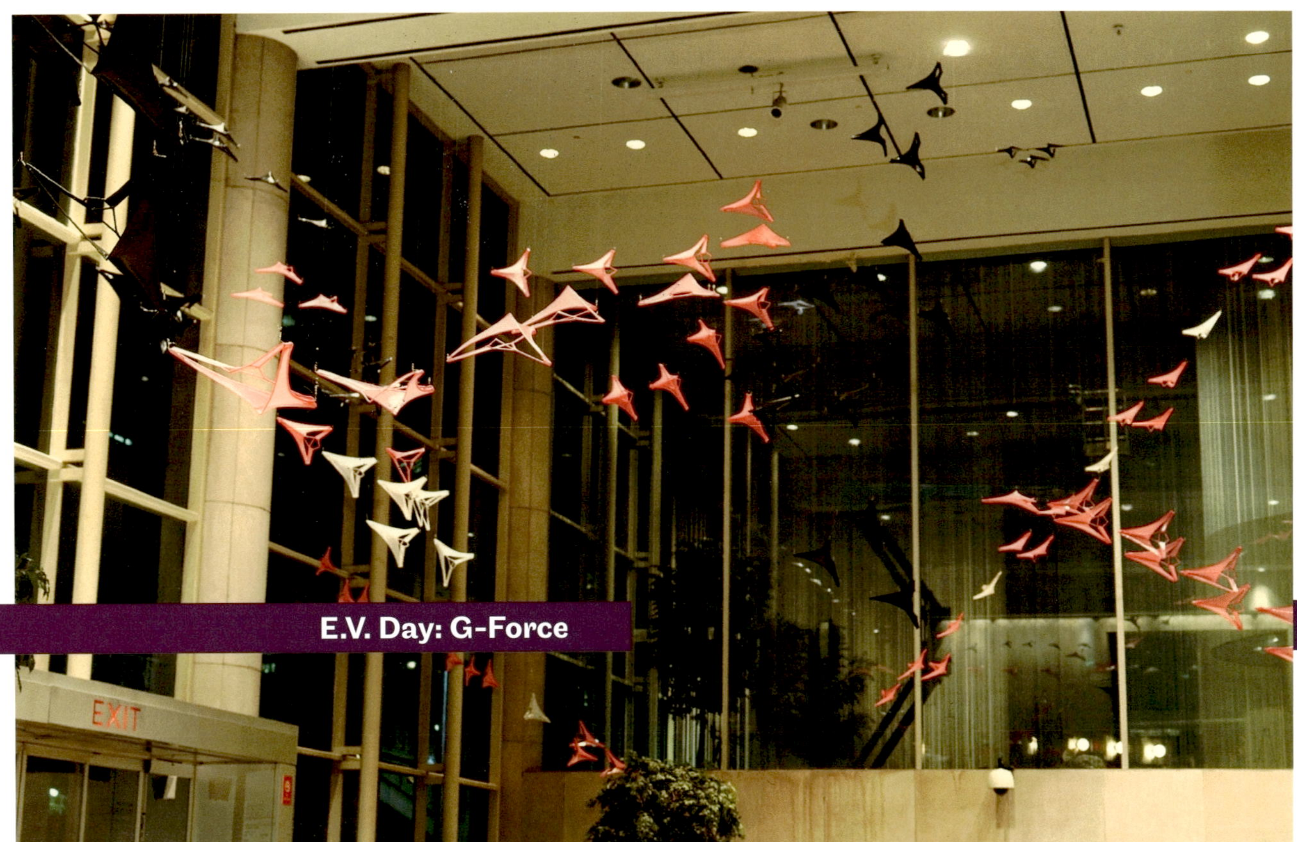

THIS PAGE AND FOLLOWING: Installation views of *E.V. Day: G-Force.*

October 5, 2001 to January 4, 2002

Speaking In Thongs

If ever an article of clothing symbolized the notions of desire and display that underlie women's fashion, it would be the thong. The thong is as ubiquitous in lingerie shops and department stores (where thongs account for ninety percent of overall panty sales) as it is in the popular imagination. As the subject of casual cocktail party conversation, countless magazine articles, and even popular rock songs, the thong is now literally talked about everywhere. Fashion-conscious women ignore its original intent—invisible underwear. Instead, thongs are flaunted, worn wrapped up high over hips with backsides exposed by low-riding pants and skirts—the brighter, the better. As with bras in the eighties, the idea of a woman's intimate apparel being an exclusively private aesthetic and erotic statement for the male gaze has been discarded. The thong has been reclaimed, and aggressively and publicly presented. Nowadays, the focus is less on who is looking than on who has decided to display.

E.V. Day's *G-Force,* a new installation in the Sculpture Court of the Whitney Museum at Philip Morris, plays off this contemporary moment and the politics of desire and display—fantasy and fashion, femininity and fetishism—that have been of issue since women first got dressed. Drawing on elements of her earlier work exploring female icons, popular culture, and fashion, Day has created configurations of sleek flying objects from multicolored thongs and G-strings (black, silver, pink, and blue) that hang in groups from the ceiling. Approximately two hundred of these forms dive and swirl through the 40-foot-high space, transforming the cold, corporate architecture of the Sculpture Court into a kind of public aviary. The thongs, stretched and then hardened with polyurethane resin, create abstractions of flight and movement that animate the boundary between indoor and outdoor space. Caught in a moment of exploration and dynamic motion, they dart through the air with a purposive trajectory, imminently departing to parts unknown.

Day was inspired to use the thong in flight when she noticed increasing numbers of women wearing externally visible thongs. Seen from behind, the typical shape of a thong rising above a waistband closely resembles a child's schematic drawing of a bird in flight, a curved letter V with a thicker middle juncture approximating the bird's body and wings. Day envisioned a fantasy world in which thongs achieve sentience and spring off women's bodies into the air of their own accord. She humorously describes this as the "liberation of the thong."[1] In a witty twist

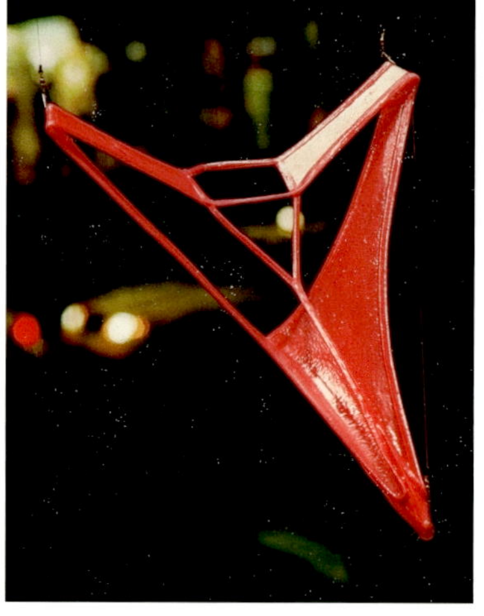

on the idea of women's empowerment, the thong is itself empowered to soar. Thongs have shed their identity as mere bodily accessories and become beings in their own right, with focus and direction.

The arrested motion in *G-Force*—thongs frozen but definitively in transit—is characteristic of Day's earlier work, which often presents her subject in a moment of transformation or transition, both spatially and conceptually. The suspended sculpture *Bombshell,* from her *Exploding Couture* series, captures an iconic object of clothing—the white dress worn by Marilyn Monroe in *The Seven Year Itch*—at the instant it explodes. The motion of the dress recalls the famous scene in which Marilyn's dress is blown up by air from a subway grate. In *Bombshell,* the force that lifted Marilyn's skirt has become aggressive and explosive. The dress shatters into pieces, caught in the air on monofilaments strung from floor to ceiling on turn buckles. The violence implicit in the piece is transformative rather than destructive. Day has isolated "a moment of release" when a woman "explodes the conventions of femininity."[2] By referencing an iconic female figure such as Marilyn Monroe, Day universalizes the possibility of breaking seemingly indestructible social constraints for all women. It is an ongoing and unfinished process, punctuated by drastic moments.

A similar logic applies to the most recent of Day's *Exploding Couture* works, *Transporter,* in which a deconstructed silver sequined dress is also caught in a moment within the process of translocation. *Transporter* might be the next step after *Bombshell*; once convention has been shattered, one is free to achieve true transcendence. *Transporter*'s silvery scraps of fabric create a vertical outline that

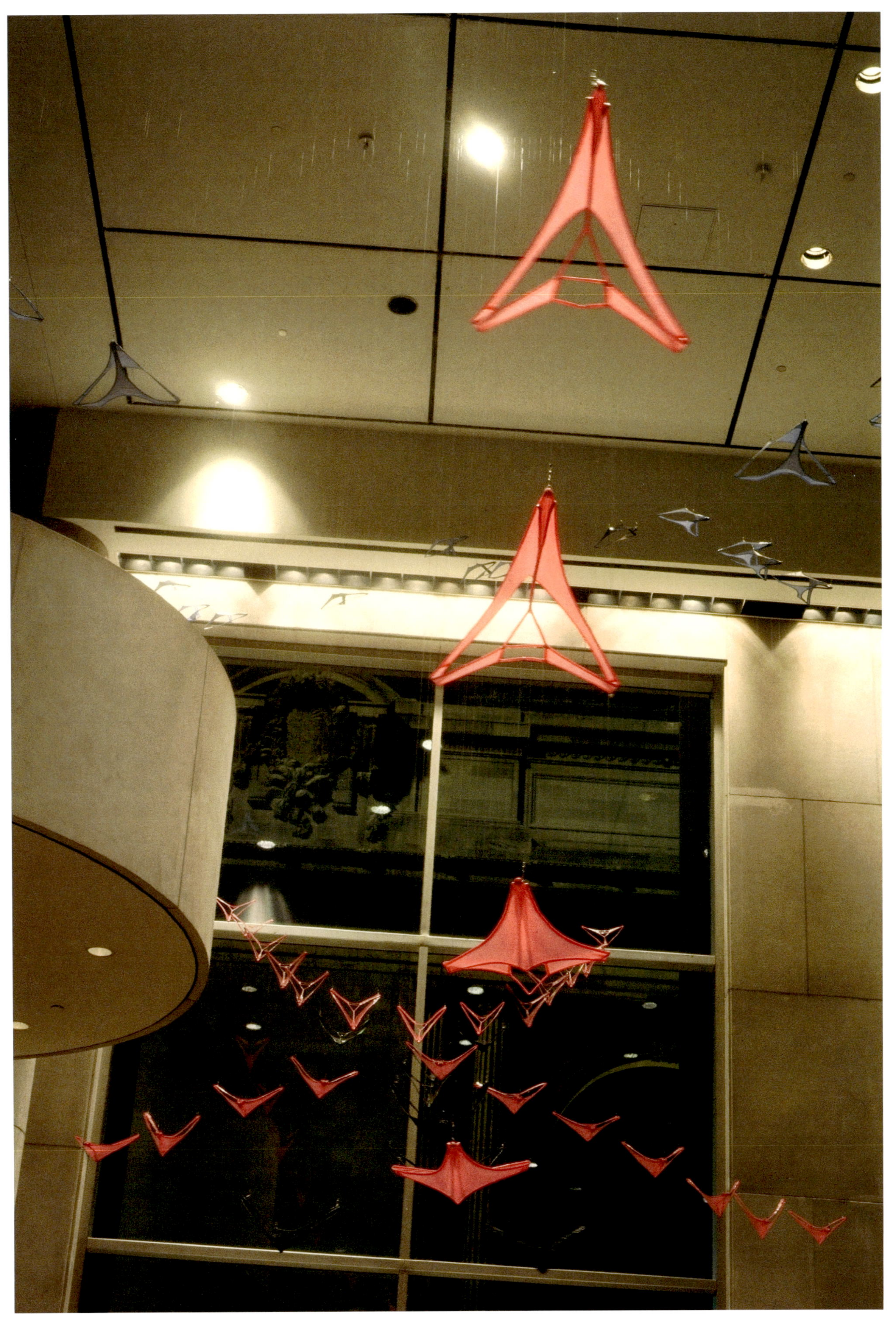

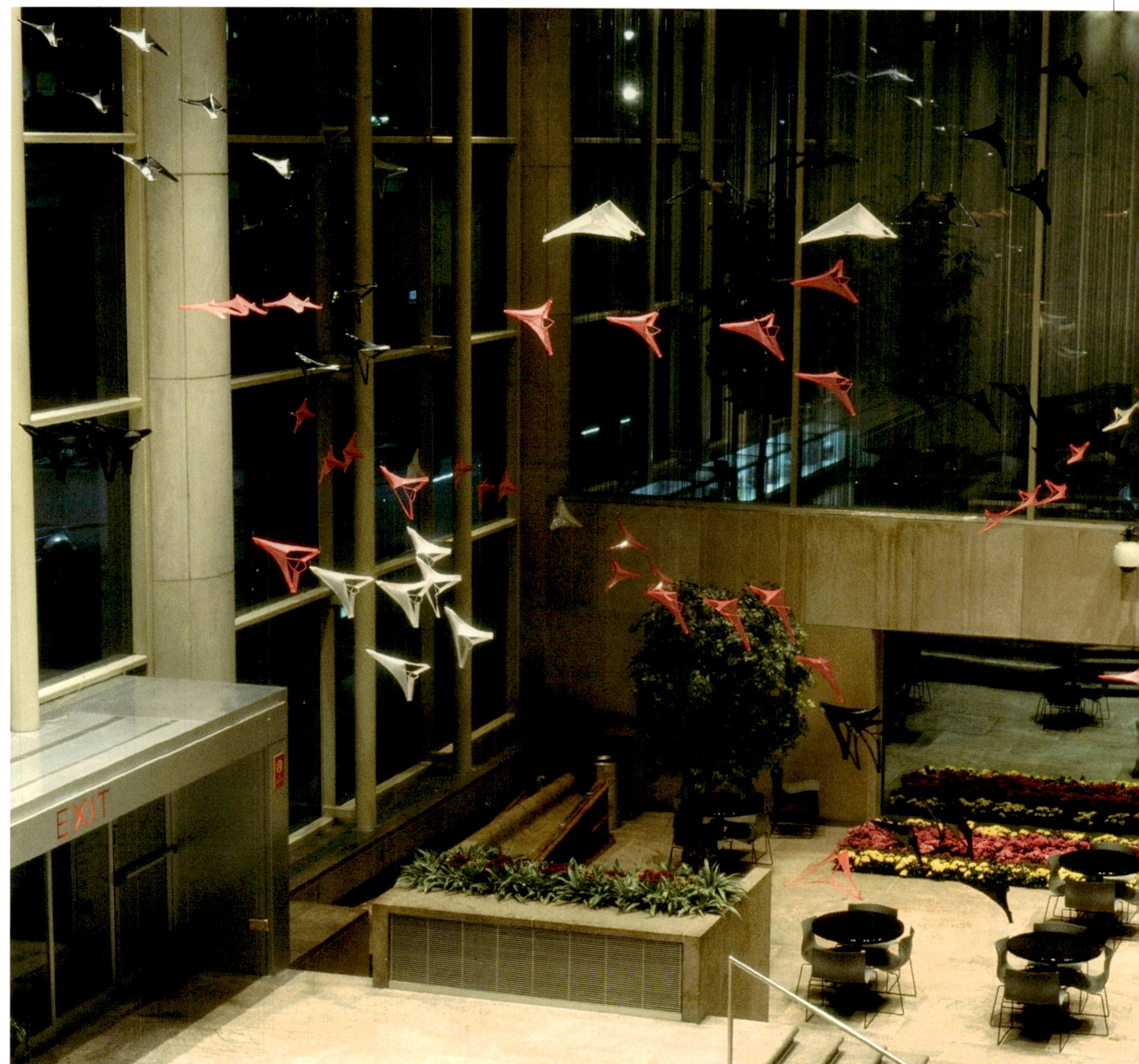

retains the essential shape of the dress, implying a transitional moment in which the dress (as woman) is dematerializing from this world to another—a sublime state of motion rather than one of violent rupture. The reference to the transporter in *Star Trek* links the work to an imagined world yet to come, a place still undefined and replete with possibility. Looking at the trajectory of Day's previous work, the thongs in *G-Force* might be the inhabitants of this other world, returning en masse in perfect, unified formation to survey the world they left behind.

The installation of *Transporter* also included a collection of Day's *Celestial Pelvis* sculptures—surgical wire shaped to suggest female genitalia and pelvic bones. Dripping with glittering drops of clear resin, the sculptures hung from the ceiling on monofilament, gently bobbing and swaying around the dematerializing silver dress. Like the thongs in *G-Force,* the pelvises glorify the female genital region, and are glamorous, self-sustaining, and self-propelled. Hung in groups that suggest a sentience similar to that of the thongs, the pelvises propose a creature

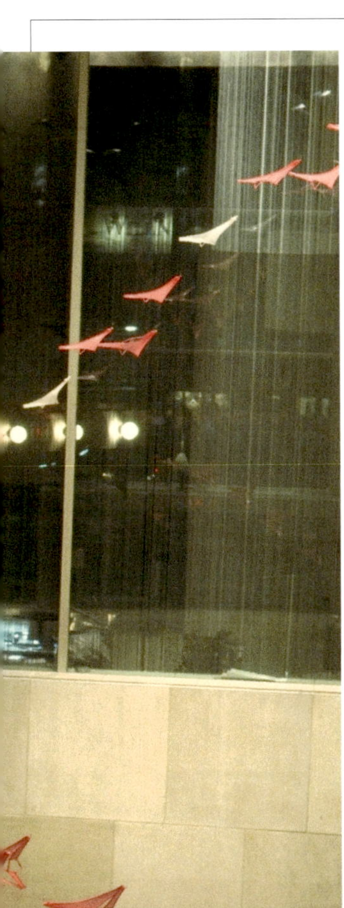

that is both familiar and alien, a hybrid state of being that suggests humanity but is clearly something else.

Like the *Celestial Pelvis* sculptures, much of Day's work explores the interface between the organic and technological that so captivates contemporary society. Day, however, rejects the moralizing nature/science dualism that commonly characterizes discussions of the issue. In her work, the pelvises, thongs, and dresses offer the possibility of beauty and transcendence. They are a potential evolutionary step forward rather than horrifying aberrations. For example, Day's wet-suit sculptures, dissected rather than exploded, are strung on surgical wire within metal, cagelike structures, that suggest the human form but as a new, artificial creature. Like peoples and societies on display at an anthropology museum, the wet suits are new beings to be observed. Yet the *Dissected Wetsuit* sculptures are not lifeless, sanitized, emotionless, and scientific—they are uncomfortably alive. The rubbery material and the suggestion of bondage or capture enhance the sexually suggestive position of the figures. Although fixed, the wet suits' various postures imply movement, bodies poised for action.

Unlike the glamorous, "feminine" materials of the *Exploding Couture* series, wet-suit fabric is technologically advanced, designed for performance enhancement rather than aesthetics. The dissected wet suits, like the dresses, suggest a moment of transformation, and offer the possibility of transcending bodily constraints through technology rather than fantasy. Day's work flirts with the questions, What is natural? What is artificial? It explores the body's limits and anticipates the inevitable desire to overcome them.

With *G-Force*, Day continues her investigation into the relationship between the organic and technological, and its inherent possibilities—both terrifying and thrilling—for transcendent synthesis. The thongs' sleek, elegant forms simultaneously suggest diving birds of prey and high-tech fighter jets. This relationship is reinforced by their configurations, which mimic the formations of fighter jets and migrating birds (on which jet patterns are based). Although the thongs' forms are streamlined, sharp, and potentially dangerous, they do not resemble the animated objects of horror and science fiction. The fleets of thongs convey purposiveness above all else, "flying with some kind of intent"[3] as they enter through the enormous windows, trace an exploratory reconnaissance around the space and then exit through the windows on the other side.

G-Force shares the fantastical aspects of Day's previous work that is anchored in popular culture by her choice of material. Like the dresses and wet suits, the thongs are re-envisioned, twisted and shaped into creatures whose basic material is not immediately recognizable. This is critical to the essential power of Day's work, which has been described as "respatializ[ing] cultural artifacts . . . expanding and re-editing their fixed cultural value."[4] Day goes further than revealing the dormant meanings embedded in these familiar objects—she transforms, and often explodes them.

Thus *G-Force* is comprised of thongs that might have been purchased and worn if not otherwise employed in the installation. Day had no interest in creating her own thongs, despite some initial difficulty in procuring the ones she wanted. To have designed her own thong would have been to create "a sculpture based on a thong,"[5] thereby weakening the installation's associative meaning by eroding its connection to the thongs' contemporary function. Using manufactured thongs also links the work to the commodification of desire and feminine sexuality, the material exchange of intangibles that underlies nearly all contemporary media.

The historical objectification of the female form, and its deconstruction by contemporary critical and cultural theorists, informs all of Day's work. However, despite the serious nature of these issues, Day never loses her appreciation for the comedic surreal or for physical, sensual impact. The interpretation of clothing as metaphor for the female body enriches the multilayered meaning of her *Exploding Couture* series, while at the same time the work embraces the idea of pleasure even as it critiques it. Day's feminism is passionately feminine, as evidenced by the delirious motion of the *Exploding Couture* dresses or the evocative glitter of the *Celestial Pelvis* sculptures. However, all the pieces have elements—the violence of the exploded dresses, the skeletal forms suggested by the dissected wet suits, and the lines of monofilament in the suspension pieces which recall gun sightlines—that carry a hint of danger and death. It is this consistent flux between sex, glamour, and violence that empowers her work. It is Day's acknowledgment of the humor inherent in that provocative and constantly changing equation that has earned her comparisons with the wry wit of Pop-era artists.

At the same time, Day's work can recall the ecstatic delirium of Baroque sculpture and painting, perhaps the first movement in which sensual pleasure in art was considered an end in itself. *Bombshell* "puts you in mind of things flying, female and climactic,"[6] and it is not far-fetched to compare it to Bernini's famous sculpture of St. Teresa, in which religious ecstasy is literalized as physical pleasure. St. Teresa's transcendent state is emphasized by Bernini's masterfully animated flying drapery (a Baroque technique often called "living drapery"). *G-Force* is entirely composed of similarly "living" articles of clothing. Like many characteristically Italian Baroque ceiling frescoes of the Virgin's or Christ's ascension, *G-Force* depicts

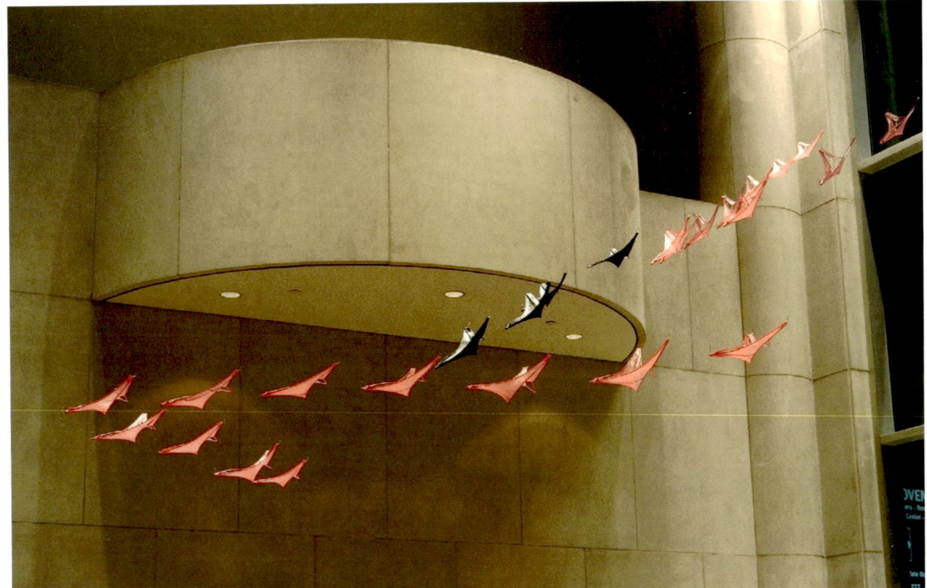

motion and drama that swirl out towards the boundaries of the composition and strain against a sense of stable centrality. The flying thongs, like the frescoes, suggest that transformation requires constant motion.

Unlike the *Exploding Couture* series, the thongs in *G-Force* do not merely substitute for the body in absence, but have been freed from the body altogether. Day reimagines the idea of a gendered object, giving the thongs a newly created sexuality. Each of the thongs is endowed with its own means to experience pleasure: during the process of stretching and coating the thongs with resin, Day inserted an iridescent pearl bead into what would have been the crotch of the panty. Though only occasionally visible to the viewer, this witty detail is characteristic of the artist's effortless tweaking of the line between humor and social critique. *G-Force* subtly unpacks one of the most prevalent contradictions of American society: the bottomless fascination with sexual display and exposure that coexists with strong undercurrents of Puritanism, and the fear of and desire to limit sexual power.

While the streamlined forms of the thongs evoke military strength and invulnerability rather than stereotypes of female passivity, Day's goal is not to project a clichéd notion of either gender. The thongs are "not there to drop bombs," nor as "feminist empowerment in the sense of women conquering, seeking, and destroying."[7] Rather, *G-Force* embodies the possibility of change where there is purpose, intent, and of course, pleasure. Real empowerment lies in the freedom to make one's own decisions. In *G-Force*, Day has endowed these formerly fetishistic objects with an ability to transcend conventions of gender and fashion in favor of agency. "The thong," as Day describes it, "is making a choice to cruise."[8]

—SHAMIM M. MOMIN, BRANCH CURATOR

1. Taped conversation with the artist, August 15, 2001.
2. From E.V. Day's notes.
3. Taped conversation with the artist, August 15, 2001.
4. Charles Beyer, introduction to "Day-Blow," interview by Stephen Sprouse, *Surface*, April 2000.
5. Taped conversation with the artist, August 15, 2001.
6. Deborah Solomon, "A Roll Call of Fresh Names and Faces," *The New York Times*, April 16, 2000.
7. Taped conversation with the artist, August 15, 2001.
8. Ibid.

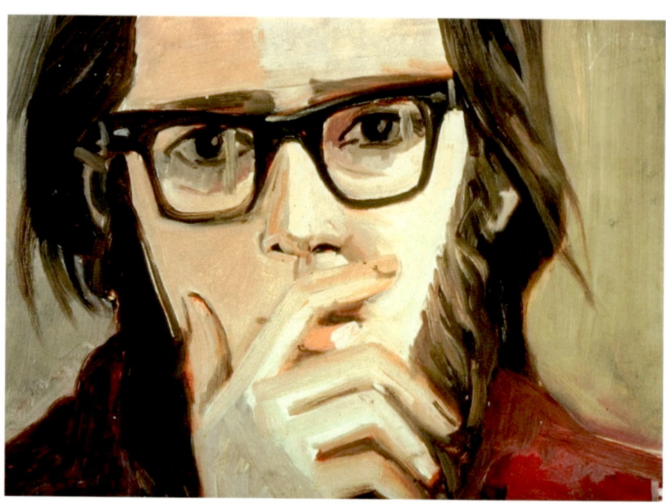

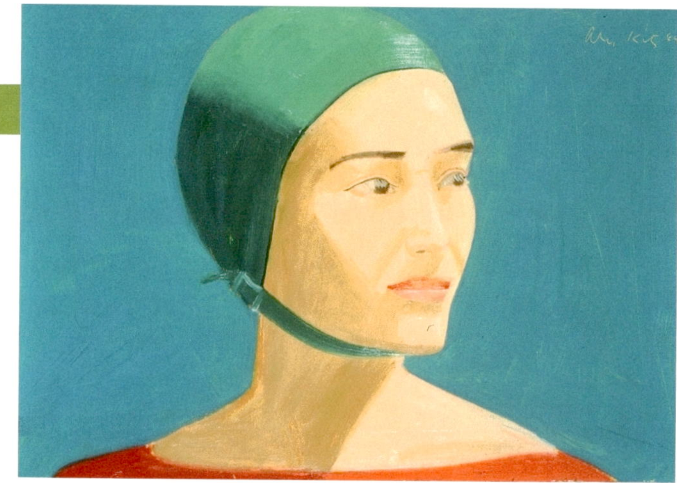

Alex Katz: Small Paintings

October 5, 2001 to January 4, 2002

Although best known for his unmistak-able large-scale images, Katz has produced a singular body of work, both monumental and small-scale, throughout his 50-year career. "Even though Katz considers the large works to be his major productions, the oil sketches reveal his initial passion for a subject . . ." said Shamim M. Momin, branch curator of the Whitney Museum of Art at Philip Morris and one of the co-organizers of the exhi-bition. "In these works, we discover that Katz is a master of intimate as well as public painting. He proves that a small surface can encompass bravura paint-ing just as well as a larger, open stretch of canvas. If Katz's big paintings are like public performances, the small oils are rehearsals that reveal not only how he works, but, more importantly, what matters most to him."

. . . In the early to mid-1950s, partly as a reaction to the large canvases of Abstract Expressionist artists, Katz be-gan painting intimate works, most measuring no more than 2 x 3 feet. In these works he developed the central focus, unmodulated colors, and flat shapes that eventually became the hall-mark of his art. Many of the works are portraits, both single-subject and figura-tive groups; portraits have been the mainstay of Katz's painting since the late 1950s. His subjects have most often been his wife Ada, his son Vincent, and his circle of friends, including many artists, poets, critics, and dancers.

Everyone knows that strange, marvelous, fleeting state between sleep and waking, when the mind is beginning to emerge from the realm of dreams into the more obdurate portion of existence we call "reality." It's a delicious moment when you can not only recall the manifold happenings of your dreams but also feel as if you comprehend their logic—that oblique, unpredictable narrative structure that, in a few minutes, will be as mysterious and incomprehensible as the script of a lost language.

This in-between state is extremely fragile. A turn of the head or a blink of the eye can be enough to make it vanish, but for as long as it lasts you seem to have been granted access to new realms of understanding. The experience of standing in front of one of Jane Hammond's thronging, multilayered, icon-rich paintings is not unlike this frontier zone of consciousness. The viewer is confronted with sets of wildly disparate images—Hammond has taken up subjects as diverse as erotic voyeurism and the life of her own grandmother— that seem to be linked by some not quite tangible order. Using brilliant visual rhymes and subtly ordered compositions, she enmeshes her fanciful figures and objects within cohesive, if sometimes bizarre, symbolic tales. Rejecting both

Jane Hammond: *Back Stage—Secrets of Scene Painting*

the irrational juxtapositions of Surrealism and the chilly disjunctions of postmodernism, Hammond crafts a unique visual syntax that, for all its imaginative leaps, invites our comprehension. —RAPHAEL RUBINSTEIN

Installation view of *Jane Hammond: Back Stage—Secrets of Scene Painting.*

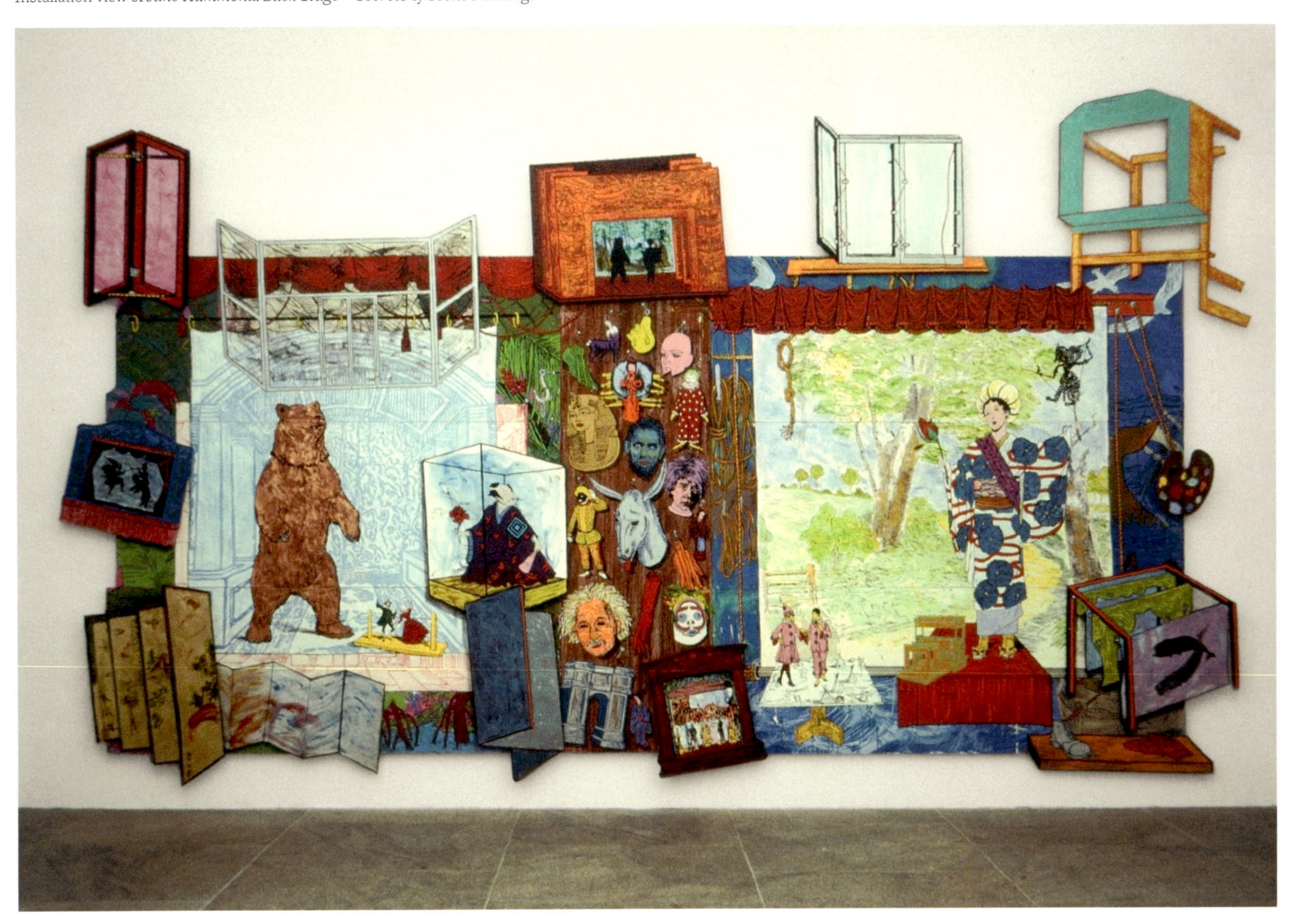

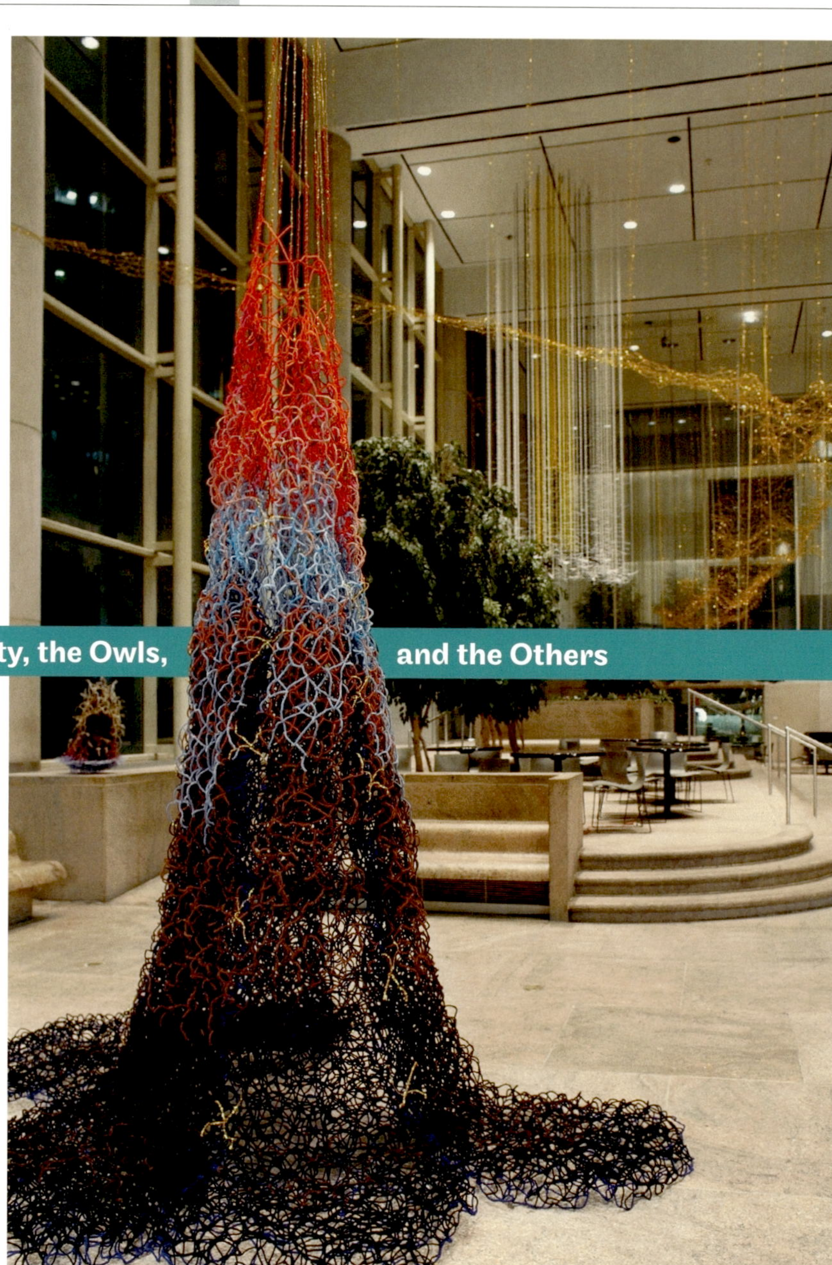

Lucky DeBellevue: Khlysty, the Owls, and the Others

January 18 to April 5, 2002

Turn away for a moment from the frenzied crowds and icy winds of midtown Manhattan and escape into the chimerical world of Lucky DeBellevue's multi-object installation *Khlysty, the Owls, and the Others*, currently inhabiting the Sculpture Court of the Whitney Museum of American Art at Philip Morris. After the disorder and claustrophobia of the street, the vast space of the Sculpture Court is especially remarkable, spanning over a hundred feet long and soaring forty feet above your head. The pink granite that cloaks the walls does little to soften the ponderously corporate effect of the architecture's powerful lines. . . .

Though all of the pieces are characterized by a painstaking attention to detail and labor-intensive creative process, they do not share any single pattern of construction. Rather, each structure's unique logic is determined incrementally, moment by moment, in a process that, while technically exacting, is notably and fundamentally human in its essence.

—SHAMIM M. MOMIN, BRANCH DIRECTOR AND CURATOR

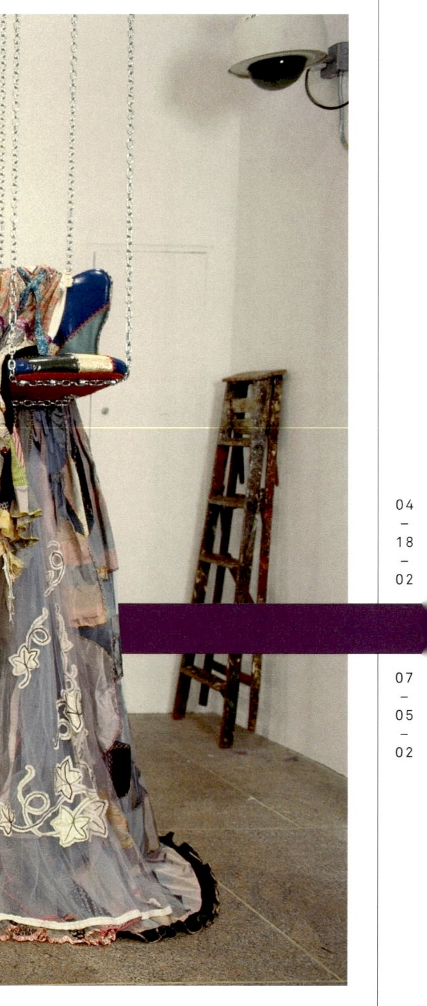

Five by Five: Contemporary Artists on Contemporary Art

April 18 to July 5, 2002

Five by Five: Contemporary Artists on Contemporary Art features new works commissioned from five contemporary artists alongside five contemporary works from the Whitney's permanent collection. Each invited artist was asked to select a contemporary work (1985–present) that he or she found personally important or influential, and then to create a work inspired by that piece. The title of the exhibition comes from a radio communiqué that numerically describes the strength and clarity of radio reception, "five by five" being the equivalent of "loud and clear." The phrase—which refers to a situation that is both complicated and changeable—recently reappeared in New York youth slang, creating a contemporary condition grounded in history. *Five by Five* visually creates a recent historical context for contemporary art while presenting a diverse and multilayered dialogue on what "contemporary" can mean.

Left to right: Mike Kelly, *More Love Hours Than Can Ever Be Repaid and Wages of Sin*, 1987; Larry Krone, *More Love Hours (No Charge)*, 2002 (installation view of *Five by Five: Contemporary Artists on Contemporary Art*).

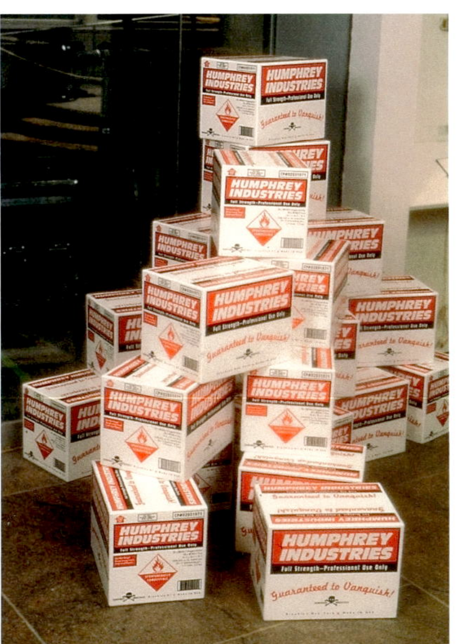

Ryan Humphrey, *Humphrey Industries Product Boxes; Humphrey T-Shirts*, 2002 (installation view of *Five by Five: Contemporary Artists on Contemporary Art*).

PERFORMERS	02

everton sylvester and searching for banjo

Ken Nintzel

Yasuko Yokoshi

David Neumann

Paul Henry Ramirez:
Space Addiction

July 18 to October 11, 2002

Seen from outside the gallery, the deep reds, pinks, and shades of orange-peach of Paul Henry Ramirez's *Space Addiction* beckon. Only upon entering the space itself, however, does the riot of color and form that comprises Ramirez's site-specific installation fully emerge. On the back wall of the gallery, three large panel paintings hover close to the floor, seemingly pushed by fingers of color extending from a velvety-matte block of red painted directly onto the wall. Soft-edged shapes, like geometric forms gone limp with satiated exhaustion, drape over one edge of this large color field. These shapes lead the eye to another set of paintings—seven rectangular panels stacked like children's blocks march-ing toward the ceiling. On the right wall, curved bars of color stretch from the floor and ceiling as if to gently support another series of canvases—concave swirls of concentric colors that create the impression of cartoon eyes peeking this way and that. Ramirez treats the wall it-self as another canvas; his wall painting extends around the entire gallery, drip-ping a large, stretchy pink form over the doorway valance, squirting up from the floor like a gush of multicolored liquid, or unfolding like a snake in thick curves of color. —SHAMIM M. MOMIN, BRANCH DIRECTOR AND CURATOR

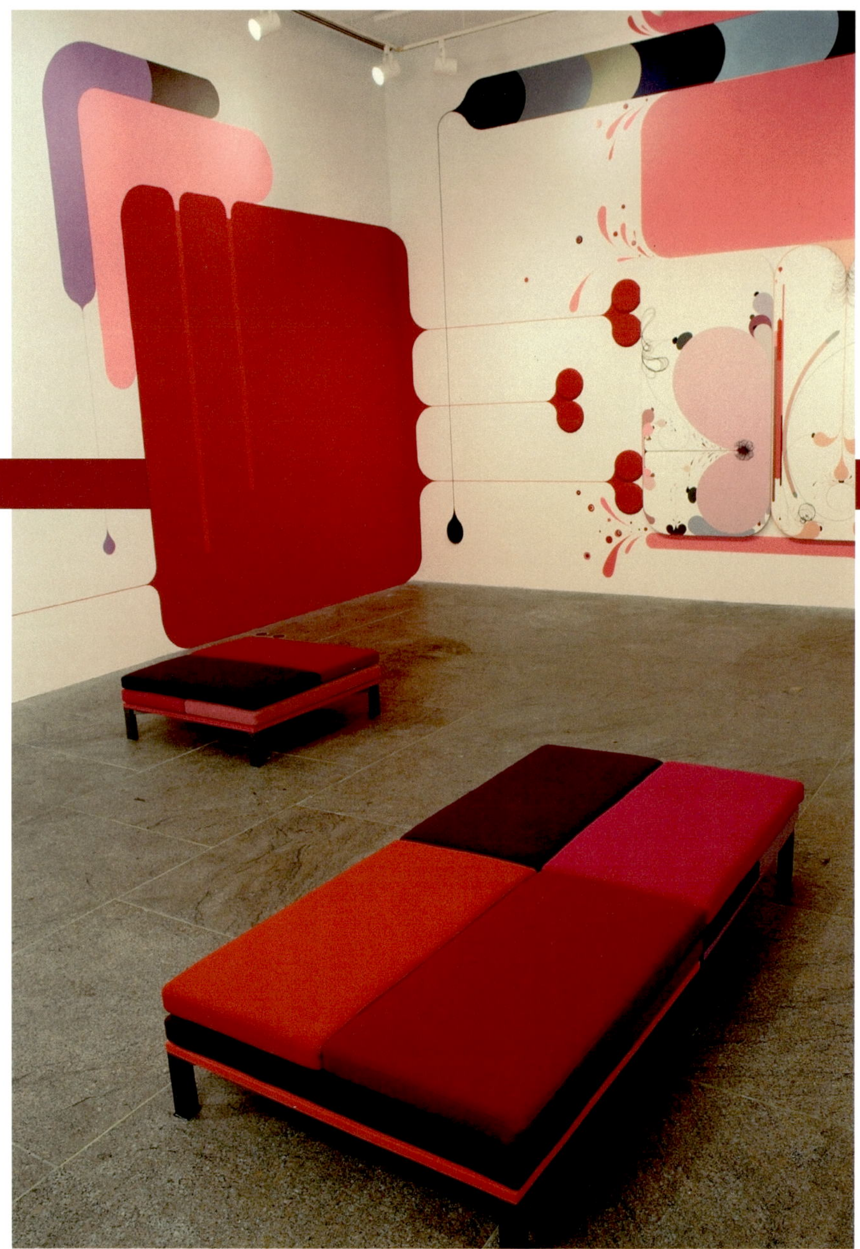

Installation view of *Paul Henry Ramirez: Space Addiction*. The seating units were created by Stuart Basseches.

July 18, 2002 to January 3, 2003

What is public urban space? Which characteristics define it, what types of activity does it offer? How does it shape the way we, as urban inhabitants, move through our daily lives? Above all, how do the spaces of the city affect our perception of ourselves and of the world around us? These questions address some of the issues that inform *Outer City, Inner Space*, an exhibition commissioned for the Whitney Museum at Philip Morris of three site-specific installations by artists whose work examines architectural and conceptual space. Teresita Fernández, Stephen Hendee, and Ester Partegàs were invited to consider the Museum's Sculpture Court and especially the specifics of its construction, function, and use. Each of these works investigates the phenomenological experience of constructed space and the perceptual and social impact of urban life on the way individuals interact with it. As public artworks that address public space, the installations negotiate a subtle shift in meaning, at the same time self-referential and integrally related to function and site. These works reflect the changing nature of contemporary public art and emphasize the critical part played by the audience and its spatial interaction with a given work—unlike many historical examples of public sculpture,

Outer City, Inner Space

which allow the viewer only a purely contemplative role. Rather than fixing on the object or the psychological state of the artist, the central conceit of this work is the experience it provokes for those who encounter it. —SHAMIM M. MOMIN, BRANCH DIRECTOR AND CURATOR

Stephen Hendee, *War Gems*, 2002
(installation views of *Outer City, Inner Space*).

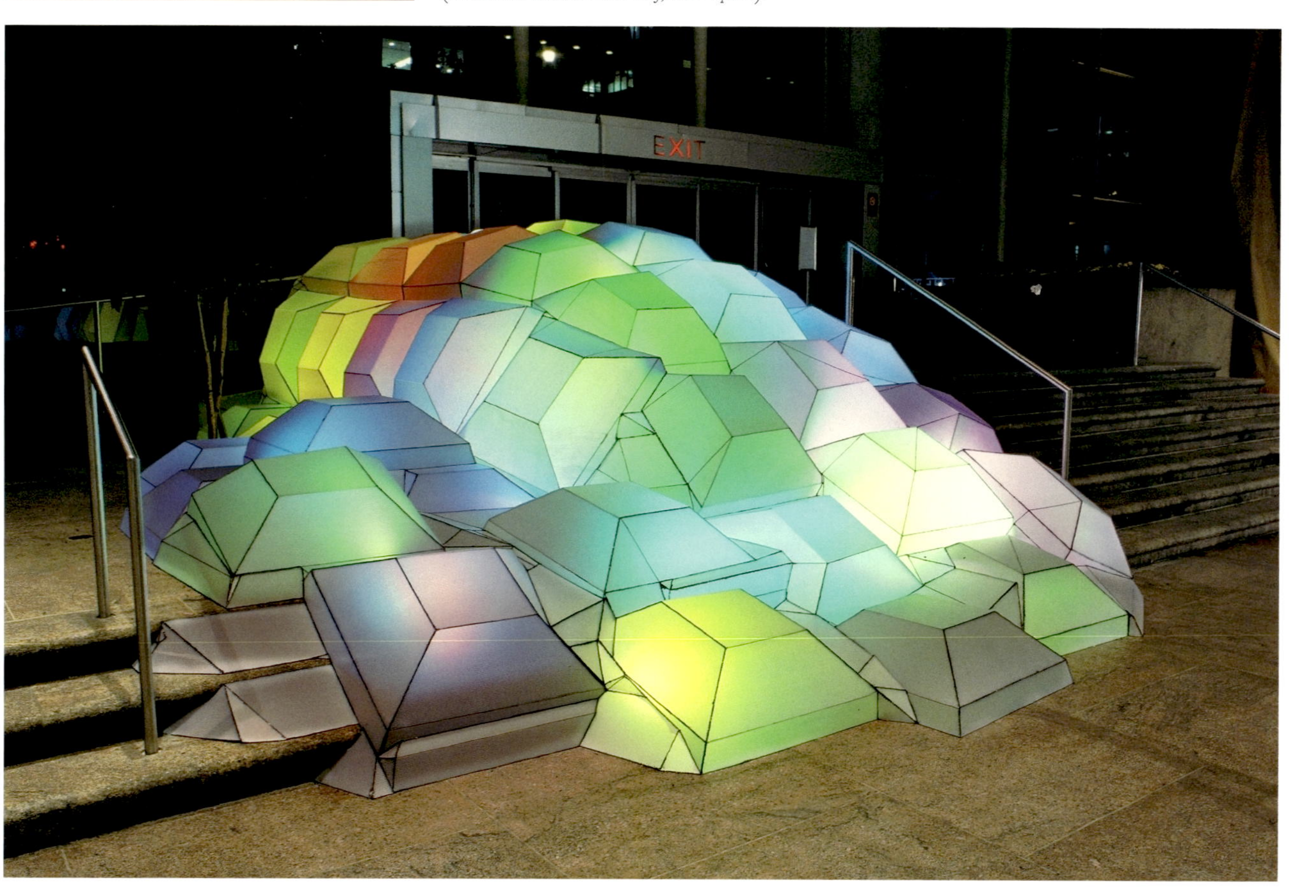

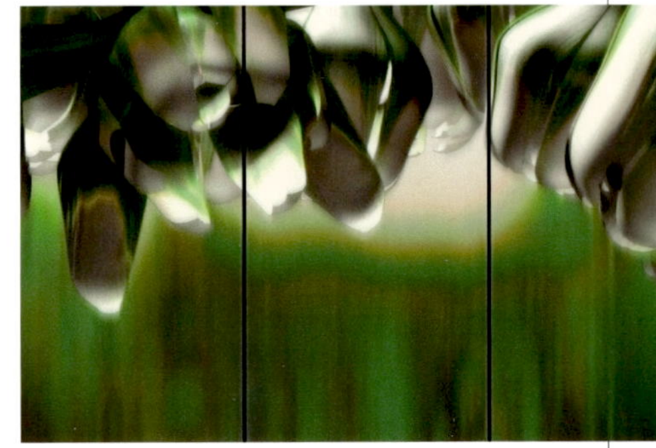

Stills from *Haluk Akakçe: Illusion of the First Time.*

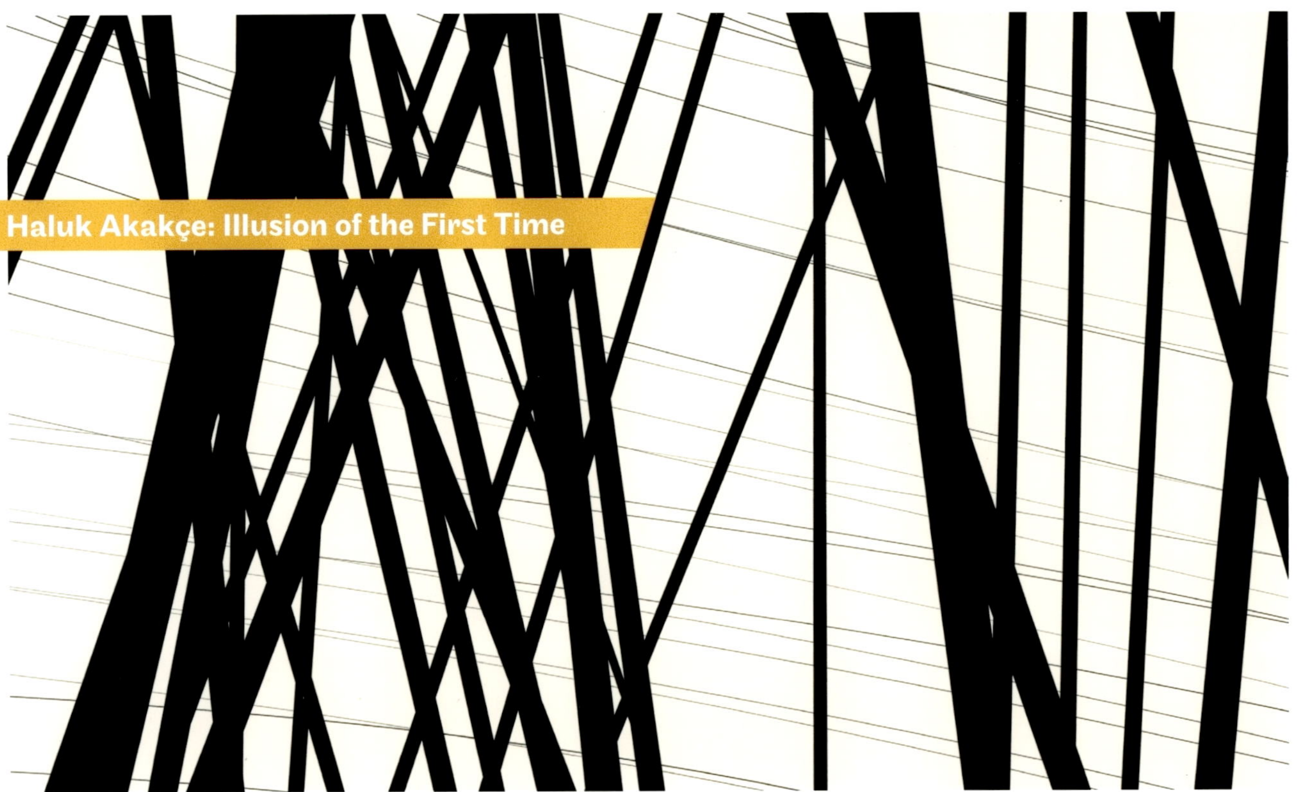

Haluk Akakçe: Illusion of the First Time

October 28, 2002 to January 10, 2003

In the gallery, the viewer enters an interior room cloaked in a soft blackness. The high ceilings and the tight dimensions of the walls form a space both intimate and reverent, intensifying the silence. On the facing wall, three large projected images merge into a single mural-size frame, cycling through three "compositions" in a symphony of shape and image. The first is silent, echoing the graphic black lines of the exterior wall but here moving in increasingly hectic motion, rushing past one another almost anxiously in every direction—both across the plane of the wall and seemingly into the depth of the surface itself. The second section evolves slowly from a deep graded darkness into shadowy, slow-moving organic shapes that drift gently down the surface with increasing density, spiraling like loosened strands of a DNA helix and accompanied by an eerie, beautiful score. The third composition is heavy with diffuse, watery color, rich to the eye after the intense gray scale of the previous two. Spinning and unfolding slowly, as if rising through water, indeterminate techno-organic objects float upward through melting greens and pinks.

—SHAMIM M. MOMIN, BRANCH DIRECTOR AND CURATOR

A Whitney for the Whitney at Altria (2003) is constructed around the Museum's recently published collection catalogue. An enormous gold frame, with the exhibition title painted overhead, borders the granite doorframe of the gallery at the branch Museum. To enter, the viewer must step over the frame and into the space beyond, effectively entering the picture. Before even opening the doors to the gallery, the viewer has engaged a critical aspect of Harvey's project, which literalizes multiple definitions of a frame: "a structure made for admitting, enclosing, or supporting something," "to give expression to," or "to fit or adjust to something in order to achieve a desired outcome or interpretation." . . .

Passing through Harvey's gold frame, the viewer enters a room constructed within the gallery made of 10-foot-high panels bearing painted copies of each of the 394 images featured in *American Visionaries*. Though painted directly onto the panels, the copies appear to hang salon-style. Roughly following the alphabetical ordering in the catalogue, each copy is scaled twice as large as its printed image. Rectangular openings in the panels reveal artworks—the actual objects, rather than painted copies— placed behind the walls at seven points. Hung as in a typical gallery, they are only visible in their entirety when the viewer stands extremely close to the corresponding cutout frame.

—SHAMIM M. MOMIN, BRANCH DIRECTOR AND CURATOR

Ellen Harvey: A Whitney for the Whitney at Altria

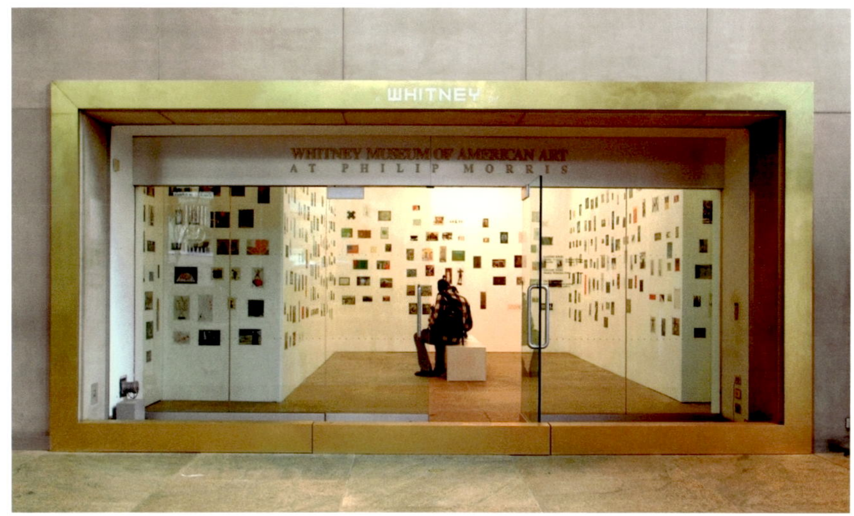

PERFORMERS	03
Elizabeth Brown	
Geoffrey Nutter	
Suzanne Wise	
Rebecca Wolff	

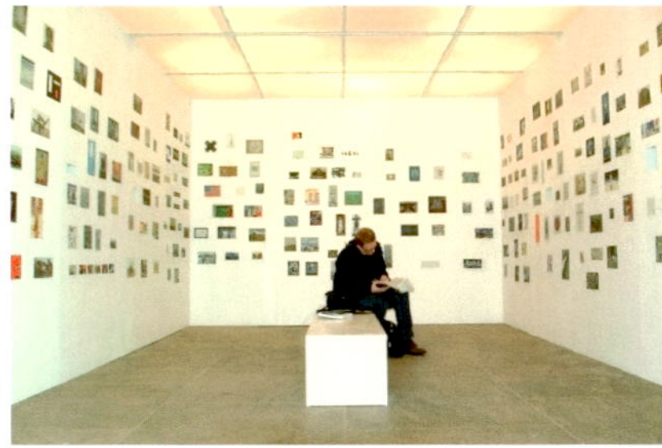

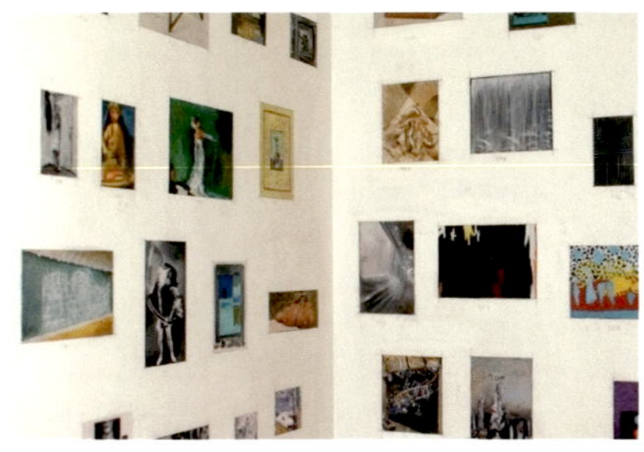

Installation views of *Ellen Harvey: A Whitney for The Whitney at Altria.*

April 17 to July 3, 2003

(Re)Making the World: Dario Robleto's Say Goodbye To Substance

If we as a generation have been given nothing but the wreckage of the past, then I say thank God for that … We are all social archaeologists now—mining raw history and actively participating in its critique and reconstruction/re-enchantment. Let the digging begin. —DARIO ROBLETO

We live in a time of extraterrestrial hopes and anxieties. —MARTIN AMIS, *INVASION OF THE SPACE INVADERS*

Are we unique? Are we something utterly special in the universe? Or are we an example of many, many different civilizations that have emerged, many, many different life forms? —SAMPLE USED IN "ARE WE HERE" BY ORBITAL, *SNIVILISATION*

Dario Robleto's work is deeply rooted in a desire for regeneration—a mad scientist's version of cultural archaeology, developing a newly envisioned song of the future with an alchemical beat. Through meticulous research into materials

Dario Robleto: Say Goodbye to Substance

and historical/pop cultural systems ranging from music to paleontology to space travel, Robleto creates enticingly intimate objects that weave a tale of an alternate world. Based deeply in the power of music and its inherent possibilities for transformation, Robleto limns his multiple narratives into propositions for the future. He likens his process to that of a DJ—mixing, sampling, recombining—but his is an evolution in aesthetic strategy, serving not so much to undermine notions of originality and authorship as to acknowledge the weight of meaning that objects and materials carry. Robleto locates the revolutionary impact of sampling as "a youth cultural movement that actually cherished history—there is no such thing as a good DJ who is historically ignorant." Similarly, his work builds narrative webs, with multiple layers of stories and ideas that reinvent the past in order to reinvigorate the future. Robleto is, above all, a master storyteller—a raconteur in the ancient way, in which pleasure and engagement are symbiotic with criticality, reinvention, and wisdom.

Robleto's wryly humorous titles and elaborate materials lists are critical aspects of the work, reflecting the way he builds his objects almost as if he were writing a complex text. The weight of information inherent in Robleto's materials and his process—what he calls "clues to the story"—is an integral part of the exhibition. The text following each entry is in the artist's voice, his own walk-through of the exhibition. My additional information and commentary in *blue* similarly gestures to Robleto's interest in layered narrative, here physically coexisting with his own story. —SHAMIM M. MOMIN, BRANCH DIRECTOR AND CURATOR

03 PERFORMERS

Cynthia Hopkins

Ben Munisteri Dance Projects

Gale Gates et al.

Ethel

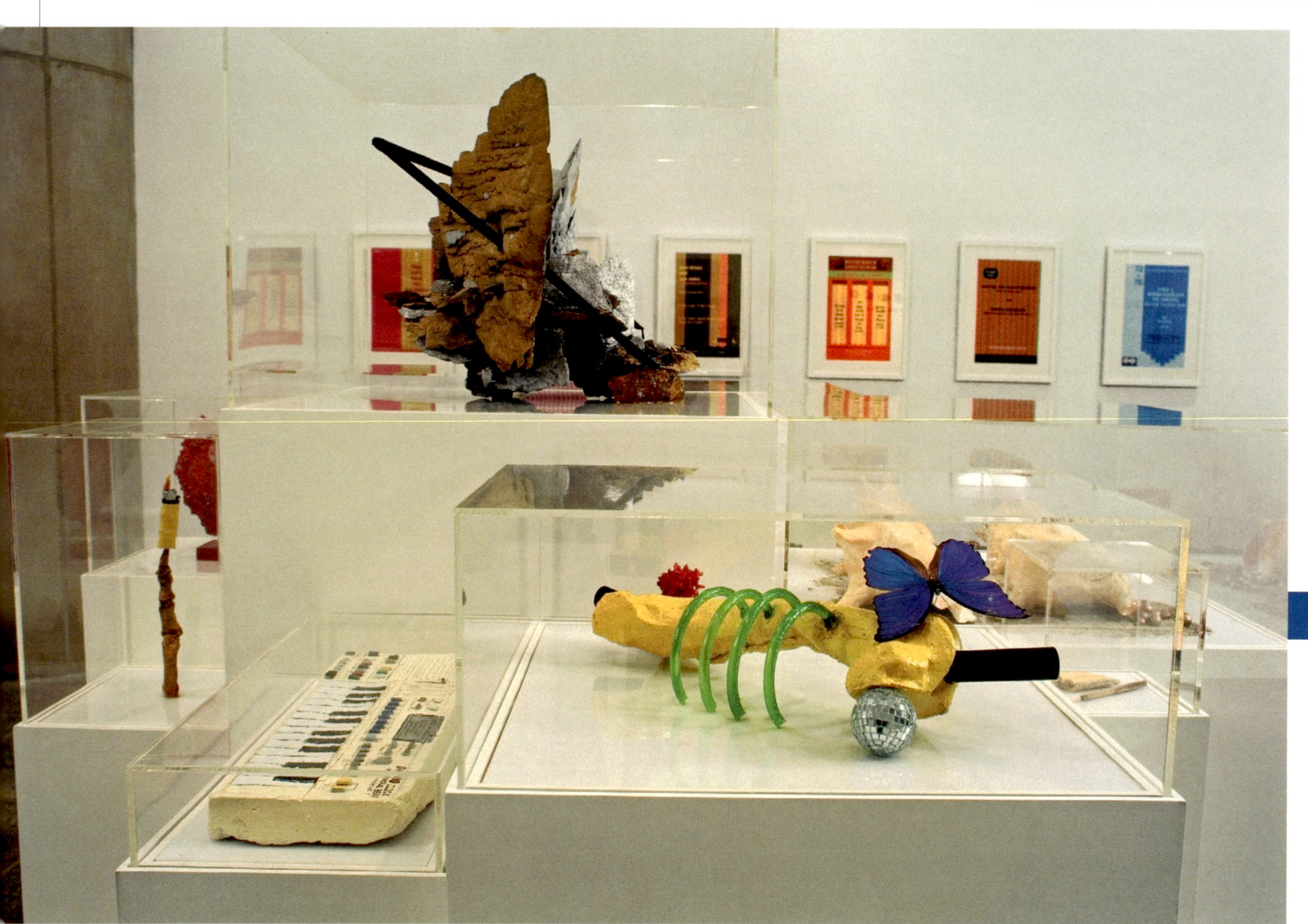

1. Voyager 1 and 2 were launched, respectively, in August and September of 1977, and were slated to arrive at Jupiter in 1979 and Saturn in 1980. Both were equipped with 12-inch, gold-plated copper records designed by Carl Sagan that were meant to convey the diversity of life and culture on Earth, should they be encountered by another civilization. A needle and cartridge accompanied the records, along with instructions in symbolic language that explained the origin of the spacecraft and indicated how the record was to be played. Each record contained 115 images and a variety of natural sounds, such as those made by surf, wind, and thunder, as well as birds, whales, and other animals. They also contained musical selections from different cultures and eras, spoken greetings in 55 languages ranging from ancient Sumerian to modern-day Chinese, and messages from President Jimmy Carter and U.N. Secretary General Kurt Waldheim. Traveling faster than its successor, Voyager 1 is presently about 11 billion kilometers from the Earth and is moving away at a speed of 17 km/s. Light from the Earth takes over 11 hours to reach Voyager 1; in the past few months, scientists have determined that we have received the last faint return signals from the ship.

The exhibition's central sculpture, Popular Hymns Will Sustain Us All (End It All), *sets the tone for the whole show, and the story that I developed for it has dictated what I have built around it.* Popular Hymns *is based on the Voyager spacecraft. I was around 8 years old when the Voyager left our solar system. There was a number you could call to hear its last message. I was excited at the idea, but when I called, it was just a series of beeps. It was such a lesson about science as science: what I had considered the romance of space was really just ones and zeroes, in a way its own romance but not what I had in mind. I've always held on to that disappointment—it felt so important, even at that age, to find that something you envision as so deep, so profound, in the end isn't quite like that.*

The spirit of the Voyager has always intrigued me: essentially, it was a mixed tape of humankind. Imagine being Carl Sagan and selecting what was to be included on that mission in the event of an alien encounter; what a privilege it must have been for him to be the DJ that sampled our world.[1] *What pressure he must have felt in making the mixed tape of humankind— you don't want to forget anything. I love that somebody at NASA thought,* just in case, let's have our story on board. Such things meant a lot to me when I was getting into science. For Popular Hymns, I wanted my own version of a mixed tape of humankind—to tell that story in sculpture. I wanted it to be a floating dance floor, with multiple platforms on each of which I attempted to address some moment or dilemma of human history. The piece is recessed at the bottom, so that it hovers slightly above the ground, and the lighting system that rhythmically illuminates the top of each pedestal makes it appear as if it is ready for liftoff. The lights alternate to four different beats of music—different popular hymns.

I limited myself to 10 sculptures, each based on preceding vinyl work but with new materials.[2] The sculpture A Dark Day For The Dinosaurs is founded on an actual cave bear digit. Many scientists believe that this particular species of cave bear was the first animal that humans pushed to extinction. The bears were competing for caves at the same significant moment that humans were exerting dominance on other species for the first time. So this is the origin of what has become a bigger problem in our history.

Of course, the vinyl records that I choose to make my objects from play an important part in telling the story. Perched on the tip of the cave bear digit is a lighter that I made from dissolved 8-track recordings of Black Sabbath's "Iron Man." The flame is made from T-Rex's "Life's A Gas." In the history of rock and roll, there is an ongoing extinction: rock is always supposedly "dead." Here I took two forms—heavy metal and glam rock—that have gone the way of dinosaurs as art forms but are still evocative of specific moments. The play on words is not just with the song titles—the ephemeral lightness of what we think so serious, coupled with the heroic celebration of humankind's aggressive nature—but also with the sculpture, which is essentially a translated version of the band names, Black Sabbath and T-Rex. The gesture being made in the sculpture is important as well—the role of the lighter in rock concerts. It comes out at the ballad or the last song, or at some heightened, dramatic moment. Here, I took the lighter out to say goodbye to the dinosaur, who is participating in his own farewell.

Another piece, entitled Falsetto Can Be A Weapon, is a small functional dart gun that I constructed. It is important to me that all my sculptures seem timeless. In this case, the gun appears to be a handcrafted, early hunter-gatherer artifact. In fact, it is hand-carved, fossilized ivory from a mammoth, another creature we pushed into extinction. Each piece of ivory is enlaced with what appears to be poison, made from melted vinyl. I used Tammy Wynette's "Stand By Your Man," suggesting that perhaps something about the song could be seen as poisonous. This is a great but also controversial song, involving the complicated issues of women's roles and feminism. How could a woman take such a subservient role as to "stand by her man," and yet who can deny the romance of such a commitment? I like the implication that this song could literally become lethal—that in your bloodstream, the vinyl would attack your system and lead to

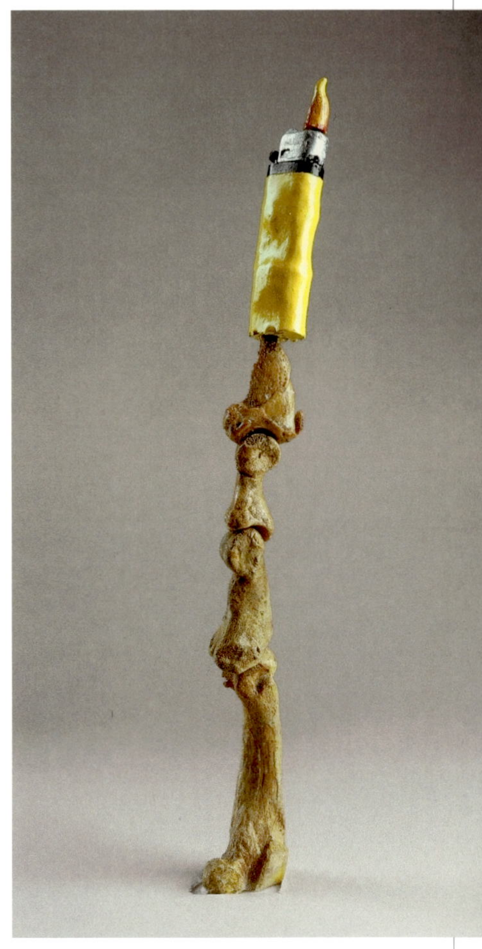

2. In his earlier work, Robleto developed a process in which he scratched vinyl records into powder and used the dust in a reconstituted medium to create his sculptures. In a sense, he aimed to capture the soul of the music through a transformation of its own medium. The layered associations of the selected songs richly evoke music's nearly universal emotional power. As his work evolved, Robleto began combining this symbolic technique with other categorical systems—science, technology, history—and other loaded media, but his attention to materials and their associative power remains as rigorous as his conceptual research.

your collapse. It is a play on what the song is about and what I am suggesting it does to your body: it may not be such a nice song after all. But it has a sort of poignant beauty in that, musically, it is also a complicated song, a particular style of country music. As the title of the overall piece implies, I wanted to represent a variety of popular forms of music in these works. [3]

The sculpture This Mineral I Call A Beat *addresses artistic endeavors specific to a particular moment. There was a wonderful moment in early electronic music and hip hop sampling when certain instruments designed by Sony and Casio started to appear for the first time—instruments that were both used and abused by musicians. The misuse of early samples of keyboards and drum machines became the backbone of new and revolutionary forms of music. I was intrigued by the idea that misuse of an instrument could blossom into a whole new musical genre, as well as the larger idea of our relationship with technology and how it transforms things in unexpected ways.* [4] This Mineral I Call A Beat *is an attempt to fulfill my desire of always wanting to have made one of those instruments. I've made this machine out of a number of raw materials and elements, as part of an investigation of how sound and material interact. For example, there is a button made of carved sulfur. What happens if you press this button? What does sulfur sound like? I am interested in the relationship between the way music is made and its direct impact on the body. A large amount of the same minerals that constitute our bodies is also found in the keyboard; so the piece also suggests the possibility that you could create someone, or something organic, by playing its keys. Or that by releasing sulfur sound, it would materialize into something else—almost transubstantiation. It is an instrument of multiple transformation, instead of merely being one for sound—one that translates into materials, into life.* [5]

3. Robleto has said that songs are "liquid"—like water cycling in the atmosphere, changing composition but never disappearing. This seems an apt metaphor for the perseverance of humanity that Popular Hymns both critiques and celebrates. As a symbolic system, music provides the perfect ambiguity through which to filter ideas; it is endlessly adaptable and relevant to specific circumstances. The story of music has always been the story of humanity, from the great epic struggles of love and death, to the minor daily skirmishes of desire and despair.

4. Robleto's view of DJ culture—specifically sampling—as a truly transformative contemporary creative process is reflective of a larger cultural change from a deconstructive, postmodern remove to a reinvented notion of creation: neo-modern perhaps, or, searching for an altogether new term, even protofuturity. Taking as its motto a line from T.S. Eliot's The Dry Salvages, "Not fare well, But fare forward, voyagers," it is characterized by a sincerity built out of deeply internalized cynicism and doubt, by hope engendered by the end of past practices, and by a renewed belief in the future—one that synthesizes the dissolution of definitions with the possibility of creating new ones. It is critically situated within a reinterpreted notion of origin that emphasizes permutation and expanded vectors rather than a linear beginning or end, with a reinvigorated desire for emotional commitment. Robleto asks, "What if one said no to boredom, and demanded romance—not for a moment, but as a social formation? This is what the aesthetics of sampling offer—a re-enchantment with the world . . . Sampling is about having a profound respect for Foucault but only falling to your knees for Patsy Cline . . . It is based on gut, on rhythm, on soul."

5. Robleto has referred to the dance floor as a "site of redemption"—a striking use of religious terminology that, coupled with the sculpture's titular reference, evokes a notion of transformation through belief. The arrangement of Popular Hymns' 10 pedestals in contiguous, semicircular form and blinking lights intended to recall a dance floor links this idea of redemption with his remaking of human history. The notion of transubstantiation offered via music modeled through This Mineral I Call A Beat also conjures a new faith through Popular Hymns overall, grounded both in the specificity of popular culture and the infinite imaginings evoked by space.

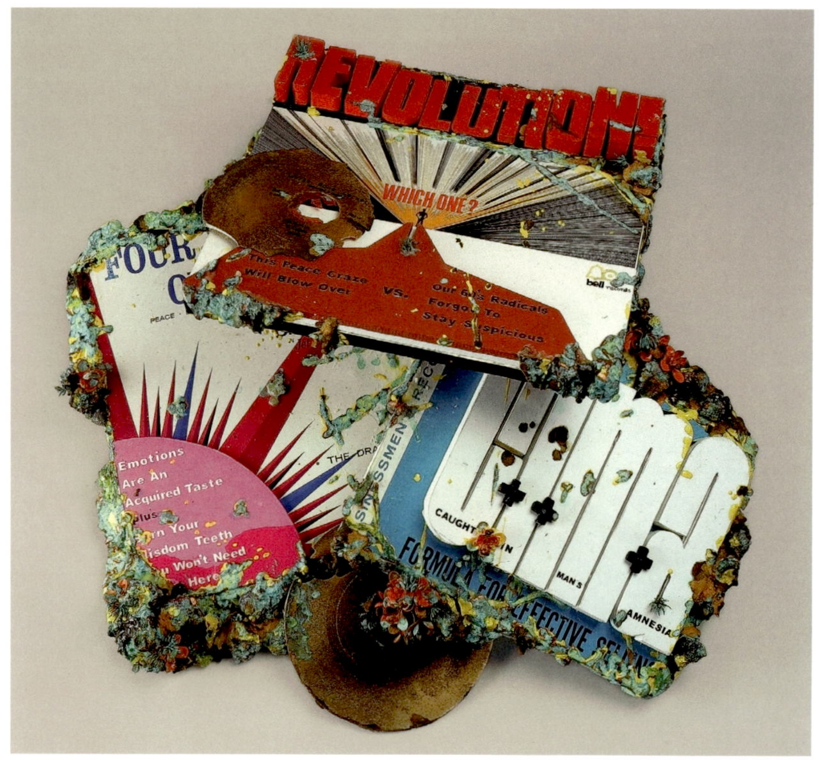

Dario Robleto, *A Pair Of Spinning Pop Stars Tethered By A Ribbon Of Gas And Dust (Lust)*, 2002. Sulfur-coated beeswax, amethyst, prehistoric Colombian amber, home-made crystals, altered record covers, paper, foamcore, glue, prehistoric whale bone dust, melted vinyl of Nirvana's record "In Bloom" and Marvin Gaye's record "Mercy Mercy Me (The Ecology)," gunpowder, antibiotics, polyester resin, letraset, and spray paint.

In Popular Hymns, *through the selection of specific songs and sculptural forms, I wanted to address humankind's problem of destroying, as well as creating. In making a mixed tape of humankind, I wanted to address some fundamental problems. When the story of humanity is told someday, these problems will have to be included.*[6]

As I mentioned, Popular Hymns *dictated the rest of the show. The diptych* Nowadays I Only Look Up To Pray *and* If A Meteorite Falls On Your Head Then God Was Aiming *were meant to function together. The ideas in these works are similar to the central theme of* Popular Hymns, *in that they involve humankind dealing with problems; yet here it takes the form of self-annihilation.*

The kaleidoscope in the first is custom-made; I worked with a toy maker to get the exact dimensions I wanted. The glass inside I treated like stained glass. It is trinitite, which is glass produced by a nuclear explosion—specifically, from the first test explosion in the United States in 1945. The physics of it is beautiful: the intense heat from the impact of the blast literally melted the desert sand into glass. It has this incredible historical resonance, being a remnant of the worst kind of explosion produced in history. Through the kaleidoscope, the viewer looks into the eye of

6. *The narrative webs that structure all of Robleto's work rely on an expanded sense of time, beyond the strictly linear. In fact,* Popular Hymns *stems specifically from Robleto's observation of the "way we are determined to control [time] by the creation of historical fantasies." In making his own version of history, Robleto conflates different notions of time, ranging from the elastic experience of musical contemplation, the curious timelessness of memory, and stratified and expansive geological time, to the emphatic present of consumer culture and the curvature of space-time. The objects themselves are formally evocative of this diverse temporality, their rough, organic contours feel authentic yet they remain resistant to being placed in a specific period.*

7. *Death, or obsolescence, is inevitable for both humans and objects, and our ever-present knowledge of that terminality defines life. The existentialist philosopher Martin Heidegger (1889–1976) termed it being-toward-death: the transitory nature of the present is not taken to show its insignificance, or to lead to a form of life in which one ignores the present in favor of either the future or the past; rather, all experience becomes present experience. Music and narrative have always functioned with this assumption in mind, recognizing that everything miraculous in the world matters because of the inevitable fact of its passing, and moments have emotional weight because they are ephemeral. There is no human subjectivity that is not structured in relationship to a profound sense of loss. Robleto's reuse and radical reinvention of pre-existing and often discarded objects acknowledge this condition, and seek at least a temporary immortality in face of this inevitable demise.*

the worst thing human beings can produce, yet it is made into an enjoyable experience, in a sense questioning how to relate to such an event.

The first piece, positioned to look down on the second, is created along similar lines but out of impact glass—glass that results from a meteorite crashing into the desert, where again the intense heat produces pure glass. I used this glass to make 10 marbles and sketched out a game being played in dust made of dinosaur and human bones. This is suggestive of how the dinosaurs died—by meteorite impact, a natural event. While this annihilation seems horrible, when viewed on a grand level it presents the idea that when one thing dies, another rises up to take its place. We are here now, and we have that meteorite to thank for it.[7]

I've made that act into a game of marbles, where the parameters are made out of the dust of the creature that the "marbles" symbolically eradicated—evoking the issues of chance and retribution. The question of whether a species might "deserve" their annihilation—relevant in considering our own fate—is generated by the relationship of the two works together. Whether we do it to ourselves or it is an act of God, somehow we will end up as dust if we are not careful.

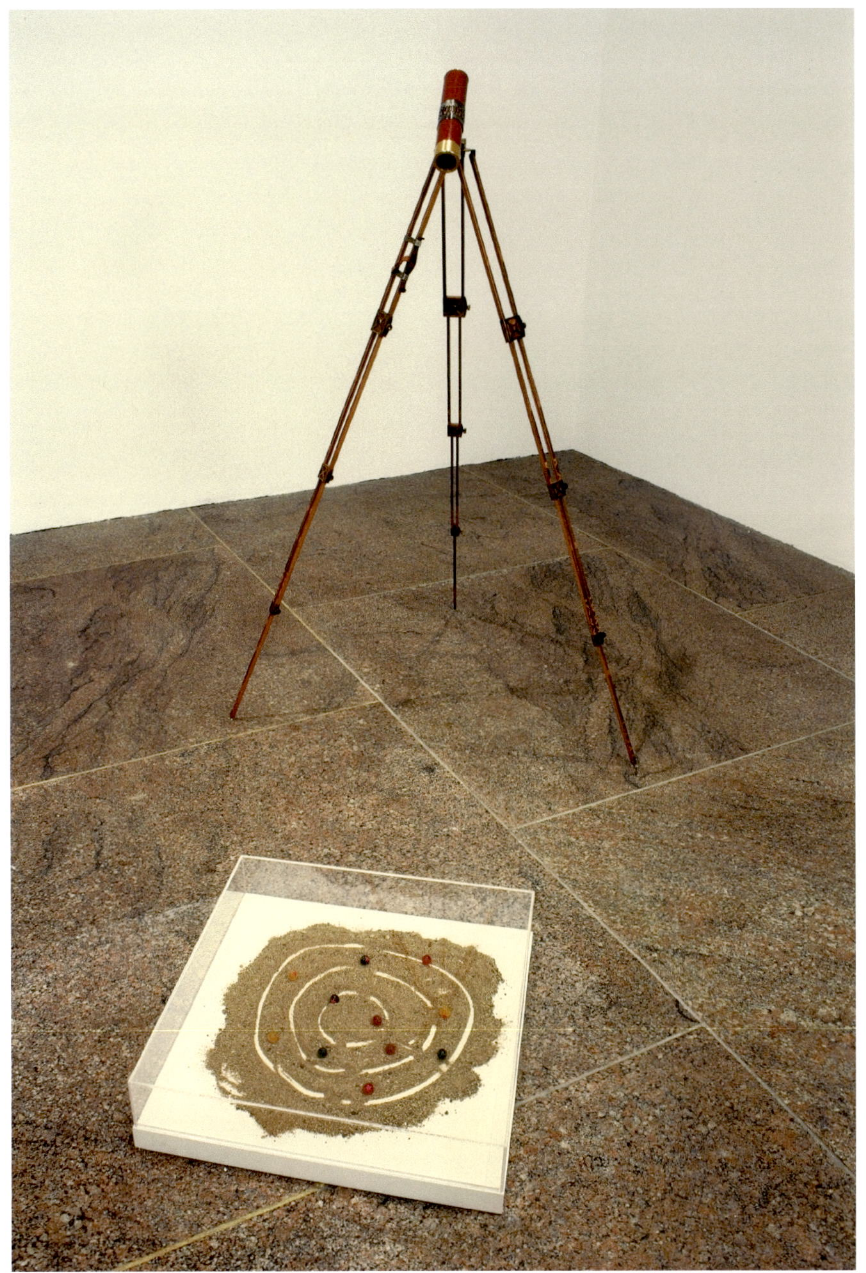

Dario Robleto, *Nowadays I Only Look Up To Pray*, 2001–02. Custom-made kaleidoscope, wood, brass, mirrors, hand-ground trinitite (glass produced during the first nuclear test explosion, when heat from the blast melted the surrounding sand), and antique wood and brass tripod, dimensions variable. Dario Robleto, *If A Meteorite Falls On Your Head Then God Was Aiming*, 2002. Marbles made from impact glass (glass produced when a meteorite strikes the Earth and melts the surrounding sand) and hand-ground human and dinosaur dust from femur bones, dimensions variable.

When I used Men Are The New Women *in a recent show, it was primarily a look at the effect of war on the body. The idea of transformation was set in the context of warfare's effects on the body, in which the soldier's body is the site of all kinds of people's politics. Less specifically, to use the body or the bones (the remains of the body) implies the destruction of the body. But when you take* Men Are The New Women *and put it in the context of* Popular Hymns, *it is pulled out of its center of gravity; I view it as a sort of bonus track.[8] It is like some B-side you didn't get on the mixed tape. The whole exhibition is, in part, a commentary on our destructive habits, and* Men Are The New Women *is the "what-if" scenario.*

Instead of warfare, the work's aspect of transformation—of remaking the origin—becomes prominent in this show. The biblical story of origin has always intrigued me: the idea of the female being produced from the male, that women didn't exist until men got lonely.[9] As someone who is interested in materials, it always struck me that in this story women weren't even given their own molecules. In Men Are The New Women, *the crucial act is taking a female rib, grinding it to dust, and recasting it as a male rib. It is a simple gesture—not technically, but rather that it can be stated so simply—and yet the ramifications are huge. I spent a great deal of time and effort making it look authentic; the idea of the piece is to present it as fact, not fiction. If the bone looks real, then the implications of it hit you much harder. If it were real, imagine how that would change the way society has evolved, based both on interpretations of gender that the creation myth was founded on in the Western world, as well as later notions of scientific truth. That was my mission—a work of art that would present an alternate route through history.*

I love that there is openness to the interpretation of this piece, and my motivation wasn't necessarily that a matriarchal world is better than a patriarchal one. Wouldn't women hate, too? My suggestion was more, how did we get here, to a place where it is necessary to start over? Why do we have to try something else? Why does it even have to be considered?

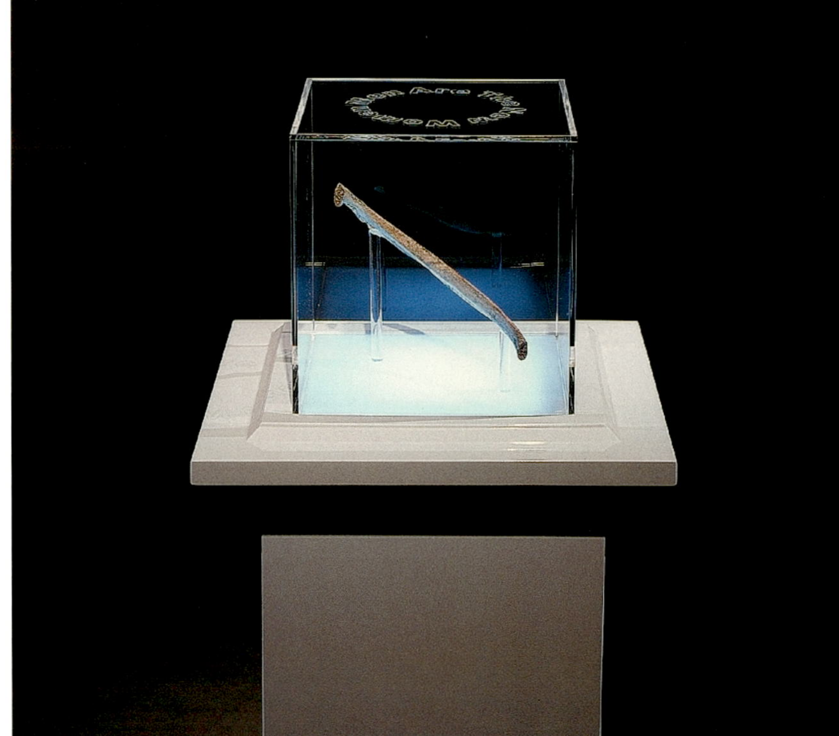

8. *Robleto applies his strategy of remixing not just within the specific objects, but also to their installation. By configuring a different set of work in each exhibition, the total group conveys an entirely new narrative based on their context. Certain conceptual threads rise to the top and become more prominent in relationship to the other works. In* Say Goodbye To Substance, *the works were installed to encourage a circumnavigation of* Popular Hymns, *and the different vantage points to other works provide the viewer with varying juxtapositions. For example, the painting* Cosmology Of Constant Sorrow *(based on an image from the Hubble telescope, manipulated both in form and palette and annotated, as if a star chart with subjective statements) hangs high on the wall opposite the entrance beyond* Popular Hymns, *perhaps implying where that "time capsule" might be headed.*

9. *". . . but for Adam there was not found a helpmate for him. And the Lord God caused a deep sleep to fall upon Adam and he slept, and he took one of his ribs and closed up the flesh instead thereof. And the rib which the Lord God had taken from man, made he a woman, and brought her unto the man. And Adam said, this is now bone of my bones, and flesh of my flesh: she shall be called Woman, because she was taken out of Man." Gen: 2:21,23*

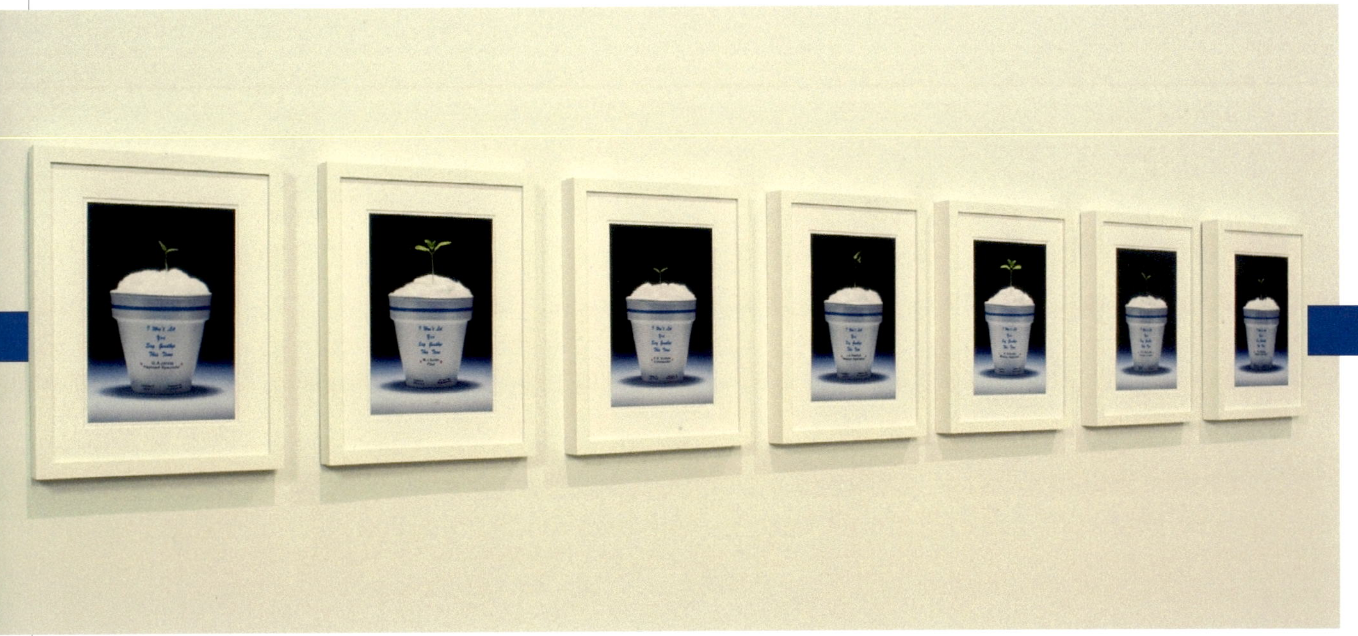

10, Both the diptych sculpture and the records used in Popular Hymns refer to ideas of creation and destruction, creative metamorphosis, and cycles of regeneration. Rather than a passive resignation that views these processes as beyond our control, the underlying idea is one of individual agency. Though viewing the world with cynicism, Robleto rejects the melancholic futility that compromises many interpretations of the intrinsic narrative to the world, leaving hope as the only option. The systems he chooses to connect and explore—pop music, science, space travel—encapsulate a similarly poignant promise, or at least longing, to change the world for the better.

This brings me to I Won't Let You Say Goodbye This Time. *Just like* with Men Are The New Women, *a lot of what I do is about the "what-if." For me, it also becomes a bigger issue: the question of what art can do. Can you expect a change? Can it right a wrong? I am trying to find ways of making that happen, and this piece is one attempt. Here, the idea is to finish something left unfinished due to things beyond my control.*[10]

In the late '70s and '80s, when the shuttle technology was introduced, part of the initial excitement was that it implied a greater accessibility to space for all of us. As a kid, I thought this incredible, and I remember that excitement so vividly. NASA saw potential in this excitement and began a PR campaign based on that accessibility. They built a probe called LDEF, which stands for the Long Duration Exposure Facility, designed to go aboard the shuttle. It had 57 compartments that they essentially opened up to the public—if you presented a proposal of what you wanted to include, it could be put on board. When you consider the security issues today, it is amazing that this could have happened. NASA literally mailed you

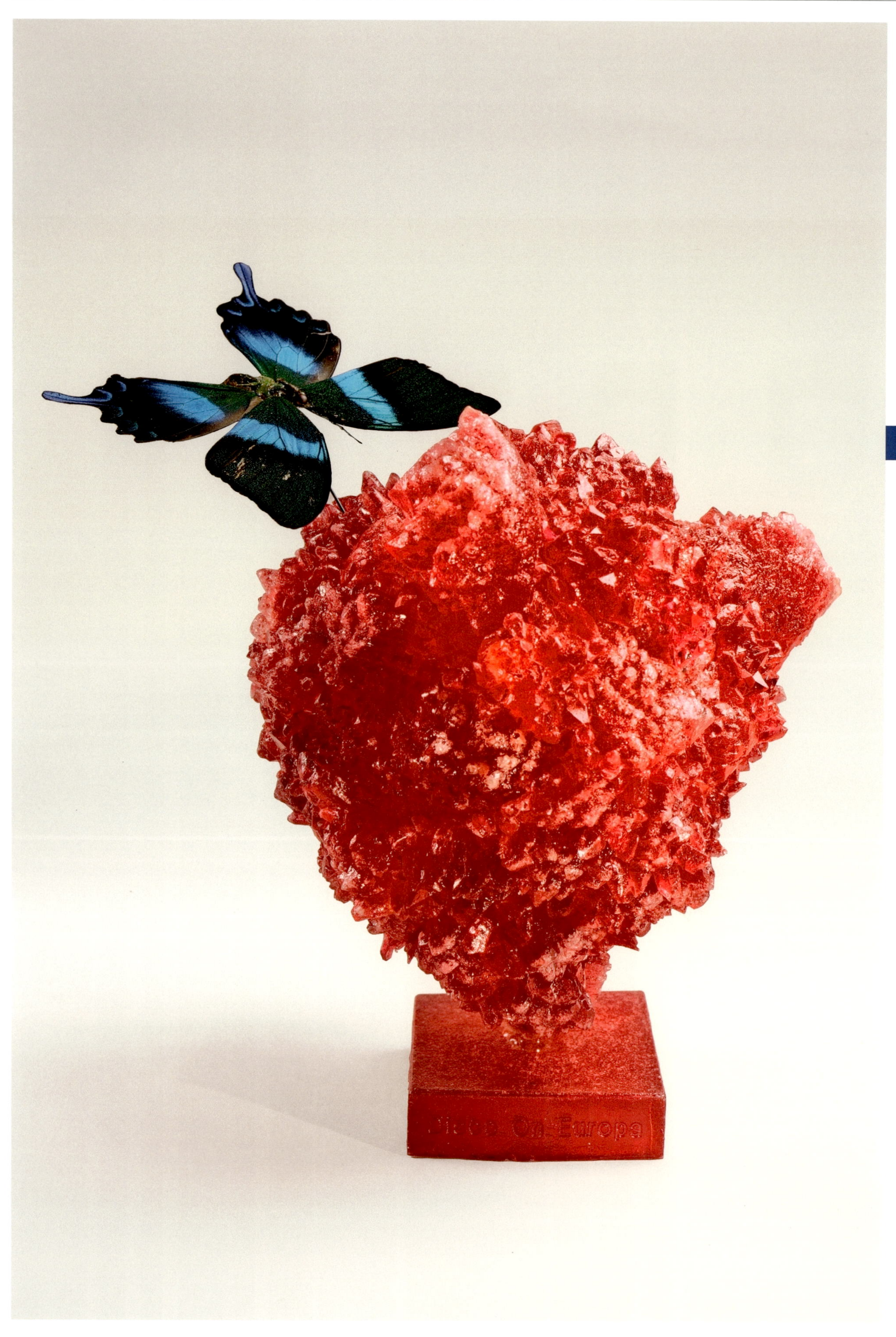

Moon On Europa

a tray, you set up your experiment and mailed it back to them, and they put it on board. I couldn't even dream of this happening today. NASA allowed so much room that the experiments ranged from the complicated, such as scientists doing tests for new materials, to a bunch of kids who said "Hey, can we put some seeds on board?" There was no hard science at stake; it really wasn't about that. It was about nurturing somebody else's imagination and belief.

The LDEF went into space in 1984 aboard the Challenger and was deployed into orbit. It was designed to be in orbit for nine months. The shuttle scheduled to pick it up was the Challenger mission that exploded. After that, everything was put on hold, and the probe sat in orbit for seven years. Even when the space program got back up, LDEF was never a priority—it just floated, essentially lost in space. Finally, in 1990, it was brought back. From what I understand, all of the kids had grown up, people had moved on, and it was just forgotten; so NASA had a lot of stuff left that they didn't know what to do with. I obtained the tomato seeds that were aboard from NASA auctions, where they also had actual material remnants of the Challenger shuttle. I got some fragments from the heat shield, the tiles that protect the shuttle from burning up upon reentry.

Is it within my power as an artist to finish something that was never completed? I wanted to regrow the plants, the way they were supposed to be—I wanted the final object to exist and live. The project is presented as a cross between classroom science and hard science. The particular language of this science was that of Styrofoam cups, names written in crayon, cotton, seeds, and a Jack-and-the-Beanstalk fascination. I made seven cups—one for each of the lost Challenger crewmembers. Designed to look like Styrofoam, they are actually custom-made porcelain. When the porcelain was still in the powder stage, the dust from the heat shields was incorporated into them. I wanted to make the cups as if they were little heat shields, mini spaceships in a way—quite delicate and special but with a protective coating, so each seed is safe from the heat of explosion.

Digital photography needed to be a component, and this was the first time I had to grapple with the idea of the art object being a photograph of my sculpture. The objective was to capture the plants at the moment of bloom in digital imagery; the deeper implication is that nothing is really dead if you can store it properly. It was 20 years from the time the seeds went up to the time I sprouted them, and I wanted to capture that moment, forever, as they tried again. In I Won't Let You Say Goodbye This Time, *my objective was to not let the past happen. This brings us back to the question of: Can art do that? Can I do that?*

Each cup contains a crewmember's name, official role, and information that NASA had sent up with the seeds. I wanted to recapture each crewmember as well, right at that moment of imminent return, when I imagine they felt nothing but hope. I wanted the lighting to appear as though they were landing, with a shadow cast as if they were touching down from their mission. There is also a subtle shift in the atmospheric quality. I want the viewer to feel them symbolically in the objects, in the careful framing and emphasis on the volume and three-dimensionality of the image. In the way they are presented, the crew can never die—at least not digitally.[11]

Dario Robleto, *Disco On Europa*. Homemade crystals, Green Blumei butterfly, butterfly antennae made of Donna Summer's vinyl record "I Feel Love," and polyester resin.

The final part of the story, where art and life collide, is that the shuttle that brought the seeds back was the Columbia. Suddenly, unintentionally, this work embraced another tragedy. One of the things I grappled with when I saw the Columbia explode was that my project did not stop anything. It didn't do what I had invested so much into, and it hit me hard that I hadn't changed anything; it didn't stop their deaths. But in talking about it with Houston-based art dealer Kerry [Inman] and Whitney curator Shamim [Momin], I realized that the idea was about trying, and there is something to be said for the gesture. If all art is just trying, then it is still valid. It is a great thing to ponder what art can do for us, the moment in which those things are going on in us: there is such horrible destruction, but I am trying to create something out of it. There are parallels to those ideas throughout the installation. You just can't stop trying.

These digital prints were designed to accompany Popular Hymns. They are also "what-if" scenarios, other versions of history like Popular Hymns, but I chose the vocabulary for the flyers from entirely fictional events. They were based on design motifs from theatrical posters of the '30s and '40s as well as the color schemes used in the flyers for raves and clubs. They advertise things that couldn't happen, but also suggest what might happen if they did.

For example, Science Is Not The Way imagines three plays by three real-life scientists: Copernicus, Ludwig Wittgenstein, and Werner Heisenberg. It plays on their personal and professional life stories; I think of them as three anarchists of science, who each fundamentally changed the way the world was perceived, such an extraordinary effect of the "what-if." At the same time, Science Is Not The Way addresses my love/hate relationship with science, and what it can and cannot offer; science is just as susceptible as anything else to context that affects the way truth is written. It is also about our roles as humans: how we affect the things that we believe to be universal truths.[12] These three men all did that in various ways. Copernicus' play is Ask Copernicus About Pushing Limits; because of him, we moved on from the idea of one supposed universal truth. When I think about being radical, I just remember what he went through, and I realize how out of his league I still am. Similarly, Heisenberg let us understand that, whether we like it or not, uncertainty is part of everything we do. The title of his play is Heisenberg May Have Slept Here.

In another print, Hey, Let's Keep The Population Down!, I addressed the desire pop stars have to save the world, related to the larger question of whether or not we can alter anything. The history of pop stars trying to change the world is littered with terrible and self-serving deeds. So what would happen if three scientists got together to write a pop song to save the world? The three scientists featured in this advertisement for that song are each singing something totally different. If Robert Oppenheimer, the father of the atomic bomb, sang "Hey, let's keep the population down," it would mean something different from Diane Fosse singing it and trying to save gorillas or the jungle. And if Jacque Cousteau sang it, he would mean something else. It is just a weird pop song, but it means nothing without knowing who's singing it.

12. "There is a difference between an idea and an ideology … ideas are not 'out there' waiting to be discovered, but are tools—like forks and knives and microchips—that people devise to cope with the world in which they find themselves … that ideas do not develop according to some inner logic of their own, but are entirely dependent, like germs, on their human carriers and environment. And … that since ideas are provisional responses to particular and unreproducable circumstances, their survival depends not on their immutability but on their adaptability." Louis Menand, The Metaphysical Club: A Story of Ideas in America, (Farrar Straus & Giroux, 2002), pp. xi-xii.

13. While obviously based in historical events and facts, the works in Robleto's Say Goodbye To Substance are reconfigured to tell a different story of humanity, one that is deeply personal and subjective, but perhaps no less true than that found in books. If history is nothing more than an agreed-upon collective memory, how do we choose to remember what has happened? Which parts of the story define us as humans? Theorist Kaja Silverman has proposed that memories are never authentic or "real" but rather are post-event constructions, a means to create social and psychic structure. (Kaja Silverman, "Back to the Future," Camera Obscura 27. (1991): 109–32.) Thus, memory provides a means to understand or justify events without necessarily having an indexical relationship to the "real." Robleto's reconstructed creation myths, his "what-ifs," are no different than the false

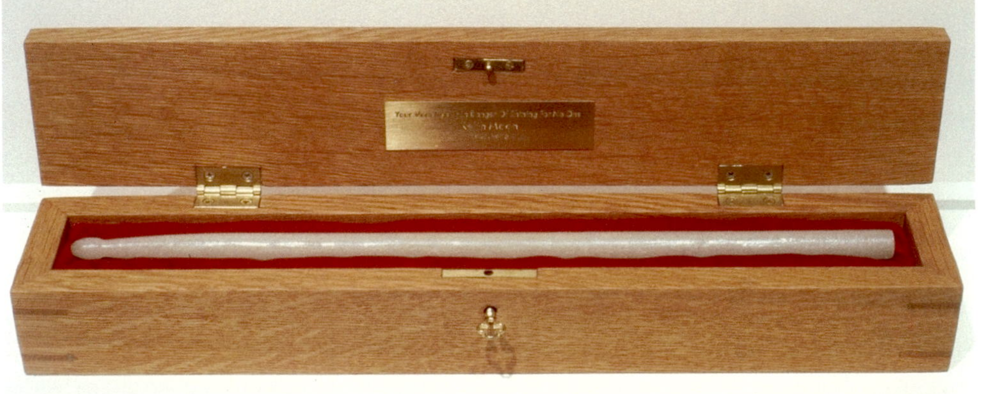

Dario Robleto, *Your Moonlight Is In Danger Of Shining For No One*, 2000-01. Custom-made maple box, glass and hand-ground trinitite (glass produced during the first nuclear test explosion, when heat from the blast melted the surrounding sand), velvet, and engraved brass label.

Your Moonlight Is In Danger Of Shining For No One uses the trinitite glass and is dedicated to Keith Moon, the drummer for The Who. He was the true rock and roll cliché, embodying the desire to "live fast, die young" in rock and roll history and mythology. He also revolutionized the art form of rock drumming, which is about sheer ferocity and aggression. It was his complete disregard for everything and yet complete focus that I was so intrigued with. He died in an explosion of his own life, because he could not sustain the level at which he was living. I wanted to make for him the Excalibur of drumsticks—one that you only pull out on special occasions. I made only one drumstick, out of the glass of the nuclear test explosion. Being made of glass, it can strike just once—but what a hit it would be. The implication is that in striking it, Moon would create this incredible explosion and obliterate himself in the process, in the same way that his own life, his drumming, did. His art was his downfall. The drumstick is presented in an open, delicate, handmade box, like a coffin—whether for presentation or use, it's hard to tell.

memories we have created to construct our own identities out of imagined pasts. Perhaps in a contemporary world where the sense of being anchored to a fixed reality has been permanently disturbed, if not totally unmoored, these subjective constructions have more weight in the proof of our own reality than other quantitative measures. This relationship between fact and fiction in Robleto's work is critical; but the real thrust lies in the impact of the work, not in its "truth." A time capsule should function as an authentic record of humankind's past, yet the selection of objects is as subjective as the viewers' interpretation of them. It is a desire to validate ourselves, to communicate our identity, rather than a real investment in truth. The knowledge of this falsity does not destroy the objects' power of evocation, in Robleto's world, the stories are real if they create individual subjectivity, meaning, and belief.

Light may be the most important underlying theme in this show. There are all kinds of light, from different sources: a nuclear explosion, a meteorite, starlight. Your Moonlight Is In Danger Of Shining For No One is that final, blinding light. It is a way of saying goodbye to Moon, and saying goodbye to a mythological understanding of rock and roll, to the romance of space, to a nostalgic belief in the perfect positivism of humanity. [13]

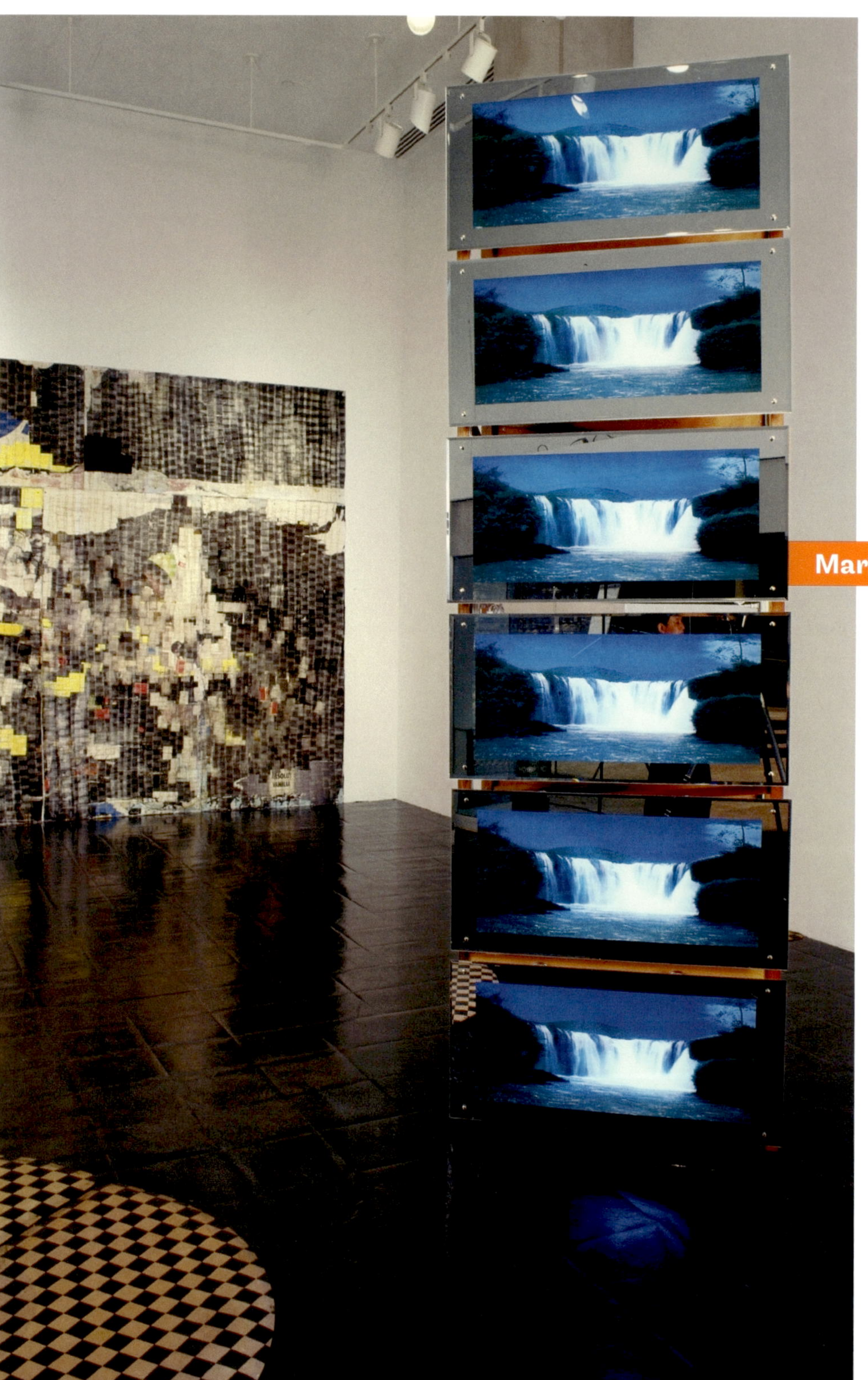

Left to right: Mark Bradford, *The Devil is Beating His Wife*, 2003; *Two Faced*, 2003. **THIS PAGE AND FOLLOWING:** Installation views of *Mark Bradford: Very Powerful Lords*.

Mark Bradford:
Very Powerful Lords

There's an abstraction that happens in the city which interests me. Simultaneous shifts in culture and meaning when you have the Mexican tacqueria next to the black wig shop across the street from the Vietnamese nail salon.
—MARK BRADFORD [1]

You cannot step into the same river twice, for fresh waters are ever flowing in upon you.
—ATTRIBUTED TO HERACLITUS
(500 BCE)

In 1493, on Columbus's second voyage, the Spanish explorer Juan Ponce de León came to the Americas. In a series of voyages from his home port of San Juan, Puerto Rico, he discovered the Bahamas and Florida. Based on his discoveries, Spain claimed all of the territory south of Virginia to Key West, and west to the Mississippi. The driving force behind much of de León's explorations was his obsession with tales of the Fountain of Youth. This mythical fountain was reputed to flow with water that cured illness and granted eternal youth. Perhaps equally important to both the explorer and his king, it was also rumored to sit amidst a treasure of gold and silver.

Mark Bradford's commissioned installation in the gallery of the Whitney Museum at Altria, *Very Powerful Lords,* was inspired by a letter written by Juan Ponce de León in 1521 in which he implores the King of Spain to continue funding his explorations. The conquistador's quest for youth, beauty, territory, and wealth provided Bradford with a tapestry of ideas aptly related to contemporary society, given the persistence of these myths and the perpetuation of these desires. Consisting of a large-scaled wall painting and several sculptures made of manipulated found objects, the exhibition brings together culturally diverse notions of ritual with Eurocentric emblems of youth and pulchritude as manifested through systems of power and commerce.

For this installation, Bradford's materials are drawn largely from products and services designed to make one look or feel good via artificial enhancement—permanent press hair papers, signage promising the transformative potential of consumer products, linoleum flooring and checkered mats lifted from standard salon décor, bottled water, and the promotion of nature as a spiritual means to transcend the burdens of culture. Bradford has used our culture's driving desire for permanent youth and beauty (acknowledging that in contemporary Western culture, one must have youth or the appearance of youth to be considered beautiful) as the central anchor to his installation. He investigates cultural systems of power, hierarchy, and control, both of the past and the present.

Bradford's paintings recall formal aspects of modernism while being grounded in the urban materials of his Los Angeles community, a synthesis of art historical concerns and popular black aesthetics. His previous work, drawn more closely from his experience as a salon stylist, centered on investigations of ethnicity, beauty and artifice, and ritual and process. His signature painting process incorporates layers of singed permanent press end papers with synthetic polymer or cellophane hair dyes to create translucent washes of color. The final paintings recall the investigations of the grid characteristic of modernist painting, such as that of Agnes Martin (whose work the artist often specifically references in titles such as *Pressin' Agnes,* and *On a Clear Day, I Can Usually See All the Way to Watts*), but invigorated with sociocultural content. Abstraction, for Bradford, becomes a semiotic vehicle to introduce an ambiguous interpretation of race and ethnicity. While the political issues of African-American hair have been extensively treated in contemporary art of the past decade, with hair functioning as a material stand-in for issues of racial representation, Bradford pushes the synecdoche a step further. By focusing on the processes and rituals associated with community, the artist both celebrates and questions culturally determined stereotypes which, however, simultaneously provide the venue to express increasingly hybrid manifestations based on those definitions.

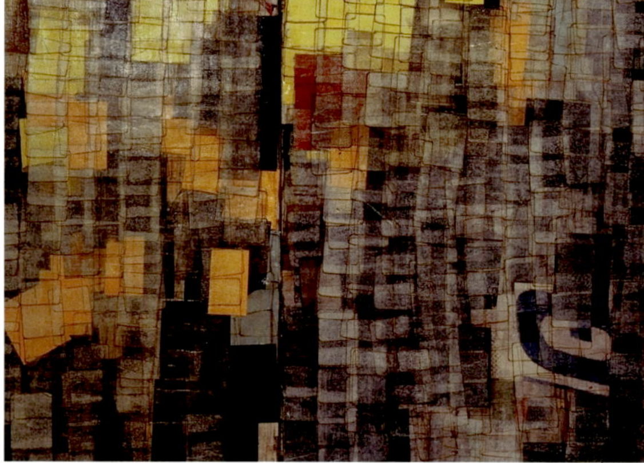
Mark Bradford, *The Devil is Beating His Wife*, 2003 (detail).

In Bradford's earlier works, his material sources and the textured, slightly scarred surface of the paintings suggested a type of skin. The work functions as a substitute for physical subjectivity, a presence-in-absence resembling the strategy of early-nineties artists' use of the painterly mark, text, or representational synecdoche to address issues of corporeality and the body. In the more recent paintings, however, the elegant spatial depth of his delicate, jittery grids has become increasingly interrupted by found-object, elements—print media such as magazine images or poster text—that disrupt the purity of the painted surface and fix his works more firmly to specific material connotations.

Bradford's engagement with the aesthetic of a specific part of the black urban community also reflects his exploration of class and trade structures within neighborhoods dominated historically by specific ethnicities. "Until about 1950, Central Avenue and the southeast part of the city were the only places blacks, and, for that matter, Mexicans could live, he explains:

> *The housing covenants started lifting and the middle class fled to*
> *the northern and western parts of the city. The urban population*
> *became imbalanced. With the absence of the professional class,*
> *the dope man and the "gangsta" became the norm, as did out*
> *and out violence on any male who was "sissy" or other. The departure*
> *of the middle class holds a lot of historical importance because*
> *they became entrenched in a new integrated model that was more*
> *palatable to the mainstream white society, and inner-city style*
> *went virtually unnoticed until the entertainment industry tapped the*
> *commercial potential of "gangsta" rap. Gangsta rap made everybody*
> *pay attention to inner-city style, if only as a new site for colonization.*
> *But inner-city style has always been here, the skeleton in the*
> *closet now worth some money, but still hardly official or respected.*

I use the aesthetic of southeast Los Angeles to highlight that region and all it carries, not in a romantic sense but to explicate its tenacity and complexity. A hybridity from within a kind of boundedness.[2]

In the Whitney exhibition, the large multipanel painting, *The Devil Is Beating His Wife* (2003), which occupies the gallery's back wall, functions as the visual anchor of the installation's multimedia elements. This new wall piece is Bradford's first which uses entirely "non-art" materials—the permanent press end papers, inexpensive fabric dye, and layers of found advertising posters and other local signage. Bradford's paintings have become increasingly scaled to the architectural environment; moving away from painting as an object, his current work more closely occupies the realm of mural. Issues of commerce, advertising, and material specificity are increasingly present in the mural, as Bradford more explicitly addresses his external environment.

Signage in particular plays a more prominent role in the painting's layered construction. While sustained viewing reveals the presence of such collage elements in his earlier work, here they take on a more active compositional presence. The painting is built up in visible layers, each remaining in traces of color or the physical thickness of the panel edges as the new layer is applied. The effect of this layering recalls the accumulation of posters and ads one often encounters on city streets, where a poster for a new rap artist lies beneath a beauty product ad, which in turn is covered by a sales announcement for the nearby liquor store. This process functions both as a formal device to achieve visual depth in the work, and also references Bradford's commitment to a truly hybrid notion of existence, that essential

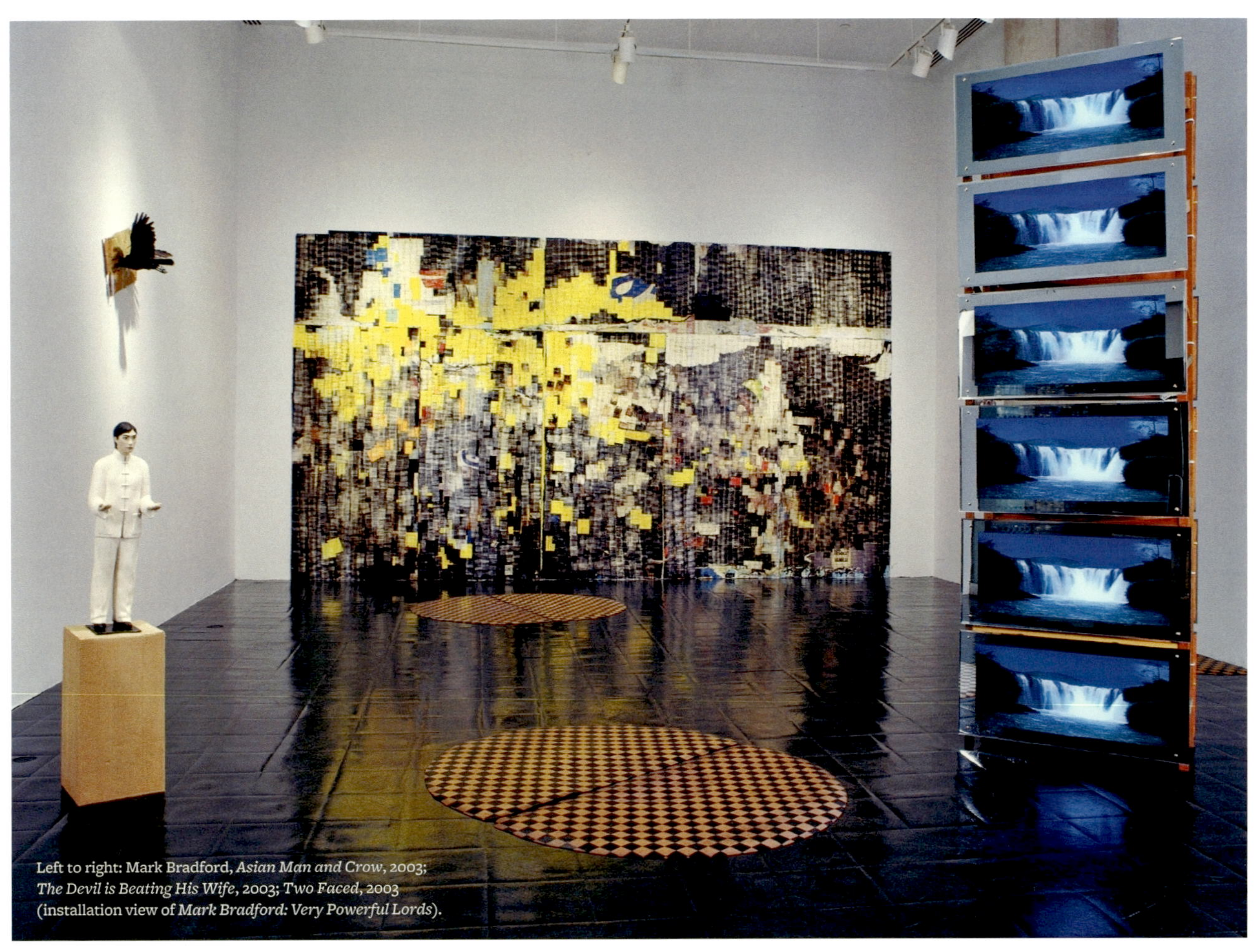

Left to right: Mark Bradford, *Asian Man and Crow*, 2003; *The Devil is Beating His Wife*, 2003; *Two Faced*, 2003 (installation view of *Mark Bradford: Very Powerful Lords*).

definitions—particularly racial or ethnic definitions—are no longer useful or accurate, if they ever were. The artwork encourages a rearticulated understanding between oneself and others, not a happy fusion of difference, but rather an insistence on the inextricable intersection of all aspects of identity.

The palette of the work's most visible layers moves away from the silvery blues, pinks, and yellows that characterized the shimmering surfaces of Bradford's earlier works, though like the posters peeking through, the blues and greens of the earlier layers (drawn from the palette of Monet's *Water Lilies* series) make appearances throughout. On the final layer, the translucent blacks and neon yellow are drawn from the familiar materials of police barriers and construction sites one often sees in a cityscape. The title refers to a black folk saying that describes the simultaneous occurrence of rain and sunshine. Building on the multivalence of material associations he is drawn to throughout his work, Bradford invokes the idea that media assume different meanings based on their context. "The signage in the hood is about something that is abandoned," Bradford explains,

> *The barricades that go up around burnt-out buildings, some of which are still not rebuilt from the 1992 riots. You learn quickly walking by these urban abstractions that wtthin the walls of those abandoned buildings lie accumulated stories, half-forgotten but retaining an energy-in-waiting. White, upper class, neighborhoods, on the other hand, usually put up barricades around potentiality— renovation, new construction, that kind of thing. Money is coming in; those same barricades in some black neighborhoods are all about money done gone.*[3]

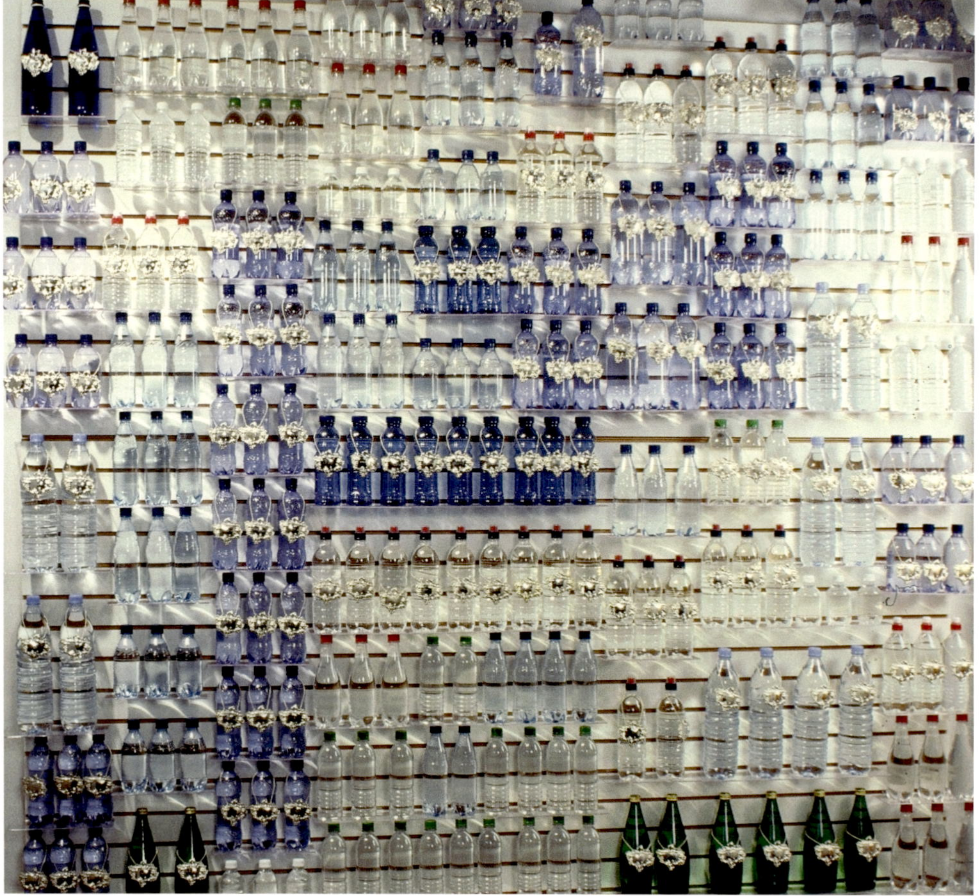

Mark Bradford, *Water Lillies*, 2003 (installation view of *Mark Bradford: Very Powerful Lords*).

The painting's layers function as a kind of urban archaeology, each stratum evoking a moment in the history of the local community while simultaneously addressing the reality of a more global history built upon the layers of its past, even when apparently cloaking or obliterating them. Describing the "ongoing erasure and rewriting of ownership that flows in the 'hood," Bradford reenacts the "constant collision of signs" that characterizes the fluid economies among culturally hybrid communities in relationship to larger trade models of a capitalist system.

Questioning commerce, a display wall of shelves lined with blue and clear water bottles glow and sparkle seductively, their curved contours unmarred by labels and their suggestively anthropomorphic forms enhanced with glimmering silver necklaces, champagne tags specially inscribed "Welcome." Entitled *Water Lilies* (2003), the work elaborates on the conflation of desire and commerce, its structure derived from the perfectly arranged shelves of a drugstore or cosmetics shop. The product saturation characteristic of capitalism is designed to entice the customer, not with the material object, but rather with its conceptual promise—the possibility of achieving the always-elusive perfection of youth and beauty. Again, Bradford engages the viewer in the actuality of our world, but troubles the neat consumer encapsulation that commodity transactions equal beauty and satisfaction. The late-twentieth-century craze for bottled water might in fact be seen as our updated version of belief in water's transformative properties: recalling everything from the physical benefits of the Fountain of Youth and the Baths of Vichy to culturally diverse examples of the spiritual healing power of sacred springs and wells ranging from ancient Greek or Hindu rituals and Native American rites to Christian baptism. Using the actual water bottles one can buy at any deli or drugstore, Bradford has transformed the products lining the shelves into a jewellike composition of blue-shaded transparencies, humorously titled after Monet's famous series depicting the Giverny gardens (itself an artificially transformed natural landscape). As part of Bradford's larger endeavor in *Very Powerful Lords, Water Lilies* plays with the boundaries of nature and culture, a waterfall of inexpensive plastic products promising access to purity and beauty, but offering only banality.

The shiny black linoleum covering the gallery floor is punctuated with checkered, hemispherical salon mats, reinforcing the construction as a stylized, artificial landscape. Streaks of neon yellow from the painting reflect in its surface as if on a body of water, while the mats double as floating lily pads. Bradford creates a total environment for the viewer to enter, but one that moves fluidly between inside and outside, reality and artifice, universal spirituality and local materiality. The central three-dimensional form, *Two Faced* (2003), is a structurally geometric wooden frame on which Bradford has mounted a slick, sharp tower of identical mirrored light boxes, each depicting the same idyllic natural landscape. Formally, the work recalls elements of Minimalist sculpture with its clean, mute form that theatrically engages the viewer with its physical presence in space. *Two Faced*'s serial construction and repetition of forms also recalls minimalist strategies, particularly in Bradford's use of industrially produced objects. However, the light boxes are preexisting found objects, an updated Duchampian gesture that questions ideas of class and aesthetics. These kitschy, decorative objects might be found, for example, in inexpensive Asian restaurants, and tend to be associated with popular, rather than refined, taste. The transformation engendered by their placement in the gallery rests on their function as a kind of art form, questioning the relationship of class (as a complicated weave of ethnicity, education, and economics) and concurrent expectations of taste.

The image of a perfectly imagined waterfall, rocks, trees, and blue sky is backlit and motorized to suggest endless cascading, accompanied by its "natural" soundtrack of moving water and chirping birds. Its attempts to re-create the natural world actually distances it from reality. The manufactured artificiality of each light box functions to signify the idea of nature, rather than depict it in actuality. The dissonance between reality and artifice is not an opposition per se, but rather a vacillating coexistence in which one may take prominence at different moments. This dissonance is echoed in the boxes' sound. Bradford has manipulated the mechanism within the boxes so that each misses a beat now and then, creating syncopated music. This slightly disjunctive soundtrack and the blurring of sound clarity resulting from the cacophonous layering of multiple light boxes short-circuits the notion of an equivalence between their pictorial surfaces and the true existence of the utopian world they depict.

Though the light box images are utopian oases in which all human presence has been carefully excluded, Bradford's structure emphasizes the inevitable egotism inherent in these conceptions of nature. Because the images in these light boxes are framed by mirrored surfaces, one cannot engage the piece without one's reflection literally framing this artificial scene. While the mirror is clearly the locus of superficial obsessions with self-image as it pertains to beauty and youth in contemporary culture, it also recalls water as the first reflective surface, the first means of understanding oneself as a discrete physical identity in the world, yet always one troubled by ideas of separation from self. The Greek myth of Narcissus, in fact—in which the protagonist was so captivated by the beauty of his own reflection (perceived as another person) that he wasted away at water's edge—is the original mirror-stage as defined by philosopher Jacques Lacan. The reflection provides an external image that gives rise to the mental representation of an individual self, but also establishes this entity as fundamentally dependent upon external objects. Isolating subjectivity in relationship to one's own recognition of perception "from the outside" establishes an interesting metaphor for the inside/outside simultaneity of Bradford's sculpture, which persists throughout the installation—the salon floor as a reflecting pool, the glittering bottles as waterfall, and the street poster as high art.

The idealized landscape portrayed in these light boxes—untouched by culture or by human hands—only underscores the artificiality of desire for a perfect, spiritually pure natural world. Like the Fountain of Youth, this notion of nature exists only as a cultural construction. Yet, the cinematic progression of repeated imagery in the stacked boxes builds an aesthetically evocative atmosphere, while the glowing blue light haloing the structure and its striking physical presence maintain the seductive possibilities of this mythic font of purity, transformation, and peace that persist in contemporary society. Despite the inconsistencies in this opposition between nature and culture, the desire to engage with a "purer" mode of existence manifests itself today in paradoxes such as the environment-destroying SUV, advertised to challenge raw roads and worlds it will never take on. As a sibling of the historical impulse for exploration and conquest, contemporary representations of the desire to reintegrate with nature—gear-laden retreats to the woods, the popularity of extreme traveling as a search for self, country houses in unspoiled villages and rustic summer escapes—are usually indicative of a system of power that privileges one culture or community over another. Bradford's work also evokes the notion of Nature associated with the exoticized Other—an elevation of and condescension to ethnic cultures regarded as direct or primal, from the pure pastoral of the noble savage, to the Zen garden of the spiritual Oriental.

On another level, *Two Faced*'s whimsical evocation of an actual fountain relates to the notion of material desire permeating the installation. Fountains can connote a kind of folly, a superstitious ritual of hopes turned into a monetary exchange—one throws a penny into the water as a symbol of the abstract wish, a less expensive version of offering material supplication to the gods to ensure the fulfillment of one's prayers. Above the sculpture, ropes of pennies twist into the lighting track, drooping down just into one's line of vision, wishes thrown and frozen in their trajectory. Ambiguously present, they recall the phrase "pennies from heaven," immortalized by Bing Crosby in a song describing the necessary coexistence of good with bad. In fact, the lyrics explicitly acknowledge a dependence on exchange to return the positive from the negative: "No one appreciated a sky that was always blue. . . . So it was planned that they would vanish now and then. And you must *pay* before you get them back again. That's what storms were made for. . . . Every time it rains it rains/ pennies from heaven." Like the barricade reference in the painting, all yin requires—and is charged for—its yang.

Bradford's current investigation expands beyond a racially specific, black/white opposition, addressing the hybrid cultural and economic exchanges of Asian and Latino communities in Los Angeles. He has explored these issues in earlier works such as *China Silk* (2001), in which he foregrounded the oddities of ethnic trade by weaving Chinese hair (the predominant source for hair extensions, generally imported and sold by Korean immigrant merchants to black women) onto the heads of Korean-American women. In another multimedia piece exploring ethnicity, class, and community, *Hooked Up* (2002), Bradford brought plaster sculptures of hands clasped in prayer to different nail salons along a particular Los Angeles boulevard, and had each salon add artificial tips adorned with their most popular design. Together, the sculptures track the mix of different communities comprising Bradford's neighborhood, while neatly encapsulating ideas of ethnocentric taste and class assumptions with the jarring visual contrasts of the bright, flashy nails against the white plaster.

In *Very Powerful Lords,* the relationship to local specificity and universal paradigms of trade and beauty is further considered in the diptych *Asian Man and Crow* (2003). Bradford found the statue locally at the same Korean wholesaler in his neighborhood where he buys other materials for his work. For this installation, Bradford selected his materials from goods "found in the stalls of the Korean merchant and purchased by blacks and Latinos" in urban communities. Here, the found statuette, stereotypically clad in a simple white garment (martial arts-cum-Buddhist-priest pajamas) poses with his hands out, welcoming you into a pseudo-spiritual garden of earthly delights. Like the light box sculpture, the artificiality of this construct is clear. The artist was also struck by the stylized gesture of the "wise Asian" as a kind of reversal of the subservient posture of a black lawn jockey sculpture, another familiar, racially typed form.[4] Again, Bradford shifts between layers of micro- and macrocosmic meaning, commenting on the Eurocentric fetish of Orientalism and pseudo-spirituality while also making a connection between the often tense relationships that exist between blacks and Koreans in his own community.

Bradford's choice of a taxidermied crow—a real animal made permanently fake—symbolically recalls the shifting superimposition of meaning and history made literal in the painting's surface. As is typical of Bradford's work, the web of ideas that reside in each piece is selectively enhanced by the presence of other objects—the product shelves of water take on aspects of a waterfall when seen against the fountain, the floor becomes a representation of a watery environment as the painting reflects in its depths, and yet remains a salon because of its material sources. That the crow functions as a diptych with the figurine of the Asian man suggests the coexistence of these alternate meanings, and enforces the ethnic hybridity of Bradford's community. The crow has its own hybrid identity, with vastly different meanings in different cultures and times. In most contemporary Western cultures, the crow symbolizes negative omens, even death, though it has also historically embodied positive concepts such as love and filial devotion and has functioned as everything from the savior of humanity, to a divine messenger or the personification of the Supreme Being.[5]

Of course, the figure of the black crow also recalls other racially charged connotations. The term Jim Crow is believed to have originated around 1830 as a minstrel show character. By the eve of the Civil War, Jim Crow was one of many stereotypes of black inferiority in the popular culture of the day.[6] The words became a racial slur in the vocabulary of many whites; and by the end of the century, legal acts of racial discrimination toward blacks were often referred to as Jim Crow laws.

The illusion of the taxidermied bird in flight crashing through the gallery wall is undermined by the presence of the cardboard packing to which it was clearly affixed for transport; similarly, the revelation of the mechanisms of the light boxes and the wooden support structure of *Two Faced* allow for constructs to coexist with illusion. The generic Asian man statuette extends his hand in welcome, perhaps, standing somewhat askew atop a box resembling the cardboard packing in which it may have arrived. Linked to the conglomeration of products underlying the materials of the overall installation, the cardboard box/pedestal also refers to art as consumption, to post-Warholian politics of the commodity. Throughout the installation, Bradford is clearly interested in the meeting of desires with products designed to appeal to them.

The clear, though delicate, relationship between the works in this diptych have the ambiguous connections characteristic of Bradford's approach. His work is deeply invested in the ephemeral, the fluid imperfections of reality, and the notion of what one might call the "almost real." The tonally ambiguous, fleeting sensibility of his work can be linked aesthetically and philosophically to Fluxus, a loosely defined mid-twentieth-century aesthetic movement that conjoined the works of experimental artists, architects, composers, and designers in an attempt to give form to the Heraclitean philosophy of flux. The ancient Greek philosopher Heraclitus first articulated the idea of impermanence as a condition of existence, where reality is thus defined as a succession of transitory states. Fluxus artists drew on notions of musical improvisation and play to create ephemeral, experimental activites

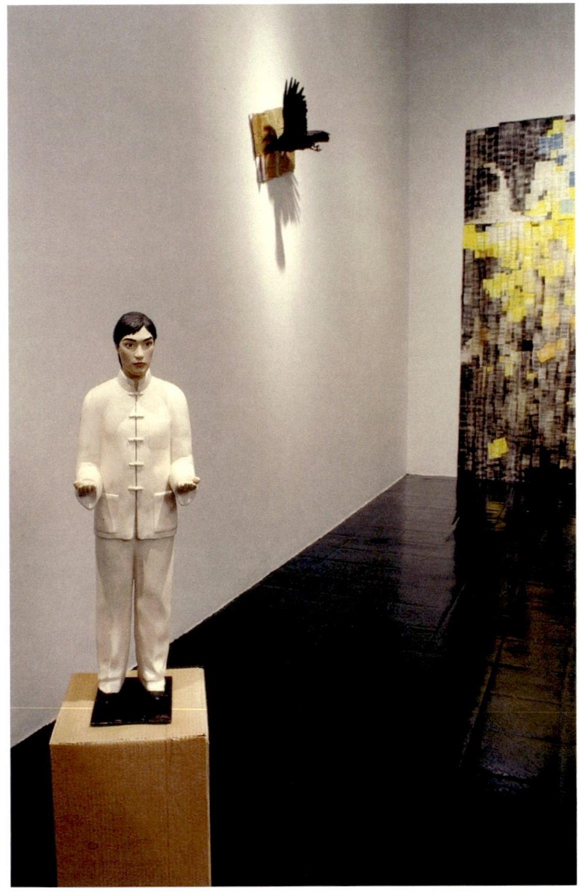

Left to right: Mark Bradford, *Asian Man and Crow*, 2003; *The Devil is Beating His Wife*, 2003 (installation view of *Mark Bradford: Very Powerful Lords*).

and "products" that proposed an alternative system of art-making. Like the Fluxists, Bradford's conceptual approach centers on the ephemeral nature of being, what he calls "the musicality of becoming," and the eternal spontaneity of the present. Though his emblematic quote implies otherwise, fire was Heraclitus's symbol of this notion of perpetual change; in *Very Powerful Lords,* Bradford has taken its opposite, water, as literal and metaphoric fluidity.

Bradford has constructed a landscape occupied by influences ranging from the economics of trade and European colonial conquest to black folklore, style, and baptism. Like Heraclitus, he focuses on the "flux and fire" of contemporary existence, rather than attempting to believe in an essential condition. Sliding effortlessly between issues of local and universal interpretation, Bradford is explicitly of his moment, in which the classically modernist era of binary logic is over: no real against artificial, no we against them, no self against other, no inside against outside. As with his approach to ethnicity, Bradford does not address these questions as dichotomies. Instead, he has disturbed the secure definitions of these concepts as opposites. As boundaries are pierced and parameters made more fluid, one wonders if the resulting hybridity might provide possibilities for emancipatory subversion through the transformation of identity from an internal essentialism to a transgression of borders. Bradford's work is grounded in our empathetic relationship to the abstract notions of beauty and power that govern, to some extent, all of our lives. His installation encourages us to reflect on our own personal engagement with these "very powerful lords" that have defined the world, and urges us to challenge them. —SHAMIM M. MOMIN, BRANCH DIRECTOR AND CURATOR

1. Email conversations with the artist, July 2003.

2. Interview with Eungie Joo, "Free Trade," Summer-Fall 2002, http://www.pomona.edu/ADWR/Museum/exhibits/20022003/bradford/joo.shtml

3. Email conversations with the artist, July 2003.

4. An example of a co-opted form is the lawn jockey, which typically depicted a blackface figure dressed in jockey's clothing, one hand in his pocket and the other reaching out a ring on which to tie one's horse—precipitated the racial slur "lawn jockey" to refer derogatorily to African-American men, particularly when trying to indicate subservience. But in the first half of the nineteenth century, escaping slaves understood then that the jockey statue would guide them to safe houses along the Underground Railroad and to freedom.

5. For ancient Celts, the crow was the evil counterpart to the swan's symbolic purity. In ancient Greece the crow was replaced by the owl as Athena's companion for being too gossipy. In the Bible the crow's selfishness keeps him from reporting to Noah that the flood was over, and in India's *Mahabharata*, the messengers of death are likened to crows. In many nomadic cultures, however, the crow assumes a positive meaning, particularly in Native American myths. In some tribes, the crow resides as the divine protagonist of creationist myths; in others, it is he who steals the sun to provide it for humanity. In yet others, he is the personification of the Supreme Being. Similarly, in Scandinavia, a pair of crows often symbolized the principle of creation. His role in Asiatic cultures is also largely positive—showing love and filial devotion. In Chinese legend the crow becomes the source of the world's light—the solar symbol and creative principle—while in Japanese mythology, the crow is often a divine messenger.

6. A white, minstrel show performer, Thomas "Daddy" Rice, blackened his face with charcoal paste or burnt cork and danced a ridiculous jig while singing the lyrics to the song, "Jump Jim Crow." Rice created this character after seeing a black slave dancing and singing a song ending with these chorus words: "Weel about and turn about and do jis so, Eb'ry time I weel about I jump Jim Crow." Some historians believe that a Mr. Crow owned the slave who inspired Rice's act—thus the reason for the Jim Crow term in the lyrics. In any case, Rice incorporated the skit into his minstrel act, and by the 1850s the "Jim Crow" character had become a standard part of the minstrel show in America.

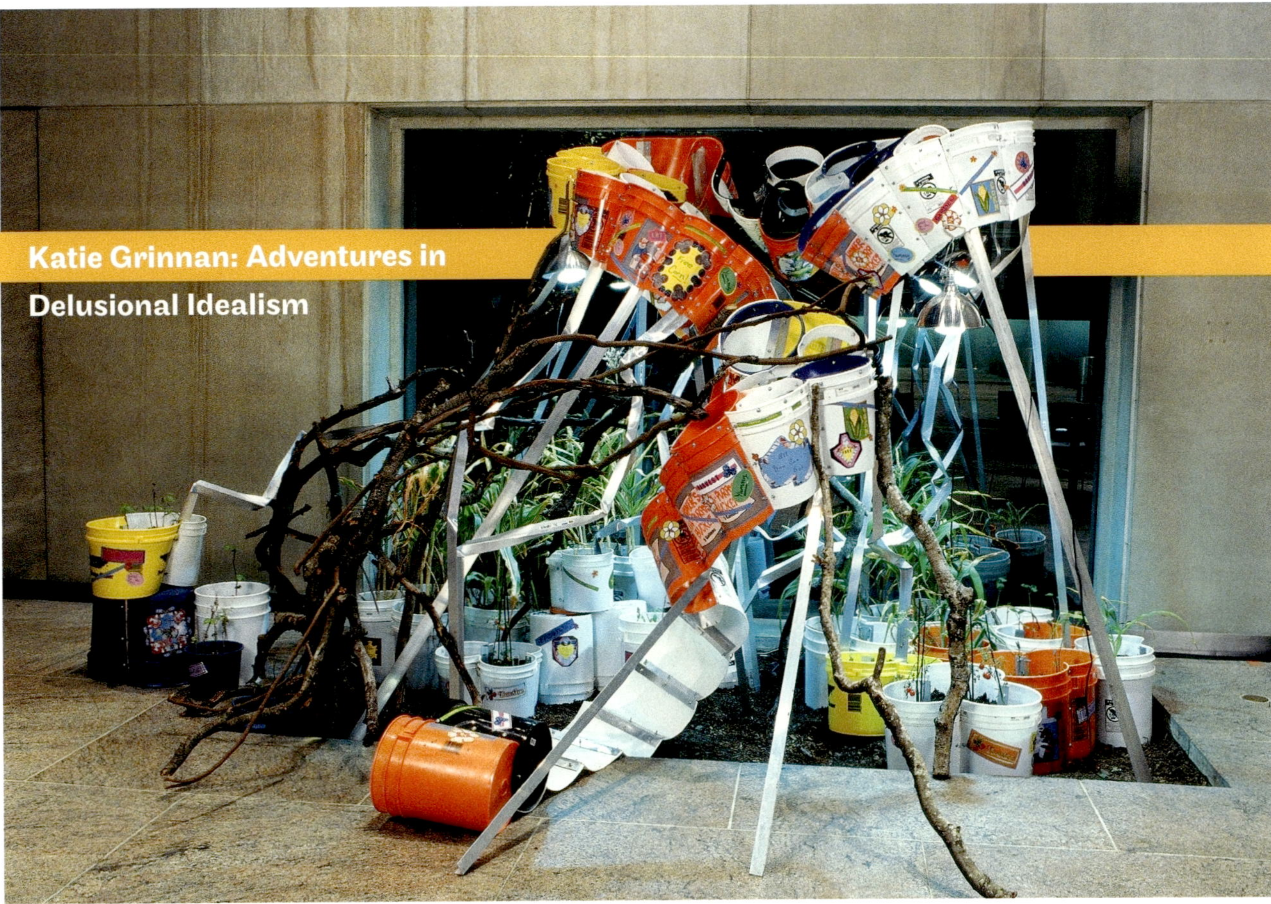

Katie Grinnan, *Salad*, 2003 (installation view of
Katie Grinnan: Adventures in Delusional Idealism).

Katie Grinnan: Adventures in Delusional Idealism

July 24, 2003 to January 4, 2004

Evoking contained, self-sustaining eco-systems and utopian communities, Katie Grinnan uses moldable plastic and computer-altered images of corporate spaces to create large-scale photo sculptures and installations that envelop the architecture of the Whitney at Altria Sculpture Court....

Grinnan's installation work spatializes the intersection of photography, sculpture, and architectural environments. By incorporating her recent research of rain forests in Costa Rica, the Great Barrier Reef, the Biosphere, and Arcosanti (a utopian community in Arizona), Grinnan draws on the site-specific aspects of the Sculpture Court to create elements of her own hybrid, self-sustaining utopian community. This includes a small crop of corn planted in the existing flower beds, and an inverted tree that is suspended from the ceiling, creating a fantastical reflection of the actual trees below. Seamlessly combining high and low-tech processes, the installation features organically contoured sculptures growing over existing architectural structures and photographic forms that mimic objects in the space. These photographic sculptures and murals are derived from images taken by Grinnan of Altria public and office spaces. The combined elements of the installation reflect a compression of distance between structure and surface and the blurring of spatial function.

Luis Gispert: Urban Myths Part II (Return of the Hypenaholics)

November 6, 2003 to March 12, 2004

For his first solo New York museum show, Luis Gispert creates a hybrid environment that fuses the stylized forms of furniture design with the material ethos of hip hop culture. Consisting of large-scale wall drawings, multipurpose sculptures, and a collaborative sound component, the installation presents improbable objects of unexpected scale and material such as a turntable arm ornamented with chains and a baseball cap that doubles as an interactive seating unit....

Gispert, whose work was included in the 2002 Whitney Biennial, makes photographs and sculptures that synthesize hip-hop's visually baroque aesthetic with art-historical references ranging from Renaissance painting to early modern furniture. The wall drawing in *Urban Myths Part II* provides a multi-dimensional landscape of towering speaker formations and stereo-shaped elements. Within this space, objects such as turntables, chrome tire rims, and boom boxes exist and sometimes meld with his design-inspired furniture structures. These objects also defy the boundaries of the gallery: one sculpture excessively ornamented with platinum chain medallions defiantly extends beyond the glass façade of the space. According to Gispert, this installation reflects a formal environment in which archetypal modernist designs relate to the consumer driven notions of portability, novelty, and cultural materialism.

Installation view of *Luis Gispert: Urban Myths Part II* (*Return of the Hyphenoholics*).

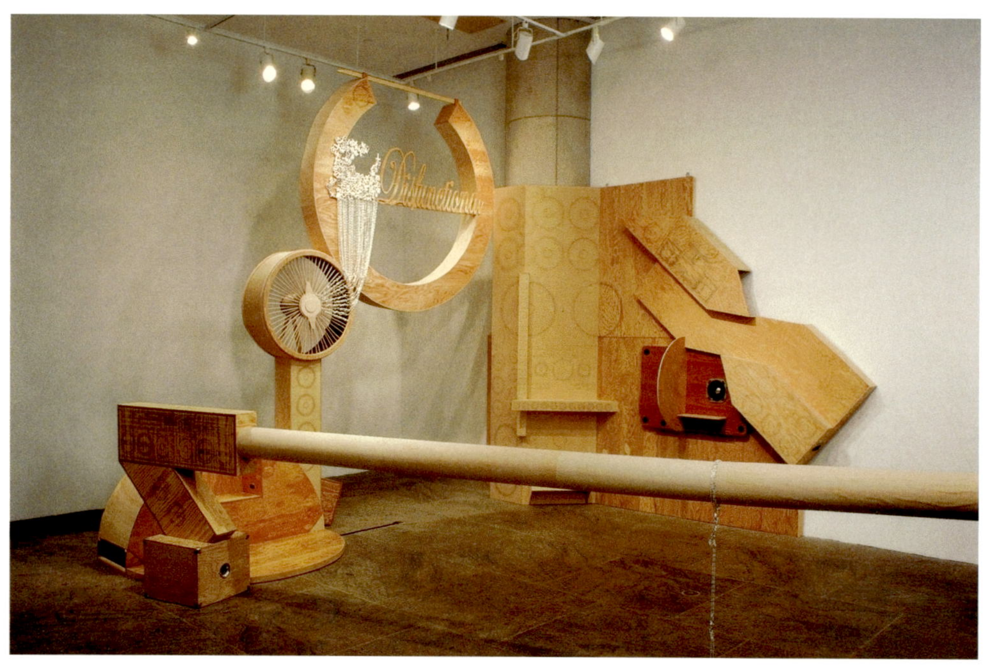

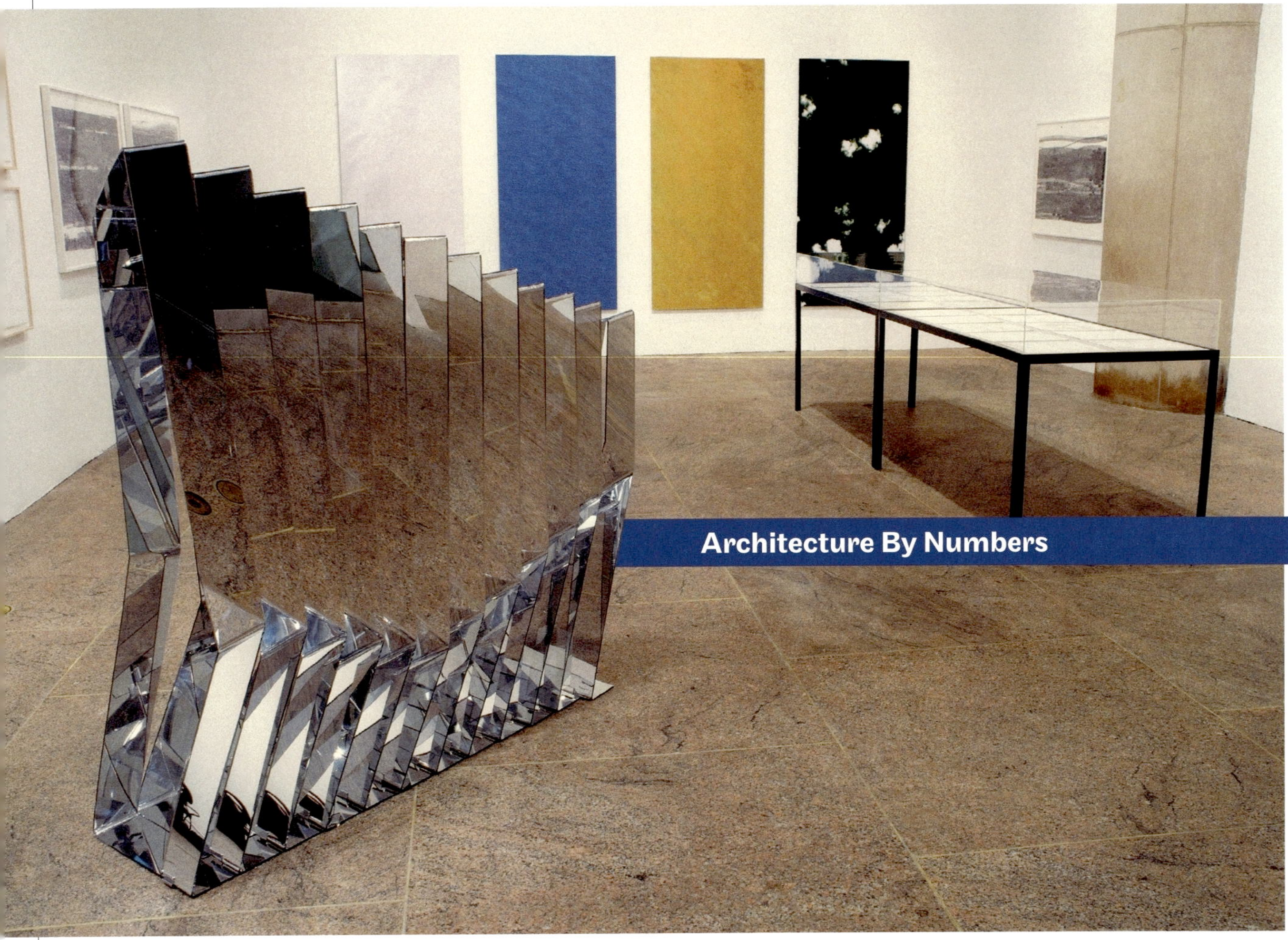

Architecture By Numbers

Clockwise from foreground: works by Michelle Fornabai, Preston Scott Cohen, Marsha Cottrell, and Laura Kurgan (installation view of *Architecture by Numbers*).

March 25 to July 9, 2004

Architecture By Numbers [is] an exhibition that investigates architecture and its essential relationship with the numerical. The exhibition includes drawings, digital prints, and three-dimensional work by Preston Scott Cohen, Marsha Cottrell, Michelle Fornabai, Laura Kurgan, and Ben Nicholson. . . .

The five architects in this exhibition seek out numerical information in the architectures of objects, places, or ideas of such singularity that some may see the projects as aberrations or even obsessions. The obsessions include the mystical numbering systems of labyrinths, the digital record of extreme landscapes, complex geometrical transformations or even the landscapes of information that can be derived from punctuation marks.

From the very beginnings of architectural theory as it emerged out of Pythagorean-Platonic philosophies of harmony and proportion, to our own time when, it seems, the entirety of our experience has become digitized, architecture has been understood as a fulcrum between the material world of things and their construction, and the transcendent mathematics of the cosmos itself. Architecture exists in these projects not as a practice of building, but as a frame for thinking about specific artistic or social problems such as authorship and production, the abstract calculations endemic to contemporary space versus the particularity of spatial experience, or sociological representation versus individual expression. Architecture exists in these projects as patterns that map culture's unconscious.

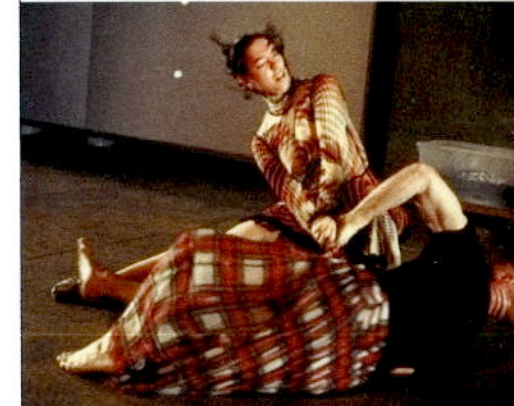

RoseAnne Spradlin, *Future Past* and *Rerrangement (or a Spell for Mortals)*, 05–19–04

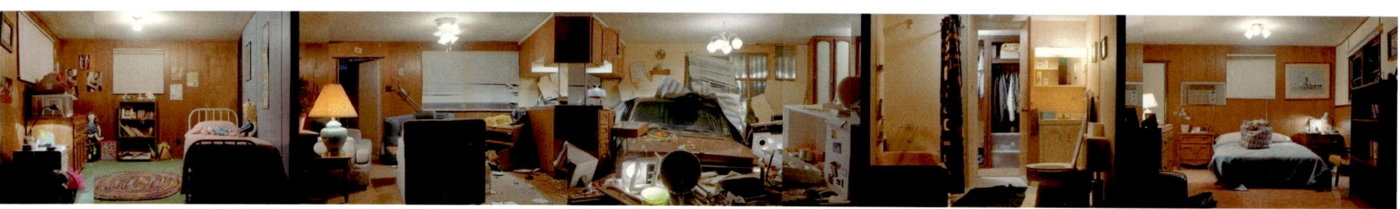

TOP: Set for *Single Wide*, 2003. C-Print on Fuji Color Crystal Archive paper. BOTTOM: *Single Wide*, 2002. High definition video transferred to DVD, sound; ten 6-minute loops.

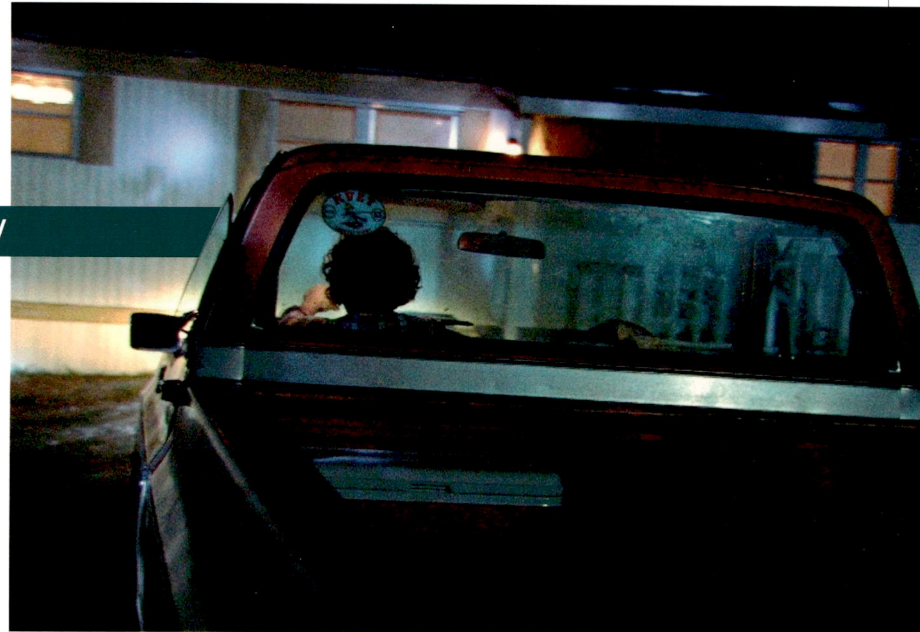

Single Wide: Teresa Hubbard/ Alexander Birchler

July 22 to October 22, 2004

Teresa Hubbard and Alexander Birchler know how to tell a story as well as they know how to untell it. Emerging from their earlier highly staged and meticulously crafted photographic work, their cinematically referential, single-pan videos ask the viewer to consider how a story arises, and how it is simultaneously constructed. Drawing on the notion of architectural space as a psychological metaphor, Hubbard and Birchler employ and, as in this installation, often exhibit precisely built models and stage sets, combining them with camera motion that confounds the viewer's expectations to explore and ultimately blur the distinctions between inside/outside, real/artificial, light/dark, and cause/effect. The tightly framed, intensely saturated imagery creates a series of almost photographic tableaux, a conscious production of framed moments heightened by the continuous motion of the spectator's gaze.

In their recent video installation *Single Wide* (2002), the slow, meditative movement of the camera traces what appears to be an evolution toward a violent event that has happened or is about to happen. The pace of the video creates dramatic tension in the implied story, but the "plot" remains ultimately unresolved as the video loops back seamlessly to its "beginning." —SHAMIM M. MOMIN, BRANCH DIRECTOR AND CURATOR

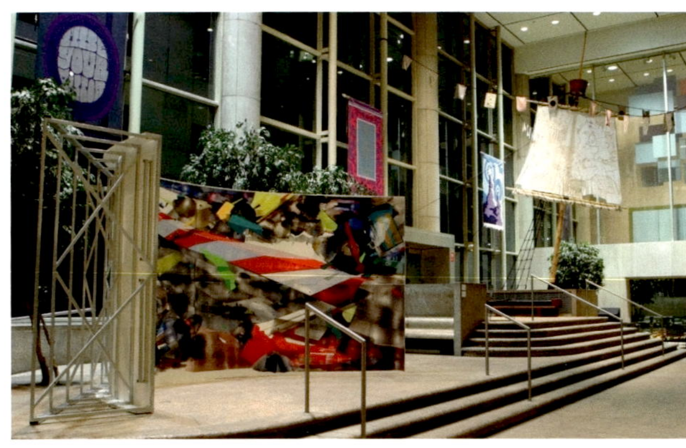

Fight or Flight

November 4, 2004 to February 18, 2005

The term "fight or flight" refers to the involuntary bodily reaction humans or animals have when faced with a sudden, unexpected threat. This exhibition draws on the pervasive discussions of fear and anxiety that have emerged in the popular press in recent years, clearly related to our turbulent times. Each of the featured artists was asked to consider this topic and respond accordingly, and in doing so, the work that was created for this exhibition engages both the scientific response and psychological application of "fight or flight."

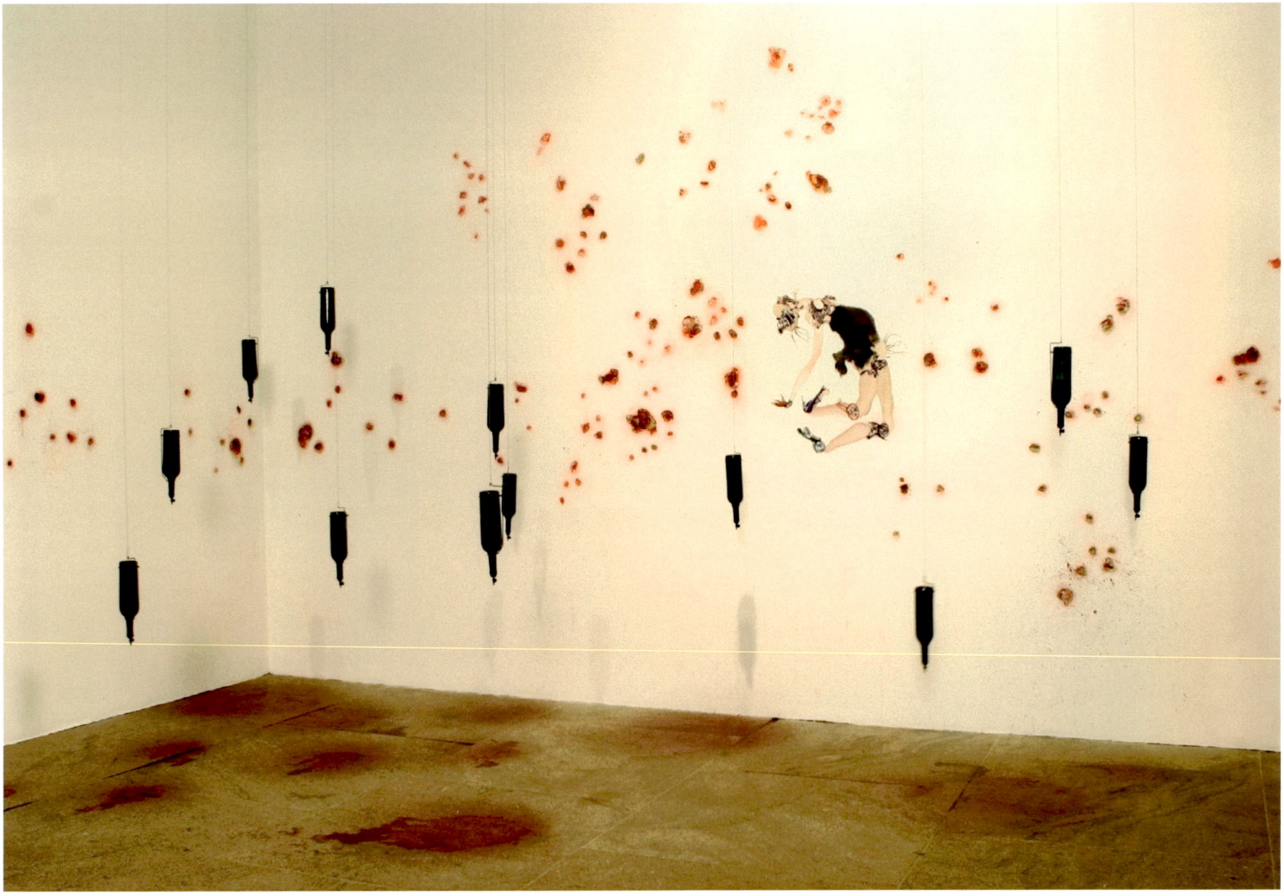

Sue de Beer: Black Sun

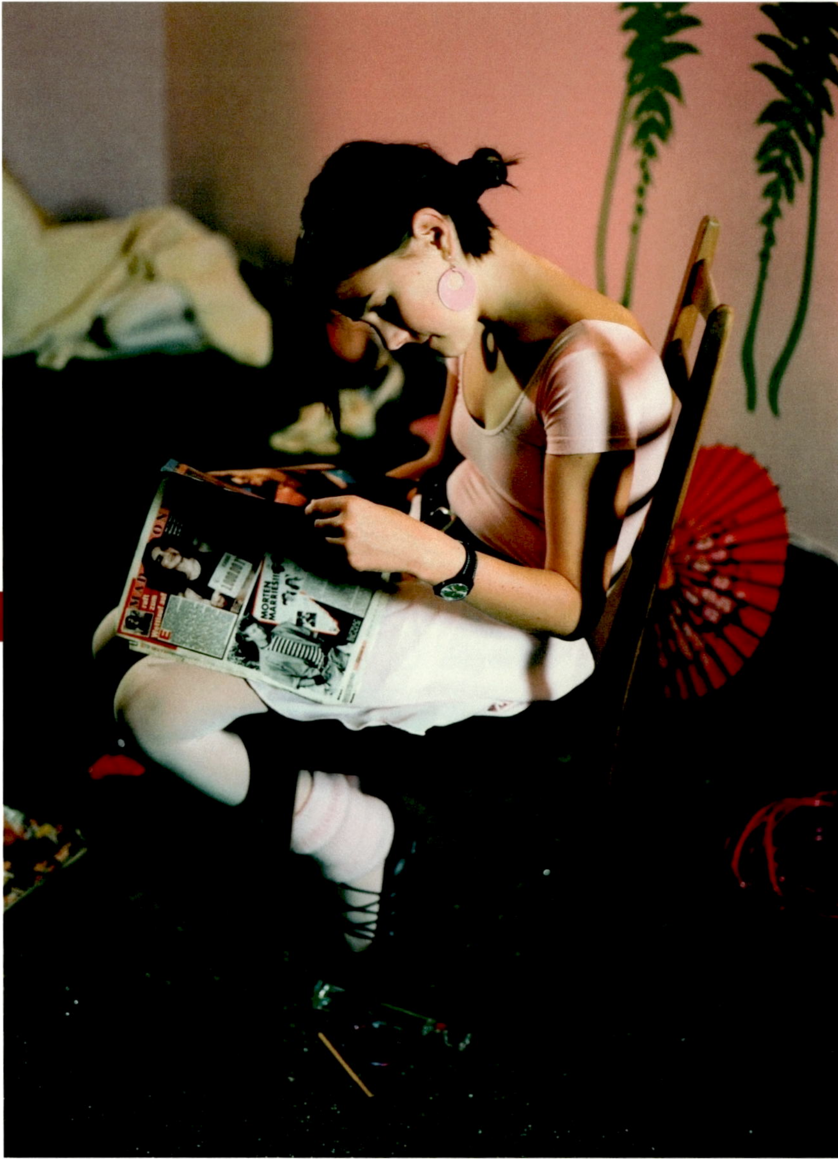

Still from *Sue de Beer: Black Sun.*

Adam Putnam

Noémie Lafrance

05   PERFORMERS

James Tenney with the
Flux Quartet

VisionIntoArt

Douglas Henderson

Vito Acconci

Los Super Elegantes

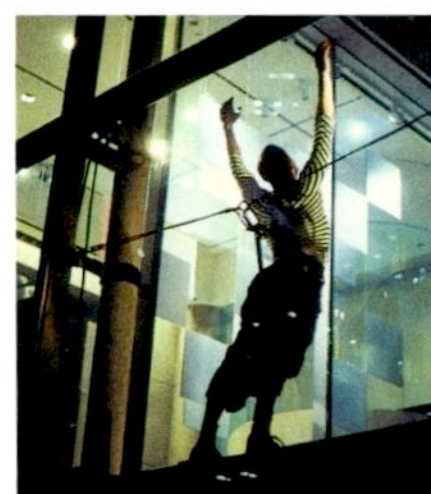

Noémie Lafrance,
Migrations, 05–04–05

March 3 to June 17, 2005

From: Shamim Momin, Altria
To: Sue de Beer
Sent: 03/16/04 10:01 am
Here's some good stuff from an article
I was reading the other day: "A central
problem of choice is what (is called)
"miswanting." Wanting . . . is 'a prediction
of liking.' Predictions are often biased,
and predictions of one's feelings are
more biased than most. Current prefer-
ences 'contaminate' future plans. . . . You
might try to draw on experience to help
you choose, but your memories aren't
to be trusted. . . . Our minds focus on the
peak and the final moments of a past
ex-perience while crowding out memories of its duration."
xxx, smm

From: Sue de Beer
To: Shamim Momin, Altria
Sent: 3/16/04 3:12 pm
What is memory? What is your experience?
How much of what defines your memory is fiction? And is the fiction something
you created or something others helped
you to create (a parent, TV, a book)?
I liked what you said also—once we were
talking about relationships and you
said, "But there are always good parts,
too, which is always so hard to remember not to forget." And when you said, "I
think being in love is a choice you make."
Both of those things speak to the consciousness of memory being something
alterable by oneself, by the feeling one
chooses to have.

July 7 to October 13, 2005

Past Presence: Childhood and Memory investigates memory, either in a personally specific way or collectively in the larger culture. The works taken together suggest the potent cultural resonance of representing memory and the formation of the self as a strategy for image-making.

The four artists [Robert Beck, Gary Simmons, Peggy Preheim, and Charles LeDray] in this exhibition explore how the objects and experience of childhood connect with culture and society to express aspects of youth through the lens of memory. The works in the exhibition evoke childhood and the individual's struggle to interpret, reinterpret, and understand its effects on the construction of personality over time and on the adult mental state.

Past Presence: Childhood and Memory

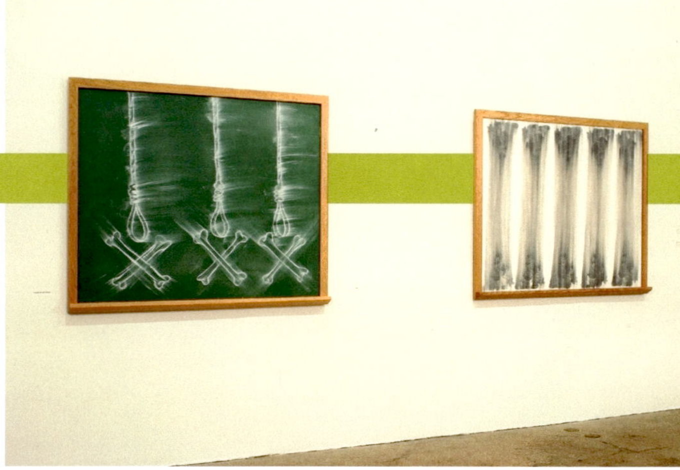

TOP: Left to right: Gary Simms, *Green Chalkboard (Triple X)*, 1993; *Hey, Hey, Hey. . .*, 1994 (installation view of *Past Presence: Childhood and Memory*). BOTTOM: Left to right: Charles LeDray, *Milk and Honey*, 1994–95; Robert Beck, *The Funnel (The Modern Man's Guide to Life by Denis Boyles, Alan Rose, Alan Rose, Alan Wellikoff)*, 2000 (installation views of *Past Presence: Childhood and Memory*).

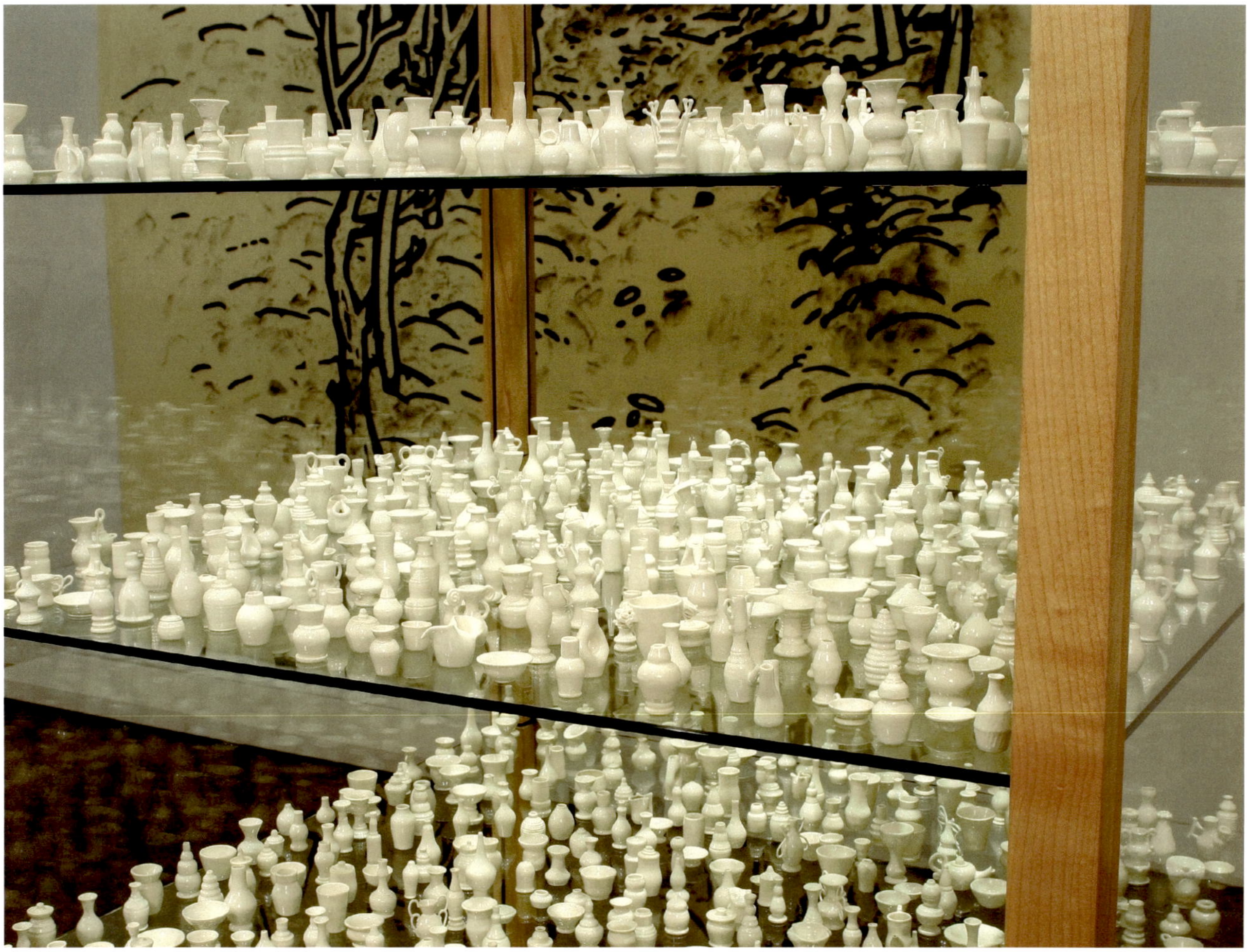

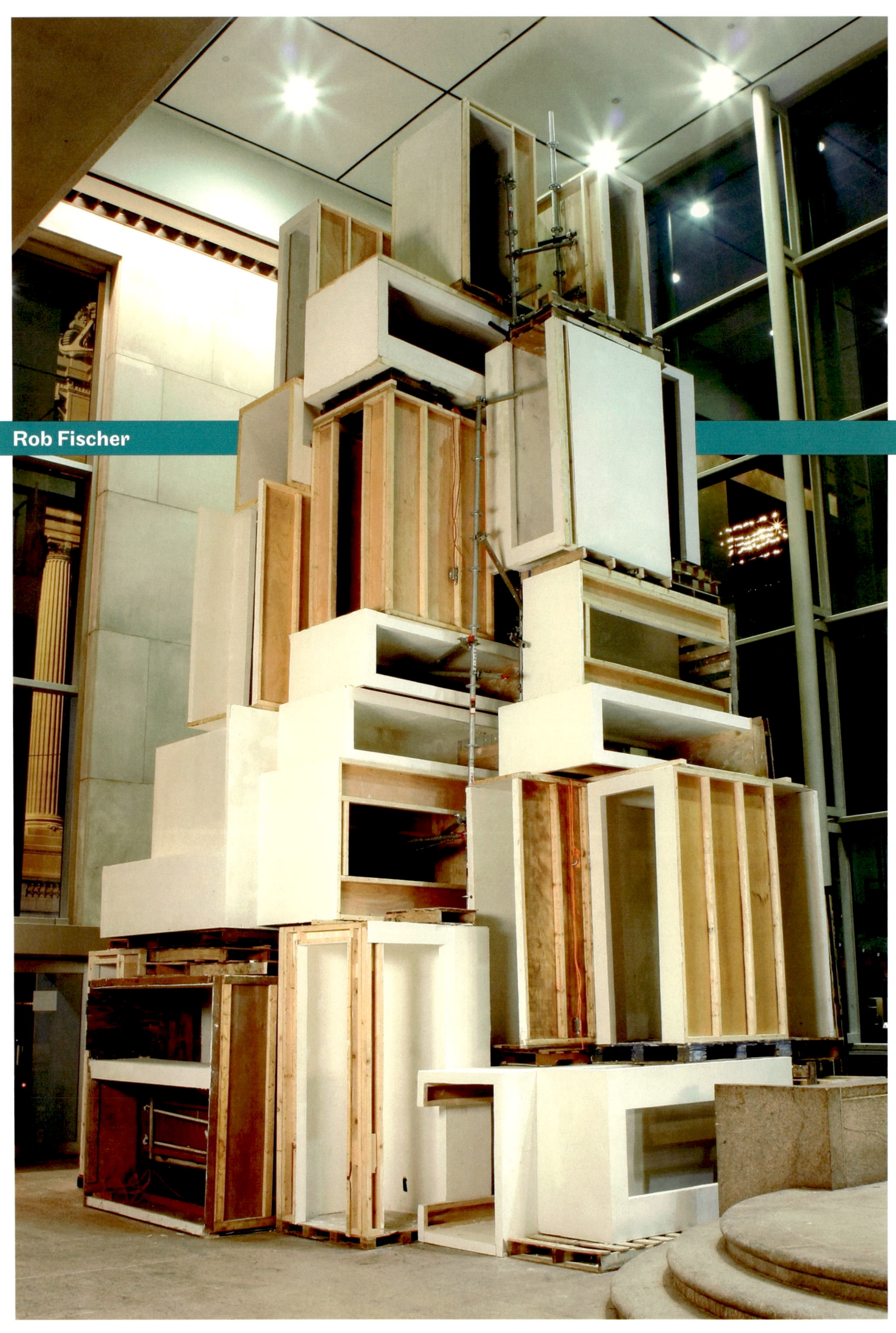
10
–
27
–
05

01
–
22
–
06

Rob Fischer

Rob Fischer: Here Is Always Somewhere Else

Men dream of flying because they thirst for a state of mind where they need not worry about the placement of their feet.
—ROBERT GROSSMAN, *THE BOOK OF LAZARUS*[1]

That's the problem, I thought—most people try to tell the many stories of their lives but are interrupted, time and again, until they begin to forget them. —GINA OCHSNER, *PEOPLE I WANTED TO BE*[2]

How do we explain a life, our own or any individual's? "How did I end up here?" These are questions that we tend to want to answer by citing a series of singular events—things that either happened to us or that were precipitated by us, a good story unfurled as a narrative of critical choices and dramatic moments that have shifted and diverted our paths according to a clear vision of who and what we would become. But in fact the trajectories are not as magisterial as we would like to believe: it is usually the minute, unnoticed decisions that shape our existence, and those are much harder to track. Failed or successful attempts to fulfill our desires require continued renegotiation and reorientation, and follow a far more elliptical, regenerative cycle than the teleological linearity of a cause-and-effect narrative. Perhaps the things that one strives to *not* be are in fact the most present, existing quietly behind those attempts toward grandeur. To further complicate things, life's stories are often swayed by our motivations to retell and make better sense of "the way it was."

Throughout his earlier practice, and most explicitly in recent sculptural installations he describes as "footnotes to an unknown story,"[3] Brooklyn-based artist Rob Fischer addresses the revisions of these contingent, aleatory histories. Fischer's sculptures have often incorporated recycled vehicle parts or vernacular architectural elements familiar to the landscape of his native Minnesota—trailers, boats, single-room cabins and houses, trucks, Dumpsters—for their formal and material qualities as well as the individual stories embedded in their histories. It is easy to imagine that the spatial relationships of the layered sculptural forms and our path through and among them (which becomes of increasing importance in his work) might suggest a diary of use. However, rather than functioning as an explicit series of true events, for Fischer the forms are cartographic, mapping specifics and deeply linked to a lived reality while also abstracted to a set of symbols that have broader and more universal meaning.

In Fischer's most recent large-scale installation of works from 2005 at the Whitney Museum at Altria, it is perhaps the smallest work—a diptych of photographs—that anchors and illuminates his media and practice. In *Highway 71 (Blur)* the two snapshot-like images of a group of parked trucks in an anonymous American countryside have clearly been taken from inside a moving vehicle. The setting sun glints on the edge of a car window, its glare challenged by a bright orange of trucks bursting into flames beyond—the color painted on the image by the artist. The blurring of the image suggests speed and escape from the destruction left behind. Throughout his career

Rob Fischer, *Your vigor for life appalls me*, 2005.
THIS PAGE AND FOLLOWING: Installation views of *Rob Fischer*.

Fischer has compiled similar photographs of common dwellings and vehicles, often abandoned, as an image library, studies for future works—and in the past few years he began to apply paint to their surfaces. Initially his painterly intervention was a protective gesture, blocking out the windows of people's houses in white to protect their privacy. Later he came to feel that the houses, essentially stand-ins for the absent people, were themselves emanating that light, a kind of "blinding spirit." More recently he has taken to depicting the internal combustion seen in *Highway 71 (Blur),* perhaps the most extreme act of protection through destruction.

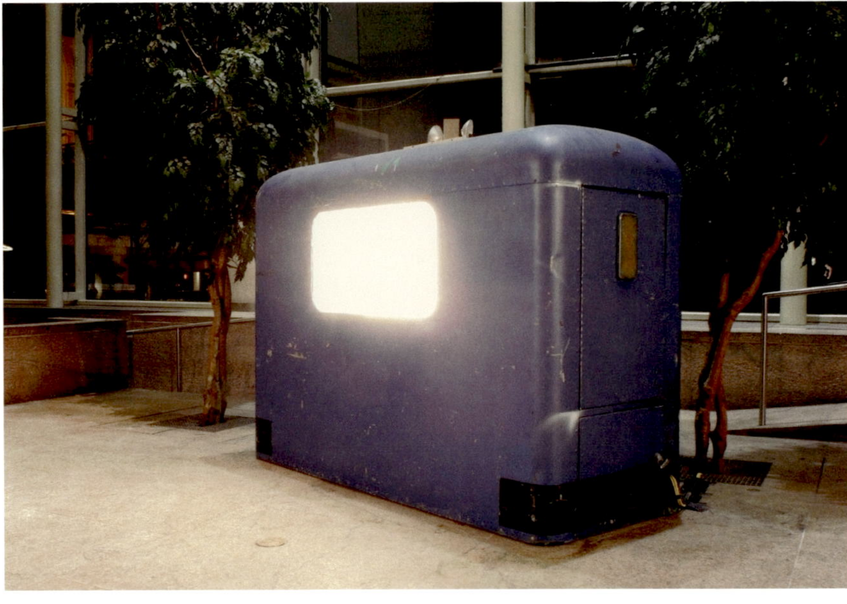

Rob Fischer, *God wrote Convoy in here,* 2005 (installation view of *Rob Fischer*).

These works embody recurrent aspects of Fischer's oeuvre: the altered photographs collapse memory, reality, and one's imagination of events witnessed and those imagined. The fleeting temporality of the snapshot form (enhanced by the viewer's vantage point inside the artist's moving car) contrasts with the painterliness (suggesting a more fixed state) of the smoke and flames, which in turn connote an immediate, transformative event. In Fischer's sculptural works, too, time is unstable and vulnerable, undermined by the tension between the urge for change and movement and the desire for stability and protection. His glimpse of violent destruction suggests the fragmentary and vestigial episodes of its anonymous and unaware victims, who would go on to interpret and retell the events. In exposing the nobility and the loss of such tragedy, Fischer sees these works as reflecting the human will for survival: "these fire paintings . . . were all about this reflection, or lack of, as a means of self-preservation. It is a blessing—memory loss. People have an amazing ability to select the memories that help them cope. It is true that people's memories of painful experiences are of them not being as bad as they thought they were at the time. Ignorance may not be bliss, but the opposite can be unbearable. Life would be overwhelming."

Outside the gallery, in the Whitney Museum at Altria atrium, a curved container of blue metal sits on one of the granite platforms, washing viewers with an intense light emitted from a translucent white opening. The work, *God wrote Convoy in here,* can be understood in part as the three-dimensional representation of Fischer's series of painted photographs. The piece, consisting of a truck's inverted sleeper cab, embodies the tension between mobility and place that underlies the photographic series as well as many of his sculptures. The decontextualized cab creates a space of protection within its hidden interior, owing both to the cab's original function as a private, mobile compartment and its reconfigured presence in a public arena. The inaccessible room glows with a beatific light, implying incubation or transformation, a spiritual transubstantiation that is denied the viewer. Just as Fischer protectively painted out the windows of houses he photographed, here he uses light to the same effect. It is so intense that, like the sun, it's difficult to look at directly. The shining whiteness is an intimate source of warmth and light within the vast, cold exterior space. The title, *God wrote Convoy in here,* adds to an idea of internal strength and resistance—Sam Peckinpah's 1978 movie *Convoy,* based on C. W. McCall's popular country song of the same name, centered on the community of support that arose around a trucker's vendetta against a corrupt sheriff. Fischer wryly evokes this reference, with the Almighty rebelliously personified and claiming his space.

The sculpture that occupies the balance of the gallery, *30 Yards (Minor Tragedies Dissected),* a revision of Fischer's 2004 Whitney Biennial submission *30 Yards (Minor Tragedies),* is made of a Dumpster quartered and stacked into a square cross-section. Each rusted quadrant is filled with a careful composition of material that integrates at least seven of his other sculptures, crushed into the whole. Sheets of bent and shaped metal intersect with scrap plumbing that angles in graphic patterns through the interiors; striped metal barrels protrude perilously from an upper section; old wood beams, overlapping like shingles, comprise a side wall as formally precise as a geometric abstraction. The rusted, skeletal remains of the Dumpster structure create four uniform frames for the compositions within, each a kind of "painting" with three-dimensional materials. Glass windowpanes in one of the sections add multiple frames within a frame.

Fischer's practice of recycling previous sculptures into newer works is less about his embrace of found objects than a reflection of his organic working process. The original *30 Yards* folded all of these layers of others' discarded objects within

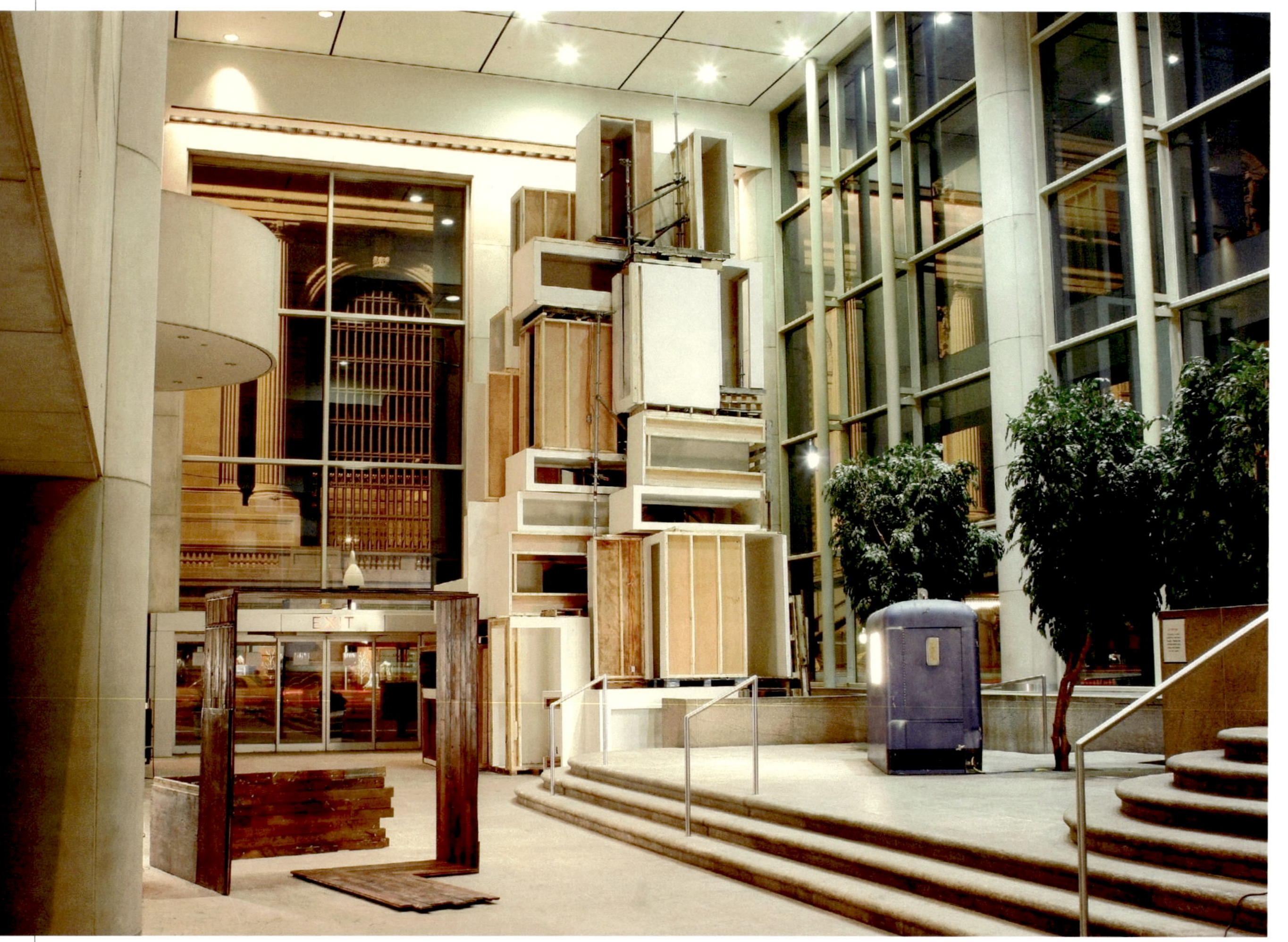

the Dumpster shell, but exposed them and the suggestions of their individual histories by replacing the steel sides with glass panels, a change that is also typical of his use of Dumpsters. In this final version of the work the artist has dissected and rearranged that collection, not in violation of its integrity but with an eye to increased clarity, getting to the "truer version" through each successive reorientation. As each permutation reuses material from past works, Fischer develops the layering of meaning he refers to as "the refusal of your own history to let you go." This connectivity is embodied in the recurring use of plumbing in Fischer's work, creating visual conduits connoting circulation and nourishment. Though it is more metaphorical in *30 Yards,* in a recent installation he joined the discrete sculptures (several of these are the empty rooms or closets that are a critical part of the artist's formal vocabulary) with pipes running between and through them, as if it were the original plumbing displaced as a house was pulled apart. It also created one visually complex linked system within the space, requiring viewers to be conscious of their movements through it as they ducked beneath or stepped over the pipes.[4]

As one moves from the gallery into the vast atrium space in the Whitney installation, the sculpture is further abstracted and conceptually focused on the tension between ambition and humility, between the desire to transcend the anonymity of life and the near-inevitable failure of that attempt. The installation is anchored on opposing sides of the sculpture court (an architectural emblem of corporate power and strength) by Fischer's own explorations of monumentality and hubris. On one side, a massive tower of stacked semi-modular cubic forms of wood and plaster climbs around a spine of steel scaffolding nearly to the 40-foot ceiling. Entitled *Your vigor for life appalls me* (from a book of letters by noir-comic master Robert Crumb), it competes for attention in scale and presence with the strident geometry of the mirror and steel sculpture on the other end, a shimmering, gridded construction that mimics the basic form of a triumphal arch. *I bet you think this song is about you* is a 20-yard Dumpster oriented vertically, the interior panels carefully sliced out to retain only the structural steel skeleton, with the balance of the planes replaced with mirrors and an "entranceway" through which we might pass. Between these two forms, five smaller discrete sculptural pieces wend their way across the multiple levels of the public space and the gallery, providing our navigational course. This suggestion of a narrative trajectory emerges as both an undercurrent of the installation and an integral reading of the

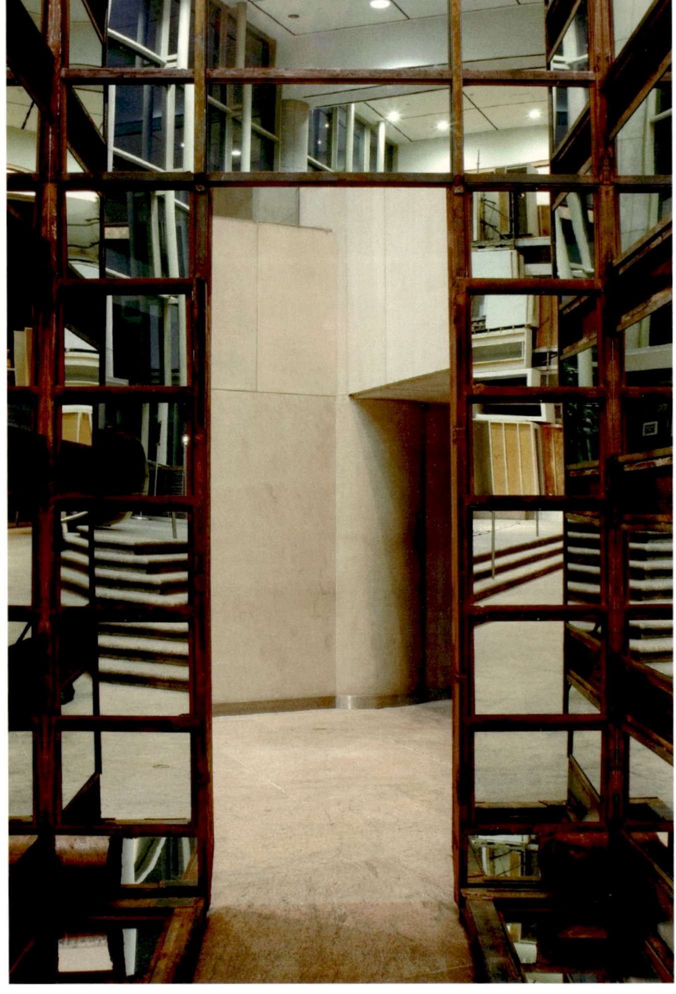

Rob Fischer, *I bet you think this song is about you,* 2005 (installation view of *Rob Fischer*).

individual works. The word *navigation* itself is emblematic of Fischer's exploration—to steer a course on, across, or through a medium, to make one's way.

As we approach the tower, it becomes impossible to view the entire construction at once, and thus the individual views of the work take on increased importance. The primary building blocks of the work are what the artist refers to as "closets and hallways"—minimal, schematized versions of those forms in a combination of plastered and unfinished wood, which, like much of Fischer's work, are oriented as needed for support and composition, thus troubling their familiar associations. Floors become walls become ceilings become coffins, amplifying their dislocation from quotidian context and allowing them to be read as purely formal elements. They are closets that don't hold things, hallways that don't lead anywhere. That each container in the enormous structure is scaled to the human body calls attention to their emptiness and sense of alienation—or, when laid horizontally, death. The accumulation of like forms suggests a community, yet the empty elements never truly merge, remaining vulnerable, exposed, and largely alone. Once we are close to the piece the interior scaffolding becomes more visible, an organic arrangement of steel poles and clamps that begins to resemble a semi-exposed spine, powerfully structural and infinitely delicate. At the same time, the minimal palette and velvety plaster against raw wood form a series of abstract, sensual compositions from different vantage points around the tower, shifting volumetric to planar. The artist in fact cites a number of painters, rather than sculptors, as influences for his thinking about space and composition—Giorgio Morandi, Luc Tuymans, Magnus von Plessen, and Kai Altoff—who layer paint and color in veiled planes of semiabstract, semirepresentational form, encouraging facile slippages between generality and specificity, flatness and depth. Fischer is particularly drawn to the fragility of how the objects and spaces they paint barely touch, a hesitancy embodied in much of his own work. Here the gentle palette of whites, grays, and neutral beiges mitigates the enormity of the piece, creating painterly interactions of ghostly monochrome that dissolve the structure from certain viewpoints, while circumnavigation disassembles the object into its volumetric parts.

Your vigor for life appalls me was initially inspired by Fischer's interest in the biblical story of the tower of Babel. As described in the book of Genesis, the original community had grown tired of being a nomadic people, so they taught themselves brickmaking and settled to build their homes. Soon they were building tall monuments, leading to evermore ambitious goals: "Come, let us build ourselves a city, with a tower that reaches to the heavens, so that we may make a name for ourselves and not be scattered over the face of the whole earth."[5] In spite of their remarkable innovations, God was displeased with their arrogance and took steps to limit such human ambition, "confounding their tongues" so they could not communicate and thus could not finish the structure.[6] Fischer was less intrigued by the dramatic result of the Babel endeavor than in its underlying human motivations: "people invariably attempt to be bigger than they are"; the heartbreak so often inherent in that ever-replenished desire; and the impossibility of some ideas to coexist without destroying themselves. He sees his tower less as a monument to a society's failed ambition, however, than to an individual's, the carapace-like vestiges of personal pride. Hope and despair lay down the unfinished walls, erect the velvety white siding, wrap the worn floorboards around a partially hidden interior, and frame out the structure of a person's existence. "You learn to live with your second skeleton," wrote artist Vito Acconci, "it moves as you move, like a shadow, a mirror image, a dancing partner, a devil."[7]

The huge scale of *Your vigor for life appalls me,* like that of the colossal mirrored Dumpster it communicates with across the atrium, inevitably recalls memorials and monuments, which are typically dedicated to the achievement of some grand success or to the celebration of noble sacrifice. Here and throughout Fischer's work, the artist pays tribute to the shadows between the imagined ideal and the smaller negotiations of our lives.[8] Franz Kafka's story "The City Coat of Arms," about the building of the tower of Babel, describes its incompletion not as an act of God, but one of man's constant struggle with an idea of progress or non-progress: as each successive generation learned more sophisticated building techniques, they would tear down what was previously built and begin again the "right" way, thus dooming the tower to terminal incompletion. Along with the personal tone that his choices of materials lend to much of Fischer's work, his practice simultaneously takes the shape of larger cultural metaphors, cycles of destruction and renewal that are reflected on all scales of experience.

Fischer attributes this fluidity between specific and universal to his own visual heritage, the rural midwestern landscape of his childhood—a different view of architecture as part of and within the landscape rather than in a position of dominating or conquering it (as more commonly conveyed within an urban environment). The artist describes how houses, farm equipment, cars, and trucks largely remain where they were abandoned, falling apart and decaying slowly until "rather than reading as a piece of human intervention in the landscape, they end up as little islands of nature in the middle of the fields again. . . . All of these things left in the fields then recycle into, regenerate, new life."

Just beyond the aggressive brightness emitted by the sleeper cab sculpture, a meager light glows within a smaller work, *Living Will.* Though minimal in structure and palette, the work nonetheless plays on many of the same conceits as in the massive tower. It rests on the floor, as if a single wood and plaster module had been removed from the tower and laid on its side. The stillness of the all-white form is enhanced by three steps rising to its top, forming a humble, empty stage. A lightbulb inside the container, just beyond comfortable viewing, calls attention to the semi-hidden interior; its proportions and orientation recall a vacant sarcophagus. As with the tower, Fischer uses absence to powerfully evoke the human form, the under-stage light giving a claustrophobic weight to the empty spaces of both sculptures.

In contrast to the near-palpable ray of *God wrote Convoy in here,* the tentative light of *Living Will* embodies the variable interpretations of the title. Of course it suggests the legal document in which an individual appoints another to make choices that we usually associate with decisions about their final life support (a last deliberate act at a moment defined by an inability to make decisions for oneself), but the title could also imply the will to life—hence the light—suggesting that idea of choice is the only constant that illuminates our movement through the world. Will has no physical nature; it is purely a composite of experience, habit, and impression that inspires an action and, here, inspires a monument. Fischer has likened the piece to Native American spirit houses that are still scattered throughout the melancholic landscape of northern Minnesota. He was particularly struck by the burial houses from the 1930s and '40s, rotted and on the verge of collapse, at the brink of no longer marking their graves. Yet as their name suggests, these memorials never held the bodies of the deceased, but rather their spirit of living—this is the will that the sculpture commemorates, even as its emptiness suggests ephemerality and loss.

The sculpture *Manyfold (Minotaur)* is likewise as densely layered with meaning and oblique connections to the other works as it is minimal in form. Constructed of found flooring from a domestic interior, the work suggests a three-dimensional section of labyrinth or a partial aerial view. The deep-brown wood planks show the vestiges of their earlier life, running parallel to the path of the labyrinth and emphasizing a sense of internalized movement. As in many of his works, Fischer employs a familiar material in uncanny ways— the flooring runs comfortably along the ground then turns up and climbs into a wall, bending sharply again to become a section of ceiling. The confusion of space evoked by a seemingly simple form is implied by its title: built by the legendary inventor Daedalus, the mythical labyrinth was to contain the monstrous offspring of woman and bull, the Minotaur. The labyrinth was a space both of protection and violence (the Minotaur's captor, King Minos, required the annual sacrifice of seven virgin girls and boys to ensure the beast's cooperation), but it also represents the despair of the infinite, of endless, lonely wandering, and of claustrophobia and containment. The story connects to ideas of hubris and destruction seen in the Tower of Babel tale: after Theseus breached the maze and killed the Minotaur, Minos imprisoned Daedalus and his son in his own invention. Sacrificing all available materials, Daedalus created a set of wax wings for his son Icarus's escape, but despite his father's warning, the boy attempted to fly too high and his wings were melted by the sun, so he plummeted to his death.[9] These two legends embody undercurrents throughout Fischer's installation—ambition and failure, creation and destruction, will and loss.

The swelling curve of a nearby piece, *Not waving but drowning,* beckons from its perch on a raised landing of the atrium, atop the stairs to the exit. Lying on its side, the rise of the metal hull of a bisected boat assumes an organic sensibility, the mottled and cracked surface like withered skin of a beached animal. As with much of Fischer's work, there is a sense of a narrative in which something went wrong. Though generally impossible to surmise exactly, the title—the refrain from a poem

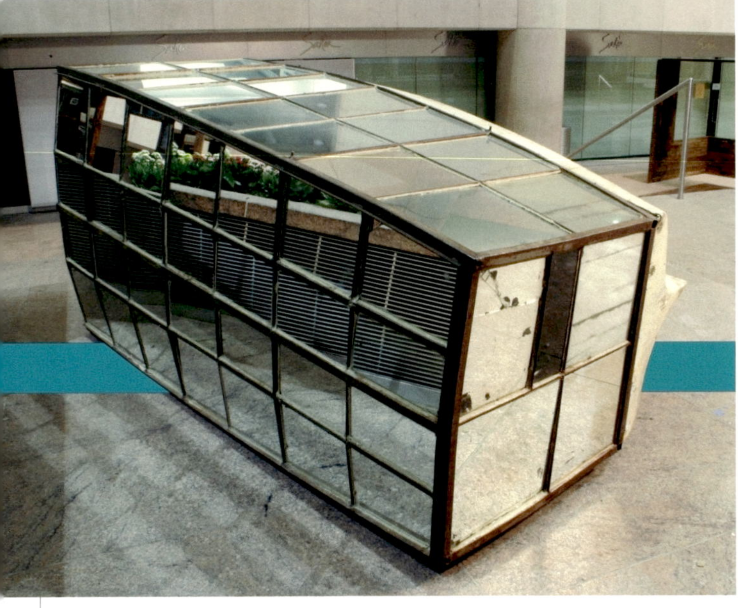

Rob Fischer, *Not waving but drowning,* 2005 (installation view of *Rob Fischer*).

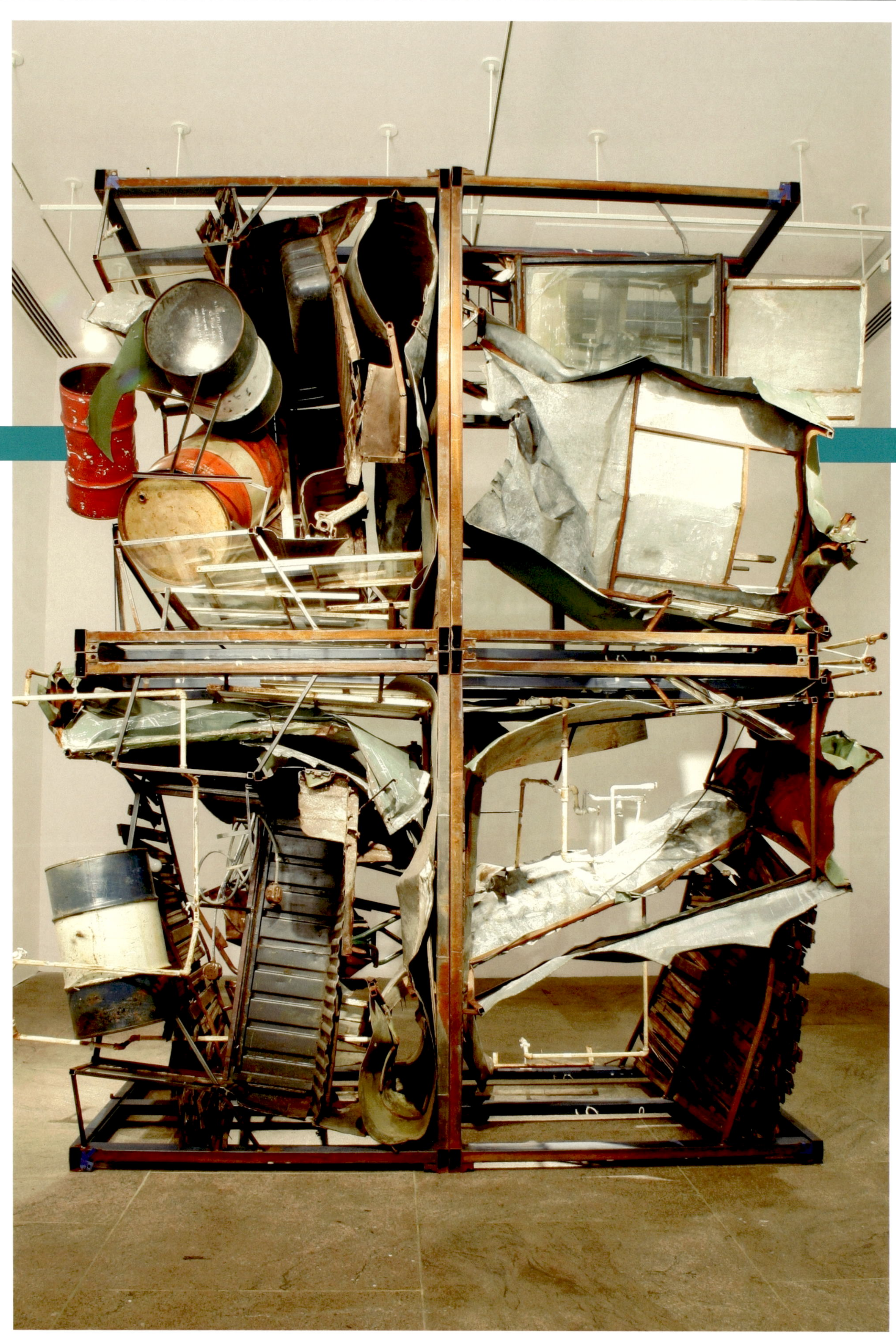

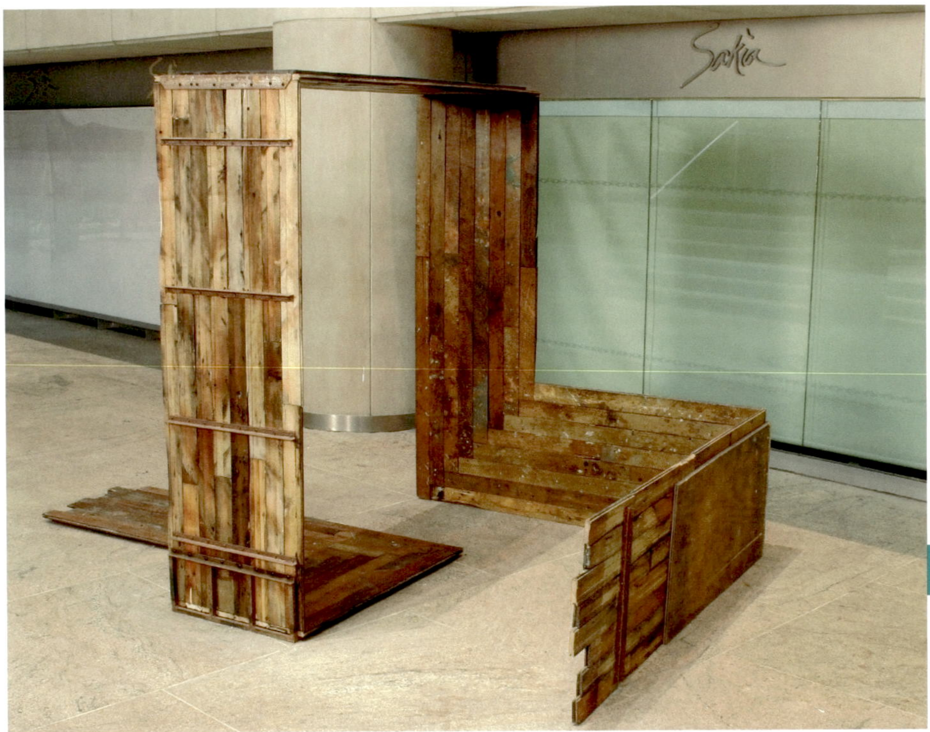

Rob Fischer, *Manyfold (Minotaur)*, 2005.
OPPOSITE: Rob Fischer, *30 Yards (Minor Tragedies Dissected)*, 2005 (installation views of *Rob Fischer*).

by British writer Stevie Smith—suggests a story of misinterpretation, the attempt to communicate gone awry.[10] The cavelike interior of the boat is closed off by panels of mirrors, melding a houselike architecture to the boat bottom. The artist's repeated use of mirrors enhances the work's placelessness; as they reflect and incorporate their environment they become subsumed within it, curiously anonymous.

While Fischer's work remains deeply tied to specific locations and geographies, whether of his native city and its environs or the desiccated backyard of his Brooklyn studio, the idea of place he describes conveys a liminal state of uncertainty. His earlier work, from when he was still living in Minnesota, had more directly referenced the tension between the desire for mobility and change, stability and place. Though the familiar and utilitarian elements were recognizable, he modified his hybrid sculptures to obscure a transparent purpose—a practice still evident in *Not waving but drowning*. Instead, such works embodied what the artist refers to as a "sort-of" purpose, a transitory state of imminent movement or complete stasis, a sense of apprehension and fallibility, where the tentative choice takes precedence over the grand gesture. More recently, works such as *Manyfold (Minotaur)*, *Living Will*, and *God wrote Convoy in here* tend toward greater abstraction, where the references are less recognizable. The simple forms of the smaller works in the Whitney installation imply a directness that is then denied by their modifications—often upending meaning by upending literally, hinting at purpose where ultimately there is none.

Looking up from the boat-house sculpture to the enormous mirrored Dumpster-archway of *I bet you think this song is about you,* it appears a cast-off element from the larger work, shed from its gridded geometry. Lined entirely with mirrors except for the human-scaled doorway, the Dumpster is at once monumental and oddly insubstantial. Again, the reflective surface dissolves the space it occupies by enfolding its environment within. As it offers an image of what surrounds it, the closed surface of the mirror also conceals, as if protecting some secret behind, much like the emanating light of *Convoy* or the painted-out windows of the photographs, and the rusty patina of the metal frame gives the work a sense of age and history recalled from other sculptures. The grid of Dumpster skeleton mimics the framework of the enormous windows of the atrium architecture, for example, while the tangle of images tilting and intersecting in the mirrored panels bankrupts the blustering machismo of its corporate modernism.

The humor of the title *I bet you think this song is about you* (a line from the Carly Simon song "You're So Vain") mitigates the unavoidably iconic presence of the piece, a reminder that it is not a monument to anything but what you see within it. The work also evokes the dangers of vanity and hubris, here turned specifically onto the viewer. For Fischer, it was necessarily constructed from a real Dumpster, maintaining a connection to its original incarnation, "in order to become something else." The archway makes it a marker of passage between states. Like the closets incorporated into *Your vigor for life appalls me,* the former container no longer contains; like the hallways that connect no rooms, it becomes about itself as a conduit. As usual, the Dumpster is reoriented—it has just stood up, the human gesture of getting on its feet. For Fischer this position is one of defiance and willful resolve, whereas the horizontal Dumpsters represent a passive motion. This adjustment suggests a spectral past composed of the refuse of lives or a place; it becomes a memorial of sorts. That the mirrored archway also feels like a massive altarpiece in the cathedral-like space of the atrium projects a reverential, sacred atmosphere that is in other works as well. While the traditional connotation of triumphal entry is blunted by its positioning at a distant wall, it announces instead one's conscious movement around and through it, framing a view of the other sculptures within its doorway. This placement reminds the viewer of the choices of space through which he or she has just passed, retelling the story just formed, in front of their own image, as memory and time insubstantially folds in on itself.

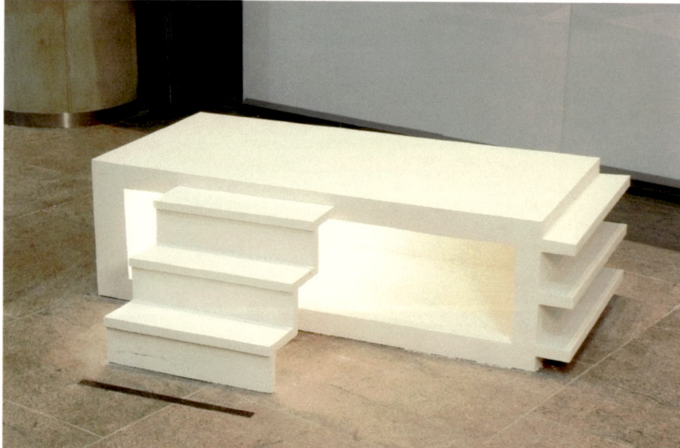

Rob Fischer, *Living Will*, 2005 (installation view of *Rob Fischer*).

Creating narrative structure, assembling life into a story, is arguably the most essential process of human consciousness—perhaps we are only able to understand the world by organizing it into these frameworks. We need these stories to attribute meaning, purpose, and a future to our lives, but they are created as much by exclusion as by what is selected. The almost incidental quality of the "not-told" is the fundamental content of Fischer's work, where beauty is found in heartbreak and solitude, what he calls a fascination with the "damaged character." The philosopher Immanuel Kant famously wrote that "out of the crooked timber of humanity, no straight thing was ever made." Fischer assembles skewed, circuitous, oblique timbers into the resonating pathos of his work in the recognition that straight things are merely someone else's way of telling the wrong story.

—SHAMIM M. MOMIN, BRANCH DIRECTOR AND CURATOR

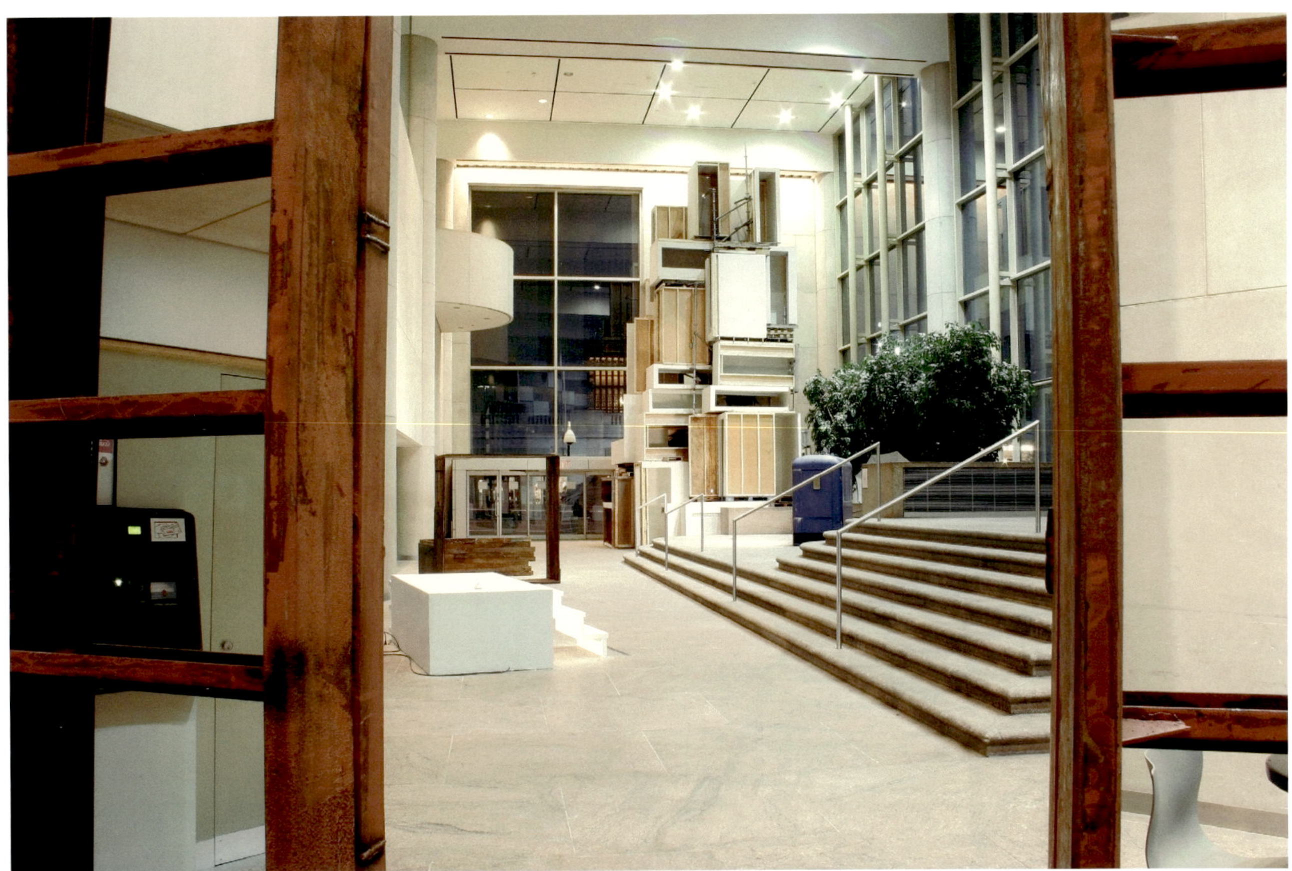

1. Robert Grossman,
The Book of Lazarus (Chicago:
Northwestern University
Press, 1997), 27.
2. Gina Ochsner, *People
I Wanted to Be* (Boston and
New York: Houghton Mifflin,
2005), 37.
3. All quotes from
conversations with the artist
on September 12, 27, and
October 26, 2005, unless
otherwise noted.
4. The artist's first sketches
for the Whitney installation
were based on schematic
versions of old city maps.
Hallways converged
elliptically on a central point
and filled the space like
veins to a heart or tree roots
to a trunk. As with the metaphor of plumbing,
these constructions rhyme
with human and natural
patterns.

5. Genesis 11.4.
6. Fischer's approach recalls
a version of the story
painted in 1563 by Peter
Bruegel the Elder (c. 1525–
1569), who was known for
his focus on the beauty
and truth inherent in daily
life. His *Tower of Babel*
illustrates a ziggurat of
earthen brick with architectural elements clinging to it
in seemingly haphazard
piles and other inexplicable
assemblages of machinery—
the human vestiges of
the event.
7. Vito Acconci, from
the work *World in your Bones*
(1998); see Vito Hannibal
Acconci Studio (exh. cat.
Musée des Beaux-Arts de
Nantes and Museu d'Art
Contemporani de Barcelona,
2004–5), 408, 410.

8. In a conversation with the
artist about the flux be-
tween the ideal and what
is settled for, he described
a hand-lettered sign he had
seen when driving in
Minnesota in the summer
of 2005 that he couldn't get
out of his head. The sign
advertised the sale of some
unknown personal property
for "500 dollars or best offer."
9. Incidentally, the morality
tale of Icarus's death was the
ostensible subject of
another painting by Pieter
Bruegel that emphasized,
like Fischer, not a recounting
of monumental events, but
how such things are largely
unremarked-upon at the
time of their happening, however defining they later become. The painting focuses
on average people going
about their business, tilling

the soil, transporting goods
on the waters—Icarus's tiny
leg disappearing beneath
the sea off to the bottom
right foreground, unnoticed.
10. *Nobody heard him, the
dead man,
But still he lay moaning:
I was much further out than
you thought
And not waving but drowning.*

*Poor chap, he always loved
larking
And now he's dead
It must have been too cold
for him his heart gave way,
They said.*

*Oh, no no no, it was
too cold always
(Still the dead one lay
moaning)
I was much too far out
all my life
And not waving but drowning.*

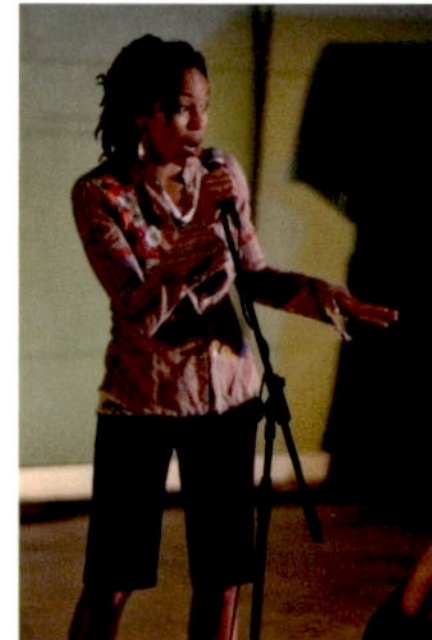

Andrea Zittel: Small Liberties

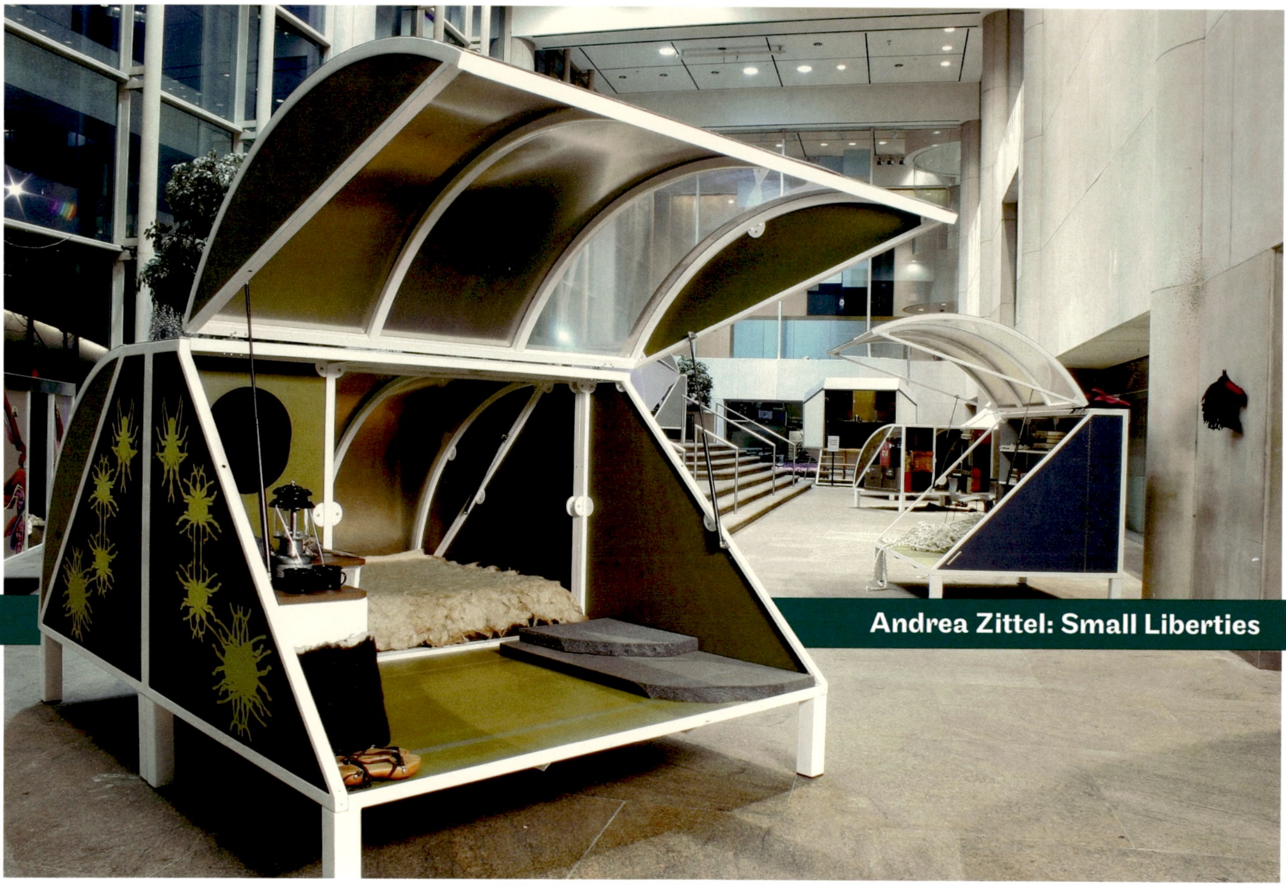

Installation view of *Andrea Zittel: Small Liberties.*

Alex Hubbard

Bill Fontana

Liza Jessie Peterson

Nicholasleichterdance
and Eisa Davis

Phil Kline

Charwei Tsai

Lizzi Bougatsos

06   PERFORMERS

Hisham Bharoocha

Julien Asfour

Mick Barr

Loris Gréaud

Nicholasleichterdance
and Eisa Davis,
Sweetwash, 05–17–06

February 9 to June 18, 2006

Ceaselessly researching, designing, and remodeling her own domestic and external environments, Andrea Zittel has created an evolving body of experimental structures and systems for living. Her work centers on the recognition that rules, while generally presented as irreproachable and inviolable, are actually fundamentally arbitrary and thus can— and should—be explored, investigated, and reconfigured to suit specific contexts. Zittel's practice seeks to balance tensions between individuality and community, beauty and usefulness, material clarity/truthfulness and conceptual rigor. The culmination of ten years of experimentation with these systems of living, Zittel's current project, A-Z West, is a fully realized compound and community sited in Joshua Tree, California.

From February 9 through June 18, 2006, the Whitney Museum of American Art at Altria, New York, presented the exhibition *Andrea Zittel: Small Liberties*, a selection of eleven Wagon Stations. These single-person living units were created at the Joshua Tree site and customized by invited individuals who have participated in the development of Zittel's desert community. Illustrating an overarching system that also represents specific, individual personalities, the Wagon Stations locate moments of the liberating contemplation suggested by the exhibition's title as they illuminate the basic tenets of Zittel's work. Transplanted to the urban landscape of New York City, the simple clarity of the overall system of the stations was highlighted, while the individuality of each object was retained.

June 30 to November 12, 2006

[Trace features] six artists who deal in various ways with the idea of the spectral trace, the absent object, and how the invisible—time, memory, desire—shapes our material reality. A pervasive sense of loss and tragedy links a number of these works, but they also possess a kind of sublime memorialization. . . .

Jedediah Caesar's geode sculptures made from resin, dust, and detritus collected from his studio constitute a material archive of time and the subtle accrual of remnant objects. . . .

Shannon Ebner's work presents two projects juxtaposing photographs of past events and text that together act as an elusive monument to contemporary political alienation. . . .

Iván Navarro's sculptural installation consists of a large-scale, black cubic space in which viewers enter to find a set of illusional mirrored sculptures infinitely reflecting text and light. Accompanied by a sound component, the work exists as both singular sculpture and also immersive environment in the Sculpture Court. . . .

Karyn Olivier employs spare sculptural interventions that evoke a consciousness of nostalgia and absence. With subtle manipulations of scale, function, and physical access, Olivier creates an equivocal location between public and private space. . . .

Michael Queenland excavates cultural and religious forms that have become detached from their original associations and functions. Drawing from diverse sources such as art history, avant-garde practices, craft legacies, and religion, Queenland creates stark associative installations involving sculpture, photography, and found objects. . . .

Karlis Rekevics' cast plaster sculptures of industrial objects from such overlooked urban spaces and objects as highway underpasses, cement traffic dividers, and sign posts render a psychologically charged landscape throughout the Sculpture Court.

Trace: New Work by Jedediah Caesar, Shannon Ebner, Karyn Olivier, Iván Navarro, Michael Queenland and Karlis Rekevics

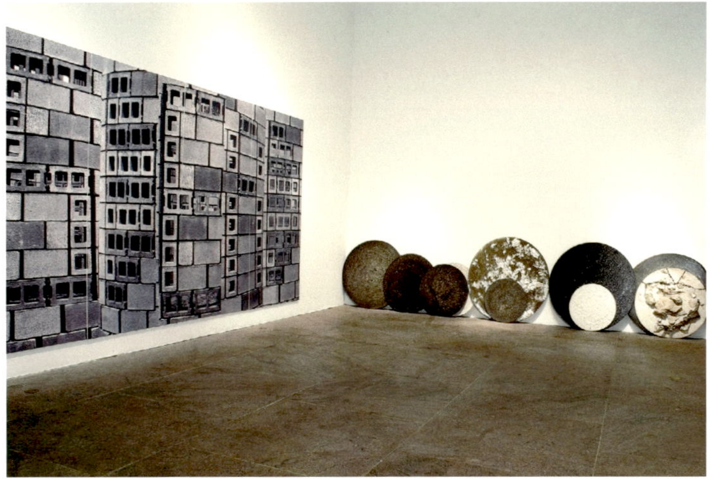

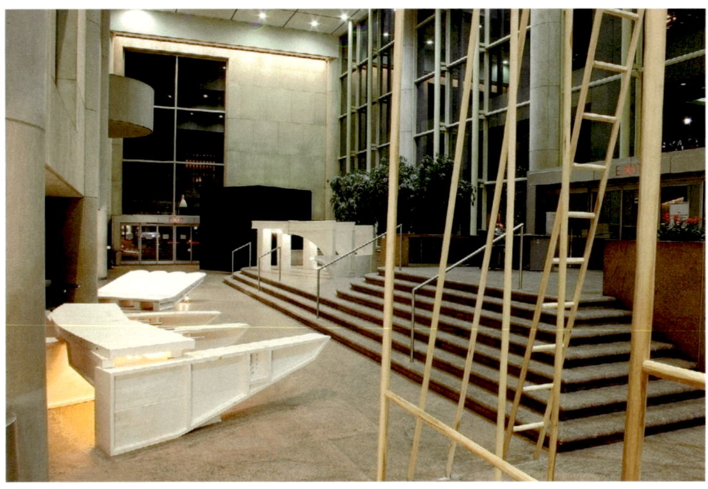

TOP: Left to right: Shannon Ebner, *"Is Dead,"* 2006; Jedediah Caesar, *0,000,000*, 2006 (installation view of *Trace: New Work by Jedediah Caesar, Shannon Ebner, Karyn Olivier, Ivan Navarro, Michael Queenland, and Karlis Rekevics*). **BOTTOM:** Left to right: Ivan Navarro, *Die again (monument for Tony Smith)*; Karlis Rekevic, *Veracity, Validity, Fabrication, Facts*; Karyn Olivier, *Junglegym*, 2006 (installation view of *Trace: New Work by Jedediah Caesar, Shannon Ebner, Karyn Olivier, Ivan Navarro, Michael Queenland, and Karlis Rekevics*).

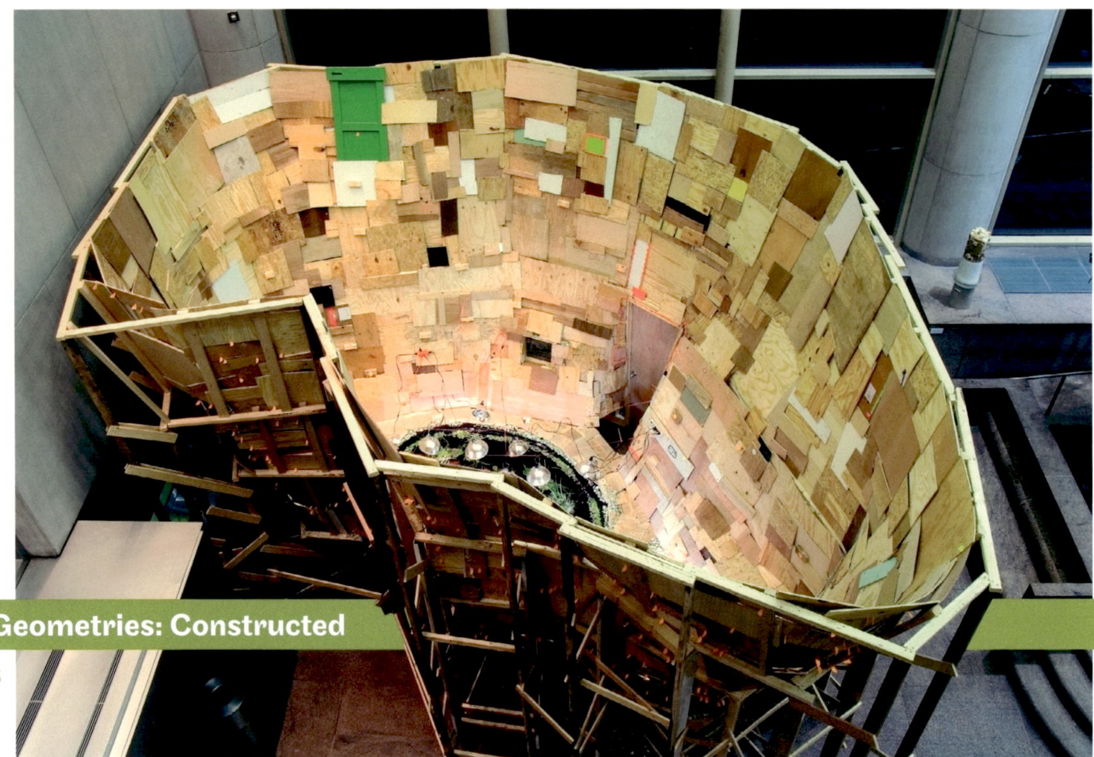

TOP: Pheobe Washburn, *Minor In-House Brain Storm*, 2006 (installation views of *Burgeoning Geometries: Constructed Abstractions*). BOTTOM: Left to right: Jane South, *Untitled (Tracing Parameters)*, 2006; Tara Donovan, *Untitled (Pins)*, 2004.

Burgeoning Geometries: Constructed Abstractions

December 7, 2006 to March 4, 2007

We live in an age where, due to exploding technological developments and our human impulse to produce, objects naturally burgeon, accrete, multiply, and serialize ad infinitum. Skyscrapers, freeways, strip malls, parking lots, radio towers, satellites, electronic circuits, wireless networks, cyberspace, these are but a few everyday examples of the disparate, expanding forms comprising our man-made environment. Anchored in a capitalist culture that revels in mass-consumerism, mass distribution, and the mass media, industrial and technological growth has reached extreme levels in the United States...

American artists have been incorporating observations of their burgeoning environment into their practice for over a half-century, most notably in Minimalist and Pop art...

Each piece begins as a simple, reductive form and, through the artists' meticulous manipulation of these common objects and materials, cumulatively becomes a complex network of abundant, interconnecting elements that delight in color, line, texture, space, and volume. Visually rich and densely layered, the works are difficult to identify as belonging exclusively to one specific category, but rather reside in the interstices between painting, drawing, sculpture, and installation. —APSARA DIQUINZIO

07	PERFORMERS

Fritz Haeg

Judith Sánchez Ruíz and Dafnis Prieto

Glenn Kaino

Praxis Studio

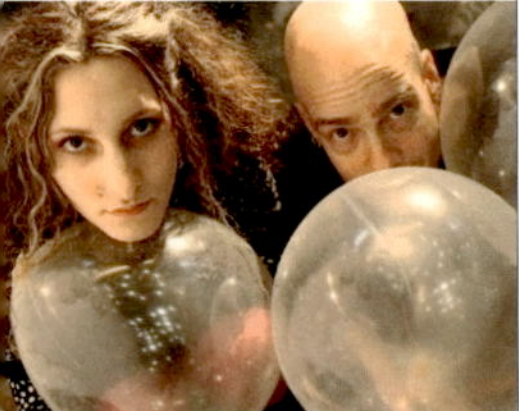

Praxis Studio, *Dreams and Possiblities*, 03–12 to 03–22–07

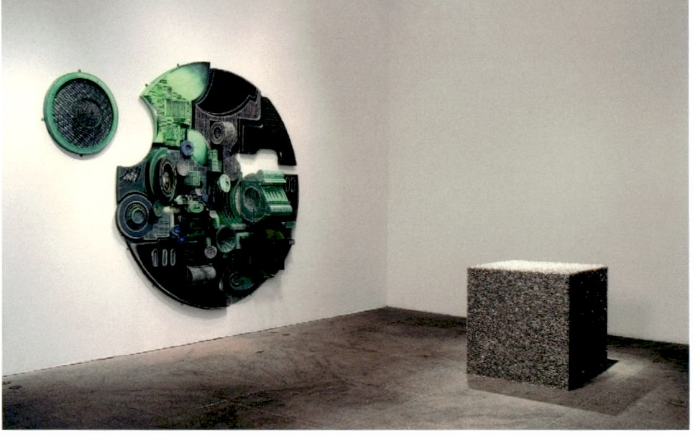

Chapter 11

Without attendant punctuation or context, Matthew Brannon's exhibition title *Where Were We* makes itself irreducible to a single interpretation. Its ambiguity and incompleteness as a phrase belies its seemingly reductive economy and alliterative simplicity. It points to a loss of bearings—uttered perhaps after an interruption in conversation, a regrettable shared experience, or a period of unconsciousness, during which we lost our expectation, register, or direction. A diversion has occurred.

Through the proliferation of speculative narratives stemming from this short indeterminate phrase, we are introduced to the nature of Brannon's artistic practice and strategies: even in the most simple and apparently vacated form, text and images are loaded with meanings that slide past and inform each other without ever fully fixing themselves or their associations. Intimated in these signifying operations is the specter of the psychological unconscious, which may be understood as being structured much like language and similarly discloses itself through

Matthew Brannon: Where Were We

jokes, slips, breakdowns, and unexpected ruptures.[1]

With a nuanced understanding of psychoanalytic theory, the artist juxtaposes image and text to bring the viewer into a play of associations between language and representation. At the same time, he has designed the exhibition to structure the viewer's visual experience around the act of reading and that which is revealed in the systems of pictures, narratives, objects, and space.

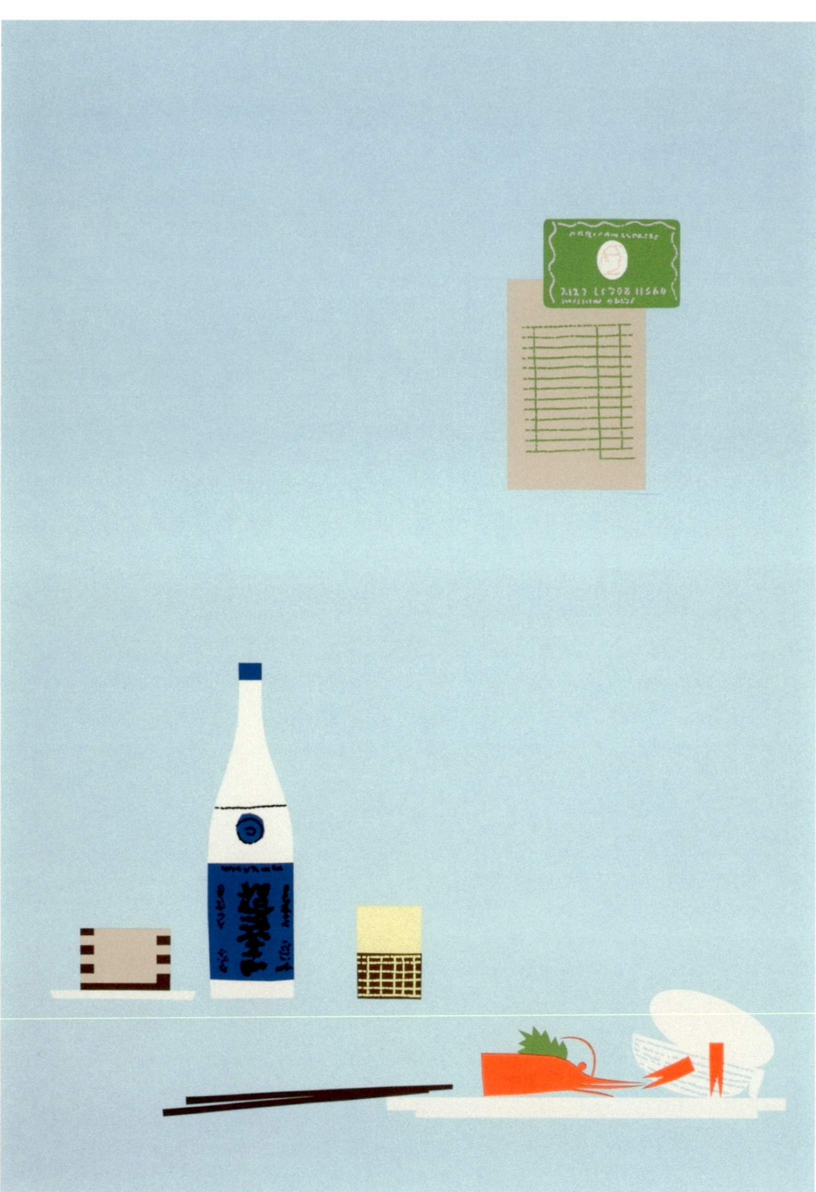

Matthew Brannon, *Who Takes Home Tonight*, 2007.
THIS PAGE AND FOLLOWING: Installation views of *Matthew Brannon: Where Were We*.

Restructuring

Brannon employs a signature combination of printed images, design strategies, and text in work that leverages the forms, visual currency, and circulation of promotional materials. The postcards, posters, and other ephemera that he creates at once announce the exhibition and comprise its formal elements, expanding the idea of what constitutes an exhibition to include all of its considered and diffuse material extensions.[2]

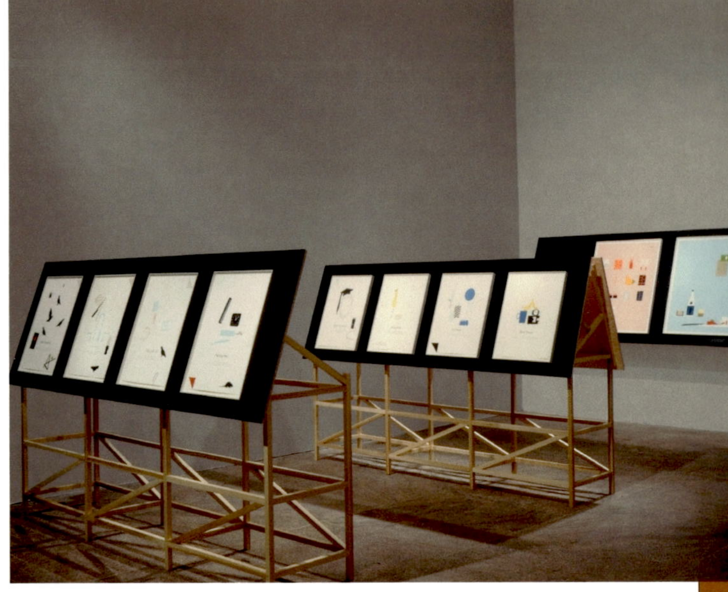

With *Where Were We,* the exhibition and the act of reading begin with the announcement and invitation, designed by the artist. The opening reception invitation, in the form of a letterpress "business card," and a poster are presented together in a custom envelope, evoking a bureaucratic aesthetic and formality. A provisional logo—a coiled black eel that is a recurring graphic motif in Brannon's work—lends the envelope and card a similar impression. The four-color poster unfolds to reveal a stark photograph of an anonymous urban office building "attached" to the page by a large trompe l'oeil paper clip, creating a representational play at hand with the metal clip actually holding the elements together.[3] Here we enter the realm of language.

The poster clearly cites the conventional information—the artist's name, the dates, location, and address of the exhibition. Where the image and exhibition credits are usually located, however, there are instead texts that simultaneously displace the announcement's authorship, function, and context. The photograph was taken by an artist (Michelle Elzay) other than Brannon and who otherwise has no presence in the exhibition; in the fine print typical of illustration captions, the text running along the left margin unexpectedly reveals itself as a short narrative:

> *Above our heads the weight of a city block. Tons of poured cement. Miles of phone and electric. Enough glass to sink a ship. Palms, ferns, soft soap, calculators, vending machines, and fluorescent lighting. Picture one person at their desk. In the very center. Pen in mouth. Slight hangover. Answering a phone call they don't want to take.*

Brannon demonstrates that in a determined form such as a promotional poster there remain spaces to inscribe content that transforms the reading of the object itself. Even the relationship of the promotional ephemera to the exhibition may be reconsidered: he typically invites artist friends to design his posters featuring their own images, subverting the reading and expectations of the exhibition with their seemingly unrelated aesthetics and subject. Previous posters have been designed by Carol Bove, Liam Gillick, Wade Guyton, Patrick Hill, Sarah Morris, Richard Phillips, Lari Pittman, and Stephen Prina.

Throughout Brannon's oeuvre, the spaces he prefers to work with tend to be marginal or overlooked in relation to the overall form, yet through his manipulations they become integral to the piece's ongoing interpretation. This pattern began with earlier works, inspired by horror films, in which he explored the movie poster form. In the area traditionally reserved for production credits, he inserted instead short text and narrative segments, as in *Sick Decisions* (2004) and *Grotesque Desperate* (2005). Sometimes Brannon's text completely overtakes the form and image, pointing to what may be happening behind the scenes as possibly the most revealing thing. An extreme example is Brannon's film *Unending Horrible* (2004), in which the scrolling introductory film credits *("KNEEJERK NEGATIVITY WITH / GREAT WHITE SHARK HEART STUDIOS AND / SHIT FUN FILMS / PRESENTS / COLD GENITALS / IN A / NIGHTS SWEATS IDEA FOR")* become the entirety of the work."[4]

From these invitation materials—a business card, a picture of an office building, and a reluctant employee—a scene is set for the exhibition.

Mergers

Brannon cites as an ongoing reference Vladimir Nabokov's *Pale Fire* (1962), an epic poem eclipsed by convoluted annotations and eventually revealed as a novel whose form Nabokov has exploited to scrutinize and expand the genre.[5] Brannon similarly uses the form of the exhibition to describe a visual field of images and text through the language of printmaking, graphic and textile design, writing, and display. Against this backdrop, he explores the underlying psychologies inherent in the production, interpretation, and distribution of image-making.

Upon entering the exhibition space, viewers immediately discover the coiled black eel graphic first seen on the invitation, now in the form of a 26-foot-tall decal on the windows of the Whitney Museum at Altria's Sculpture Court, facing 42nd Street. The massive presence, stark black against muted gray concrete surroundings, here confounds its previous manifestation as an ad hoc graphic logo. With the addition of a title, *The Price of Admission* (2007), the piece attains a new, binary status as artwork and symbol. Viewable from both outside and inside the Whitney at Altria, a corporate building in the heart of midtown and the Times Square area, the eel takes on the promotional proportions of commercial street signage. For the artist, the eel continues to develop as a symbol of abjectness, refinement, and wealth—its conflicted meanings in contrast to its simple and alluring graphic manifestation. Brannon also relates the eel graphic to the image of a coiled whip, which he has employed in other works to evoke the psychological dynamics of power and domination.

The main gallery features three scaffoldlike display structures, designed by the artist and inspired by director's chairs (also a recurring symbol in Brannon's work), on which Brannon's framed letterpress and silkscreen prints are arranged in

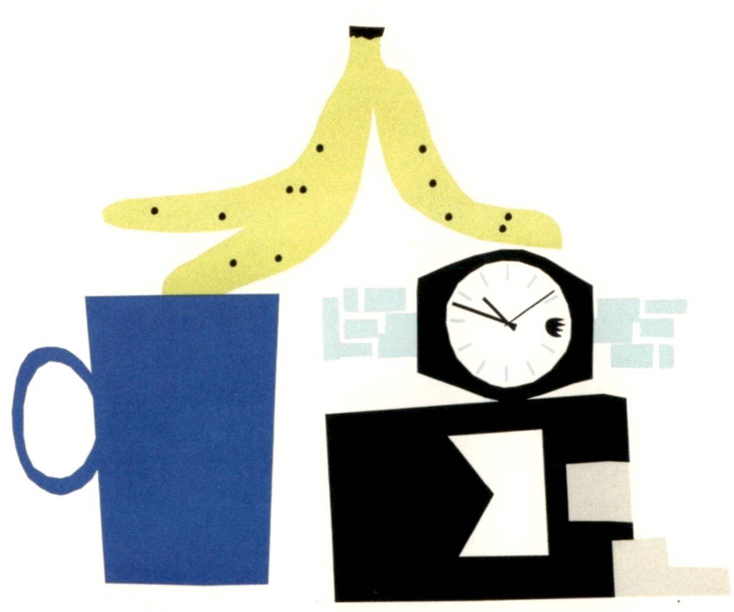

Steak Dinner

· THIS YEAR TELL HER YOU LOVE HER ALL OVER AGAIN ·
· WITH A GRAB BAG OF DIAMONDS · WITH MOUTHFULS OF CAVIAR · WITH YOUR RENT IN CLOTHES · A CREDIT CARD OF HOTEL ROOMS ·
· STOCKINGS · CHAMPAGNE · PLANE TICKETS · AND A SOFT SLAP ON HER BARE ASS ·

rows. A single gray wall matching the hues found in both the announcement poster and the exhibited prints serves as a cool, neutral background for the graphic black surfaces. The structures provide the support and spatial organization for the framed prints, creating what Brannon refers to as a "cadence" in viewing akin to reading pages arranged in chapters with no particular sequence.

A transitional moment occurs with the third display structure, which is fixed to the wall. Whereas the two freestanding structures have usurped the default display function of the gallery walls, this one has assimilated itself into the wall, creating an unusual doubling effect: a display surface supporting another display surface. These shifts in presentation, including the two works in the exhibition which are hung on the wall itself (*untitled*, 1993, and *Signature*, 2007), accentuate the varying contexts at play in the viewer's experience and interpretation of the exhibition.

Misconduct

Psychoanalysis suggests that much of our fascination with image culture, including advertising, art, and cinema, is informed by the concept of cathexis—the ways we invest emotional energy in objects, ideas, or other people.

Brannon employs reflexive operations to explore how these psychological impulses can become overinvested and repressed, manifesting in such obsessive pathologies as megalomania, self-destruction, and perversion. He begins with a presentational form, such as an exhibition and its promotional materials, graphic elements, objects, and publication. Then he introduces what he refers to as an "irritant," a disjunctive text/narrative or a formal/compositional aberration that displaces the interpretation of the work—sometimes overtaking it entirely. As we see here, such devices include inviting other artists to occupy his promotional posters and allowing his accompanying text (including titles) to commandeer the reading of his visual images.

Where Were We draws its initial contextual and visual narrative from its location in commercial midtown and the constructed imagery that Brannon presents. Each print in the exhibition features a simple graphic composition that evokes a generic and stylistically anachronistic iconography of corporate, commuter, and after-hours cosmopolitan lifestyles. The color palette is decorative and modern in flat, unmodulated colors and with a nostalgic Pop patina. *Steak Dinner* (2007) presents a deadpan arrangement of a limp yellow banana peel resting on top of a coffee mug, a luxury watch, and a pack of cigarettes; *Raw Bar* (2007) features a suggestive configuration of goods including a stiletto-heeled shoe, lowball glass, hotel key, and coat-check ticket.

With the addition of Brannon's fractured texts, what appear to be simple assortments of office stationery, commuter accoutrements, and luxury items and comestibles become loaded compositions detailing personality disorders, status anxiety, private transgressions, and other dysfunctions and trespasses. The text in *Pigs, Like Us* (2007) turns what could be a coffee-stained desktop strewn with pen-

Matthew Brannon, *Steak Dinner*, 2007.

cils and an iPod into a tainted scene recounting spiraling self-indulgence and negligence. A large silkscreen diptych flatly depicting a sushi dinner is betrayed by its title, *Who Takes Who Home Tonight* (2007), which renders the tableau a disingenuous prelude to sexual indiscretion.

In the transition from the works on the display structures to the pieces on the gallery wall, formal abstraction appears in the work, creating a dramatic, schizophrenic foil for the hard-edged graphic figuration. Drawing from a canon of aesthetic abstraction including Expressionist mark-making (*untitled*, 1993), Optical art (*Signature*, 2007), and Geometric Minimalism (*Pigeon*, 2007), Brannon stages a slippery moment in which an artwork doubles as domestic decoration or an emblem of a lifestyle. This juxtaposition highlights our perception of "art" and the values we assign to certain aesthetics, display strategies, and modes of production. The twist is that all the prints in the exhibition are unique and made with the same methods, leveling expectations both of the endless reproducibility of poster works and of the privileging of one aesthetic over the other.

Accountability

In *Where Were We,* a single voice is not apparent. Even within individual pieces the point of view is constantly shifting and ambiguous, conflating fragments of personal dialogue, anonymous verbal affronts, imaginary advertising copy, and narrative. Separated into short sentences and text segments, the story, like the images, relies on the viewer to string together words and phrases to form uniquely subjective associations and interpretations.

Pulling Out (2007) considers:

A BIT AGGRESSIVE / WOULDN'T YOU SAY? / DIDN'T SEE THAT COMING / THE WAY HE SEEMED PREPARED TO ARGUE AT EVERY TURN / AND WHERE DID HE EVER GET THAT ABOUT YOU KNOW WHAT / SO ANGRY / SOMEWHAT LOST I FEAR / WORRIES ME THOUGH / IT'S AS IF HE'S DETERMINED TO DRAG US DOWN WITH HIM

Themes materialize and coalesce throughout Brannon's work as his constructions focus on the psychology of display and promotion in relation to power, ambition, art, and taste. In *Where Were We,* Brannon delineates an Everyman beset by job anxieties, material desires, and personal dysfunction—a typology especially salient in the context of the exhibition's corporate midtown location. At the same time, the text reveals an alternate voice that self-consciously speaks about the act of writing and artmaking—even addressing the viewer about the work itself. *Adult Education* (2007) contends:

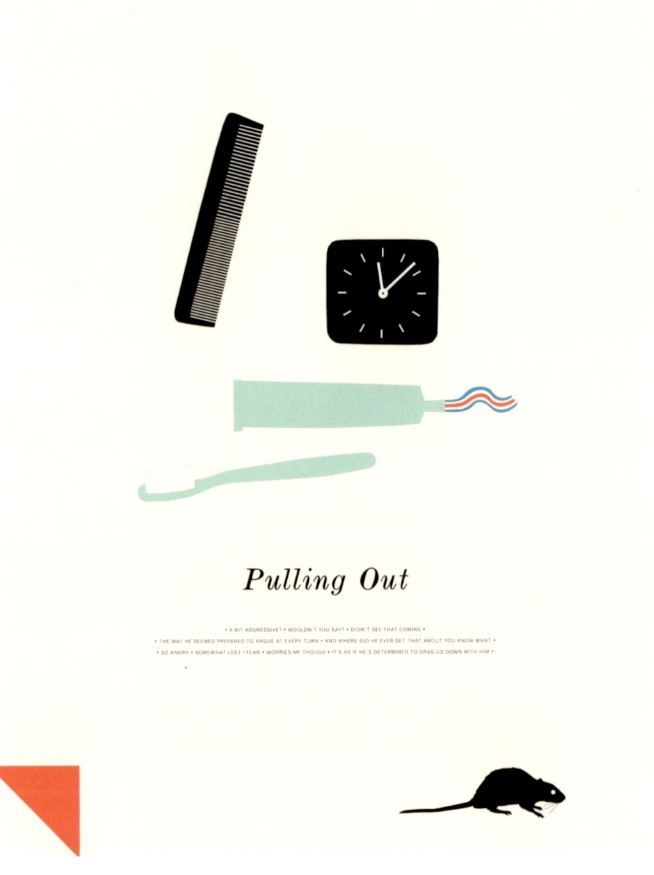

Matthew Brannon, *Pulling Out*, 2007.

IT'S ABSTRACT / IT'S TOTALLY ABSTRACT / I COPIED IT / I STOLE IT FROM YOU / I RIPPED THE PAGE RIGHT OUT OF THE BOOK / WORD FOR WORD / YOU WEREN'T DOING MUCH WITH IT ANYWAY . . .

With the fusing of these narratives, the subject, form, and interpretation of the work are addressed all at once.

This series of identification and misrecognition is central to Brannon's text and image constructions, underlining the psychoanalytic and linguistic considerations of his work. Similar to the narrative voice, the implied reader is not fully determined but is revealed individually through the process of interpretation and inferences drawn.[6] By actively responding to the pieces, filling in visual and narrative gaps, the viewer becomes situated in the construction of meaning of the work and the installation.

Termination Procedures

The interruptions and diversions implied by the title *Where Were We* may refer as well to the gaps and disjunctions we negotiate throughout the exhibition. They invite a chain of symbols and meanings that must be sutured together, much like cinema as an experience is derived from a narrative space of successive, discrete images. Through constructed scenarios and mise-en-scènes, it requires us to synthesize our viewing experience as a coherent whole while remaining subconsciously aware of its fragmented visual and narrative elements. Another reminder of how Brannon's ongoing interest in cinema can be seen as influencing his entire body of work, the cinema as a metaphor may also describe the way we (mis)identify ourselves with the images presented to us. *Where Were We* is similarly an active textual space that takes the form of and reflects our anxieties about misrecognition and uncertainty of meaning. If our unconscious is truly structured like language, Brannon posits, much is to be revealed in the ways we read ourselves and our surroundings together.

—HOWIE CHEN, BRANCH MANAGER, SENIOR CURATORIAL COORDINATOR

1. Jacques Lacan, *The Four Fundamental Concepts of Psycho-Analysis*, ed. Jacques-Alain Miller, trans. Alan Sheridan (New York: W. W. Norton and Company, 1998); originally published as *Les quatre concepts fundamenteaux de la psychoanalyse* (1973).
2. Brannon considers exhibitions' announcement materials discrete works in themselves that provide a space for both image and information. Matthew Brannon, interview by Roger White (*Brooklyn Rail,* April 2004).
3. The building is Renzo Piano's New York Times building, partially lit and still under construction, as it appears from Brannon's studio window.
4. "You don't have to watch the film to know the story. It's about sex, money, and power. It's about self-destructive impulses and fear. You don't have to watch the film to know the story." From the artist's statement for *The Unending Horrible,* Southfirst, Brooklyn, 2004.
5. This type of rhetorical de-vice, using one medium of art to describe another as a way of illuminating the former, is known as "ecphrasis."
6. See Wolfgang Iser, *The Act of Reading: A Theory of Aesthetic Response* (Baltimore: The Johns Hopkins University Press, 1978); originally published as *Der Akt des Lesens* (1976).

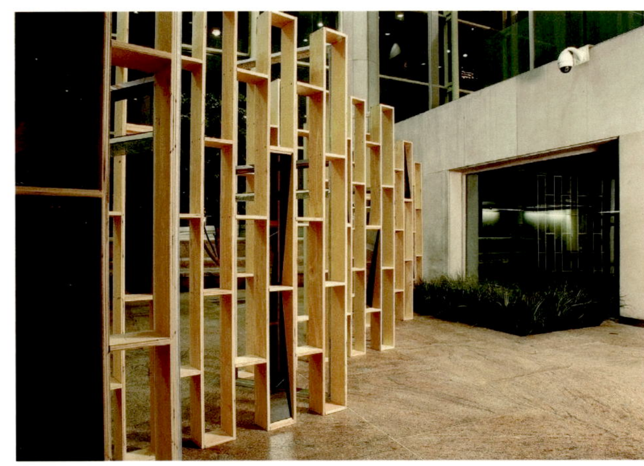

TOP: Heather Rowe, *Screen (for the rooms behind)*, 2007 (installation view of *Undone*). BOTTOM: Tom Holmes, *The Most American Problem or Something About Reducing One to Zero*, 2007 (installation view of *Undone*). OPPOSITE: Tony Matelli, *Abandon*, 2007 (installation view of *Undone*).

Undone

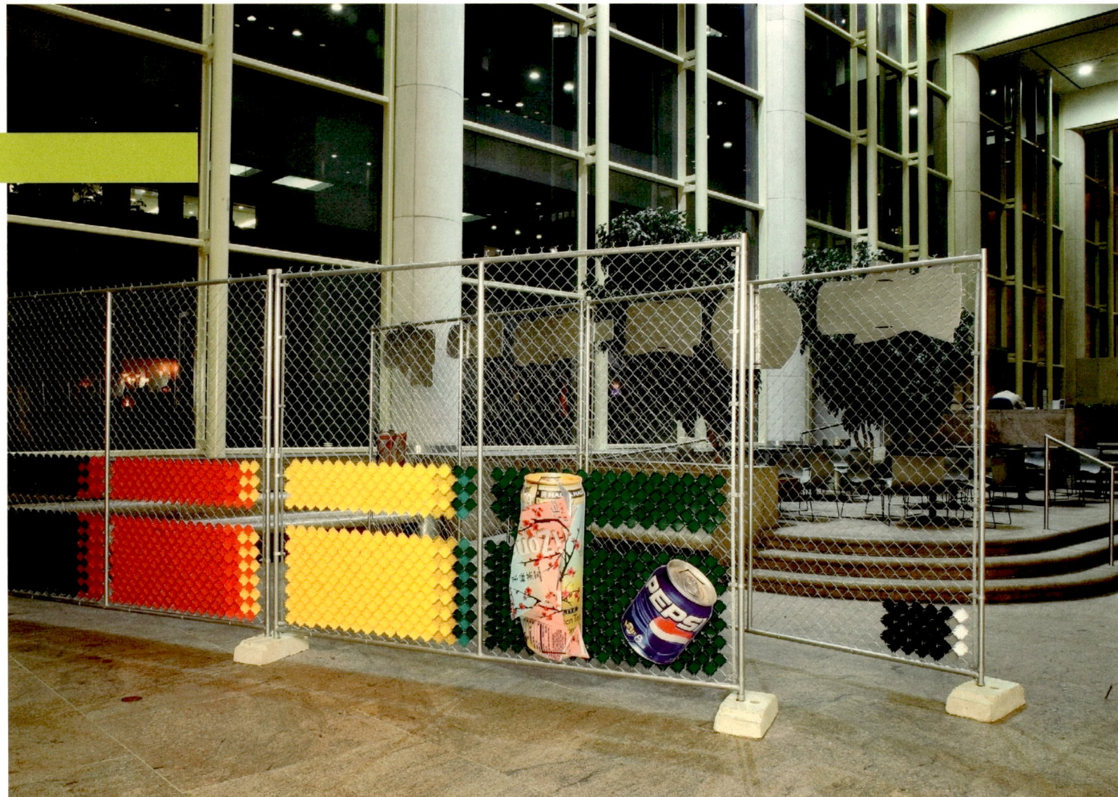

September 20, 2007 to January 29, 2008

In *Undone,* the perceived completeness of form, space, or identity is defined by its own fragmented, unfinished, or unraveling condition. Commissioned for this exhibition, the works subvert viewers' expectations about medium and exhibition space. By employing often contradictory content, scale, materials, and representation, the artists—Tom Holmes, Tony Matelli, Eileen Quinlan, and Heather Rowe—create work that draws on the context of the Whitney Museum at Altria Gallery and Sculpture Court to construct moments of unexpected transformation and "undoing" of sculpture, photography, and architecture.

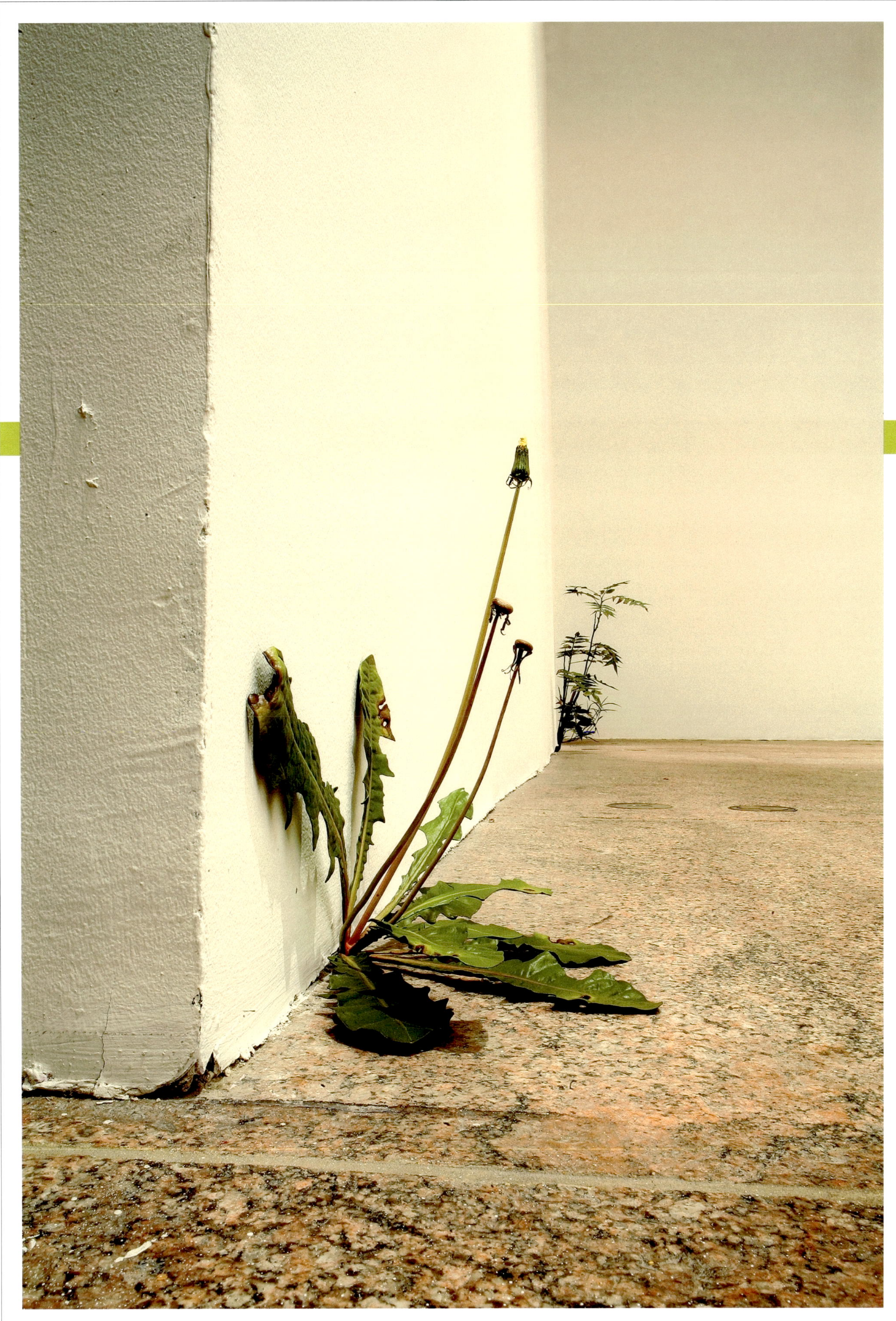

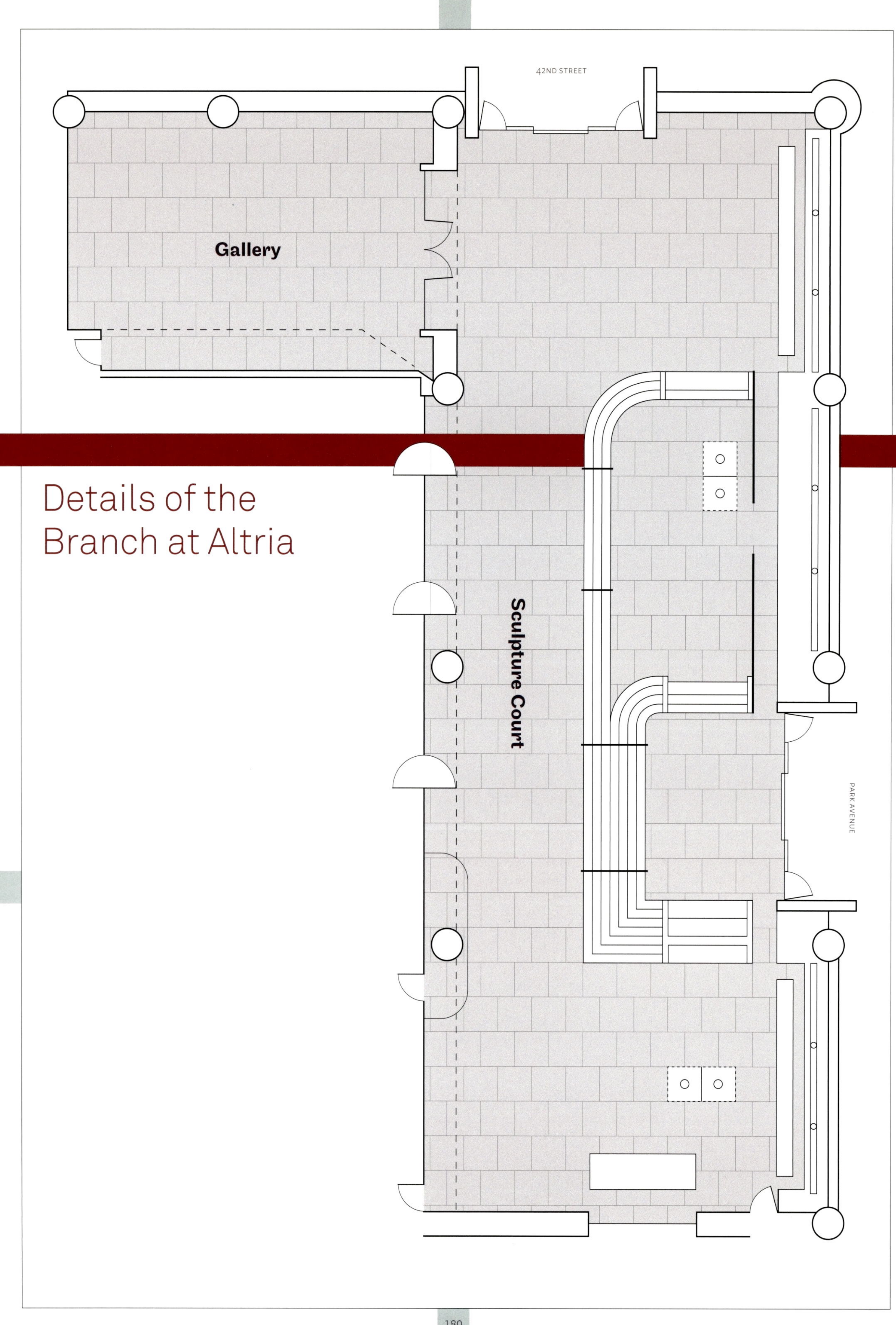

Details of the
Branch at Altria

Location

Street-level plaza of new headquarters building of Altria Group [formerly Philip Morris], Inc., Park Avenue at 42nd Street, across from Grand Central Terminal

Ulrich Franzen, Architect
Jaros, Baum and Holies, Engineers
Designed 1978; built 1980–83; opened April 8, 1983

Materials

Walls: limestone and glass in Sculpture Court; gypsum board and glass in Gallery
Floors and benches: granite
Ceilings: plaster
Entrances: aluminum

Installation Measurements/Requirements

SCULPTURE COURT
Width and length of Sculpture Court:
37 ft. 6 3/4 in. x 120 ft.
Height of Sculpture Court ceiling: (floor to ceiling) 42 ft. Height and width of Sculpture Court entrances: North—6 ft. 11 1/2 in. x 18 ft. 3 in., East—6 ft. 7 in. x 20 ft.
Exact weight limitations for Sculpture Court floor: 150 lbs. per sq. ft.
Exact weight limitations for hanging (per hook) in Sculpture Court: maximum loading one hook used = 1000 lbs.; more than one hook used for hanging one object = 500 lbs. per hook
Subject to restrictions and prior written approval of structural engineer.

GALLERY
Width and length of Gallery: 23 ft. 5 1/2 in. x 30 ft. 10 1/2 in.
Height of Gallery ceiling: (floor to ceiling) 17 ft. 5 3/4 in.
Distance from ceiling to lighting grid in Gallery: 1 ft. 6 in.
Height and width of Gallery doors: 6 ft. 8 in. x 18 ft.
Exact weight limitations for Gallery floors: 150 lbs. per sq. ft.
Exact weight limitations for hanging in ceiling or walls: not permitted unless approved by structural engineer beforehand.

The entries below are structured thus:

Exhibition Title

Artists

LOCATION [GALLERY, SCULPTURE COURT, OR BOTH]: DATES

CURATOR

*An * indicates information that could not be confirmed at the time of printing. The Archive of Whitney Museum of American Art at Altria is housed in the Museum Archives of the Frances Mulhall Achilles Library, Whitney Museum of American Art, New York.*

Twentieth-Century Sculpture: Process and Presence

Lynda Bengalis, Louise Bourgeois, Alexander Calder, John Chamberlain, Mark di Suvero, Robert Graham, Bryan Hunt, Gaston Lachaise, Roy Lichtenstein, Robert Morris, Elie Nadelman, Louise Nevelson, Isamu Noguchi, Claes Oldenburg, Theodore Roszak, Lucas Samaras, Alan Saret, Joel Shapiro, David Smith, John

---

Exhibition History

Storrs, George Sugarman, Jackie Winsor
GALLERY: 04-08-83—05-11-83
LISA PHILLIPS

The Forum Exhibition: Selections and Additions

Ben Benn, Thomas Hart Benton, Oscar Bluemner, Andrew Dasburg, Arthur G. Dove, Marsden Hartley, Stanton Macdonald-Wright, John Marin, Alfred Maurer, Henry Lee McFee, George F. Of, Man Ray, Morgan Russell, Charles Sheeler, A. [Abraham] Walkowitz, Marguerite Zorach, William Zorach
GALLERY: 05-18-83—06-22-83
ANNE HARRELL WITH ELLEN MAHONEY, HELENA RUBINSTEIN FELLOWS, WHITNEY MUSEUM OF AMERICAN ART INDEPENDENT STUDY PROGRAM, 1981–82

Reginald Marsh's New York

GALLERY: 06-29-83—08-24-83
MARILYN COHEN

Three American Families: A Tradition of Artistic Pursuit

Gerrit Duyckinck I, Evert Duyckinck III, Gerardus Duyckinck I, Charles Willson Peale, James Peale, Charles Peale Polk, Raphaelle Peale, Rembrandt Peale, Rubens Peale, Margaretta Angelica Peale, Titian Ramsey Peale, Sarah Miriam Peale, Robert Walter Weir, John Ferguson Weir, J. Alden Weir
GALLERY: 09-08-83—10-26-83
SUSAN LUBOWSKY

Still Life: Hollywood Photographs

Images by anonymous photographers and Virgil Apger, Bob Beerman, Harold Bennett, Arnold Johnson, Bert Parry, Bert Six
GALLERY: 11-02-83—12-30-83
DIANE KEATON AND MARVIN HEIFERMAN

Raymond Hood: City of Towers

GALLERY: 01-07-84—03-07-84
CAROL WILLIS, PRESENTED IN COOPERATION WITH THE INSTITUTE FOR ARCHITECTURE AND URBAN STUDIES

Flowers in Folk Art

Works by anonymous artists and Ransom

Cook, William Fellini, F. H. Hanson, Collata Holcomb, David Huebner, Elizabeth Jefferis, Anny Mohler, Nancy Perkins, John Scholl, Rachel Trundle, Henry Young
GALLERY: 03-15-84—05-09-84
SUSAN LUBOWSKY

Calder: Selections from the Permanent Collection of the Whitney Museum of American Art

Alexander Calder
GALLERY AND SCULPTURE COURT:
05-17-84—07-11-84
PAMELA GRUNINGER PERKINS AND SUSAN LUBOWSKY

The Art of Music: American Paintings & Musical Instruments 1770-1910

Painters: Frank W. Benson, I. John Bradley, John George Brown, Dennis Miller Bunker, Jefferson David Chalfant, James Goodwyn Clonney, Arthur B. Davies, Thomas W. Dewing, Thomas Eakins, Ralph Earl, Whetten Ehninger, William M. Harnett, John Eastman Johnson, Charles Bird King, Alphonse-Léon Noël, George Henry Story, Stacy Tolman, Benjamin West
GALLERY: 07-19-84—09-19-84
ORGANIZED BY THE FRED L. EMERSON GALLERY, HAMILTON COLLEGE, CLINTON, NEW YORK

On 42nd Street: Artists' Visions

Christo, Chryssa, Howard Cook, Robert Cottingham, Jane Dickson, Fritz Eichenberg, Richard Estes, William J. Glackens, Red Grooms, Richard Haas, Childe Hassam, John Held Jr., Earl Horter, Alex Katz, Joyce Kozloff, Ernest Lawson, John Marin, Mary Miss, Claes Oldenburg, Russell Patterson, Theodore Roszak, Saul Steinberg, Mark Tobey
GALLERY: 09-26-84—12-05-84
SUSAN LUBOWSKY

Modern Masks

Robert Arneson, Robert Brady, Roger Brown, Craig Coleman, Rafael Ferrer, David Finn, Nancy Graves, Rodney Alan Greenblat, Nancy Grossman, Marisol, Terry Rosenberg, Susan Rothenberg, Joseph Schactman, Ursula Schneider, Robert Sherman, Kiki Smith and David Wojnarowicz, Saul Steinberg, Jeff Way, Karl Wirsum, Daisy Youngblood
GALLERY: 12-13-84—02-07-85
SUSAN LUBOWSKY

The Box Transformed

Richard Artschwager, Joseph Cornell, Eva Hesse, Donald Judd, Sol LeWitt, Louise Nevelson, Nam June Paik, Lucas Samaras, Robert Smithson, Jackie Winsor
GALLERY: 02-15-85—04-25-85
CORRINE DISERENS, PAM MASLANSKY, AMY MIZRAHI, ELIZABETH SHRIVER, AND ZIBA DE WECK, HELENA RUBINSTEIN FELLOWS, WHITNEY MUSEUM OF AMERICAN ART INDEPENDENT STUDY PROGRAM

The Surreal City: 1930s-1950s

George Ault, Peter Blume, Jewett Campbell, Francis Criss, Philip Evergood, O. Louis Guglielmi, James Guy, Henry Koerner, Alice Neel, Kay Sage, George Tooker
GALLERY: 05-03-85—07-11-85
SUSAN LUBOWSKY

Art for the Masses 1911–1917: A Radical Magazine and Its Graphics

John Barber, Cornelia Barns, Maurice Becker, George Bellows, Kenneth Russell Chamberlain, Glenn O. Coleman, Arthur B. Davies, Stuart Davis, Al Frueh, Henry Glintenkamp, Robert Henri, Robert Minor, Boardman Robinson, John Sloan, Maurice Sterne, John Storrs, Art Young
GALLERY: 07–19–85—10–03–85
REBECCA ZURIER, TRAVELING EXHIBITION
ORGANIZED BY THE YALE UNIVERSITY ART GALLERY,
NEW HAVEN

Modern Machines: Recent Kinetic Sculpture

Alice Aycock, Jonathan Borofsky, Chris Burden, Rodney Alan Greenblat, Perry Hoberman, Kristin Jones and Andrew Ginzel, Gary Justis, Jon Kessler, Robert Longo, Dennis Oppenheim, Gary Perkins, Carolee Schneemann
SCULPTURE COURT: 10–11–85—12–05–85
SUSAN LUBOWSKY

The Photography of Imogen Cunningham: A Centennial Selection

GALLERY: 12–13–85—01–30–86
SUSAN EHRENS AND LELAND RICE, EXHIBITION
ORGANIZED BY THE AMERICAN FEDERATION
OF ARTS, NEW YORK

Urban Pleasures: New York 1900–1940

George Bellows, Paul Cadmus, Glenn O. Coleman, James Daugherty, Adolf Dehn, Guy Pène Du Bois, Wood Gaylor, William J. Glackens, George Luks, Reginald Marsh, Maurice Prendergast, Everett Shinn, John Sloan, William Zorach
GALLERY: 02–07–86—04–03–86
SUSAN LUBOWSKY AND PATTERSON SIMS

Yasuo Kuniyoshi

GALLERY: 04–11–86—06–19–86
SUSAN LUBOWSKY

The Changing Likeness: Twentieth-Century Portrait Drawings, Selections from the Permanent Collection of the Whitney Museum of American Art

Peggy Bacon, Will Barnet, Leonard Baskin, Cecilia Beaux, Thomas Hart Benton, Albert Bloch, Adolphe Borie, Bryon Browne, David Burliuk, Fedrico Castellon, Chuck Close, Philip Evergood, Arshile Gorky, John D. Graham, Edward Hopper, Alex Katz, Yasuo Kuniyoshi, Gaston Lachaise, Rico Lebrun, Richard Lindner, George Luks, Reginald Marsh, Elie Nadelman, Ed Paschke, Theodore Roszak, Lucas Samaras, John Singer Sargent, Charles Sheeler, Saul Steinberg, Joseph Stella, Andy Warhol, Charles White, John Wilde, Karl Wirsum
GALLERY: 06–27–86—09–04–86
PAUL CUMMINGS

Walter Murch

GALLERY: 09–12–86—11–18–86
JUDY COLLISCHAN VAN WAGNER, EXHIBITION
ORGANIZED BY THE HILLWOOD ART GALLERY, LONG
ISLAND UNIVERSITY, GREENVALE, NEW YORK

Contemporary Cutouts

Jonathan Borofsky, Howard Finster, Rodney Alan Greenblat, Red Grooms, Alex Katz, Roy Lichtenstein, David Montgomery, William Mutter, Larry Rivers, Judith Shea, Anton Van Dalen, Tom Wesselmann, Karl Wirsum, Timothy Woodman
GALLERY AND SCULPTURE COURT:
11–26–86—02–17–87
SUSAN LUBOWSKY AND RONI FEINSTEIN

Monotypes by Maurice Prendergast from the Terra Museum of American Art

GALLERY: 02–26–87—04–22–87
ORGANIZED BY THE TERRA MUSEUM
OF AMERICAN ART, EVANSTON, ILLINOIS

The Viewer as Voyeur

Laurie Anderson, Ida Applebroog, John Baldessari, Joseph Cornell, Jane Dickson, Walker Evans, Eric Fischl, Dan Graham, Connie Hatch, Edward Hopper, Mary Kelly, Silvia Kolbowski, Reginald Marsh, Richard Prince, Aimee Rankin, Weegee (Arthur Fellig)
GALLERY: 04–30–87—07–08–87
ANDREA INSELMANN, GRANT KESTER, JAMES PETO,
AND CHARLES A. WRIGHT, JR., HELENA RUBINSTEIN
FELLOWS, WHITNEY MUSEUM OF AMERICAN ART
INDEPENDENT STUDY PROGRAM

The Social Graces, 1905–1944: Prints and Drawings from the Permanent Collection of the Whitney Museum of American Art

Peggy Bacon, Julius Bloch, James H. Daugherty, Stuart Davis, Aldolf Dehn, Julian de Miskey, Guy Pène du Bois, Philip Evergood, William J. Glackens, Rube Goldberg, Benjamin Kopman, Charles Locke, Reginald Marsh, Marjorie Organ, Boardman Robinson, Joan Sloan
GALLERY: 07–16–87—09–24–87
SUSAN LUBOWSKY

Stuart Davis: An American in Paris

GALLERY: 10–02–87—12–10–87
LEWIS KACHUR

Elements: Five Installations

Petah Coyne, Mineko Grimmer, Ann Hamilton, Eric Orr, Peter Shelton
GALLERY AND SCULPTURE COURT:
12–18–87—02–18–88
KATHLEEN MONAGHAN

Precisionist Perspectives: Prints and Drawings

James E. Allen, Henry Billings, Howard Cook, Ralston Crawford, Charles Demuth, Elsie Driggs, Albert Heckman, Paul Landacre, Armin Landeck, Louis Lozowick, William C. McNulty, Otis Oldfield, Arnold Ronnebeck, Morton Schamberg, William S. Schwartz, Charles Sheeler, Niles Spencer, Benton Spruance, Joseph Stella, Harry Sternberg, Miklos Suba
GALLERY: 03–02–88—04–28–88
SUSAN LUBOWSKY

Real Faces

Bill Burke, Nan Goldin, Birney Imes, Judith Joy Ross
GALLERY: 05–06–88—09–22–88
MAX KOZLOFF

Urban Figures

John Ahearn with Rigoberto Torres, Jonathan Borofsky, Viola Frey, Duane Hanson, Alex Katz, Marisol, Deborah Masters, Alison Saar, George Segal
GALLERY: 11–17–88—02–15–89
SCULPTURE COURT: 11–01–88—11–01–89*
JOSEPHINE GEAR

From the Model: Selections from the Permanent Collection of the Whitney Museum of American Art

William Bailey, Jack Beal, William Beckman, Thomas Hart Benton, Isabel Bishop, James H. Daugherty, Mary Frank, Sidney Goodman, Gaston Lachaise, Alice Neel, Philip Pearlstein, George Segal, John Sloan, Abraham Walkowitz, Tom Wesselmann, William Zorach
GALLERY: 02–24–89—05–03–89
JOSEPHINE GEAR

Straphangers

Isabel Bishop, Paul Cadmus, Lily Furedi, Armin Landeck, Edward Laning, Michael Loew, Louis Lozowick, Reginald Marsh, William Pachner, John Sloan, Joseph Solman, Raphael Soyer, Benton Spruance, George Tooker
GALLERY: 05–12–89—07–22–89
JOSEPHINE GEAR

Miniature Environments

Tony Berlant, Lynne Clibanoff, James Connor, Joseph Cornell, Mark Dean, Tom Foolery, Richard Haas, Paul Hunter, Michael Hurson, Susan Leopold, Michael McMillen, Aimee Rankin, Charles Simonds
GALLERY: 08–02–89—09–27–89
JOSEPHINE GEAR

Isamu Noguchi: Portrait Sculpture

GALLERY: 10–06–89—12–06–89*
ORGANIZED BY THE NATIONAL PORTRAIT GALLERY,
SMITHSONIAN INSTITUTION, WASHINGTON, D.C.

Out of Wood: Recent Sculpture

Gallery: Jene Highstein, Mel Kendrick, Ursula Von Rydingsvard; Sculpture Court: Raoul Hague, Jene Highstein, Mel Kendrick, Michael Lekakis, Ursula Von Rydingsvard
GALLERY: 12–15–89—02–20–90
SCULPTURE COURT: 12–89—12–90 (WITH ROTATIONS)
JOSEPHINE GEAR

Cadmus, French, & Tooker: The Early Years

Paul Cadmus, Jared French, George Tooker
GALLERY: 03–01–90—05–05–90
JOSEPHINE GEAR

The (Un)Making of Nature: Installations by Michael Paha

GALLERY: 05–16–90—07–11–90
JULIO EINSPRUCH, ELIZABETH FINCH, JAMES
MARCOVITZ, HELEN MOLESWORTH, AND LYDIA YEE,
HELENA RUBINSTEIN FELLOWS, WHITNEY MUSEUM
OF AMERICAN ART INDEPENDENT STUDY PROGRAM

With the Grain: Contemporary Panel Painting

Vikky Alexander, Richard Artschwager, Ford Beckman, Michael Byron, Carroll Dunham, Julie Fromme, Robert Helm, Sherrie Levine, Russell Maltz, Michael Mazur, Jim Napierala, Ray Smith, Ned Smyth, Starn Twins (Douglas and Michael), John R. Thompson, John Torreano
GALLERY: 07–25–90—09–26–90
RONI FEINSTEIN

Abstract Expressionism:
Other Dimensions
*William Baziotes, Rollin Crampton, Willem
De Kooning, Sam Francis, Adolph Gottlieb,
Hans Hofmann, Gerome Kamrowski, Franz
Kline, Lee Krasner, Knud Merrild, Robert
Motherwell, Barnett Newman, Vincent Pepi,
Jackson Pollock, Richard Pousette-Dart,
Clayton S. Price, Ralph Rosenborg, Mark
Rothko, Ethel Schwabacher, Sonia Sekula,
Charles Seliger, Harold Shapinsky, Sal Sirugo,
Janet Sobel, Theodoros Stamos, Mark Tobey,
Bradley Walker Tomlin*
GALLERY: 10-05-90—12-05-90
JEFFREY WECHSLER, EXHIBITION ORGANIZED
BY THE JANE VOORHEES ZIMMERLI ART MUSEUM,
RUTGERS UNIVERSITY, NEW BRUNSWICK,
NEW JERSEY

Painted Forms: Recent Metal Sculpture
*John Chamberlain, Melvin Edwards, Nancy
Graves, Steve Keister, Judy Pfaff, George
Sugarman, David Winter*
GALLERY: 12-19-90—02-20-91
SCULPTURE COURT: 12-19-90—12-91*
JOSEPHINE GEAR

Abstraction Before 1930: Selections from
the Permanent Collection of the Whitney
Museum of American Art
*Tom Benrimo, Thomas Hart Benton, Oscar
Bluemner, Patrick Henry Bruce, Arthur B.
Carles, John Covert, Konrad Cramer, Stuart
Davis, Charles Demuth, Arthur G. Dove,
Marsden Hartley, Louis Lozowick, Stanton
Macdonald-Wright, John Marin, Jan Matulka,
Alfred H. Maurer, Georgia O'Keeffe, Man
Ray, Morgan Russell, Morton Schamberg,
Joseph Stella, John Storrs, Abraham
Walkowitz, Max Weber*
GALLERY: 03-01-91—05-01-91*
KATHLEEN MONAGHAN

Drawing Acquisitions, 1980-91: Selections
from the Permanent Collection of the
Whitney Museum of American Art
*Richard Artschwager, Jean-Michel Basquiat,
Robert Bechtle, Stuart Davis, Willem de
Kooning, Arshile Gorky, Philip Guston, Eva
Hesse, Ralph Humphrey, Jasper Johns, Mike
Kelley, Lee Krasner, Gaston Lachaise, Barry
Le Va, John Marin, Reginald Marsh, Stephen
Mueller, Elizabeth Murray, Elie Nadelman,
Georgia O'Keeffe, Jackson Pollock, Robert
Rauschenberg, Alan Saret, Myron Stout, Mark
Tobey, Cy Twombly, Christopher Wool*
GALLERY: 06-12-91—09-05-91
KLAUS KERTESS

Immaterial Objects: Works from
the Permanent Collection of the Whitney
Museum of American Art
Mary Lucier
GALLERY: 09-14-91—11-16-91
RICHARD MARSHALL

Ellen Driscoll: The Loophole of Retreat
GALLERY: 12-04-91—02-08-92
THELMA GOLDEN

Judith Shea: Monuments and Statues
SCULPTURE COURT: 02-20-92—06-20-92
THELMA GOLDEN

Alison Saar: Slow Boat
GALLERY: 02-20-92—04-20-92
THELMA GOLDEN

Gary Simmons: The Garden of Hate
GALLERY: 05-07-92—07-02-92
THELMA GOLDEN

Y. David Chung: Turtle Boat Head
GALLERY: 07-17-92—09-25-92
THELMA GOLDEN

Glenn Ligon: Good Mirrors Are Not Cheap
SCULPTURE COURT: 07-17-92—01-01-93*
THELMA GOLDEN

Suzanne McClelland: Painting
GALLERY: 10-29-92—12-31-92
THELMA GOLDEN

Amalia Mesa-Bains: Venus Envy Chapter
One (or the First Holy Communion
Moments Before the End)
GALLERY: 01-19-93—04-05-93*
THELMA GOLDEN

Maren Hassinger: Window Boxes
SCULPTURE COURT: 01-19-93—07-30-93
THELMA GOLDEN

Expanding the Collection: Biennial
Acquisitions
*John Baldessari, Oscar Bluemner, Paul Cadmus,
Stuart Davis, Ashile Gorky, Hans Hofmann,
Jenny Holzer, Jasper Johns, Jacob Lawrence,
Glenn Ligon, James Rosenquist*
GALLERY: 05-03-93—09-03-93*
THELMA GOLDEN

Sylvia Plachy: The Call of the Street:
Photographs of New York City
GALLERY: 09-28-93—12-31-93
THELMA GOLDEN

Lorna Simpson: Standing in the water
GALLERY: 01-19-94—03-25-94
THELMA GOLDEN, IN COLLABORATION WITH THE
FABRIC WORKSHOP/MUSEUM, PHILADELPHIA

Sam Gilliam: Golden Element Inside Gold
SCULPTURE COURT: 01-20-94—07-01-94
THELMA GOLDEN

Leone & Macdonald: Double Foolscap
Hillary Leone and Jennifer Macdonald
GALLERY: 04-08-94—07-01-94
THELMA GOLDEN

Works on Paper: Selections from
the Permanent Collection of the Whitney
Museum of American Art
*Jean-Michel Basquiat, Ross Bleckner, Bruce
Conner, Carroll Dunham, Robert Gober,
April Gornik, Sol LeWitt, Glenn Ligon, Brice
Marden, Suzanne McClelland, Donald Moffett,
Stephen Mueller, Tom Otterness, Martin
Puryear, Michael Rees, Jim Shaw, Kiki Smith,
Philip Taaffe, Sue Williams*
GALLERY: 07-13-94—10-14-94
THELMA GOLDEN

Photographs: Selections from
the Permanent Collection of the Whitney
Museum of American Art
*John Baldessari, Dawoud Bey, Nancy Burson,
John Chamberlain, John Coplans, William*

*Eggleston, Adam Fuss, Anthony Hernandez,
Zoe Leonard, Sally Mann, Ana Mendieta,
Catherine Opie, Jack Pierson, Lucas
Samaras, Cindy Sherman, Michael Spano,
William Wegman, James Welling*
GALLERY: 10-20-94—12-30-94
THELMA GOLDEN

Jacob Lawrence: War Series
GALLERY: 01-11-95—03-31-95
THELMA GOLDEN

Double Take: Views of Modern Life
by Stuart Davis and Reginald Marsh
GALLERY: 04-10-95—07-07-95
EUGENIE TSAI

Carmen Lomas Garza
GALLERY: 07-19-95—09-22-95
THELMA GOLDEN

Altered and Irrational: Selections
from the Permanent Collection
of the Whitney Museum of American Art
*Jared Bark, Michael Byron, Jim Love, Rona
Pondick, Lucas Samaras, Cindy Sherman, Kiki
Smith, Mike Todd, May Wilson, Joel-Peter Witkin*
GALLERY: 10-12-95—01-05-96
BETH VENN

Terry Adkins: Firmament RHA
SCULPTURE COURT: 10-18-95—03-29-96
THELMA GOLDEN

Matthew McCaslin: Harnessing Nature
GALLERY: 01-17-96—03-29-96
MATTHEW YOKOBOSKY AND THELMA GOLDEN

Jane Dickson: Paradise Alley
SCULPTURE COURT: 04-11-96—07-28-96
THELMA GOLDEN

Ik-Joong Kang: 8490 Days of Memory
GALLERY: 07-12-96—09-27-96
EUGENIE TSAI

Beverly Semmes: She Moves
GALLERY: 10-17-96—01-04-97
THELMA GOLDEN

Romare Bearden in Black-and-White:
Photomontage Projections 1964
GALLERY: 01-17-97—03-20-97
GAIL GELBURD, EXHIBITION ORGANIZED BY
THE COUNCIL FOR CREATIVE PROJECTS, NEW YORK

Quicker Than A Wink: The Photographs
of Harold Edgerton
GALLERY: 03-31-97—06-27-97
EUGENIE TSAI

Tunnel Visions: Photographs by
Accra Shepp
GALLERY: 07-01-97—10-10-97
EUGENIE TSAI

Pictures at an Exhibition:
An Installation by Christian Marclay
GALLERY: 10-24-97—01-25-98
EUGENIE TSAI

Garden of Qián, by Ming Fay
GALLERY AND SCULPTURE COURT:
02-06-98—04-17-98
EUGENIE TSAI

1983

Premier Performance Series
SARAH WARREN, PRODUCER
06–15: S.E.M Ensemble; Petr Kotik (director)
06–23: New York Grand Opera Singers
06–28,30: Hanne Tierney, *Drama for Voice and
Strings*
07–07: Bill and Mary Buchen, *sound sculpture*

Holiday Concert Series
12–14: *Amahl and the Night Vistors and other
holiday music*, New York Grand Opera Singers

Performance History

1984

05–18,19,22: Mel Wong Dance Company in
collaboration with environmental light sculptor
Cathey Billian; SARAH WARREN

05–29,30: Sally Gross, choreographer;
SARAH WARREN

06–06: S.E.M Ensemble; Petr Kotik (director);
SARAH WARREN

06–14: Music by Peter Griggs with Iris Brooks
and Glen Velez; SARAH WARREN

06–19: The New York Kammermusiker;
Ilonna Pederson (director); SARAH WARREN

06–26,28: Margaret Leng Tam, pianist;
SARAH WARREN

**In conjunction with *On 42nd Street:
Artists' Visions***
JEANETTE VUOCOLO, PRODUCER
10–09: Concert by the New England Bach
Festival Ensemble
10–11: "42nd Street: A Pagan Paradise,"
lecture by Brendan Gill
10–18: "The Unseen Architecture of 42nd
Street," lecture by Dr. Gerard Wolfe
10–23: "The Six Cities of 42nd Street,"
lecture by Kent Barwick
10–30: *Films about 42nd Street by independent filmmakers*

12–18: Joan Jonas with special guests in
the premiere of *Saga*, in conjunction with
Modern Masks; JANICE KRASNOW

1985

In conjunction with *Modern Masks*
*Theodora Skipitares & Company
01–10: Jeff Way in *Transformation*
01–28: Robert Sherman with dancer Janey
Savage and percussionist Michael Blair,
Journey to the Land of Souls: A Claymask Ritual

02–21,28: Films and videotapes featuring
artists at work, in conjunction with *The Box*

Transformed, JEANETTE VUOCOLO

05–09: The Microscopic Septet; JANICE
KRASNOW

05–16: Scott Johnson; JEANETTE VUOCOLO

05–20: Blondell Cummings in collaboration
with Kit-Yin Snyder; JEANETTE VUOCOLO

05–22: Elodie Lauten; JANICE KRASNOW

06–04: Metropolitan All Stars with Jann
Parker and Art Blakey, Jr.; JANICE KRASNOW

10–28: The Bronzino Duo; JANICE KRASNOW

11–04: Lenny Pickett; JANICE KRASNOW

11–18: Marco Rizo and His Latin-Jazz Quartet;
JANICE KRASNOW

11–25: Susan Marshall & Company; JANICE
KRASNOW

12–02: Perry Hoberman; JANICE KRASNOW

1986

05–01: The Ordinaires—Ton Simons and
Dancers; JEANETTE VUOCOLO

05–13: Fred Houn and The Asian American
Art Ensemble, *Excerpts from Bamboo That
Snaps Back: A Performance Art Odyssey*;
JEANETTE VUOCOLO

05–22: Bebe Miller and Company; JEANETTE
VUOCOLO

05–27: Neil B. Rolnick; JEANETTE VUOCOLO

06–05: S.E.M Ensemble; Petr Kotik (director);
JEANETTE VUOCOLO

09–17: David Tudor with Jacqueline Monier
and Molly Davies; JEANETTE VUOCOLO

* 09–28, 30 + 10–18: Uwe Mengel, *Plaster of
Paris, The most beautiful hypocrites in town*;
JEANETTE VUOCOLO

10–15: Dianne Ruth McIntyre's Sounds in
Motion Dance Company with Oluy Dara and
the Okra Orchestra, *Color-Toned Studies
on a Free Common Theme*; JEANETTE VUOCOLO

11–12: Johann Carlo and Michael Butler,
It's Still Life; JEANETTE VUOCOLO

12–03: Frankie Mann; JEANETTE VUOCOLO

* 12–19: John Zorn; JEANETTE VUOCOLO

1987

03–25: Tom Johnson; JEANETTE VUOCOLO

04–01: "Blue" Gene Tyranny; JEANETTE
VUOCOLO

04–08: Ellen Fisher and Ensemble; JEANETTE
VUOCOLO

04–15: Leroy Jenkins amd Julie Fraad [Leroy
Jenkins' Sting]; JEANETTE VUOCOLO

04–22: Women of the Calabash; JEANETTE
VUOCOLO

05–06: Wendy Perron Dance Company;
JEANETTE VUOCOLO

10–21: Akbar Ale and the Black Swan Quartet,
Black and White Exposure; JEANETTE VUOCOLO

10–28: Yoshiko Chuma and The School of
Hard Knocks, *The Big Picture*; JEANETTE
VUOCOLO

11–11: Urban Bush Women, *in Process Re:
Heat*; JEANETTE VUOCOLO

11–18: David Moss Desne Band, *Slow Talking
and Slant Lines*; JEANETTE VUOCOLO

12–02: Merián Soto and Pepón Osorio,
Wish You Were Here; JEANETTE VUOCOLO

1988

05–11: The Reggie Workman Ensemble with
The Maya Milenovic Dancers, *Synthesis III*;
JEANETTE VUOCOLO

05–18: Fast Forward and Ishmael Houston-
Jones, *Slow Motion Suicide*; JEANETTE
VUOCOLO

05–25,26: Alice Farley and Company, ANG-
GREK, *the human life of plants*; JEANETTE
VUOCOLO

06–01: Horvitz, Morris, Previte Trio with the
Horvitz and Holcomb Duo, *Duo and Trio
Works*; JEANETTE VUOCOLO

06–08: Guy Klucevsek, *Accordion for New
Ears*; JEANETTE VUOCOLO

06–15: Edwina Lee Tyler & A Piece of the
World, *DrumDrama*; JEANETTE VUOCOLO

11–02: Amina Claudine Myers and
David Peaston, *Music from the Inner Space*;
JEANETTE VUOCOLO

11–15: *Special Project: Fifth Anniversary
Celebration*, Sound environment by David
Behrman and excerpts from *Real People*,
choreographed by Ann Carlson

11–16: Ann Carlson, *Real People*; JEANETTE
VUOCOLO

11–30: Steve Turre and Explorations, *Modern
Root Music*; JEANETTE VUOCOLO

12–07: Eva Gasteazoro, *Conjuros*; David
Zambrano, *Reina Pepiada*; JEANETTE VUOCOLO

12–14: Pat Oleszko and The Usual Suspects
ARTFOOL RAPPING: *Revel Without Claus*;
JEANETTE VUOCOLO

1989

05–03: Linda Mussmann's Time & Space
Limited, with Claudia Bruce, and Semih
Firincioglu, *Lincoln Speak*; JEANETTE VUOCOLO

05–24: New Winds, *The Cliff*; JEANETTE
VUOCOLO

06–07: Jalalu-Kalvert Nelson and Trumpets of
Desire, with TUBATIME, and The Devastators,
Moving Music; JEANETTE VUOCOLO

06–14: Boogie Down: Miracle on the Deuce
A Henry Chalfant and Teodoro Pepe Esposito
production, with street artists A-1, Joel BUDA

Bevacqua, ESTOS, MARE 139, PHASE 2, Lee Quinones, Ricardo Rodriguez, and VULCAN (visual artists); Access Bronx, Andre, Cherry, Deo and Crew, Mitch TMD, and WANE (fashion); Aaron/Quest, The Infamous O.P., K.C., Latin Empire, and Rammellzee (Rap MC's); Chovie Chove, DJ Breakdown, DJ Delta, Antonio Pepe Esposito, Marcellus James, DJ Plasticman, and Albert ALBE Ragusa (DJ's); Fresh Kid Dancers, Elite Society Dance Troupe, and Justice (dancers); Raymond Betts, Precautions Team, Flip City, Jeremy Henderson, Vy Higginsen's Jump Sister Jump, Joe Humeres, and Larry Wright; JEANETTE VUOCOLO

06-21: Reno, *Raging*; JEANETTE VUOCOLO

11-11—11-16: Lawrence "Butch" Morris: Artist-in-Residence, *Conduction #15: Where Music Goes II*; JEANETTE VUOCOLO

1990
By Word of Mouth and Hand— New American Storytelling
JEANETTE VUOCOLO, PRODUCER
05-16: Malika Lee Whitney's The Pickney Players, with guest artists Hazelle Goodman, Mary Lou Lollis, Peggy Pettitt, and Thomas Osha Pinnock, *Speaking in Tongues: A Celebration of the Oral Tradition*
05-23: Fred Hopkins, Diedre Murray, and Richard "Shake-A-Leg" Thomas, *Grid Art in Grid Lock*
05-30: Brenda Wong Aoki, OBAKE! *Spirits Past and Present*
06-06: Constance De Jong, *Vanishing Acts*; Peter Gordon, *The City of the Passion: A Tone Poem*
06-13: Peter Cook and Kenny Lerner, *Flying Words Project*
06-20: Helen Thorington and artists from *New American Radio*; *Audio Lunch*, with tapes by Maurice Kenny, Gregory Whitehead, The Sleight of Mind Group, Jacki Apple and Bruce Fowler, David Moss, Helen Thorington, Sheila Davies, Hildegard Westerkamp, Harris Skibell and Susan Lepsetter, Tom Johnson, Jerri Allyn, Rinde Eckert, Charles Amirkhanian, Keith Antar Mason with Jacki Apple, Christine Baczewska, Dan Lander, Don Joyce & Negativland, Rachel Rosenthal, and Arsenije Javonovic
06-19—06-21: Live performance of *New American Radio* works by Jerri Allyn, Jacki Apple, and Gregory Whitehead; hosted by Valerie Smaldone

1991
8 in 7: New Ventures in American Music,
JEANETTE VUOCOLO, PRODUCER
03-06: Mickey Davidson, Jeanne Lee, and Ntozake Shange, *A Sense of Breath*; Commissioned by and co-presented with *The Fifth Annual Festival of Women Improvisers*
03-07: *Five Artists—Five Views: A Panel Discussion on Improvisation in Music* with Tiye Giraud, Sheila Jordan, Tania León, Diedre Murray, Pauline Oliveros; Lucy Summer, moderator; CO-PRODUCED AND CO-PRESENTED WITH THE FIFTH ANNUAL FESTIVAL OF WOMEN IMPROVISERS

03-13: Lambs Eat Ivy
03-19: Carol Emanuel and Zeena Perkins
03-27: Geri Allen and Don Pullen, *Piano Magic*
04-03,10: Dierdre Murray, *Unending Pain*; Commissioned and co-presented by The Performing Garage
04-17: Zella Jackson Price, *Keep Working for the Master*

1992
Performing Bodies and Smart Machines
A series concerned with images of the future and our interfaces with technology. Featuring new works by multi-media performing artists, a panel of science fiction writers and theorists, and speculations by a scientist/robotics specialist; JEANETTE VUOCOLO, PRODUCER; ORGANIZED WITH TONI DOVE AND HELEN THORINGTON
03-13: Toni Dove, *The Blessed Abyss—A Tale of Unmanageable Ecstasies*; Helen Thorington, *Partial Perceptions*
03-18: Matt Heckert, *Horse on Lava*; Hans Moravec, *The Universal Robot*
03-25: *Writers on the Future of the Body and Technology*, Panel: Pat Cadigan, Manuel DeLanda, Samuel Delany, Arthur and Marilouise Kroker with Steve Gibon, and David Skal
04-01: The Wooster Group, *Rae Whitfield and the Johnsons Present Dances from the Wuji Islands*
04-08: Perry Hoberman, *Runway*
04-22: Rachel Rosenthal, *filename:* FUTURFAX
04-29: Sussan Deyhim, *Oblique Intentions and the Vertical Weight of a Gaze*; Richard Horowitz, *WARP IV for Solo Ney and Tuned Breath*

1993
Say What?: The 1993 Biennial Performance/Theater Project
JEANETTE VUOCOLO, PRODUCER
03-31: Marga Gomez, *Marga Gomez is Pretty, Witty, and Gay*
04-21: James Luna, *James Luna— UNPLUGGED: The Shame-Man*
04-28: Kip Fulbeck, *banana split & other mix-ups*
05-12: Robbie McCauley, *Mississippi Freedom: In Perspective*
05-26: Mac Wellman, *The Land of Fog and Whistles*
06-02: John Kelly, *Cocteau & Barbette, excerpts from a work-in-progress*

Winter Projects
11-29—12-10: James Lo, *Incidental Harmonies and Found Bottle Caps*, (audio installation)
12-31: Frank Conversano, Diedre Murray, Fred Hopkins, Lawrence "Butch" Morris, Ruth Fugistaller, *Conduction #27: A Chorus of Poets*

1994
The Space Between Saints
04-13: Sledgehammer Theatre, *No Time Like the Present (A Rosary to Mary Frankenstein on the Occasion of the Rapture)*
04-20: Donna Uchizono, *Angels on Granite*
04-27: Dawn Chiang and Eric Cornwell, *deLights: Art on 5 Outlets*

05-18: *Ex Statics, A Processional for Audience*, Derek Bernstein and Amy Sue Rosen, Mary Griffin and Joe Hannan, Leroy Jenkins, Jill Kroesen, and "Blue" Gene Tyranny
05-25: Susan Marshall & Company, *Private Worlds in Public View: First Appearance*
06-01: 8 Bold Souls, *Ant Farm*

1995
Territorial Rites
03-01 (performance): Cunningham Dance Foundation, *Beach Birds for Camera: A Music Video Event*
03-02, 03 (installation)
03-15—03-19: Leni Schwendinger and Ben Rubin, *Not Dreaming in Public*
04-12: Andy Bey, *Best Kept Secrets*
04-26: George Emilio Sanchez, *Border/Door with $trictly Business in Keep It Real/ To the Fullest*
04-17: Ronald K. Brown/Evidence, *Short Stories*
04-24: Carla Kirkwood, *Bodies of Evidence*

Winter Projects
12-18, 19: Ronald K. Brown/Evidence, *Lessons: A Site-Specific Installation*

1996
Winter Projects
01-04: Terry Adkins, *Mirliton—Last Trumpet and Other Works*

Second Sight
03-22: Lé Thi Diem Thúy, Le Tuan Hung and Dang Kim Hiem, and The Far East Side Band, *East/West/East*
05-10: The Mark Hennen/Toby Kasavan Piano Duo; The Cooper-Moore/John Blum Duo; notated works by Kitty Brazelton, David Lang, Terry Winter Owens, Louis V Vierk, and Eva Eiener as performed by Double Edge (Edmund Niemann and Nurit Tilles) and by Anthony de Mare and Kathleen Supové; host: Anthony Davis; co-organized with Toby Kasavan, *80 Fingers: The Duo Piano Mini-Festival*

Banana Split
A two-day event incorporating dance, music, and text, Patricia Hoffbauer and Company
05-22: *Banana Split: Carmenland, the saga continues...*, Collaborators: Liz Prince and Zé Luis Oliveira; with Eva Gasteazoro, Kelly Munn, Peter Richards, *Nami Yamamoto
05-23: *Banana Split: Art Festa*; "Are We Still Juggling Bananas?: Hybrid Cultures and the Latina/o Performance", Panel: Eloise de Leon, George Emilio Sanchez, Ellas Shoat, Helena Solberg, Karla Turcios; moderator: Maria Hinojosa

06-12: Shelley Hirsch, *For Jerry*

Winter Projects
12-18, 19: *Reserved for Artists: Excerpts of New and Developing Works*: "The Architecture of Seeing" by Patricia Hoffbauer and George Emilio Sanchez, "Glass Walls" by Diedre Murray, "War Diaries" by Carla Kirkwood

screenings of works by Dan Graham, Jonathan Horowitz, Bruce Nauman, Jim O'Rourke, Oliver Payne and Nick Relph, Stephen Prina, and Catherine Sullivan; HOWIE CHEN WITH GABRIELLE GIATTINO AND JAY SANDERS

2007

Breakout Sessions: Artists Event Series

01-17: *Dancing Nine to Five and Edible Estates, Sundown Schoolhouse and the Homosexual Home* (Whitney's Architectural Dialogues series); Fritz Haeg; FRANK SMIGIEL
01-31: Judith Sánchez Ruíz and Dafnis Prieto *...the only personal thing I do...*; LIMOR TOMER
02-20: Glenn Kaino, *Burning Boards*; SHAMIM M. MOMIN
03-12—03-22: *Praxis Studio: Dreams and Possibilities*; LIMOR TOMER

Grab It! The Music of JacobTV

LIMOR TOMER, PRODUCER
05-02: *Pitch Black with PRISM Saxophone Quartet and Miro Dance Theatre*
05-03: *Artists on Art: JacobTV and America*
05-04: *Grab It! Instrumental and Multimedia Work of JacobTV*

PAMELA JOHNSON, Gallery Receptionist, 1985–86; Gallery Assistant, 1986–89
CARA KEEGAN, Research Clerk, 1986–87
ANDREA MORIARTY, Secretary to Head, Branch Museums, 1986–87; Coordinator Building Program, 1986–87
PAMELA GRUNINGER PERKINS, Head, Branch Museums, 1985– ; Coordinator Building Program, 1986–
JEANETTE VUOCOLO, Branch Manager, 1985–97
CHARLES WRIGHT, Saturday Receptionist, 1986–87

1987–1990

JOSEPHINE GEAR, Branch Director, 1987–90

AMY DION, Gallery Coordinator, 1986–89
PAMELA JOHNSON, Gallery Assistant, 1986–89
ALLISON HAYS LANE, Secretary to Head, Branch Museums, 1989–90
PETER NAUMANN, Gallery Assistant, 1988–89; Gallery Coordinator, 1989–90
PAMELA GRUNINGER PERKINS, Head, Branch Museums, 1985–93; Coordinator Building Program, 1986–91
CLARE SPINDLER, Gallery Assistant, 1989–90
JEANETTE VUOCOLO, Branch Manager, 1985–97
DIANE WITTNER, Gallery Assistant, 1987–89
GIOIA WHITTEMORE, Secretary to Head, Branch Museums, 1988–89; Coordinator Building Program, 1988–89
SUSAN WOODS, Secretary to Head, Branch Museums, and Coordinator Building Program, 1987–89

1990–1997

THELMA GOLDEN, Associate Curator and Branch Director, 1994–97; Branch Director, 1990–93

LISA ARCHAMBEAU, Gallery Assistant, Exhibition Programs, 1994–96; Senior Gallery Assistant, Exhibition Programs, 1995–97
LISA DENT, Gallery Assistant, 1993–95
ALEXA GRIFFITH, Secretary to Head, Branch Museums, and Coordinator Building Program, 1990; Gallery Assistant, 1992; Gallery Coordinator, 1992–94

ALLISON SMITH, Gallery Assistant, Educations Programs, 1995–96; Senior Gallery Assistant, Education Programs, 1996–97
JEANETTE VUOCOLO, Branch Manager, 1985–97

1997–1999

EUGENIE TSAI, Associate Curator and Curator of Branches, 1997–98; Senior Curator and Curator of Branches, 1998–99

THELMA GOLDEN, Curator and Director of Branches , 1997–99

JEFF HOPKINS, Gallery Receptionist, 1994–98; Gallery Assistant, Operations, 1996–97; Gallery Assistant, Education, 1997–98; Gallery Coordinator, Education, 1998–

ANNA LEE, Gallery Assistant, Exhibitions, 1997–98; Gallery Coordinator, Exhibitions, 1998–99

MIN LEE, Gallery Assistant, Exhibitions, 1998–
DEBRA SINGER, Branch Manager, 1997–99

1999–2000

DEBRA SINGER, Branch Curator, 1999–2000; Branch Manager, 1997–99

EVELYN HANKINS, Gallery Assistant, Exhibitons, 1999–2000; Curatorial Assistant, 2000–01
JEFF HOPKINS, Gallery Receptionist, 1994–98; Gallery Assistant, Operations, 1996–97 Gallery Assistant, Education, 1997–98; Gallery Coordinator, Education, 1998–2001; Senior Gallery Coordinator, Education, 2001–02
MOLLY LARKEY, Curatorial Assistant, 2000–02
MIN LEE, Gallery Assistant, Exhibitions, 1998–2000
SHAMIM M. MOMIN, Assistant Curator and Manager, Branch Programs, 1999–2000
BETH VENN, Curator, Touring Exhibitions, and Director of Branch Museums, 1999–2000

2001–2008

SHAMIM M. MOMIN, Branch Director and Curator, 2002–08; Branch Curator, 2000–02; Assistant Curator and Manager, Branch Programs, 1999–2000; Gallery Assistant, Exhibition Programs, 1996–97

HOWIE CHEN, Gallery/Curatorial Assistant, 2001–02; Gallery/Curatorial Coordinator, 2002–03; Branch Manager, 2004–07; Senior Curatorial Coordinator, 2006–08
LEE CLARK, Gallery Assistant, 2002–04; Gallery/ Curatorial Coordinator, 2004–07
GRAHAM COREIL-ALLEN, Gallery Assistant, 2008
CLAIRE CUNO, Temporary Gallery Assistant, 2007
JEFF HOPKINS, Gallery Receptionist, 1994–98; Gallery Assistant, Operations, 1996–97 Gallery Assistant, Education, 1997–98; Gallery Coordinator, Education,1998–2001; Senior Gallery Coordinator, Education, 2001–02
MOLLY LARKEY, Curatorial Assistant, 2000–02
LISA LIBICKI, Gallery/Education Coordinator, 2004–05
ELIZABETH LOVERO, Curatorial Coordinator, 2007–08
ALLISON WEISBERG, Gallery/Education Coordinator, 2005–07
AUSTIN YANG, Gallery/Educational Assistant, 2001–02; Gallery/Educational Coordinator, 2002–04

Branch Staff History

1983–1985

LISA PHILLIPS, Associate Curator and Head, Branch Museums, 1983–85

JANIS KRASNOW, Gallery Attendant, 1982; Gallery Assistant, 1983–84; Assistant Branch Manager, 1984–85
SUSAN LUBOWSKY, Branch Manager, 1982–84
CHARLOTTE MEEHAN, Gallery Assistant, 1984–85
NANCY PRINCENTAHL, Assistant to Head, Branch Museums, 1983–85
SARAH WARREN, Assistant to Branch Manager, 1982–84

1985–1987

SUSAN LUBOWKY, Branch Director, 1985–87

AMY DION, Gallery Assistant, 1985–86; Gallery Coordinator, 1986–89

DINA HELAL, Gallery Assistant, 1990–92; Coordinator Family and Community Programs, 1992–96
JEFF HOPKINS, Gallery Receptionist, 1994– ; Gallery Assistant, Operations, 1996–97
ALLISON HAYS LANE, Secretary to Head, Branch Museums, 1989–90; Gallery Coordinator, 1990
SHAMIM M. MOMIN, Gallery Assistant, Exhibition Programs, 1996–97
PAMELA GRUNINGER PERKINS, Head, Branch Museums, 1985–93; Coordinator Building Program, 1986–91
DEBRA SINGER, Branch Manager, 1997–99

Index of Visual Artists

Whitney Staff List

As of April 14, 2008

Colophon

This publication was produced by the Publications Department at the Whitney Museum of American Art, New York: Rachel de W. Wixom: head of publications; Beth Huseman: editor; Beth Turk: assistant editor; Anita Duquette: manager, rights and reproductions; Berit Potter: rights and reproductions assistant; Jessa Farkas: rights and reproductions assistant.

Project Manager: Howie Chen
Project Assistant: Marianna Pegno
Editor: Beth Turk
Catalogue Design: Barbara Glauber & Erika Nishizato/Heavy Meta

Set in Maple, Akkurat, and Freight
Printed on 148 GSM Fortune Matte

Production: Nerissa Dominguez Vales, The Working Dog Press
Printing: Gist and Herlin Press

Printed and bound in the United States.

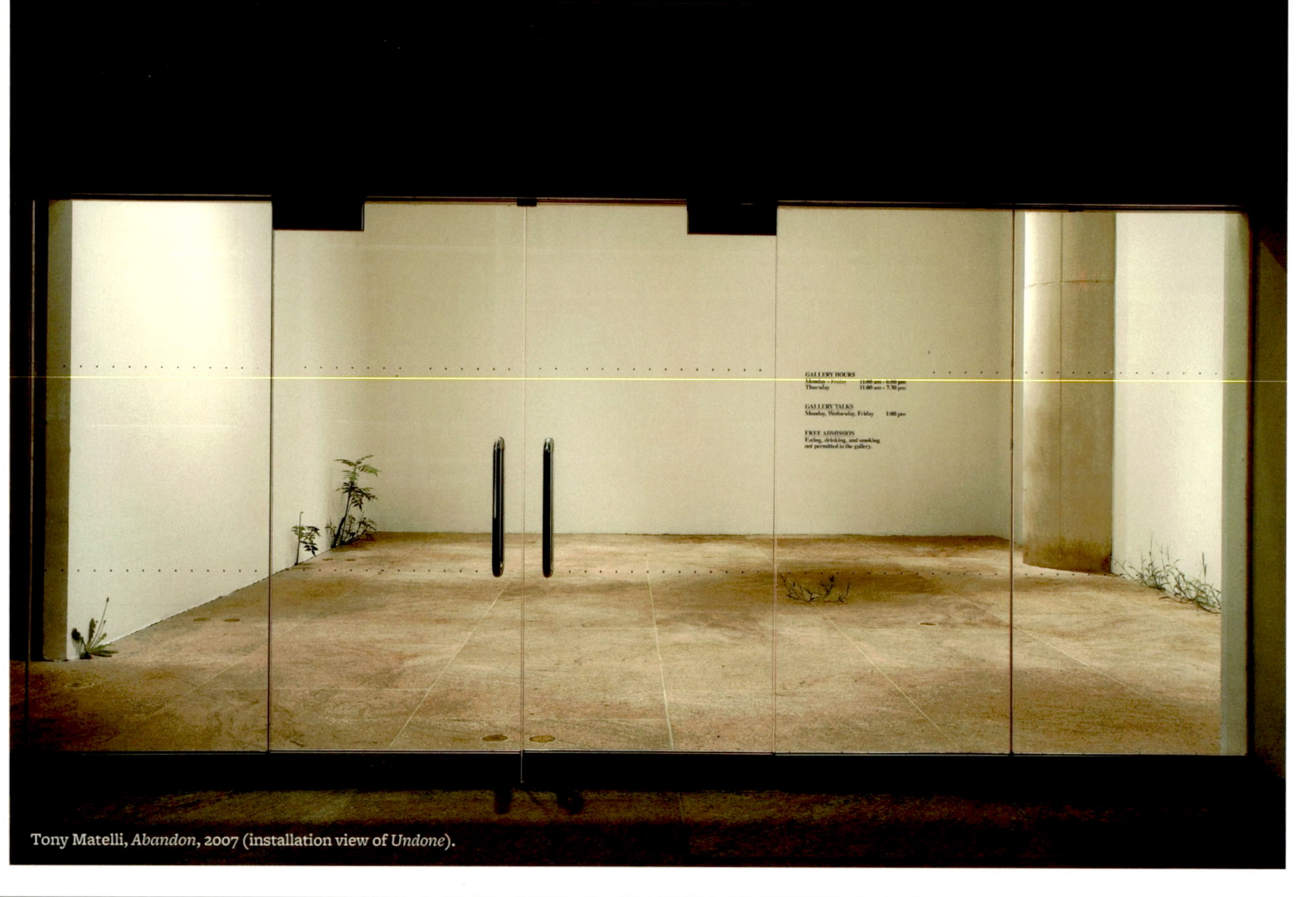

Tony Matelli, *Abandon*, 2007 (installation view of *Undone*).

entieth-Century Sculpture: Process and Presence ▪ The Forum
ee American Families: A Tradition of Artistic Pursuit ▪ Sti
wers in Folk Art ▪ Alexander Calder ▪ The Art of Music: Ameri
ists' Visions ▪ Modern Masks ▪ The Box Transformed ▪ The Su
gazine and Its Graphics ▪ Modern Machines: Recent Kine
asures: New York 1900–1940 ▪ Yasuo Kuniyoshi ▪ The Changi
ntemporary Cutouts ▪ Monotypes by Maurice Prendergast ▪
awings ▪ Stuart Davis: An American in Paris ▪ Elements: Fiv
al Faces ▪ Urban Figures ▪ From the Model ▪ Straphangers ▪
Wood: Recent Sculpture ▪ Cadmus, French, & Tooker: The
na ▪ With the Grain: Contemporary Panel Painting ▪ Abstract
ulpture ▪ Abstraction Before 1930 ▪ Drawing Acquisitions,
reat ▪ Judith Shea: Monuments and Statues ▪ Alison Saar:
tle Boat Head ▪ Glenn Ligon: Good Mirrors Are Not Cheap ▪
apter One (or the First Holy Communion Moments Before the
nnial Acquisitions ▪ Sylvia Plachy: The Call of the Street:
ter ▪ Sam Gilliam: Golden Element Inside Gold ▪ Leone & Mac
wrence: War Series ▪ Double Take: Views of Modern Life by S
d Irrational ▪ Terry Adkins: Firmament RHA ▪ Matthew McCa
ng: 8490 Days of Memory ▪ Beverly Semmes: She Moves ▪
64 ▪ Quicker Than a Wink: The Photographs of Harold Edge
Exhibition: An Installation by Christian Marclay ▪ Garden o
rrie Mae Weems ▪ Hope Sandrow: Water Life ▪ Shirin Neshat:
mamoto ▪ Wall Drawings by Byron Kim ▪ Jeanne Silverthorne
aselli: Gravity's Rainbow ▪ Correspondences: Isamu Noguchi
o! ▪ Expanding Horizons: Landscape Photographs ▪ Sowon Kw
e ▪ Miranda Lichtenstein: Sanctuary for a Wild Child ▪ E.V. D
ge—Secrets of Scene Painting ▪ Lucky DeBellevue: Khlysty,
ntemporary Art: Reed Anderson, Rina Banerjee, Susan Gra
diction ▪ Outer City, Inner Space: Teresita Fernández, Stephen
en Harvey: A Whitney for the Whitney at Altria ▪ Dario Robleto
ie Grinnan: Adventures in Delusional Idealism ▪ Luis Gisper
Numbers ▪ Single Wide: Teresa Hubbard/Alexander Birchler ▪
tu, Marc Swanson, Ivan Witenstein ▪ Sue de Beer: Black Su
el: Small Liberties ▪ Trace: New Work by Jedediah Caesar, Sha
evics ▪ Burgeoning Geometries: Constructed Abstractions,
th Phoebe Washburn, Matthew Brannon: Where Were We